Heron Books

CHARLES DICKENS

COMPLETE
WORKS

CENTENNIAL EDITION

Charles Dickens

CHARLES DICKENS

SKETCHES BY BOZ

ILLUSTRATIVE OF EVERY-DAY LIFE
AND EVERY-DAY PEOPLE

I

Introduction by
Thea Holme

HERON BOOKS

*The introduction to this book
was originally published for the
Oxford Illustrated Dickens,
published by
the Oxford University Press*

I.S.B.N. for this volume:
o 86225 093 5

*Illustrations by
George Cruikshank and Phiz*

*Printed in England by
Hazell Watson & Viney Limited
Aylesbury, Bucks*

INTRODUCTION

One evening in the autumn of 1832 the manuscript of a fictional sketch entitled 'A Sunday out of Town' was dropped 'with fear and trembling into a dark letter-box in a dark office up a dark court in Fleet Street'. Its author, describing the event to a friend, gives a picture of the sequel. We see him in a Strand bookshop, hurriedly searching through a copy of The Monthly Magazine. *He pauses, gazing at the page before him. His sketch – its name 'transmogrified' to 'A Dinner at Poplar Walk' – is there, 'in all the glory of print'. Thrusting his way through the crowded Strand, the young Charles Dickens hurries blindly towards Westminster Hall where he may pace in solitude – 'my eyes so dimmed with pride and joy, that they could not bear the street, and were not fit to be seen'.*

The delight of seeing his work in print was the only reward offered by The Monthly Magazine, *whose Editor presently sent a 'polite and flattering communication' asking for more. He was duly supplied with 'Horatio Sparkins', 'The Bloomsbury Christening', and 'The Boarding House'. This last was the first sketch to bear the author's signature – 'Boz'. The pseudonym was, as he afterwards put it, 'the nickname of a pet child, a younger brother whom I had dubbed Moses, in honour of* The Vicar of Wakefield;

VII

*which, being facetiously pronounced through the nose, became
Boses, and, being shortened, became Boz'.*

*The following year, Dickens, who was now twenty-one and
earning five guineas a week as a reporter on* The Morning Chronicle, *was sent to review a new farce at the Adelphi Theatre. He
found that the author, J. B. Buckstone, had unashamedly used the
plot and many of the jokes from his own sketch, 'The Bloomsbury
Christening'. Already he had been paid the doubtful compliment
of plagiarism.*

*By now several influential men were becoming aware of young
Boz, among them the successful author Harrison Ainsworth, who
introduced him to his own publisher, Macrone. One night, after
spending the evening at Ainsworth's house in Willesden, Dickens
and Macrone walked back into the city together. The publisher
declared that the* Sketches, *of which twenty or so had now appeared
in* The Morning Chronicle *and other papers, were 'capital value';
and suggested their being collected into a volume for publication.
Cruikshank the cartoonist, he added casually, might be the man to
illustrate them. It is not difficult to imagine the enthusiasm with
which this suggestion was received, or the eagerness with which
Boz – in the spare time snatched from his travels as a parliamentary reporter in election time – was to fling himself into the production of a quantity of new sketches to complete the two volumes
finally commissioned by Macrone. His mind was filled with ideas:
he wrote with speed. In the end it was Cruikshank, not Dickens,
who held up publication.*

*At last, on 7 February 1836, its author's twenty-fourth birth-
day, the First Series of* Sketches by Boz *was published. Its immediate success was almost immediately eclipsed; for some six weeks
later the first number of* The Pickwick Papers *appeared. After a
doubtful start this serial was to achieve, with the introduction of
Sam Weller, a swift and enduring fame. By the time the Second
Series of his* Sketches *appeared, Boz and* Pickwick *were household words.*

'Perhaps', said Cranford's *Miss Jenkyns, 'the author is young.
Let him persevere, and who knows what he may become if he will
take the great Doctor for his model.' 'Doctor Johnson's style', she
reiterated later – after listening 'with patient gravity' to a chapter*

INTRODUCTION

of Pickwick – '*Doctor Johnson's style is a model for young beginners.*'

It is true that Mrs. Gaskell, in introducing Boz as a bone of contention between two of her characters, was incidentally paying a witty compliment to the Editor who had commissioned her work. But the fictitious Miss Jenkyns's attitude may well have had its counterpart in reality. The impact of Dickens upon the more reactionary of his readers must have been startling. After the rolling phrases, the remote philosophizing characters of Johnson; the exotic phantasmagoria of Gothic romance; even after the fastidious realism of Jane Austen – '*Let other pens dwell on guilt and misery. I quit such odious subjects as soon as I can*' – the contrast is remarkable. Here was Boz, reflecting a completely new outlook, the outlook of the man in the street; setting down in his Sketches all the small events in the everyday life of common persons – bank clerks, shop assistants, omnibus drivers; laundresses, market women, and kidney-pie sellers: directing his powers of observation and description upon scenes and characters within the daily scope of any loiterer in London. '*I thought I knew something of the town*', commented one of his fellow clerks in the law firm of Ellis and Blackmore; '*but after a little talk with Dickens I found that I knew nothing. He knew it all, from Bow to Brentford.... He could imitate, in a manner I never saw equalled, the low population of the streets of London in all their varieties.*'

In these sketches we see a reflection of the tremendous social changes that were beginning to take place. On the one hand Dickens depicts in relentless detail the horrors of poverty, disease, and crime – legacy of eighteenth-century London; on the other the prosperous vulgarity of the rapidly rising middle class. The young Boz stood, as it were, between two worlds; and we are reminded that Dickens the Eminent Victorian was born in the reign of George the Third. Through his eyes we watch Hogarthian scenes of misery and despair, offset by brightly coloured pictures of mass jollification reminiscent of Frith's '*Derby Day*'.

The heat is intense this afternoon, and the people, of whom there are additional parties arriving every moment, look as warm as the tables which have been recently painted, and have the appearance of being red-hot. What a dust and noise! Men and women – boys and *girls – sweethearts and married people.... Gentlemen in alarming waistcoats, and steel watchguards, promenading about, three abreast ... ladies, with great, long, white pocket-handkerchiefs like small table-cloths in their hands, chasing one another on the grass in the most playful and interesting manner, with the view of attracting the attention of the aforesaid gentlemen – husbands in perspective ordering bottles of ginger-beer for the objects of their affections, with a lavish disregard of expense; and the said objects washing down huge quantities of shrimps and winkles, with an equal disregard of their own bodily health and subsequent discomfort – boys, with great silk hats just balanced on the top of their heads, smoking cigars, and trying to look as if they liked them – gentlemen in pink shirts and blue waistcoats, occasionally upsetting either themselves, or somebody else, with their own canes.*

I suppose it is almost inevitable that one should consider these sketches in terms of painting, for their writer is already a master of pictorial description. He lays on his colours boldly, giving us sharp contrasts of light and darkness in his 'Visit to Newgate', and bringing to life with vivid touches his portraits such as 'The Last Cab Driver' who is described as 'a brown-whiskered, white-hatted, no-coated cabman; his nose was generally red, and his bright blue eye not unfrequently stood out in bold relief against a black border of artificial workmanship'. His neck, we are told, 'was usually garnished with a bright yellow handkerchief. In summer he carried in his mouth a flower; in winter, a straw – slight, but, to a contemplative mind, certain indications of a love of nature, and a taste for botany.'

It is difficult to make a fair assessement of the literary value of these early sketches because, in doing so, one must temporarily forget the masterpieces of which they were the harbinger, and of which one is so frequently reminded by small inspired touches, or by the foreshadowing of characters as yet unborn. Dickens himself, years later, described his first book as 'often being extremely crude and ill-considered, and bearing obvious marks of haste and inexperience'. This may indeed be true of some of the 'Tales', such as 'Mr. Minns and His Cousin' (the original 'A Sunday out of Town'), which, after an amusing and carefully contrived start, ends with such suddenness that one wonder if the author had run out of paper; and also of the irritating humours of 'The Mudfog Associ-

INTRODUCTION

ation' in which the comic genius of Boz seems to have lost its way.

But as an example of what is now called 'documentary' the Sketches *deserve a unique place in literature. It has been pointed out elsewhere that more than half this volume's contents are facts: facts observed with an astonishing precision and wealth of detail. But Boz is no objective reporter: the facts he presents are invested with his own reaction to them, and in some cases are lifted by his imagination into tragedy or fantasy. An example of this is to be found in 'Meditations in Monmouth Street', where, speculating upon the contents of a second-hand clothes shop, he creates the life story of a wastrel from some of the garments displayed; and then, 'by way of restoring the naturally cheerful tone of our thoughts', begins to fit 'visionary feet and legs into a cellar-board full of boots and shoes'. With a swift stroke of invention he brings to life a whole cast of characters, imagines their relationships one with the other, and sets them before us in a sort of comic ballet.*

It is interesting to note that at the time of their publication, the two Sketches *singled out for praise were concerned with tragedy –* 'The Black Veil' *and* 'A Visit to Newgate'. *The former, which is included among the Tales, is a highly dramatic, not to say melodramatic, story, of which the theme is a recurrent one throughout the Sketches: the ruin of a woman's life by the worthlessness of the man to whom she has devoted it. In this case it is a mother whose fruitless efforts to save her son from the gallows have driven her insane. We are spared few of the horrors of this woeful tale; there are moments when the dialogue is worthy of the Radclyffian title.*

'Who was he?' *inquired the surgeon.*

'My son', *rejoined the woman; and fell senseless at his feet.*

But in contrast we find masterly passages such as that describing 'the back part of Walworth'; *and the* 'corpulent round-headed boy' *at the opening might be a rough sketch of the fat boy in* Pickwick.

Dickens admitted that he found Newgate Prison 'a very difficult subject'. *There is little doubt that he found it a heart-rending one. Reading this account one cannot fail to be aware of the pity with which his imagination works upon the mournful groups he describes: the women conversing through the bars of* 'a kind of iron

cage... *through which the friends of the female prisoners communicate with them'; the three condemned murderers – one of them
entertaining some hopes of reprieve, and holding aloof from his
two companions, who, as the turnkey intimated in a confident
undertone, 'were dead men'. After a pitiful description of fourteen
infant pickpockets 'drawn up in line for our inspection' in the
prison school, he writes, 'There was not one redeeming feature among them – not a glance of honesty – not a wink expressive of
anything but the gallows and the hulks, in the whole collection';
and concludes, 'We have never looked upon a more disagreeable
sight, because we never saw fourteen such hopeless creatures of
neglect, before.' Here, surely, is something greater than pity and
horror: the imaginative insight into the cause of crime which was
later to inspire his relentless exposure of social evils. Already, it
would seem, the foundations have been laid for* Oliver Twist; *and
the images of Fagin and his gang have peered at their creator from
out of the shadows of Newgate.*

*It is for the glimpses they afford us of their author that these
sketches have a special fascination: not only in foreshadowings of
future greatness but in those touches which reveal the young Boz
himself. In 'Making a Night of It' he gives us what is thought to be
a self portrait. He is the romantic Smithers in his 'brown hat, very
much turned up at the sides', who found his appreciation of a
theatrical performance somewhat marred by the effects of Scotch
whiskey and Havannah cigars. Young Boz must undoubtedly
have met 'The Theatrical Young Gentleman' who is the subject of
another sketch, and who called Drury Lane the lane, and the Victoria the vic. His own interest in theatrical matters is unquestionable; and in 'Private Theatres' it is clear that his knowledge of these
places of entertainment extended backstage.*

*In the National Portrait Gallery there hangs a painting by
Maclise, of which Thackeray declared, 'Here we have the real
identical man, Dickens.' It shows a youthful figure seated in a
crimson and gilt armchair before a writing desk, his left hand
firmly placed upon a manuscript – an attitude which seems to
suggest that he is playing, with enjoyment, the part of a famous
writer. The pale smooth face is turned, like an actor's, full into the
light. One observes the elegant folds of his black satin cravat, the*

neatness of his small well-polished boots. Then, drawing nearer, one becomes aware of the power and vitality in that face with its strong nose and sensuous, sensitive mouth – and the large brilliant eyes which, turned away from the artist, gaze thoughtfully out of the window. These are the eyes which observed the tragedy and comedy of life in such vivid detail; which saw and recorded brutality and pathos, courage and despair, and all the innumerable absurdities of human behaviour.

This portrait was painted three years after the publication of Sketches by Boz, *when its subject was assured of fame; but it is not difficult to recognize the author of these early works. It is in company with this same youthful, energetic figure that, reading them, we walk the streets and visit the entertainments and institutions of the London of William the Fourth. There are many rewarding discoveries for the explorer among these pages; many opportunities to exclaim in echo of Thackeray, 'Here we have the real identical man, Dickens!'*

Thea Holme

CONTENTS

OUR PARISH

CONTENTS

SCENES

CONTENTS

XVII

CONTENTS

CONTENTS

CHAPTER V

CONTENTS

TALES

LIST OF ILLUSTRATIONS

PREFACE

The whole of these Sketches were written and published, one by one, when I was a very young man. They were collected and republished while I was still a very young man; and sent into the world with all their imperfections (a good many) on their heads.

They comprise my first attempts at authorship—with the exception of certain tragedies achieved at the mature age of eight or ten, and represented with great applause to overflowing nurseries. I am conscious of their often being extremely crude and ill-considered, and bearing obvious marks of haste and inexperience; particularly in that section of the present volume which is comprised under the general head of Tales.

But as this collection is not originated now, and was very leniently and favourably received when it was first made, I have not felt it right either to remodel or expunge, beyond a few words and phrases here and there.

OUR PARISH

CHAPTER I

THE BEADLE. THE PARISH ENGINE. THE SCHOOLMASTER

How much is conveyed in those two short words—"The Parish!" And with how many tales of distress and misery, of broken fortune and ruined hopes, too often of unrelieved wretchedness and successful knavery, are they associated! A poor man, with small earnings, and a large family, just manages to live on from hand to mouth, and to procure food from day to day; he has barely sufficient to satisfy the present cravings of nature, and can take no heed of the future. His taxes are in arrear, quarter-day passes by, another quarter-day arrives: he can procure no more quarter for himself, and is summoned by—the parish. His goods are distrained, his children are crying with cold and hunger, and the very bed on which his sick wife is lying, is dragged from beneath her. What can he do? To whom is he to apply for relief? To private charity? To benevolent individuals? Certainly not—there is his parish. There are the parish vestry, the parish infirmary, the parish surgeon, the parish officers, the parish beadle. Excellent institutions, and gentle,

1

kind-hearted men. The woman dies—she is buried by the parish. The children have no protector—they are taken care of by the parish. The man first neglects, and afterwards cannot obtain, work—he is relieved by the parish; and when distress and drunkenness have done their work upon him, he is maintained, a harmless babbling idiot, in the parish asylum.

The parish beadle is one of the most, perhaps *the* most, important member of the local administration. He is not so well off as the churchwardens, certainly, nor is he so learned as the vestry-clerk, nor does he order things quite so much his own way as either of them. But his power is very great, notwithstanding; and the dignity of his office is never impaired by the absence of efforts on his part to maintain it. The beadle of our parish is a splendid fellow. It is quite delightful to hear him, as he explains the state of the existing poor laws to the deaf old women in the board-room passage on business nights; and to hear what he said to the senior churchwarden, and what the senior churchwarden said to him; and what "we" (the beadle and the other gentlemen) came to the determination of doing. A miserable-looking woman is called into the board-room, and represents a case of extreme destitution, affecting herself—a widow, with six small children. "Where do you live?" inquires one of the overseers. "I rents a two-pair back, gentlemen, at Mrs. Brown's, Number 3, Little King William's-alley, which has lived there this fifteen year, and knows me to be very hard-working and industrious, and when my poor husband was alive, gentlemen, as died in the hospital"—"Well, well," interrupts the overseer, taking a note of the address, "I'll send Simmons, the beadle, to-morrow morning, to ascertain whether your story is correct; and if so, I suppose you must have an order into the House—Simmons, go to this woman's the first thing to-morrow morning, will you?" Simmons bows assent, and ushers the woman out. Her previous admiration of "the board" (who all sit behind great books, and with

2

THE BEADLE

their hats on) fades into nothing before her respect for her lace-trimmed conductor; and her account of what has passed inside, increases—if that be possible—the marks of respect, shown by the assembled crowd, to that solemn functionary. As to taking out a summons, it's quite a hopeless case if Simmons attends it, on behalf of the parish. He knows all the titles of the Lord Mayor by heart; states the case without a single stammer: and it is even reported that on one occasion he ventured to make a joke, which the Lord Mayor's head footman (who happened to be present) afterwards told an intimate friend, confidentially, was almost equal to one of Mr. Hobler's.

See him again on Sunday in his state-coat and cocked-hat, with a large-headed staff for show in his left hand, and a small cane for use in his right. How pompously he marshals the children into their places! and how demurely the little urchins look at him askance as he surveys them when they are all seated, with a glare of the eye peculiar to beadles! The churchwardens and overseers being duly installed in their curtained pews, he seats himself on a mahogany bracket, erected expressly for him at the top of the aisle, and divides his attention between his prayer-book and the boys. Suddenly, just at the commencement of the communion service, when the whole congregation is hushed into a profound silence, broken only by the voice of the officiating clergyman, a penny is heard to ring on the stone floor of the aisle with astounding clearness. Observe the generalship of the beadle. His involuntary look of horror is instantly changed into one of perfect indifference, as if he were the only person present who had not heard the noise. The artifice succeeds. After putting forth his right leg now and then, as a feeler, the victim who dropped the money ventures to make one or two distinct dives after it; and the beadle, gliding softly round, salutes his little round head, when it again appears above the seat, with divers double knocks, administered with the cane before noticed, to the intense

3

delight of three young men in an adjacent pew, who cough violently at intervals until the conclusion of the sermon.

Such are a few traits of the importance and gravity of a parish beadle—a gravity which has never been disturbed in any case that has come under our observation, except when the services of that particularly useful machine, a parish fire-engine, are required: then indeed all is bustle. Two little boys run to the beadle as fast as their legs will carry them, and report from their own personal observation that some neighbouring chimney is on fire; the engine is hastily got out, and a plentiful supply of boys being obtained, and harnessed to it with ropes, away they rattle over the pavement, the beadle, running—we do not exaggerate—running at the side, until they arrive at some house, smelling strongly of soot, at the door of which the beadle knocks with considerable gravity for half-an-hour. No attention being paid to these manual applications, and the turn-cock having turned on the water, the engine turns off amidst the shouts of the boys; it pulls up once more at the workhouse, and the beadle "pulls up" the unfortunate householder next day, for the amount of his legal reward. We never saw a parish engine at a regular fire but once. It came up in gallant style— three miles and a half an hour, at least; there was a capital supply of water, and it was first on the spot. Bang went the pumps—the people cheered—the beadle perspired profusely; but it was unfortunately discovered, just as they were going to put the fire out, that nobody understood the process by which the engine was filled with water; and that eighteen boys, and a man, had exhausted themselves in pumping for twenty minutes, without producing the slightest effect!

The personages next in importance to the beadle, are the master of the workhouse and the parish schoolmaster. The vestry-clerk, as everybody knows, is a short, pudgy little man, in black, with a thick gold watch-chain of considerable length, terminating in two large seals and a key. He is an

4

attorney, and generally in a bustle; at no time more so, than when he is hurrying to some parochial meeting, with his gloves crumpled up in one hand, and a large red book under the other arm. As to the churchwardens and overseers, we exclude them altogether, because all we know of them is, that they are usually respectable tradesmen, who wear hats with brims inclined to flatness, and who occasionally testify in gilt letters on a blue ground, in some conspicuous part of the church, to the important fact of a gallery having being enlarged and beautified, or an organ rebuilt.

The master of the workhouse is not, in our parish—nor is he usually in any other—one of that class of men the better part of whose existence has passed away, and who drag out the remainder in some inferior situation, with just enough thought of the past, to feel degraded by, and discontented with, the present. We are unable to guess precisely to our own satisfaction what station the man can have occupied before; we should think he had been an inferior sort of attorney's clerk, or else the master of a national school— whatever he was, it is clear his present position is a change for the better. His income is small certainly, as the rusty black coat and threadbare velvet collar demonstrate: but then he lives free of house-rent, has a limited allowance of coals and candles, and an almost unlimited allowance of authority in his petty kingdom. He is a tall, thin, bony man; always wears shoes and black cotton stockings with his surtout; and eyes you, as you pass his parlour-window, as if he wished you were a pauper, just to give you a specimen of his power. He is an admirable specimen of a small tyrant: morose, brutish, and ill-tempered; bullying to his inferiors, cringing to his superiors, and jealous of the influence and authority of the beadle.

Our schoolmaster is just the very reverse of this amiable official. He has been one of those men one occasionally hears of, on whom misfortune seems to have set her mark; nothing he ever did, or was concerned in, appears to have

5

prospered. A rich old relation who had brought him up, and openly announced his intention of providing for him, left him 10,000*l.* in his will, and revoked the bequest in a codicil. Thus unexpectedly reduced to the necessity of providing for himself, he procured a situation in a public office. The young clerks below him, died off as if there were a plague among them; but the old fellows over his head, for the reversion of whose places he was anxiously waiting, lived on and on, as if they were immortal. He speculated and lost. He speculated again and won—but never got his money. His talents were great; his disposition, easy, generous and liberal. His friends profited by the one, and abused the other. Loss succeeded loss; misfortune crowded on misfortune; each successive day brought him nearer the verge of hopeless penury, and the quondam friends who had been warmest in their professions, grew strangely cold and indifferent. He had children whom he loved, and a wife on whom he doted. The former turned their backs on him; the latter died broken-hearted. He went with the stream—it had ever been his failing, and he had not courage sufficient to bear up against so many shocks—he had never cared for himself, and the only being who had cared for him, in his poverty and distress, was spared to him no longer. It was at this period that he applied for parochial relief. Some kind-hearted man who had known him in happier times, chanced to be church-warden that year, and through his interest he was appointed to his present situation.

He is an old man now. Of the many who once crowded round him in all the hollow friendship of boon-companionship, some have died, some have fallen like himself, some have prospered—all have forgotten him. Time and misfortune have mercifully been permitted to impair his memory, and use has habituated him to his present condition. Meek, un-complaining, and zealous in the discharge of his duties, he has been allowed to hold his situation long beyond the usual period; and he will no doubt continue to hold it, until

THE PAUPER SCHOOLMASTER

infirmity renders him incapable, or death releases him. As the grey-headed old man feebly paces up and down the sunny side of the little court-yard between school hours, it would be difficult, indeed, for the most intimate of his former friends to recognise their once gay and happy associate, in the person of the Pauper Schoolmaster.

CHAPTER II

WE commenced our last chapter with the beadle of our parish, because we are deeply sensible of the importance and dignity of his office. We will begin the present, with the clergyman. Our curate is a young gentleman of such pre-possessing appearance, and fascinating manners, that within one month after his first appearance in the parish, half the young-lady inhabitants were melancholy with religion, and the other half, desponding with love. Never were so many young ladies seen in our parish church on Sunday before; and never had the little round angels' faces on Mr. Tomkins's monument in the side aisle, beheld such devotion on earth as they all exhibited. He was about five-and-twenty when he first came to astonish the parishioners. He parted his hair on the centre of his forehead in the form of a Norman arch, wore a brilliant of the first water on the fourth finger of his left hand (which he always applied to his left cheek when he read prayers), and had a deep sepulchral voice of unusual solemnity. Innumerable were the calls made by prudent mammas on our new curate, and innumerable the invitations with which he was assailed, and which, to do him justice, he readily accepted. If his manner in the pulpit had created an impression in his favour, the sensation was increased tenfold, by his appearance in private circles. Pews in the immediate vicinity of the pulpit or reading-desk rose in value; sittings

in the centre aisle were at a premium: an inch of room in
the front row of the gallery could not be procured for love
or money; and some people even went so far as to assert, that
the three Miss Browns, who had an obscure family pew just
behind the churchwardens', were detected, one Sunday, in
the free seats by the communion-table, actually lying in wait
for the curate as he passed to the vestry! He began to
preach extempore sermons, and even grave papas caught the
infection. He got out of bed at half-past twelve o'clock one
winter's night, to half-baptise a washerwoman's child in a
slop-basin, and the gratitude of the parishioners knew no
bounds—the very churchwardens grew generous, and insisted
on the parish defraying the expense of the watch-box on
wheels, which the new curate had ordered for himself, to
perform the funeral service in, in wet weather. He sent
three pints of gruel and a quarter of a pound of tea to a
poor woman who had been brought to bed of four small
children, all at once—the parish were charmed. He got up
a subscription for her—the woman's fortune was made. He
spoke for one hour and twenty-five minutes, at an anti-slavery
meeting at the Goat and Boots—the enthusiasm was at its
height. A proposal was set on foot for presenting the curate
with a piece of plate, as a mark of esteem for his valuable
services rendered to the parish. The list of subscriptions
was filled up in no time; the contest was, not who should
escape the contribution, but who should be the foremost to
subscribe. A splendid silver inkstand was made, and engraved
with an appropriate inscription; the curate was invited to a
public breakfast, at the before-mentioned Goat and Boots;
the inkstand was presented in a neat speech by Mr. Gubbins,
the ex-churchwarden, and acknowledged by the curate in
terms which drew tears into the eyes of all present—the very
waiters were melted.

One would have supposed that, by this time, the theme
of universal admiration was lifted to the very pinnacle of
popularity. No such thing. The curate began to cough;

four fits of coughing one morning between the Litany and the Epistle, and five in the afternoon service. Here was a discovery—the curate was consumptive. How interestingly melancholy! If the young ladies were energetic before, their sympathy and solicitude now knew no bounds. Such a man as the curate—such a dear—such a perfect love—to be consumptive! It was too much. Anonymous presents of black-currant jam, and lozenges, elastic waistcoats, bosom friends, and warm stockings, poured in upon the curate until he was as completely fitted out with winter clothing, as if he were on the verge of an expedition to the North Pole: verbal bulletins of the state of his health were circulated throughout the parish half-a-dozen times a day; and the curate was in the very zenith of his popularity.

About this period, a change came over the spirit of the parish. A very quiet, respectable, dozing old gentleman, who had officiated in our chapel-of-ease for twelve years previously, died one fine morning, without having given any notice whatever of his intention. This circumstance gave rise to counter-sensation the first; and the arrival of his successor occasioned counter-sensation the second. He was a pale, thin, cadaverous man, with large black eyes, and long straggling black hair: his dress was slovenly in the extreme, his manner ungainly, his doctrines startling; in short, he was in every respect the antipodes of the curate. Crowds of our female parishioners flocked to hear him; at first, because he was *so* odd-looking, then because his face was *so* expressive, then because he preached *so* well; and at last, because they really thought that, after all, there was something about him which it was quite impossible to describe. As to the curate, he was all very well; but certainly, after all, there was no denying that—that—in short, the curate wasn't a novelty, and the other clergyman was. The inconstancy of public opinion is proverbial: the congregation migrated one by one. The curate coughed till he was black in the face—it was in vain. He respired with difficulty—it was equally ineffectual in

awakening sympathy. Seats are once again to be had in
any part of our parish church, and the chapel-of-ease is going
to be enlarged, as it is crowded to suffocation every Sunday!

The best known and most respected among our parishioners,
is an old lady, who resided in our parish long before our
name was registered in the list of baptisms. Our parish is a
suburban one, and the old lady lives in a neat row of houses
in the most airy and pleasant part of it. The house is her
own; and it, and everything about it, except the old lady
herself, who looks a little older than she did ten years ago,
is in just the same state as when the old gentleman was
living. The little front parlour, which is the old lady's
ordinary sitting-room, is a perfect picture of quiet neatness;
the carpet is covered with brown Holland, the glass and
picture-frames are carefully enveloped in yellow muslin; the
table-covers are never taken off, except when the leaves are
turpentined and bees'-waxed, an operation which is regularly
commenced every other morning at half-past nine o'clock—
and the little nicknacks are always arranged in precisely the
same manner. The greater part of these are presents from
little girls whose parents live in the same row; but some of
them, such as the two old-fashioned watches (which never
keep the same time, one being always a quarter of an hour
too slow, and the other a quarter of an hour too fast), the
little picture of the Princess Charlotte and Prince Leopold
as they appeared in the Royal Box at Drury Lane Theatre,
and others of the same class, have been in the old lady's
possession for many years. Here the old lady sits with her
spectacles on, busily engaged in needlework—near the window
in summer time; and if she sees you coming up the steps,
and you happen to be a favourite, she trots out to open the
street-door for you before you knock, and as you must be
fatigued after that hot walk, insists on your swallowing two
glasses of sherry before you exert yourself by talking. If
you call in the evening you will find her cheerful, but rather
more serious than usual, with an open Bible on the table,

11

before her, of which "Sarah," who is just as neat and methodical as her mistress, regularly reads two or three chapters in the parlour aloud.

The old lady sees scarcely any company, except the little girls before noticed, each of whom has always a regular fixed day for a periodical tea-drinking with her, to which the child looks forward as the greatest treat of its existence. She seldom visits at a greater distance than the next door but one on either side; and when she drinks tea here, Sarah runs out first and knocks a double-knock, to prevent the possibility of her "Missis's" catching cold by having to wait at the door. She is very scrupulous in returning these little invitations, and when she asks Mr. and Mrs. So-and-so, to meet Mr. and Mrs. Somebody-else, Sarah and she dust the urn, and the best china tea-service, and the Pope Joan board; and the visitors are received in the drawing-room in great state. She has but few relations, and they are scattered about in different parts of the country, and she seldom sees them. She has a son in India, whom she always describes to you as a fine, handsome fellow—so like the profile of his poor dear father over the sideboard, but the old lady adds, with a mournful shake of the head, that he has always been one of her greatest trials; and that indeed he once almost broke her heart; but it pleased God to enable her to get the better of it, and she would prefer your never mentioning the subject to her again. She has a great number of pensioners: and on Saturday, after she comes back from market, there is a regular levee of old men and women in the passage, waiting for their weekly gratuity. Her name always heads the list of any benevolent subscriptions, and hers are always the most liberal donations to the Winter Coal and Soup Distribution Society. She subscribed twenty pounds towards the erection of an organ in our parish church, and was so overcome the first Sunday the children sang to it, that she was obliged to be carried out by the pew-opener. Her entrance into church on Sunday is always the signal for a little bustle in the side aisle,

THE CAPTAIN

occasioned by a general rise among the poor people, who bow
and curtsey until the pew-opener has ushered the old lady into
her accustomed seat, dropped a respectful curtsey, and shut
the door: and the same ceremony is repeated on her leaving
church, when she walks home with the family next door but
one, and talks about the sermon all the way, invariably
opening the conversation by asking the youngest boy where
the text was.

Thus, with the annual variation of a trip to some quiet
place on the sea-coast, passes the old lady's life. It has
rolled on in the same unvarying and benevolent course for
many years now, and must at no distant period be brought
to its final close. She looks forward to its termination, with
calmness and without apprehension. She has everything to
hope and nothing to fear.

A very different personage, but one who has rendered himself very conspicuous in our parish, is one of the old lady's
next-door neighbours. He is an old naval officer on half-
pay, and his bluff and unceremonious behaviour disturbs
the old lady's domestic economy, not a little. In the first
place, he *will* smoke cigars in the front court, and when he
wants something to drink with them—which is by no means
an uncommon circumstance—he lifts up the old lady's knocker
with his walking-stick, and demands to have a glass of table
ale, handed over the rails. In addition to this cool proceeding,
he is a bit of a Jack of all trades, or to use his own words,
"a regular Robinson Crusoe;" and nothing delights him
better than to experimentalise on the old lady's property.
One morning he got up early, and planted three or four
roots of full-grown marigolds in every bed of her front
garden, to the inconceivable astonishment of the old lady,
who actually thought when she got up and looked out of
the window, that it was some strange eruption which had
come out in the night. Another time he took to pieces the
eight-day clock on the front landing, under pretence of
cleaning the works, which he put together again, by some

13

undiscovered process, in so wonderful a manner, that the large hand has done nothing but trip up the little one ever since. Then he took to breeding silk-worms, which he *would* bring in two or three times a day, in little paper boxes, to show the old lady, generally dropping a worm or two at every visit. The consequence was, that one morning a very stout silk-worm was discovered in the act of walking up-stairs—probably with the view of inquiring after his friends, for, on further inspection, it appeared that some of his companions had already found their way to every room in the house. The old lady went to the seaside in despair, and during her absence he completely effaced the name from her brass door-plate, in his attempts to polish it with aqua-fortis.

But all this is nothing to his seditious conduct in public life. He attends every vestry meeting that is held; always opposes the constituted authorities of the parish, denounces the profligacy of the churchwardens, contests legal points against the vestry-clerk, *will* make the tax-gatherer call for his money till he won't call any longer, and then he sends it: finds fault with the sermon every Sunday, says that the organist ought to be ashamed of himself, offers to back himself for any amount to sing the psalms better than all the children put together, male and female; and, in short, conducts himself in the most turbulent and uproarious manner. The worst of it is, that having a high regard for the old lady, he wants to make her a convert to his views, and therefore walks into her little parlour with his newspaper in his hand, and talks violent politics by the hour. He is a charitable, open-hearted old fellow at bottom, after all; so, although he puts the old lady a little out occasionally, they agree very well in the main, and she laughs as much at each feat of his handiwork when it is all over, as anybody else.

CHAPTER III

THE row of houses in which the old lady and her troublesome neighbour reside, comprises, beyond all doubt, a greater number of characters within its circumscribed limits, than all the rest of the parish put together. As we cannot, consistently with our present plan, however, extend the number of our parochial sketches beyond six, it will be better perhaps, to select the most peculiar, and to introduce them at once without further preface.

The four Miss Willises, then, settled in our parish thirteen years ago. It is a melancholy reflection that the old adage, " time and tide wait for no man," applies with equal force to the fairer portion of the creation ; and willingly would we conceal the fact, that even thirteen years ago the Miss Willises were far from juvenile. Our duty as faithful parochial chroniclers, however, is paramount to every other consideration, and we are bound to state, that thirteen years since, the authorities in matrimonial cases, considered the youngest Miss Willis in a very precarious state, while the eldest sister was positively given over, as being far beyond all human hope. Well, the Miss Willises took a lease of the house ; it was fresh painted and papered from top to bottom : the paint inside was all wainscoted, the marble all cleaned, the old grates taken down, and register-stoves, you could see to dress by, put up ; four trees were planted in

15

the back garden, several small baskets of gravel sprinkled over the front one, vans of elegant furniture arrived, spring blinds were fitted to the windows, carpenters who had been employed in the various preparations, alterations, and repairs, made confidential statements to the different maid-servants in the row, relative to the magnificent scale on which the Miss Willises were commencing; the maid-servants told their ."Missises," the Missises told their friends, and vague rumours were circulated throughout the parish, that No. 25, in Gordon-place, had been taken by four maiden ladies of immense property.

At last, the Miss Willises moved in; and then the "calling" began. The house was the perfection of neatness—so were the four Miss Willises. Everything was formal, stiff, and cold—so were the four Miss Willises. Not a single chair of the whole set was ever seen out of its place—not a single Miss Willis of the whole four was ever seen out of hers. There they always sat, in the same places, doing precisely the same things at the same hour. The eldest Miss Willis used to knit, the second to draw, the two others to play duets on the piano. They seemed to have no separate existence, but to have made up their minds just to winter through life together. They were three long graces in drapery, with the addition, like a school-dinner, of another long grace after-wards—the three fates with another sister—the Siamese twins multiplied by two. The eldest Miss Willis grew bilious—the four Miss Willises grew bilious immediately. The eldest Miss Willis grew ill-tempered and religious—the four Miss Willises were ill-tempered and religious directly. Whatever the eldest did, the others did, and whatever anybody else did, they all disapproved of; and thus they vegetated—living in Polar harmony among themselves, and, as they sometimes went out, or saw company "in a quiet-way" at home, occasionally icing the neighbours. Three years passed over in this way, when an unlooked for and extraordinary phe-nomenon occurred. The Miss Willises showed symptoms of

16

summer, the frost gradually broke up; a complete thaw took place. Was it possible? one of the four Miss Willises was going to be married!

Now, where on earth the husband came from, by what feelings the poor man could have been actuated, or by what process of reasoning the four Miss Willises succeeded in persuading themselves that it was possible for a man to marry one of them, without marrying them all, are questions too profound for us to resolve: certain it is, however, that the visits of Mr. Robinson (a gentleman in a public office, with a good salary and a little property of his own, besides) were received—that the four Miss Willises were courted in due form by the said Mr. Robinson—that the neighbours were perfectly frantic in their anxiety to discover which of the four Miss Willises was the fortunate fair, and that the difficulty they experienced in solving the problem was not at all lessened by the announcement of the eldest Miss Willis, —" *We* are going to marry Mr. Robinson."

It was very extraordinary. They were so completely identified, the one with the other, that the curiosity of the whole row—even of the old lady herself—was roused almost beyond endurance. The subject was discussed at every little card-table and tea-drinking. The old gentleman of silk-worm notoriety did not hesitate to express his decided opinion that Mr. Robinson was of Eastern descent, and contemplated marrying the whole family at once; and the row, generally, shook their heads with considerable gravity, and declared the business to be very mysterious. They hoped it might all end well;—it certainly had a very singular appearance, but still it would be uncharitable to express any opinion without good grounds to go upon, and certainly the Miss Willises were *quite* old enough to judge for themselves, and to be sure people ought to know their own business best, and so forth.

At last, one fine morning, at a quarter before eight o'clock, A.M., two glass-coaches drove up to the Miss Willises' door, at which Mr. Robinson had arrived in a cab ten minutes before, dressed in a light-blue coat and double-milled kersey pantaloons, white neckerchief, pumps, and dress-gloves, his manner denoting, as appeared from the evidence of the housemaid at No. 23, who was sweeping the door-steps at the time, a considerable degree of nervous excitement. It was also hastily reported on the same testimony, that the cook who opened the door, wore a large white bow of unusual dimensions, in a much smarter head-dress than the regulation cap to which the Miss Willises invariably restricted the somewhat excursive tastes of female servants in general.

The intelligence spread rapidly from house to house. It was quite clear that the eventful morning had at length arrived; the whole row stationed themselves behind their first and second floor blinds, and waited the result in breathless expectation.

At last the Miss Willises' door opened; the door of the first glass-coach did the same. Two gentlemen, and a pair of ladies to correspond—friends of the family, no doubt; up went the steps, bang went the door, off went the first glass-coach, and up came the second.

The street door opened again; the excitement of the whole row increased—Mr. Robinson and the eldest Miss Willis. "I thought so," said the lady at No. 19; "I always said it was *Miss* Willis!"—"Well, I never!" ejaculated the young lady at No. 18 to the young lady at No. 17.—"Did you ever, dear!" responded the young lady at No. 17 to the young lady at No. 18. "It's too ridiculous!" exclaimed a spinster of an *un*certain age, at No. 16, joining in the conversation. But who shall portray the astonishment of Gordon-place, when Mr. Robinson handed in *all* the Miss Willises, one after the other, and then squeezed himself into an acute angle of the glass-coach, which forthwith proceeded at a brisk pace, after the other glass-coach, which other glass-coach had itself proceeded, at a brisk pace, in the direction of the parish church! Who shall depict the perplexity of the

18

clergyman, when *all* the Miss Willises knelt down at the communion-table, and repeated the responses incidental to the marriage service in an audible voice—or who shall describe the confusion which prevailed, when—even after the difficulties thus occasioned had been adjusted—*all* the Miss Willises went into hysterics at the conclusion of the ceremony, until the sacred edifice resounded with their united wailings!

As the four sisters and Mr. Robinson continued to occupy the same house after this memorable occasion, and as the married sister, whoever she was, never appeared in public without the other three, we are not quite clear that the neighbours ever would have discovered the real Mrs. Robinson, but for a circumstance of the most gratifying description, which *will* happen occasionally in the best-regulated families. Three quarter-days elapsed, and the row, on whom a new light appeared to have been bursting for some time, began to speak with a sort of implied confidence on the subject, and to wonder how Mrs. Robinson—the youngest Miss Willis that was—got on; and servants might be seen running up the steps, about nine or ten o'clock every morning, with "Missis's compliments, and wishes to know how Mrs. Robinson finds herself this morning?" And the answer always was, "Mrs. Robinson's compliments, and she's in very good spirits, and doesn't find herself any worse." The piano was heard no longer, the knitting-needles were laid aside, drawing was neglected, and mantua-making and millinery, on the smallest scale imaginable, appeared to have become the favourite amusement of the whole family. The parlour wasn't quite as tidy as it used to be, and if you called in the morning, you would see lying on a table, with an old newspaper carelessly thrown over them, two or three particularly small caps, rather larger than if they had been made for a moderate-sized doll, with a small piece of lace, in the shape of a horse-shoe, let in behind: or perhaps a white robe, not very large in circumference, but very much out of proportion in point of length, with a little tucker round the top, and a frill round the bottom; and once when we called, we saw a long white roller, with a kind of blue margin down each side, the probable use of which, we were at a loss to conjecture. Then we fancied that Mr. Dawson, the surgeon, &c., who displays a large lamp with a different colour in every pane of glass, at the corner of the row, began to be knocked up at night oftener than he used to be; and once we were very much alarmed by hearing a hackney-coach stop at Mrs. Robinson's door, at half-past two o'clock in the morning, out of which there emerged a fat old woman, in a cloak and nightcap, with a bundle in one hand, and a pair of pattens in the other, who looked as if she had been suddenly knocked up out of bed for some very special purpose.

When we got up in the morning we saw that the knocker was tied up in an old white kid glove; and we, in our innocence (we were in a state of bachelorship then), wondered what on earth it all meant, until we heard the eldest Miss Willis, *in propriâ personâ*, say, with great dignity, in answer to the next inquiry, " *My* compliments, and Mrs. Robinson's doing as well as can be expected, and the little girl thrives wonderfully." And then, in common with the rest of the row, our curiosity was satisfied, and we began to wonder it had never occurred to us what the matter was, before.

CHAPTER IV

A GREAT event has recently occurred in our parish. A contest of paramount interest has just terminated; a parochial convulsion has taken place. It has been succeeded by a glorious triumph, which the country—or at least the parish—it is all the same—will long remember. We have had an election; an election for beadle. The supporters of the old beadle system have been defeated in their stronghold, and the advocates of the great new beadle principles have achieved a proud victory.

Our parish, which, like all other parishes, is a little world of its own, has long been divided into two parties, whose contentions, slumbering for a while, have never failed to burst forth with unabated vigour, on any occasion on which they could by possibility be renewed. Watching-rates, lighting-rates, paving-rates, sewer's-rates, church-rates, poor's-rates—all sorts of rates, have been in their turns the subjects of a grand struggle; and as to questions of patronage, the asperity and determination with which they have been contested is scarcely credible.

The leader of the official party—the steady advocate of the churchwardens, and the unflinching supporter of the overseers—is an old gentleman who lives in our row. He owns some half a dozen houses in it, and always walks on the opposite side of the way, so that he may be able to take in

21

a view of the whole of his property at once. He is a tall, thin, bony man, with an interrogative nose, and little restless perking eyes, which appear to have been given him for the sole purpose of peeping into other people's affairs with. He is deeply impressed with the importance of our parish business, and prides himself, not a little, on his style of addressing the parishioners in vestry assembled. His views are rather confined than extensive; his principles more narrow than liberal. He has been heard to declaim very loudly in favour of the liberty of the press, and advocates the repeal of the stamp duty on newspapers, because the daily journals who now have a monopoly of the public, never give *verbatim* reports of vestry meetings. He would not appear egotistical for the world, but at the same time he must say, that there *are* speeches—that celebrated speech of his own, on the emoluments of the sexton, and the duties of the office, for instance—which might be communicated to the public, greatly to their improvement and advantage.

His great opponent in public life is Captain Purday, the old naval officer on half-pay, to whom we have already introduced our readers. The captain being a determined opponent of the constituted authorities, whoever they may chance to be, and our other friend being their steady supporter, with an equal disregard of their individual merits, it will readily be supposed, that occasions for their coming into direct collision are neither few nor far between. They divided the vestry fourteen times on a motion for heating the church with warm water instead of coals : and made speeches about liberty and expenditure, and prodigality and hot water, which threw the whole parish into a state of excitement. Then the captain, when he was on the visiting committee, and his opponent overseer, brought forward certain distinct and specific charges relative to the management of the workhouse, boldly expressed his total want of confidence in the existing authorities, and moved for "a copy of the recipe by which the paupers' soup was prepared, together with any documents

22

THE CANDIDATES

relating thereto." This the overseer steadily resisted; he fortified himself by precedent, appealed to the established usage, and declined to produce the papers, on the ground of the injury that would be done to the public service, if documents of a strictly private nature, passing between the master of the workhouse and the cook, were to be thus dragged to light on the motion of any individual member of the vestry. The motion was lost by a majority of two; and then the captain, who never allows himself to be defeated, moved for a commitee of inquiry into the whole subject. The affair grew serious: the question was discussed at meeting after meeting, and vestry after vestry; speeches were made, attacks repudiated, personal defiances exchanged, explanations received, and the greatest excitement prevailed, until at last, just as the question was going to be finally decided, the vestry found that somehow or other, they had become entangled in a point of form, from which it was impossible to escape with propriety. So, the motion was dropped, and everybody looked extremely important, and seemed quite satisfied with the meritorious nature of the whole proceeding.

This was the state of affairs in our parish a week or two since, when Simmons, the beadle, suddenly died. The lamented deceased had over-exerted himself, a day or two previously, in conveying an aged female, highly intoxicated, to the strong room of the workhouse. The excitement thus occasioned, added to a severe cold, which this indefatigable officer had caught in his capacity of director of the parish engine, by inadvertently playing over himself instead of a fire, proved too much for a constitution already enfeebled by age; and the intelligence was conveyed to the Board one evening that Simmons had died, and left his respects.

The breath was scarcely out of the body of the deceased functionary, when the field was filled with competitors for the vacant office, each of whom rested his claims to public support, entirely on the number and extent of his family, as if the office of beadle were originally instituted as an

23

encouragement for the propagation of the human species. "Bung for Beadle. Five small children!"—"Hopkins for Beadle. Seven small children!!"—"Timkins for Beadle. Nine small children!!!" Such were the placards in large black letters on a white ground, which were plentifully pasted on the walls, and posted in the windows of the principal shops. Timkins's success was considered certain: several mothers of families half promised their votes, and the nine small children would have run over the course, but for the production of another placard, announcing the appearance of a still more meritorious candidate. " Spruggins for Beadle. Ten small children (two of them twins), and a wife!!!" There was no resisting this; ten small children would have been almost irresistible in themselves, without the twins, but the touching parenthesis about that interesting production of nature, and the still more touching allusion to Mrs. Spruggins, must ensure success. Spruggins was the favourite at once, and the appearance of his lady, as she went about to solicit votes (which encouraged confident hopes of a still further addition to the house of Spruggins at no remote period), increased the general prepossession in his favour. The other candidates, Bung alone excepted, resigned in despair. The day of election was fixed; and the canvass proceeded with briskness and perseverance on both sides.

The members of the vestry could not be supposed to escape the contagious excitement inseparable from the occasion. The majority of the lady inhabitants of the parish declared at once for Spruggins; and the *quondam* overseer took the same side, on the ground that men with large families always had been elected to the office, and that although he must admit, that, in other respects, Spruggins was the least qualified candidate of the two, still it was an old practice, and he saw no reason why an old practice should be departed from. This was enough for the captain. He immediately sided with Bung, canvassed for him personally in all directions, wrote squibs on Spruggins, and got his butcher to skewer them up on conspicuous joints in his shop-front; frightened his neighbour, the old lady, into a palpitation of the heart, by his awful denunciations of Spruggins's party; and bounced in and out, and up and down, and backwards and forwards, until all the sober inhabitants of the parish thought it inevitable that he must die of a brain fever, long before the election began.

The day of election arrived. It was no longer an individual struggle, but a party contest between the ins and outs. The question was, whether the withering influence of the overseers, the domination of the churchwardens, and the blighting despotism of the vestry-clerk, should be allowed to render the election of beadle a form—a nullity: whether they should impose a vestry-elected beadle on the parish, to do their bidding and forward their views, or whether the parishioners, fearlessly asserting their undoubted rights, should elect an independent beadle of their own.

The nomination was fixed to take place in the vestry, but so great was the throng of anxious spectators, that it was found necessary to adjourn to the church, where the ceremony commenced with due solemnity. The appearance of the churchwardens and overseers, and the ex-churchwardens and ex-overseers, with Spruggins in the rear, excited general attention. Spruggins was a little thin man, in rusty black, with a long pale face, and a countenance expressive of care and fatigue, which might either be attributed to the extent of his family or the anxiety of his feelings. His opponent appeared in a cast-off coat of the captain's—a blue coat with bright buttons: white trousers, and that description of shoes familiarly known by the appellation of "high-lows." There was a serenity in the open countenance of Bung—a kind of moral dignity in his confident air—an "I wish you may get it" sort of expression in his eye—which infused animation into his supporters, and evidently dispirited his opponents.

The ex-churchwarden rose to propose Thomas Spruggins for beadle. He had known him long. He had had his eye upon him closely for years; he had watched him with two-fold vigilance for months. (A parishioner here suggested that this might be termed "taking a double sight," but the observation was drowned in loud cries of "Order!") He would repeat that he had had his eye upon him for years, and this he would say, that a more well-conducted, a more well-behaved, a more sober, a more quiet man, with a more well-regulated mind, he had never met with. A man with a larger family he had never known (cheers). The parish required a man who could be depended on ("Hear!" from the Spruggins side, answered by ironical cheers from the Bung party). Such a man he now proposed ("No," "Yes"). He would not allude to individuals (the ex-churchwarden continued, in the celebrated negative style adopted by great speakers). He would not advert to a gentleman who had once held a high rank in the service of his majesty; he would not say, that that gentleman was no gentleman; he would not assert, that that man was no man; he would not say, that he was a turbulent parishioner; he would not say, that he had grossly misbehaved himself, not only on this, but on all former occasions; he would not say, that he was one of those discontented and treasonable spirits, who carried confusion and disorder wherever they went; he would not say, that he harboured in his heart envy, and hatred, and malice, and all uncharitableness. No! He wished to have everything comfortable and pleasant, and therefore, he would say—nothing about him (cheers).

The captain replied in a similar parliamentary style. He would not say, he was astonished at the speech they had just heard; he would not say, he was disgusted (cheers). He would not retort the epithets which had been hurled against him (renewed cheering); he would not allude to men once in office, but now happily out of it, who had mismanaged the workhouse, ground the paupers, diluted the beer, slack-baked the bread, boned the meat, heightened the work, and lowered the soup (tremendous cheers). He would not ask what such men deserved (a voice, "Nothing a-day, and find themselves!"). He would not say, that one burst of general indignation should drive them from the parish they polluted with their presence ("Give it him!"). He would not allude to the unfortunate man who had been proposed—he would not say, as the vestry's tool, but as Beadle. He would not advert to that individual's family; he would not say, that nine children, twins, and a wife, were very bad examples for pauper imitation (loud cheers). He would not advert in detail to the qualifications of Bung. The man stood before him, and he would not say in his presence, what he might be disposed to say of him, if he were absent. (Here Mr. Bung telegraphed to a friend near him, under cover of his hat, by contracting his left eye, and applying his right thumb to the tip of his nose). It had been objected to Bung that he had only five children ("Hear, hear!" from the opposition). Well; he had yet to learn that the legislature had affixed any precise amount of infantine qualification to the office of beadle; but taking it for granted that an extensive family were a great requisite, he entreated them to look to facts, and compare *data*, about which there could be no mistake. Bung was 35 years of age. Spruggins—of whom he wished to speak with all possible respect—was 50. Was it not more than possible—was it not very probable—that by the time Bung attained the latter age, he might see around him a family, even exceeding in number and extent, that to which Spruggins at present laid claim (deafening cheers and waving of handkerchiefs)? The captain concluded, amidst loud applause, by calling upon the parishioners to sound the tocsin, rush to the poll, free themselves from dictation, or be slaves for ever.

On the following day the polling began, and we never have had such a bustle in our parish since we got up our famous anti-slavery petition, which was such an important one, that the House of Commons ordered it to be printed, on the motion of the member for the district. The captain engaged

two hackney-coaches and a cab for Bung's people—the cab
for the drunken voters, and the two coaches for the old
ladies, the greater portion of whom, owing to the captain's
impetuosity, were driven up to the poll and home again,
before they recovered from their flurry sufficiently to know,
with any degree of clearness, what they had been doing.
The opposite party wholly neglected these precautions, and
the consequence was, that a great many ladies who were
walking leisurely up to the church—for it was a very hot
day—to vote for Spruggins, were artfully decoyed into the
coaches, and voted for Bung. The captain's arguments, too,
had produced considerable effect : the attempted influence of
the vestry produced a greater. A threat of exclusive dealing
was clearly established against the vestry-clerk—a case of
heartless and profligate atrocity. It appeared that the delin-
quent had been in the habit of purchasing six penn'orth of
muffins, weekly, from an old woman who rents a small house
in the parish, and resides among the original settlers ; on her
last weekly visit, a message was conveyed to her through
the medium of the cook, couched in mysterious terms, but
indicating with sufficient clearness, that the vestry-clerk's
appetite for muffins, in future, depended entirely on her vote
on the beadleship. This was sufficient : the stream had been
turning previously, and the impulse thus administered directed
its final course. The Bung party ordered one shilling's-
worth of muffins weekly for the remainder of the old woman's
natural life ; the parishioners were loud in their exclamations ;
and the fate of Spruggins was sealed.

It was in vain that the twins were exhibited in dresses of
the same pattern, and night-caps, to match, at the church
door : the boy in Mrs. Spruggins's right arm, and the girl in
her left—even Mrs. Spruggins herself failed to be an object
of sympathy any longer. The majority attained by Bung
on the gross poll was four hundred and twenty-eight, and
the cause of the parishioners triumphed.

CHAPTER V

THE excitement of the late election has subsided, and our parish being once again restored to a state of comparative tranquillity, we are enabled to devote our attention to those parishioners who take little share in our party contests or in the turmoil and bustle of public life. And we feel sincere pleasure in acknowledging here, that in collecting materials for this task we have been greatly assisted by Mr. Bung himself, who has imposed on us a debt of obligation which we fear we can never repay. The life of this gentleman has been one of a very chequered description: he has undergone transitions—not from grave to gay, for he never was grave —not from lively to severe, for severity forms no part of his disposition; his fluctuations have been between poverty in the extreme, and poverty modified, or, to use his own emphatic language, "between nothing to eat and just half enough." He is not, as he forcibly remarks, "one of those fortunate men who, if they were to dive under one side of a barge stark-naked, would come up on the other with a new suit of clothes on, and a ticket for soup in the waistcoat-pocket:" neither is he one of those, whose spirit has been broken beyond redemption by misfortune and want. He is just one of the careless, good-for-nothing, happy fellows, who float, cork-like, on the surface, for the world to play at hockey with: knocked here, and there, and

29

everywhere: now to the right, then to the left, again up in the air, and anon to the bottom, but always reappearing and bounding with the stream buoyantly and merrily along. Some few months before he was prevailed upon to stand a contested election for the office of beadle, necessity attached him to the service of a broker; and on the opportunities he here acquired of ascertaining the condition of most of the poorer inhabitants of the parish, his patron, the captain, first grounded his claims to public support. Chance threw the man in our way a short time since. We were, in the first instance, attracted by his prepossessing impudence at the election; we were not surprised, on further acquaintance, to find him a shrewd, knowing fellow, with no inconsiderable power of observation; and, after conversing with him a little, were somewhat struck (as we dare say our readers have frequently been in other cases) with the power some men seem to have, not only of sympathising with, but to all appearance of understanding feelings to which they themselves are entire strangers. We had been expressing to the new functionary our surprise that he should ever have served in the capacity to which we have just adverted, when we gradually led him into one or two professional anecdotes. As we are induced to think, on reflection, that they will tell better in nearly his own words, than with any attempted embellishments of ours, we will at once entitle them

Mr. Bung's Narrative.

"It's very true, as you say, sir," Mr. Bung commenced, "that a broker's man's is not a life to be envied; and in course you know as well as I do, though you don't say it, that people hate and scout 'em because they're the ministers of wretchedness, like, to poor people. But what could I do, sir? The thing was no worse because I did it, instead of somebody else; and if putting me in possession of a house would put me in possession of three and sixpence a day, and levying a distress on another man's goods would relieve my distress and that of my family, it can't be expected but what I'd take the job and go through with it. I never liked it, God knows; I always looked out for something else, and the moment I got other work to do, I left it. If there is anything wrong in being the agent in such matters—not the principal, mind you—I'm sure the business, to a beginner like I was, at all events, carries its own punishment along with it. I wished again and again that the people would only blow me up, or pitch into me—that I wouldn't have minded, it's all in my way; but it's the being shut up by yourself in one room for five days, without so much as an old newspaper to look at, or anything to see out o' the winder but the roofs and chimneys at the back of the house, or anything to listen to, but the ticking, perhaps, of an old Dutch clock, the sobbing of the missis, now and then, the low talking of friends in the next room, who speak in whispers, lest 'the man' should overhear them, or perhaps the occasional opening of the door, as a child peeps in to look at you, and then runs half-frightened away—it's all this, that makes you feel sneaking somehow, and ashamed of yourself; and then, if it's winter-time, they just give you fire enough to make you think you'd like more, and bring in your grub as if they wished it 'ud choke you—as I dare say they do, for the matter of that, most heartily. If they're very civil, they make you up a bed in the room at night, and if they don't, your master sends one in for you; but there you are, without being washed or shaved all the time, shunned by everybody, and spoken to by no one, unless some one comes in at dinner-time, and asks you whether you want any more, in a tone as much to say, 'I hope you don't,' or, in the evening, to inquire whether you wouldn't rather have a candle, after you've been sitting in the dark half the night. When I was left in this way, I used to sit, think, think, thinking, till I felt as lonesome as a kitten in a wash-house copper with the lid on; but I believe the old brokers' men who are regularly trained to it, never think at all. I have heard some on 'em say, indeed, that they don't know how!

"I put in a good many distresses in my time (continued Mr. Bung), and in course I wasn't long in finding, that some people are not as much to be pitied as others are, and that people with good incomes who get into difficulties, which they keep patching up day after day, and week after week, get so used to these sort of things in time, that at last they come scarcely to feel them at all. I remember the very first place I was put in possession of, was a gentleman's house in this parish here, that everybody would suppose couldn't help having money if he tried. I went with old Fixem, my old master, 'bout half arter eight in the morning; rang the area-bell; servant in livery opened the door: 'Governor at home?' —'Yes, he is,' says the man; 'but he's breakfasting just now.' 'Never mind,' says Fixem, 'just you tell him there's a gentleman here, as wants to speak to him partickler.' So the servant he opens his eyes, and stares about him all ways—looking for the gentleman, as it struck me, for I don't think anybody but a man as was stone-blind would mistake Fixem for one; and as for me, I was as seedy as a cheap cowcumber. Hows'ever, he turns round, and goes to the breakfast-parlour, which was a little snug sort of room at the end of the passage, and Fixem (as we always did in that profession), without waiting to be announced, walks in arter him, and before the servant could get out, 'Please, sir, here's a man as wants to speak to you,' looks in at the door as familiar and pleasant as may be. 'Who the devil are you, and how dare you walk into a gentleman's house without leave?' says the master, as fierce as a bull in fits. 'My name,' says Fixem, winking to the master to send the servant away, and putting the warrant into his hands folded up like a note, 'My name's Smith,' says he, 'and I called from Johnson's about that business of Thompson's.'—'Oh,' says the other, quite down on him directly, 'How *is* Thompson?' says he; 'Pray sit down, Mr. Smith: John, leave the room.' Out went the servant; and the gentleman and Fixem looked at one another till they couldn't look any longer, and then they varied the amusements by looking at me, who had been standing on the mat all this time. 'Hundred and fifty pounds, I see,' said the gentleman at last. 'Hundred and fifty pound,' said Fixem, 'besides cost of levy, sheriff's poundage, and all other incidental expenses.'—'Um,' says the gentleman, 'I shan't be able to settle this before to-morrow afternoon.'—'Very sorry ; but I shall be obliged to leave my man here till then,' replies Fixem, pretending to look very miserable over it. 'That's very unfort'nate,' says the gentleman, 'for I have got a large party here to-night, and I'm ruined if those fellows of mine get an inkling of the matter—just step here, Mr. Smith,' says he, after a short pause. So Fixem walks with him up to the window, and after a good deal of whispering, and a little chinking of suverins, and looking at me, he comes back and says, 'Bung, you're a handy fellow, and very honest I know. This gentleman wants an assistant to clean the plate and wait at table to-day, and if you're not particularly engaged,' says old Fixem, grinning like mad, and shoving a couple of suverins into my hand, 'he'll be very glad to avail himself of your services.' Well, I laughed: and the gentleman laughed, and we all laughed; and I went home and cleaned myself, leaving Fixem there, and when I went back, Fixem went away, and I polished up the plate, and waited at table, and gammoned the servants, and nobody had the least idea I was in possession, though it very nearly came out after all; for one of the last gentlemen who remained, came down-stairs into the hall where I was sitting pretty late at night, and putting half-a-crown into my hand, says, 'Here, my man,' says he, 'run and get me a coach, will you?' I thought it was a do, to get me out of the house, and was just going to say so, sulkily enough, when the gentleman (who was up to everything) came running down-stairs, as if he was in great anxiety. 'Bung,' says he, pretending to be in a consuming passion. 'Sir,' says I. 'Why the devil an't you looking

33

after that plate?'—'I was just going to send him for a coach for me,' says the other gentleman. 'And I was just a-going to say,' says I—'Anybody else, my dear fellow,' interrupts the master of the house, pushing me down the passage to get out of the way—'anybody else; but I have put this man in possession of all the plate and valuables, and I cannot allow him on any consideration whatever, to leave the house. Bung, you scoundrel, go and count those forks in the break-fast-parlour instantly.' You may be sure I went laughing pretty hearty when I found it was all right. The money was paid next day, with the addition of something else for myself, and that was the best job that I (and I suspect old Fixem too) ever got in that line.

"But this is the bright side of the picture, sir, after all," resumed Mr. Bung, laying aside the knowing look and flash air, with which he had repeated the previous anecdote—"and I'm sorry to say, it's the side one sees very, very seldom, in comparison with the dark one. The civility which money will purchase, is rarely extended to those who have none; and there's a consolation even in being able to patch up one difficulty, to make way for another, to which very poor people are strangers. I was once put into a house down George's-yard—that little dirty court at the back of the gas-works; and I never shall forget the misery of them people, dear me! It was a distress for half a year's rent—two pound ten, I think. There was only two rooms in the house, and as there was no passage, the lodgers up-stairs always went through the room of the people of the house, as they passed in and out; and every time they did so—which, on the average, was about four times every quarter of an hour—they blowed up quite frightful: for their things had been seized too, and included in the inventory. There was a little piece of en-closed dust in front of the house, with a cinder-path leading up to the door, and an open rain-water butt on one side. A dirty striped curtain, on a very slack string, hung in the window, and a little triangular bit of broken looking-glass

34

rested on the sill inside. I suppose it was meant for the people's use, but their appearance was so wretched, and so miserable, that I'm certain they never could have plucked up courage to look themselves in the face a second time, if they survived the fright of doing so once. There was two or three chairs, that might have been worth, in their best days, from eightpence to a shilling a-piece; a small deal table, an old corner cupboard with nothing in it, and one of those bedsteads which turn up half way, and leave the bottom legs sticking out for you to knock your head against, or hang your hat upon; no bed, no bedding. There was an old sack, by way of rug, before the fireplace, and four or five children were grovelling about, among the sand on the floor. The execution was only put in, to get 'em out of the house, for there was nothing to take to pay the expenses; and here I stopped for three days, though that was a mere form too: for, in course, I knew, and we all knew, they could never pay the money. In one of the chairs, by the side of the place where the fire ought to have been, was an old 'ooman—the ugliest and dirtiest I ever see—who sat rocking herself backwards and forwards, backwards and forwards, without once stopping, except for an instant now and then, to clasp together the withered hands which, with these exceptions, she kept constantly rubbing upon her knees, just raising and depressing her fingers convulsively, in time to the rocking of the chair. On the other side sat the mother with an infant in her arms, which cried till it cried itself to sleep, and when it 'woke, cried till it cried itself off again. The old 'ooman's voice I never heard: she seemed completely stupefied; and as to the mother's, it would have been better if she had been so too, for misery had changed her to a devil. If you had heard how she cursed the little naked children as was rolling on the floor, and seen how savagely she struck the infant when it cried with hunger, you'd have shuddered as much as I did. There they remained all the time: the children ate a morsel of bread once or twice, and I gave 'em best part of the dinners my missis brought me, but the woman ate nothing; they never even laid on the bedstead, nor was the room swept or cleaned all the time. The neighbours were all too poor themselves to take any notice of 'em, but from what I could make out from the abuse of the woman up-stairs, it seemed the husband had been transported a few weeks before. When the time was up, the landlord and old Fixem too, got rather frightened about the family, and so they made a stir about it, and had 'em taken to the workhouse. They sent the sick couch for the old 'ooman, and Simmons took the children away at night. The old 'ooman went into the infirmary, and very soon died. The children are all in the house to this day, and very comfortable they are in comparison. As to the mother, there was no taming her at all. She had been a quiet, hard-working woman, I believe, but her misery had actually drove her wild; so after she had been sent to the house of correction half-a-dozen times, for throwing inkstands at the overseers, blaspheming the churchwardens, and smashing everybody as come near her, she burst a blood-vessel one mornin', and died too; and a happy release it was, both for herself and the old paupers, male and female, which she used to tip over in all directions, as if they were so many skittles, and she the ball.

"Now this was bad enough," resumed Mr. Bung, taking a half-step towards the door, as if to intimate that he had nearly concluded. "This was bad enough, but there was a sort of quiet misery—if you understand what I mean by that, sir—about a lady at one house I was put into, as touched me a good deal more. It doesn't matter where it was exactly: indeed, I'd rather not say, but it was the same sort o' job. I went with Fixem in the usual way—there was a year's rent in arrear; a very small servant-girl opened the door, and three or four fine-looking little children was in the front parlour we were shown into, which was very clean, but very scantily furnished, much like the children themselves. 'Bung,' says Fixem to me, in a low voice, when we were left alone for a minute, 'I know something about this here family, and my opinion is, it's no go.' 'Do you think they can't settle?' says I, quite anxiously; for I liked the looks of them children. Fixem shook his head, and was just about to reply, when the door opened, and in come a lady, as white as ever I see any one in my days, except about the eyes, which were red with crying. She walked in, as firm as I could have done; shut the door carefully after her, and sat herself down with a face as composed as if it was made of stone. 'What is the matter, gentlemen?' says she, in a surprisin' steady voice. '*Is* this an execution?' 'It is, mum,' says Fixem. The lady looked at him as steady as ever: she didn't seem to have understood him. 'It is, mum,' says Fixem again; 'this is my warrant of distress, mum,' says he, handing it over as polite as if it was a newspaper which had been bespoke arter the next gentleman.

"The lady's lip trembled as she took the printed paper. She cast her eye over it, and old Fixem began to explain the form, but I saw she wasn't reading it, plain enough, poor thing. 'Oh, my God!' says she, suddenly a-bursting out crying, letting the warrant fall, and hiding her face in her hands. 'Oh, my God! what will become of us!' The noise she made, brought in a young lady of about nineteen or twenty, who, I suppose, had been a-listening at the door, and who had got a little boy in her arms: she sat him down in the lady's lap, without speaking, and she hugged the poor little fellow to her bosom, and cried over him, till even old Fixem put on his blue spectacles to hide the two tears, that was a-trickling down, one on each side of his dirty face. 'Now, dear ma,' says the young lady, 'you know how much you have borne. For all our sakes—for pa's sake,' says she, 'don't give way to this!'— 'No, no, I won't!' says the lady, gathering herself up, hastily, and drying her eyes; 'I am very foolish, but I'm better now —much better.' And then she roused herself up, went with us into every room while we took the inventory, opened all the drawers of her own accord, sorted the children's little

37

clothes to make the work easier; and, except doing everything in a strange sort of hurry, seemed as calm and composed as if nothing had happened. When we came down-stairs again, she hesitated a minute or two, and at last says, 'Gentlemen,' says she, 'I am afraid I have done wrong, and perhaps it may bring you into trouble. I secreted just now,' she says, 'the only trinket I have left in the world—here it is.' So she lays down on the table a little miniature mounted in gold. 'It's a miniature,' she says, 'of my poor dear father! I little thought once, that I should ever thank God for depriving me of the original, but I do, and have done for years back, most fervently. Take it away, sir,' she says, 'it's a face that never turned from me in sickness or distress, and I can hardly bear to turn from it now, when, God knows, I suffer both in no ordinary degree.' I couldn't say nothing, but I raised my head from the inventory which I was filling up, and looked at Fixem; the old fellow nodded to me significantly, so I ran my pen through the 'Mini' I had just written, and left the miniature on the table.

"Well, sir, to make short of a long story, I was left in possession, and in possession I remained; and though I was an ignorant man, and the master of the house a clever one, I saw what he never did, but what he would give worlds now (if he had 'em) to have seen in time. I saw, sir, that his wife was wasting away, beneath cares of which she never complained, and griefs she never told. I saw that she was dying before his eyes; I knew that one exertion from him might have saved her, but he never made it. I don't blame him: I don't think he *could* rouse himself. She had so long anticipated all his wishes, and acted for him, that he was a lost man when left to himself. I used to think when I caught sight of her, in the clothes she used to wear, which looked shabby even upon her, and would have been scarcely decent on any one else, that if I was a gentleman it would wring my very heart to see the woman that was a smart and merry girl when I courted her, so altered through her love

for me. Bitter cold and damp weather it was, yet, though
her dress was thin, and her shoes none of the best, during
the whole three days, from morning to night, she was out of
doors running about to try and raise the money. The money
was raised and the execution was paid out. The whole family
crowded into the room where I was, when the money arrived.
The father was quite happy as the inconvenience was
removed—I dare say he didn't know how; the children looked
merry and cheerful again; the eldest girl was bustling about,
making preparations for the first comfortable meal they had
had since the distress was put in; and the mother looked
pleased to see them all so. But if ever I saw death in a
woman's face, I saw it in hers that night.

"I was right, sir," continued Mr. Bung, hurriedly passing
his coat-sleeve over his face; "the family grew more
prosperous, and good fortune arrived. But it was too late.
Those children are motherless now, and their father would
give up all he has since gained—house, home, goods, money:
all that he has, or ever can have, to restore the wife he
has lost."

CHAPTER VI

THE LADIES' SOCIETIES

OUR Parish is very prolific in ladies' charitable institutions. In winter, when wet feet are common, and colds not scarce, we have the ladies' soup distribution society, the ladies' coal distribution society, and the ladies' blanket distribution society; in summer, when stone fruits flourish and stomach aches prevail, we have the ladies' dispensary, and the ladies' sick visitation committee; and all the year round we have the ladies' child's examination society, the ladies' bible and prayer-book circulation society, and the ladies' childbed-linen monthly loan society. The two latter are decidedly the most important; whether they are productive of more benefit than the rest, it is not for us to say, but we can take upon ourselves to affirm, with the utmost solemnity, that they create a greater stir and more bustle, than all the others put together.

We should be disposed to affirm, on the first blush of the matter, that the bible and prayer-book society is not so popular as the childbed-linen society; the bible and prayer-book society has, however, considerably increased in importance within the last year or two, having derived some adventitious aid from the factious opposition of the child's examination society; which factious opposition originated in manner following:—When the young curate was popular, and all the unmarried ladies in the parish took a serious turn,

40

THE THREE MISS BROWNS

the charity children all at once became objects of peculiar and especial interest. The three Miss Browns (enthusiastic admirers of the curate) taught, and exercised, and examined, and re-examined the unfortunate children, until the boys grew pale, and the girls consumptive with study and fatigue. The three Miss Browns stood it out very well, because they relieved each other; but the children, having no relief at all, exhibited decided symptoms of weariness and care. The unthinking part of the parishioners laughed at all this, but the more reflective portion of the inhabitants abstained from expressing any opinion on the subject until that of the curate had been clearly ascertained.

The opportunity was not long wanting. The curate preached a charity sermon on behalf of the charity school, and in the charity sermon aforesaid, expatiated in glowing terms on the praiseworthy and indefatigable exertions of certain estimable individuals. Sobs were heard to issue from the three Miss Browns' pew; the pew-opener of the division was seen to hurry down the centre aisle to the vestry door, and to return immediately, bearing a glass of water in her hand. A low moaning ensued; two more pew-openers rushed to the spot, and the three Miss Browns, each supported by a pew-opener, were led out of the church, and led in again after the lapse of five minutes with white pocket-handkerchiefs to their eyes, as if they had been attending a funeral in the churchyard adjoining. If any doubt had for a moment existed, as to whom the allusion was intended to apply, it was at once removed. The wish to enlighten the charity children became universal, and the three Miss Browns were unanimously besought to divide the school into classes, and to assign each class to the superintendence of two young ladies.

A little learning is a dangerous thing, but a little patronage is more so; the three Miss Browns appointed all the old maids, and carefully excluded the young ones. Maiden aunts triumphed, mammas were reduced to the lowest depths of

41

despair, and there is no telling in what act of violence the general indignation against the three Miss Browns might have vented itself, had not a perfectly providential occurrence changed the tide of public feeling. Mrs. Johnson Parker, the mother of seven extremely fine girls—all unmarried—hastily reported to several other mammas of several other unmarried families, that five old men, six old women, and children innumerable, in the free seats near her pew, were in the habit of coming to church every Sunday, without either bible or prayer-book. Was this to be borne in a civilised country? Could such things be tolerated in a Christian land? Never! A ladies' bible and prayer-book distribution society was instantly formed: president, Mrs. Johnson Parker; treasurers, auditors, and secretary, the Misses Johnson Parker: subscriptions were entered into, books were bought, all the free-seat people provided therewith, and when the first lesson was given out, on the first Sunday succeeding these events, there was such a dropping of books, and rustling of leaves, that it was morally impossible to hear one word of the service for five minutes afterwards.

The three Miss Browns, and their party, saw the approaching danger, and endeavoured to avert it by ridicule and sarcasm. Neither the old men nor the old women could read their books, now they had got them, said the three Miss Browns. Never mind; they could learn, replied Mrs. Johnson Parker. The children couldn't read either, suggested the three Miss Browns. No matter; they could be taught, retorted Mrs. Johnson Parker. A balance of parties took place. The Miss Browns publicly examined—popular feeling inclined to the child's examination society. The Miss Johnson Parkers publicly distributed—a reaction took place in favour of the prayer-book distribution. A feather would have turned the scale, and a feather did turn it. A missionary returned from the West Indies; he was to be presented to the Dissenters' Missionary Society on his marriage with a wealthy widow. Overtures were made to

42

THE MONTHLY LOAN SOCIETY

the Dissenters by the Johnson Parkers. Their object was the same, and why not have a joint meeting of the two societies? The proposition was accepted. The meeting was duly heralded by public announcement, and the room was crowded to suffocation. The Missionary appeared on the platform; he was hailed with enthusiasm. He repeated a dialogue he had heard between two negroes, behind a hedge, on the subject of distribution societies; the approbation was tumultuous. He gave an imitation of the two negroes in broken English; the roof was rent with applause. From that period we date (with one trifling exception) a daily increase in the popularity of the distribution society, and an increase of popularity, which the feeble and impotent opposition of the examination party, has only tended to augment.

Now, the great points about the childbed-linen monthly loan society are, that it is less dependent on the fluctuations of public opinion than either the distribution or the child's examination; and that, come what may, there is never any lack of objects on which to exercise its benevolence. Our parish is a very populous one, and, if anything, contributes, we should be disposed to say, rather more than its due share to the aggregate amount of births in the metropolis and its environs. The consequence is, that the monthly loan society flourishes, and invests its members with a most enviable amount of bustling patronage. The society (whose only notion of dividing time, would appear to be its allotment into months) holds monthly tea-drinkings, at which the monthly report is received, a secretary elected for the month ensuing, and such of the monthly boxes as may not happen to be out on loan for the month, carefully examined.

We were never present at one of these meetings, from all of which it is scarcely necessary to say, gentlemen are carefully excluded; but Mr. Bung has been called before the board once or twice, and we have his authority for stating, that its proceedings are conducted with great order and regularity:

not more than four members being allowed to speak at one time on any pretence whatever. The regular committee is composed exclusively of married ladies, but a vast number of young unmarried ladies of from eighteen to twenty-five years of age, respectively, are admitted as honorary members, partly because they are very useful in replenishing the boxes, and visiting the confined ; partly because it is highly desirable that they should be initiated, at an early period, into the more serious and matronly duties of after-life; and partly, because prudent mammas have not unfrequently been known to turn this circumstance to wonderfully good account in matrimonial speculations.

In addition to the loan of the monthly boxes (which are always painted blue, with the name of the society in large white letters on the lid), the society dispense occasional grants of beef-tea, and a composition of warm beer, spice, eggs, and sugar, commonly known by the name of "caudle," to its patients. And here again the services of the honorary members are called into requisition, and most cheerfully conceded. Deputations of twos or threes are sent out to visit the patients, and on these occasions there is such a tasting of caudle and beef-tea, such a stirring about of little messes in tiny saucepans on the hob, such a dressing and undressing of infants, such a tying, and folding, and pinning; such a nursing and warming of little legs and feet before the fire, such a delightful confusion of talking and cooking, bustle, importance, and officiousness, as never can be enjoyed in its full extent but on similar occasions.

In rivalry of these two institutions, and as a last expiring effort to acquire parochial popularity, the child's examination people determined, the other day, on having a grand public examination of the pupils; and the large school-room of the national seminary was, by and with the consent of the parish authorities, devoted to the purpose. Invitation circulars were forwarded to all the principal parishioners, including, of course, the heads of the other two societies, for whose especial behoof and edification the display was intended; and a large audience was confidently anticipated on the occasion. The floor was carefully scrubbed the day before, under the immediate superintendence of the three Miss Browns; forms were placed across the room for the accommodation of the visitors, specimens in writing were carefully selected, and as carefully patched and touched up, until they astonished the children who had written them, rather more than the company who read them; sums in compound addition were rehearsed and re-rehearsed until all the children had the totals by heart; and the preparations altogether were on the most laborious and most comprehensive scale. The morning arrived: the children were yellow-soaped and flannelled, and towelled, till their faces shone again; every pupil's hair was carefully combed into his or her eyes, as the case might be; the girls were adorned with snow-white tippets, and caps bound round the head by a single purple ribbon: the necks of the elder boys were fixed into collars of startling dimensions.

The doors were thrown open, and the Misses Brown and Co. were discovered in plain white muslin dresses, and caps of the same—the child's examination uniform. The room filled: the greetings of the company were loud and cordial. The distributionists trembled, for their popularity was at stake. The eldest boy fell forward, and delivered a propitiatory address from behind his collar. It was from the pen of Mr. Henry Brown; the applause was universal, and the Johnson Parkers were aghast. The examination proceeded with success, and terminated in triumph. The child's examination society gained a momentary victory, and the Johnson Parkers retreated in despair.

A secret council of the distributionists was held that night, with Mrs. Johnson Parker in the chair, to consider of the best means of recovering the ground they had lost in the favour of the parish. What could be done? Another meeting! Alas! who was to attend it? The Missionary would not do twice; and the slaves were emancipated. A bold step must be taken.

The parish must be astonished in some way or other; but no one was able to suggest what the step should be. At length, a very old lady was heard to mumble, in indistinct tones, " Exeter Hall." A sudden light broke in upon the meeting. It was unanimously resolved, that a deputation of old ladies should wait upon a celebrated orator, imploring his assistance, and the favour of a speech; and the deputation should also wait on two or three other imbecile old women, not resident in the parish, and entreat their attendance. The application was successful, the meeting was held; the orator (an Irishman) came. He talked of green isles—other shores—vast Atlantic —bosom of the deep—Christian charity—blood and extermi- nation—mercy in hearts—arms in hands—altars and homes —household gods. He wiped his eyes, he blew his nose, and he quoted Latin. The effect was tremendous—the Latin was a decided hit. Nobody knew exactly what it was about, but everybody knew it must be affecting, because even the orator was overcome. The popularity of the distribution society among the ladies of our parish is unprecedented; and the child's examination is going fast to decay.

CHAPTER VII

OUR NEXT-DOOR NEIGHBOUR

WE are very fond of speculating as we walk through a street, on the character and pursuits of the people who inhabit it; and nothing so materially assists us in these speculations as the appearance of the house doors. The various expressions of the human countenance afford a beautiful and interesting study; but there is something in the physiognomy of street-door knockers, almost as characteristic, and nearly as infallible. Whenever we visit a man for the first time, we contemplate the features of his knocker with the greatest curiosity, for we well know, that between the man and his knocker, there will inevitably be a greater or less degree of resemblance and sympathy.

For instance, there is one description of knocker that used to be common enough, but which is fast passing away—a large round one, with the jolly face of a convivial lion smiling blandly at you, as you twist the sides of your hair into a curl or pull up your shirt-collar while you are waiting for the door to be opened; we never saw that knocker on the door of a churlish man—so far as our experience is concerned, it invariably bespoke hospitality and another bottle.

No man ever saw this knocker on the door of a small attorney or bill-broker; they always patronise the other lion; a heavy ferocious-looking fellow, with a countenance expressive of savage stupidity—a sort of grand master among the knockers, and a great favourite with the selfish and brutal.

Then there is a little pert Egyptian knocker, with a long thin face, a pinched-up nose, and a very sharp chin ; he is most in vogue with your government-office people, in light drabs and starched cravats; little spare, priggish men, who are perfectly satisfied with their own opinions, and consider themselves of paramount importance.

We were greatly troubled a few years ago, by the innovation of a new kind of knocker, without any face at all, composed of a wreath depending from a hand or small truncheon. A little trouble and attention, however, enabled us to overcome this difficulty, and to reconcile the new system to our favourite theory. You will invariably find this knocker on the doors of cold and formal people, who always ask you why you *don't* come, and never say *do*.

Everybody knows the brass knocker is common to suburban villas, and extensive boarding-schools ; and having noticed this genus we have recapitulated all the most prominent and strongly-defined species.

Some phrenologists affirm, that the agitation of a man's brain by different passions, produces corresponding developments in the form of his skull. Do not let us be understood as pushing our theory to the full length of asserting, that any alteration in a man's disposition would produce a visible effect on the feature of his knocker. Our position merely is, that in such a case, the magnetism which must exist between a man and his knocker, would induce the man to remove, and seek some knocker more congenial to his altered feelings. If you ever find a man changing his habitation without any reasonable pretext, depend upon it, that, although he may not be aware of the fact himself, it is because he and his knocker are at variance. This is a new theory, but we venture to launch it, nevertheless, as being quite as ingenious and infallible as many thousands of the learned speculations which are daily broached for public good and private fortune-making.

Entertaining these feelings on the subject of knockers, it

will be readily imagined with what consternation we viewed the entire removal of the knocker from the door of the next house to the one we lived in, some time ago, and the substitution of a bell. This was a calamity we had never anticipated. The bare idea of anybody being able to exist without a knocker, appeared so wild and visionary, that it had never for one instant entered our imagination.

We sauntered moodily from the spot, and bent our steps towards Eaton-square, then just building. What was our astonishment and indignation to find that bells were fast becoming the rule, and knockers the exception! Our theory trembled beneath the shock. We hastened home; and fancying we foresaw in the swift progress of events, its entire abolition, resolved from that day forward to vent our speculations on our next-door neighbours in person. The house adjoining ours on the left hand was uninhabited, and we had, therefore, plenty of leisure to observe our next-door neighbours on the other side.

The house without the knocker was in the occupation of a city clerk, and there was a neatly-written bill in the parlour window intimating that lodgings for a single gentleman were to be let within.

It was a neat, dull little house, on the shady side of the way, with new, narrow floorcloth in the passage, and new, narrow stair-carpets up to the first floor. The paper was new, and the paint was new, and the furniture was new; and all three, paper, paint, and furniture, bespoke the limited means of the tenant. There was a little red and black carpet in the drawing-room, with a border of flooring all the way round; a few stained chairs and a pembroke table. A pink shell was displayed on each of the little sideboards, which, with the addition of a tea-tray and caddy, a few more shells on the mantelpiece, and three peacock's feathers tastefully arranged above them, completed the decorative furniture of the apartment.

This was the room destined for the reception of the single

gentleman during the day, and a little back room on the same floor was assigned as his sleeping apartment by night.

The bill had not been long in the window, when a stout, good-humoured looking gentleman, of about five-and-thirty, appeared as a candidate for the tenancy. Terms were soon arranged, for the bill was taken down immediately after his first visit. In a day or two the single gentleman came in, and shortly afterwards his real character came out.

First of all, he displayed a most extraordinary partiality for sitting up till three or four o'clock in the morning, drinking whiskey-and-water, and smoking cigars; then he invited friends home, who used to come at ten o'clock, and begin to get happy about the small hours, when they evinced their perfect contentment by singing songs with half-a-dozen verses of two lines each, and a chorus of ten, which chorus used to be shouted forth by the whole strength of the company, in the most enthusiastic and vociferous manner, to the great annoyance of the neighbours, and the special discomfort of another single gentleman overhead.

Now, this was bad enough, occurring as it did three times a week on the average, but this was not all; for when the company *did* go away, instead of walking quietly down the street, as anybody else's company would have done, they amused themselves by making alarming and frightful noises, and counterfeiting the shrieks of females in distress; and one night, a red-faced gentleman in a white hat knocked in the most urgent manner at the door of the powdered-headed old gentleman at No. 3, and when the powdered-headed old gentleman, who thought one of his married daughters must have been taken ill prematurely, had groped down-stairs, and after a great deal of unbolting and key-turning, opened the street door, the red-faced man in the white hat said he hoped he'd excuse his giving him so much trouble, but he'd feel obliged if he'd favour him with a glass of cold spring water, and the loan of a shilling for a cab to take him home, on which the old gentleman slammed the door and went up-

stairs, and threw the contents of his water jug out of window
—very straight, only it went over the wrong man; and the
whole street was involved in confusion.

A joke's a joke; and even practical jests are very capital
in their way, if you can only get the other party to see the
fun of them; but the population of our street were so dull
of apprehension, as to be quite lost to a sense of the drollery
of this proceeding : and the consequence was, that our next-
door neighbour was obliged to tell the single gentleman, that
unless he gave up entertaining his friends at home, he really
must be compelled to part with him. The single gentleman
received the remonstrance with great good-humour, and
promised from that time forward, to spend his evenings at
a coffee-house—a determination which afforded general and
unmixed satisfaction.

The next night passed off very well, everybody being
delighted with the change; but on the next, the noises were
renewed with greater spirit than ever. The single gentleman's friends being unable to see him in his own house every
alternate night, had come to the determination of seeing him
home every night; and what with the discordant greetings of
the friends at parting, and the noise created by the single
gentleman in his passage up-stairs, and his subsequent
struggles to get his boots off, the evil was not to be borne.
So, our next-door neighbour gave the single gentleman, who
was a very good lodger in other respects, notice to quit; and
the single gentleman went away, and entertained his friends
in other lodgings.

The next applicant for the vacant first floor, was of a very
different character from the troublesome single gentleman
who had just quitted it. He was a tall, thin, young gentleman, with a profusion of brown hair, reddish whiskers, and
very slightly developed moustaches. He wore a braided
surtout, with frogs behind, light grey trousers, and wash-
leather gloves, and had altogether rather a military appearance. So unlike the roystering single gentleman. Such

insinuating manners, and such a delightful address! So seriously disposed, too! When he first came to look at the lodgings, he inquired most particularly whether he was sure to be able to get a seat in the parish church; and when he had agreed to take them, he requested to have a list of the different local charities, as he intended to subscribe his mite to the most deserving among them.

Our next-door neighbour was now perfectly happy. He had got a lodger at last, of just his own way of thinking—a serious, well-disposed man, who abhorred gaiety, and loved retirement. He took down the bill with a light heart, and pictured in imagination a long series of quiet Sundays, on which he and his lodger would exchange mutual civilities and Sunday papers.

The serious man arrived, and his luggage was to arrive from the country next morning. He borrowed a clean shirt, and a prayer-book, from our next-door neighbour, and retired to rest at an early hour, requesting that he might be called punctually at ten o'clock next morning—not before, as he was much fatigued.

He *was* called, and did not answer: he was called again, but there was no reply. Our next-door neighbour became alarmed, and burst the door open. The serious man had left the house mysteriously; carrying with him the shirt, the prayer-book, a teaspoon, and the bedclothes.

Whether this occurrence, coupled with the irregularities of his former lodger, gave our next-door neighbour an aversion to single gentlemen, we know not; we only know that the next bill which made its appearance in the parlour window intimated generally, that there were furnished apartments to let on the first floor. The bill was soon removed. The new lodgers at first attracted our curiosity, and afterwards excited our interest.

They were a young lad of eighteen or nineteen, and his mother, a lady of about fifty, or it might be less. The mother wore a widow's weeds, and the boy was also clothed in deep mourning. They were poor—very poor; for their only means of support arose from the pittance the boy earned, by copying writings, and translating for booksellers.

They had removed from some country place and settled in London; partly because it afforded better chances of employment for the boy, and partly, perhaps, with the natural desire to leave a place where they had been in better circumstances, and where their poverty was known. They were proud under their reverses, and above revealing their wants and privations to strangers. How bitter those privations were, and how hard the boy worked to remove them, no one ever knew but themselves. Night after night, two, three, four hours after midnight, could we hear the occasional raking up of the scanty fire, or the hollow and half-stifled cough, which indicated his being still at work; and day after day, could we see more plainly that nature had set that unearthly light in his plaintive face, which is the beacon of her worst disease.

Actuated, we hope, by a higher feeling than mere curiosity, we contrived to establish, first an acquaintance, and then a close intimacy, with the poor strangers. Our worst fears were realised; the boy was sinking fast. Through a part of the winter, and the whole of the following spring and summer, his labours were unceasingly prolonged: and the mother attempted to procure needlework, embroidery—anything for bread.

A few shillings now and then, were all she could earn. The boy worked steadily on; dying by minutes, but never once giving utterance to complaint or murmur.

One beautiful autumn evening we went to pay our customary visit to the invalid. His little remaining strength had been decreasing rapidly for two or three days preceding, and he was lying on the sofa at the open window, gazing at the setting sun. His mother had been reading the Bible to him, for she closed the book as we entered, and advanced to meet us.

"I was telling William," she said, "that we must manage to take him into the country somewhere, so that he may get quite well. He is not ill, you know, but he is not very strong, and has exerted himself too much lately." Poor thing! The tears that streamed through her fingers, as she turned aside, as if to adjust her close widow's cap, too plainly showed how fruitless was the attempt to deceive herself.

We sat down by the head of the sofa, but said nothing, for we saw the breath of life was passing gently but rapidly from the young form before us. At every respiration, his heart beat more slowly.

The boy placed one hand in ours, grasped his mother's arm with the other, drew her hastily towards him, and fervently kissed her cheek. There was a pause. He sunk back upon his pillow, and looked long and earnestly in his mother's face.

"William, William!" murmured the mother, after a long interval, "don't look at me so—speak to me, dear!"

The boy smiled languidly, but an instant afterwards his features resolved into the same cold, solemn gaze.

"William, dear William! rouse yourself; don't look at me so, love—pray don't! Oh, my God! what shall I do!" cried the widow, clasping her hands in agony—"my dear boy! he is dying!"

The boy raised himself by a violent effort, and folded his hands together—"Mother! dear, dear mother, bury me in the open fields—anywhere but in these dreadful streets. I should like to be where you can see my grave, but not in these close crowded streets; they have killed me; kiss me again, mother; put your arm round my neck——"

He fell back, and a strange expression stole upon his features; not of pain or suffering, but an indescribable fixing of every line and muscle.

The boy was dead.

SCENES

CHAPTER I

THE appearance presented by the streets of London an hour before sunrise, on a summer's morning, is most striking even to the few whose unfortunate pursuits of pleasure, or scarcely less unfortunate pursuits of business, cause them to be well acquainted with the scene. There is an air of cold, solitary desolation about the noiseless streets which we are accustomed to see thronged at other times by a busy, eager crowd, and over the quiet, closely-shut buildings, which throughout the day are swarming with life and bustle, that is very impressive.

The last drunken man, who shall find his way home before sunlight, has just staggered heavily along, roaring out the burden of the drinking song of the previous night: the last houseless vagrant whom penury and police have left in the streets, has coiled up his chilly limbs in some paved corner, to dream of food and warmth. The drunken, the dissipated, and the wretched have disappeared; the more sober and orderly part of the population have not yet awakened to the labours of the day, and the stillness of death is over the streets; its very hue seems to be imparted to them, cold and lifeless as they look in the grey, sombre light of daybreak.

55

The coach-stands in the larger thoroughfares are deserted: the night-houses are closed; and the chosen promenades of profligate misery are empty.

An occasional policeman may alone be seen at the street corners, listlessly gazing on the deserted prospect before him; and now and then a rakish-looking cat runs stealthily across the road and descends his own area with as much caution and slyness—bounding first on the water-butt, then on the dust-hole, and then alighting on the flag-stones—as if he were conscious that his character depended on his gallantry of the preceding night escaping public observation. A partially opened bedroom-window here and there, bespeaks the heat of the weather, and the uneasy slumbers of its occupant; and the dim scanty flicker of the rushlight, through the window-blind, denotes the chamber of watching or sickness. With these few exceptions, the streets present no signs of life, nor the houses of habitation.

An hour wears away; the spires of the churches and roofs of the principal buildings are faintly tinged with the light of the rising sun; and the streets, by almost imperceptible degrees, begin to resume their bustle and animation. Market-carts roll slowly along: the sleepy waggoner impatiently urging on his tired horses, or vainly endeavouring to awaken the boy, who, luxuriously stretched on the top of the fruit-baskets, forgets, in happy oblivion, his long-cherished curiosity to behold the wonders of London.

Rough, sleepy-looking animals of strange appearance, something between ostlers and hackney-coachmen, begin to take down the shutters of early public-houses; and little deal tables, with the ordinary preparations for a street breakfast, make their appearance at the customary stations. Numbers of men and women (principally the latter), carrying upon their heads heavy baskets of fruit, toil down the park side of Piccadilly, on their way to Covent-garden, and, following each other in rapid succession, form a long straggling line from thence to the turn of the road at Knightsbridge.

George Cruikshank

The Streets—Morning

AN HOUR AFTER DAYBREAK

Here and there, a bricklayer's labourer, with the day's dinner tied up in a handkerchief, walks briskly to his work, and occasionally a little knot of three or four schoolboys on a stolen bathing expedition rattle merrily over the pavement, their boisterous mirth contrasting forcibly with the demeanour of the little sweep, who, having knocked and rung till his arm aches, and being interdicted by a merciful legislature from endangering his lungs by calling out, sits patiently down on the door-step, until the housemaid may happen to awake.

Covent-garden market, and the avenues leading to it, are thronged with carts of all sorts, sizes, and descriptions, from the heavy lumbering waggon, with its four stout horses, to the jingling costermonger's cart, with its consumptive donkey. The pavement is already strewed with decayed cabbage-leaves, broken hay-bands, and all the indescribable litter of a vegetable market; men are shouting, carts backing, horses neighing, boys fighting, basket-women talking, piemen expatiating on the excellence of their pastry, and donkeys braying. These and a hundred other sounds form a compound discordant enough to a Londoner's ears, and remarkably disagreeable to those of country gentlemen who are sleeping at the Hummums for the first time.

Another hour passes away, and the day begins in good earnest. The servant of all work, who, under the plea of sleeping very soundly, has utterly disregarded "Missis's" ringing for half an hour previously, is warned by Master (whom Missis has sent up in his drapery to the landing-place for that purpose), that it's half-past six, whereupon she awakes all of a sudden, with well-feigned astonishment, and goes down-stairs very sulkily, wishing, while she strikes a light, that the principle of spontaneous combustion would extend itself to coals and kitchen range. When the fire is lighted, she opens the street-door to take in the milk, when, by the most singular coincidence in the world, she discovers that the servant next door has just taken in her milk too, and that Mr. Todd's young man over the way, is, by an

57

equally extraordinary chance, taking down his master's shutters. The inevitable consequence is, that she just steps, milk-jug in hand, as far as next door, just to say "good morning" to Betsy Clark, and that Mr. Todd's young man just steps over the way to say "good morning" to both of 'em; and as the aforesaid Mr. Todd's young man is almost as good-looking and fascinating as the baker himself, the conversation quickly becomes very interesting, and probably would become more so, if Betsy Clark's Missis, who always will be a-followin' her about, didn't give an angry tap at her bedroom window, on which Mr. Todd's young man tries to whistle coolly, as he goes back to his shop much faster than he came from it; and the two girls run back to their respective places, and shut their street-doors with surprising softness, each of them poking their heads out of the front parlour window, a minute afterwards, however, ostensibly with the view of looking at the mail which just then passes by, but really for the purpose of catching another glimpse of Mr. Todd's young man, who being fond of mails, but more of females, takes a short look at the mails, and a long look at the girls, much to the satisfaction of all parties concerned.

The mail itself goes on to the coach-office in due course, and the passengers who are going out by the early coach, stare with astonishment at the passengers who are coming in by the early coach, who look blue and dismal, and are evidently under the influence of that odd feeling produced by travelling, which makes the events of yesterday morning seem as if they had happened at least six months ago, and induces people to wonder with considerable gravity whether the friends and relations they took leave of a fortnight before, have altered much since they have left them. The coach-office is all alive, and the coaches which are just going out, are surrounded by the usual crowd of Jews and nondescripts, who seem to consider, Heaven knows why, that it is quite impossible any man can mount a coach without requiring at least sixpenny-worth of oranges, a penknife, a pocket-book, a last year's annual, a pencil-case, a piece of sponge, and a small series of caricatures.

Half an hour more, and the sun darts his bright rays cheerfully down the still half-empty streets, and shines with sufficient force to rouse the dismal laziness of the apprentice, who pauses every other minute from his task of sweeping out the shop and watering the pavement in front of it, to tell another apprentice similarly employed, how hot it will be to-day, or to stand with his right hand shading his eyes, and his left resting on the broom, gazing at the "Wonder," or the "Tally-ho," or the "Nimrod," or some other fast coach, till it is out of sight, when he re-enters the shop, envying the passengers on the outside of the fast coach, and thinking of the old red brick house "down in the country," where he went to school: the miseries of the milk and water, and thick bread and scrapings, fading into nothing before the pleasant recollection of the green field the boys used to play in, and the green pond he was caned for presuming to fall into, and other schoolboy associations.

Cabs, with trunks and band-boxes between the drivers' legs and outside the apron, rattle briskly up and down the streets on their way to the coach-offices or steam-packet wharfs; and the cab-drivers and hackney-coachmen who are on the stand polish up the ornamental part of their dingy vehicles—the former wondering how people can prefer "them wild beast cariwans of homnibuses, to a riglar cab with a fast trotter," and the latter admiring how people can trust their necks into one of "them crazy cabs, when they can have a 'spectable 'ackney cotche with a pair of 'orses as von't run away with no vun;" a consolation unquestionably founded on fact, seeing that a hackney-coach horse never was known to run at all, "except," as the smart cabman in front of the rank observes, "except one, and *he* run back'ards."

The shops are now completely opened, and apprentices and shopmen are busily engaged in cleaning and decking the windows for the day. The bakers' shops in town are filled with servants and children waiting for the drawing of the first batch of rolls—an operation which was performed a full hour ago in the suburbs: for the early clerk population of Somers and Camden towns, Islington, and Pentonville, are fast pouring into the city, or directing their steps towards Chancery-lane and the Inns of Court. Middle-aged men, whose salaries have by no means increased in the same proportion as their families, plod steadily along, apparently with no object in view but the counting-house; knowing by sight almost everybody they meet or overtake, for they have seen them every morning (Sundays excepted) during the last twenty years, but speaking to no one. If they do happen to overtake a personal acquaintance, they just exchange a hurried salutation, and keep walking on either by his side, or in front of him, as his rate of walking may chance to be. As to stopping to shake hands, or to take the friend's arm, they seem to think that as it is not included in their salary, they have no right to do it. Small office lads in large hats, who are made men before they are boys, hurry along in pairs, with their first coat carefully brushed, and the white trousers of last Sunday plentifully besmeared with dust and ink. It evidently requires a considerable mental struggle to avoid investing part of the day's dinner-money in the purchase of the stale tarts so temptingly exposed in dusty tins at the pastry-cooks' doors; but a consciousness of their own importance and the receipt of seven shillings a-week, with the prospect of an early rise to eight, comes to their aid, and they accordingly put their hats a little more on one side, and look under the bonnets of all the milliners' and staymakers' apprentices they meet—poor girls!—the hardest worked, the worst paid, and too often, the worst used class of the community.

Eleven o'clock, and a new set of people fill the streets. The goods in the shop-windows are invitingly arranged; the shopmen in their white neckerchiefs and spruce coats, look as if they couldn't clean a window if their lives depended on it; the carts have disappeared from Covent-garden; the wag-goners have returned, and the costermongers repaired to their ordinary "beats" in the suburbs; clerks are at their offices, and gigs, cabs, omnibuses, and saddle-horses, are conveying their masters to the same destination. The streets are thronged with a vast concourse of people, gay and shabby, rich and poor, idle and industrious; and we come to the heat, bustle, and activity of NOON.

CHAPTER II

But the streets of London, to be beheld in the very height of their glory, should be seen on a dark, dull, murky winter's night, when there is just enough damp gently stealing down to make the pavement greasy, without cleansing it of any of its impurities; and when the heavy lazy mist, which hangs over every object, makes the gas-lamps look brighter, and the brilliantly-lighted shops more splendid, from the contrast they present to the darkness around. All the people who are at home on such a night as this, seem disposed to make themselves as snug and comfortable as possible; and the passengers in the streets have excellent reason to envy the fortunate individuals who are seated by their own firesides.

In the larger and better kind of streets, dining parlour curtains are closely drawn, kitchen fires blaze brightly up, and savoury steams of hot dinners salute the nostrils of the hungry wayfarer, as he plods wearily by the area railings. In the suburbs, the muffin boy rings his way down the little street, much more slowly than he is wont to do; for Mrs. Macklin, of No. 4, has no sooner opened her little street-door, and screamed out "Muffins!" with all her might, than Mrs. Walker, at No. 5, puts her head out of the parlour-window, and screams "Muffins!" too; and Mrs. Walker has scarcely got the words out of her lips, than Mrs. Peplow, over the way, lets loose Master Peplow, who darts down the

George Cruikshank

The Streets—Night

street, with a velocity which nothing but buttered muffins
in perspective could possibly inspire, and drags the boy back
by main force, whereupon Mrs. Macklin and Mrs. Walker,
just to save the boy trouble, and to say a few neighbourly
words to Mrs. Peplow at the same time, run over the way
and buy their muffins at Mrs. Peplow's door, when it appears
from the voluntary statement of Mrs. Walker, that her
"kittle's jist a-biling, and the cups and sarsers ready laid,"
and that, as it was such a wretched night out o' doors, she'd
made up her mind to have a nice, hot, comfortable cup o'
tea—a determination at which, by the most singular coincidence, the other two ladies had simultaneously arrived.

After a little conversation about the wretchedness of the
weather and the merits of tea, with a digression relative to
the viciousness of boys as a rule, and the amiability of
Master Peplow as an exception, Mrs. Walker sees her
husband coming down the street; and as he must want his
tea, poor man, after his dirty walk from the Docks, she
instantly runs across, muffins in hand, and Mrs. Macklin
does the same, and after a few words to Mrs. Walker, they
all pop into their little houses, and slam their little street-
doors, which are not opened again for the remainder of the
evening, except to the nine o'clock "beer," who comes round
with a lantern in front of his tray, and says, as he lends
Mrs. Walker "Yesterday's 'Tiser," that he's blessed if he
can hardly hold the pot, much less feel the paper, for it's
one of the bitterest nights he ever felt, 'cept the night when
the man was frozen to death in the Brick-field.

After a little prophetic conversation with the policeman at
the street-corner, touching a probable change in the weather,
and the setting-in of a hard frost, the nine o'clock beer
returns to his master's house, and employs himself for the
remainder of the evening, in assiduously stirring the tap-
room fire, and deferentially taking part in the conversation
of the worthies assembled round it.

The streets in the vicinity of the Marsh-gate and Victoria

Theatre present an appearance of dirt and discomfort on such a night, which the groups who lounge about them in no degree tend to diminish. Even the little block-tin temple sacred to baked potatoes, surmounted by a splendid design in variegated lamps, looks less gay than usual; and as to the kidney-pie stand, its glory has quite departed. The candle in the transparent lamp, manufactured of oil-paper, embellished with "characters," has been blown out fifty times, so the kidney-pie merchant, tired with running backwards and forwards to the next wine-vaults, to get a light, has given up the idea of illumination in despair, and the only signs of his "whereabout," are the bright sparks, of which a long irregular train is whirled down the street every time he opens his portable oven to hand a hot kidney-pie to a customer.

Flat-fish, oyster, and fruit vendors linger hopelessly in the kennel, in vain endeavouring to attract customers; and the ragged boys who usually disport themselves about the streets, stand crouched in little knots in some projecting doorway, or under the canvas blind of a cheesemonger's, where great flaring gas-lights, unshaded by any glass, display huge piles of bright red and pale yellow cheeses, mingled with little fivepenny dabs of dingy bacon, various tubs of weekly Dorset, and cloudy rolls of "best fresh."

Here they amuse themselves with theatrical converse, arising out of their last half-price visit to the Victoria gallery, admire the terrific combat, which is nightly encored, and expatiate on the inimitable manner in which Bill Thompson can "come the double monkey," or go through the mysterious involutions of a sailor's hornpipe.

It is nearly eleven o'clock, and the cold thin rain which has been drizzling so long, is beginning to pour down in good earnest; the baked-potato man has departed—the kidney-pie man has just walked away with his warehouse on his arm—the cheesemonger has drawn in his blind, and the boys have dispersed. The constant clicking of pattens on the slippy and uneven pavement, and the rustling of umbrellas, as the wind blows against the shop-windows, bear testimony to the inclemency of the night; and the policeman, with his oilskin cape buttoned closely round him, seems as he holds his hat on his head, and turns round to avoid the gust of wind and rain which drives against him at the street-corner, to be very far from congratulating himself on the prospect before him.

The little chandler's shop with the cracked bell behind the door, whose melancholy tinkling has been regulated by the demand for quarterns of sugar and half-ounces of coffee, is shutting up. The crowds which have been passing to and fro during the whole day, are rapidly dwindling away; and the noise of shouting and quarrelling which issues from the public-houses, is almost the only sound that breaks the melancholy stillness of the night.

There was another, but it has ceased. That wretched woman with the infant in her arms, round whose meagre form the remnant of her own scanty shawl is carefully wrapped, has been attempting to sing some popular ballad, in the hope of wringing a few pence from the compassionate passer-by. A brutal laugh at her weak voice is all she has gained. The tears fall thick and fast down her own pale face; the child is cold and hungry, and its low half-stifled wailing adds to the misery of its wretched mother, as she moans aloud, and sinks despairingly down, on a cold damp door-step.

Singing! How few of those who pass such a miserable creature as this, think of the anguish of heart, the sinking of soul and spirit, which the very effort of singing produces. Bitter mockery! Disease, neglect, and starvation, faintly articulating the words of the joyous ditty, that has enlivened your hours of feasting and merriment, God knows how often! It is no subject of jeering. The weak tremulous voice tells a fearful tale of want and famishing; and the feeble singer of this roaring song may turn away, only to die of cold and hunger.

One o'clock! Parties returning from the different theatres foot it through the muddy streets; cabs, hackney-coaches, carriages, and theatre omnibuses, roll swiftly by; watermen with dim dirty lanterns in their hands, and large brass plates upon their breasts, who have been shouting and rushing about for the last two hours, retire to their watering-houses, to solace themselves with the creature comforts of pipes and purl; the half-price pit and box frequenters of the theatres throng to the different houses of refreshment; and chops, kidneys, rabbits, oysters, stout, cigars, and "goes" innumerable, are served up amidst a noise and confusion of smoking, running, knife-clattering, and waiter-chattering, perfectly indescribable.

The more musical portion of the play-going community betake themselves to some harmonic meeting. As a matter of curiosity let us follow them thither for a few moments.

In a lofty room of spacious dimensions, are seated some eighty or a hundred guests knocking little pewter measures on the tables, and hammering away, with the handles of their knives, as if they were so many trunk-makers. They are applauding a glee, which has just been executed by the three "professional gentlemen" at the top of the centre table, one of whom is in the chair—the little pompous man with the bald head just emerging from the collar of his green coat. The others are seated on either side of him—the stout man with the small voice, and the thin-faced dark man in black. The little man in the chair is a most amusing personage,— *such* condescending grandeur, and *such* a voice!

"Bass!" as the young gentleman near us with the blue stock forcibly remarks to his companion, "bass! I b'lieve you; he can go down lower than any man: so low sometimes that you can't hear him." And so he does. To hear him growling away, gradually lower and lower down, till he can't get back again, is the most delightful thing in the world, and it is quite impossible to witness unmoved the impressive

66

solemnity with which he pours forth his soul in "My 'art's in the 'ighlands," or "The brave old Hoak." The stout man is also addicted to sentimentality, and warbles "Fly, fly from the world, my Bessy, with me," or some such song, with lady-like sweetness, and in the most seductive tones imaginable.

"Pray give your orders, gen'l'm'n—pray give your orders," —says the pale-faced man with the red head; and demands for "goes" of gin and "goes" of brandy, and pints of stout, and cigars of peculiar mildness, are vociferously made from all parts of the room. The "professional gentlemen" are in the very height of their glory, and bestow condescending nods, or even a word or two of recognition, on the better-known frequenters of the room, in the most bland and patronising manner possible.

That little round-faced man, with the small brown surtout, white stockings and shoes, is in the comic line; the mixed air of self-denial, and mental consciousness of his own powers, with which he acknowledges the call of the chair, is particularly gratifying. "Gen'l'men," says the little pompous man, accompanying the word with a knock of the president's hammer on the table—"Gen'l'men, allow me to claim your attention —our friend, Mr. Smuggins, will oblige."—"Bravo!" shout the company; and Smuggins, after a considerable quantity of coughing by way of symphony, and a most facetious sniff or two, which afford general delight, sings a comic song, with a fal-de-ral—tol-de-ral chorus at the end of every verse, much longer than the verse itself. It is received with unbounded applause, and after some aspiring genius has volunteered a recitation, and failed dismally therein, the little pompous man gives another knock, and says "Gen'l'men, we will attempt a glee, if you please." This announcement calls forth tumultuous applause, and the more energetic spirits express the unqualified approbation it affords them, by knocking one or two stout glasses off their legs—a humorous device; but one which frequently occasions some slight altercation when the form of paying the damage is proposed to be gone through by the waiter.

Scenes like these are continued until three or four o'clock in the morning; and even when they close, fresh ones open to the inquisitive novice. But as a description of all of them, however slight, would require a volume, the contents of which, however instructive, would be by no means pleasing, we make our bow, and drop the curtain.

CHAPTER III

WHAT inexhaustible food for speculation, do the streets of London afford! We never were able to agree with Sterne in pitying the man who could travel from Dan to Beersheba, and say that all was barren; we have not the slightest commiseration for the man who can take up his hat and stick, and walk from Covent-garden to St. Paul's Churchyard, and back into the bargain, without deriving some amusement —we had almost said instruction—from his perambulation. And yet there are such beings: we meet them every day. Large black stocks and light waistcoats, jet canes and discontented countenances, are the characteristics of the race; other people brush quickly by you, steadily plodding on to business, or cheerfully running after pleasure. These men linger listlessly past, looking as happy and animated as a policeman on duty. Nothing seems to make an impression on their minds: nothing short of being knocked down by a porter, or run over by a cab, will disturb their equanimity. You will meet them on a fine day in any of the leading thoroughfares: peep through the window of a west-end cigar shop in the evening, if you can manage to get a glimpse between the blue curtains which intercept the vulgar gaze, and you see them in their only enjoyment of existence. There they are lounging about, on round tubs and pipe boxes, in all the dignity of whiskers, and

69

gilt watch-guards; whispering soft nothings to the young lady in amber, with the large ear-rings, who, as she sits behind the counter in a blaze of adoration and gas-light, is the admiration of all the female servants in the neighbourhood, and the envy of every milliner's apprentice within two miles round.

One of our principal amusements is to watch the gradual progress—the rise or fall—of particular shops. We have formed an intimate acquaintance with several, in different parts of town, and are perfectly acquainted with their whole history. We could name off-hand, twenty at least, which we are quite sure have paid no taxes for the last six years. They are never inhabited for more than two months consecutively, and, we verily believe, have witnessed every retail trade in the directory.

There is one, whose history is a sample of the rest, in whose fate we have taken especial interest, having had the pleasure of knowing it ever since it has been a shop. It is on the Surrey side of the water—a little distance beyond the Marsh-gate. It was originally a substantial, good-looking private house enough; the landlord got into difficulties, the house got into Chancery, the tenant went away, and the house went to ruin. At this period our acquaintance with it commenced; the paint was all worn off; the windows were broken, the area was green with neglect and the overflowings of the water-butt; the butt itself was without a lid, and the street-door was the very picture of misery. The chief pastime of the children in the vicinity had been to assemble in a body on the steps, and to take it in turn to knock loud double knocks at the door, to the great satisfaction of the neighbours generally, and especially of the nervous old lady next door but one. Numerous complaints were made, and several small basins of water discharged over the offenders, but without effect. In this state of things, the marine-store dealer at the corner of the street, in the most obliging manner took the knocker off,

and sold it : and the unfortunate house looked more wretched
than ever.

We deserted our friend for a few weeks. What was our
surprise, on our return, to find no trace of its existence ! In
its place was a handsome shop, fast approaching to a state
of completion, and on the shutters were large bills, informing
the public that it would shortly be opened with " an extensive
stock of linen-drapery and haberdashery." It opened in due
course ; there was the name of the proprietor "and Co." in
gilt letters, almost too dazzling to look at. Such ribbons and
shawls ! and two such elegant young men behind the counter,
each in a clean collar and white neckcloth, like the lover in
a farce. As to the proprietor, he did nothing but walk up
and down the shop, and hand seats to the ladies, and hold
important conversations with the handsomest of the young
men, who was shrewdly suspected by the neighbours to be
the " Co." We saw all this with sorrow ; we felt a fatal presentiment that the shop was doomed—and so it was. Its
decay was slow, but sure. Tickets gradually appeared in the
windows ; then rolls of flannel, with labels on them, were
stuck outside the door ; then a bill was pasted on the street-
door, intimating that the first floor was to let *un*furnished ;
then one of the young men disappeared altogether, and the
other took to a black neckerchief, and the proprietor took
to drinking. The shop became dirty, broken panes of glass
remained unmended, and the stock disappeared piecemeal. At
last the company's man came to cut off the water, and then
the linen-draper cut off himself, leaving the landlord his
compliments and the key.

The next occupant was a fancy stationer. The shop was
more modestly painted than before, still it was neat ; but
somehow we always thought, as we passed, that it looked
like a poor and struggling concern. We wished the man
well, but we trembled for his success. He was a widower
evidently, and had employment elsewhere, for he passed us
every morning on his road to the city. The business was

carried on by his eldest daughter. Poor girl! she needed no assistance. We occasionally caught a glimpse of two or three children, in mourning like herself, as they sat in the little parlour behind the shop; and we never passed at night without seeing the eldest girl at work, either for them, or in making some elegant little trifle for sale. We often thought, as her pale face looked more sad and pensive in the dim candle-light, that if those thoughtless females who interfere with the miserable market of poor creatures such as these, knew but one-half of the misery they suffer, and the bitter privations they endure, in their honourable attempts to earn a scanty subsistence, they would, perhaps, resign even opportunities for the gratification of vanity, and an immodest love of self-display, rather than drive them to a last dreadful resource, which it would shock the delicate feelings of these *charitable* ladies to hear named.

But we are forgetting the shop. Well, we continued to watch it, and every day showed too clearly the increasing poverty of its inmates. The children were clean, it is true, but their clothes were threadbare and shabby; no tenant had been procured for the upper part of the house, from the letting of which, a portion of the means of paying the rent was to have been derived. and a slow, wasting consumption prevented the eldest girl from continuing her exertions. Quarter-day arrived. The landlord had suffered from the extravagance of his last tenant, and he had no compassion for the struggles of his successor; he put in an execution. As we passed one morning, the broker's men were removing the little furniture there was in the house, and a newly-posted bill informed us it was again "To Let." What became of the last tenant we never could learn; we believe the girl is past all suffering, and beyond all sorrow. God help her! We hope she is.

We were somewhat curious to ascertain what would be the next stage—for that the place had no chance of succeeding now, was perfectly clear. The bill was soon taken down, and some alterations were being made in the interior of the shop. We were in a fever of expectation; we exhausted conjecture—we imagined all possible trades, none of which were perfectly reconcilable with our idea of the gradual decay of the tenement. It opened, and we wondered why we had not guessed at the real state of the case before. The shop—not a large one at the best of times—had been converted into two: one was a bonnet-shape maker's, the other was opened by a tobacconist, who also dealt in walking-sticks and Sunday newspapers; the two were separated by a thin partition, covered with tawdry striped paper.

The tobacconist remained in possession longer than any tenant within our recollection. He was a red-faced, impudent, good-for-nothing dog, evidently accustomed to take things as they came, and to make the best of a bad job. He sold as many cigars as he could, and smoked the rest. He occupied the shop as long as he could make peace with the landlord, and when he could no longer live in quiet, he very coolly locked the door, and bolted himself. From this period, the two little dens have undergone innumerable changes. The tobacconist was succeeded by a theatrical hair-dresser, who ornamented the window with a great variety of " characters," and terrific combats. The bonnet-shape maker gave place to a green-grocer, and the histrionic barber was succeeded, in his turn, by a tailor. So numerous have been the changes, that we have of late done little more than mark the peculiar but certain indications of a house being poorly inhabited. It has been progressing by almost imperceptible degrees. The occupiers of the shops have gradually given up room after room, until they have only reserved the little parlour for themselves. First there appeared a brass plate on the private door, with " Ladies' School " legibly engraved thereon ; shortly afterwards we observed a second brass plate, then a bell, and then another bell.

When we paused in front of our old friend, and observed these signs of poverty, which are not to be mistaken, we

73

thought as we turned away, that the house had attained its lowest pitch of degradation. We were wrong. When we last passed it, a "dairy" was established in the area, and a party of melancholy-looking fowls were amusing themselves by running in at the front door, and out at the back one.

CHAPTER IV

SCOTLAND-YARD is a small—a very small—tract of land, bounded on one side by the river Thames, on the other by the gardens of Northumberland House: abutting at one end on the bottom of Northumberland-street, at the other on the back of Whitehall-place. When this territory was first accidentally discovered by a country gentleman who lost his way in the Strand, some years ago, the original settlers were found to be a tailor, a publican, two eating-house keepers, and a fruit-pie maker; and it was also found to contain a race of strong and bulky men, who repaired to the wharfs in Scotland-yard regularly every morning, about five or six o'clock, to fill heavy waggons with coal, with which they proceeded to distant places up the country, and supplied the inhabitants with fuel. When they had emptied their waggons, they again returned for a fresh supply; and this trade was continued throughout the year.

As the settlers derived their subsistence from ministering to the wants of these primitive traders, the articles exposed for sale, and the places where they were sold, bore strong outward marks of being expressly adapted to their tastes and wishes. The tailor displayed in his window a Lilliputian pair of leather gaiters, and a diminutive round frock, while each doorpost was appropriately garnished with a model of a coal-sack. The two eating-house keepers

75

exhibited joints of a magnitude, and puddings of a solidity, which coalheavers alone could appreciate; and the fruit-pie maker displayed on his well-scrubbed window-board large white compositions of flour and dripping, ornamented with pink stains, giving rich promise of the fruit within, which made their huge mouths water, as they lingered past.

But the choicest spot in all Scotland-yard was the old public-house in the corner. Here, in a dark wainscoted-room of ancient appearance, cheered by the glow of a mighty fire, and decorated with an enormous clock, whereof the face was white, and the figures black, sat the lusty coalheavers, quaffing large draughts of Barclay's best, and puffing forth volumes of smoke, which wreathed heavily above their heads, and involved the room in a thick dark cloud. From this apartment might their voices be heard on a winter's night, penetrating to the very bank of the river, as they shouted out some sturdy chorus, or roared forth the burden of a popular song; dwelling upon the last few words with a strength and length of emphasis which made the very roof tremble above them.

Here, too, would they tell old legends of what the Thames was in ancient times, when the Patent Shot Manufactory wasn't built, and Waterloo-bridge had never been thought of; and then they would shake their heads with portentous looks, to the deep edification of the rising generation of heavers, who crowded round them, and wondered where all this would end; whereat the tailor would take his pipe solemnly from his mouth, and say, how that he hoped it might end well, but he very much doubted whether it would or not, and couldn't rightly tell what to make of it—a mysterious expression of opinion, delivered with a semi-prophetic air, which never failed to elicit the fullest concurrence of the assembled company; and so they would go on drinking and wondering till ten o'clock came, and with it the tailor's wife to fetch him home, when the little party broke up, to meet again in the same room, and say and do

George Cruikshank

Scotland-Yard

precisely the same things, on the following evening at the same hour.

About this time the barges that came up the river began to bring vague rumours to Scotland-yard of somebody in the city having been heard to say, that the Lord Mayor had threatened in so many words to pull down the old London-bridge, and build up a new one. At first these rumours were disregarded as idle tales, wholly destitute of foundation, for nobody in Scotland-yard doubted that if the Lord Mayor contemplated any such dark design, he would just be clapped up in the Tower for a week or two, and then killed off for high treason.

By degrees, however, the reports grew stronger, and more frequent, and at last a barge, laden with numerous chaldrons of the best Wallsend, brought up the positive intelligence that several of the arches of the old bridge were stopped, and that preparations were actually in progress for constructing the new one. What an excitement was visible in the old tap-room on that memorable night! Each man looked into his neighbour's face, pale with alarm and astonishment, and read therein an echo of the sentiments which filled his own breast. The oldest heaver present proved to demonstration, that the moment the piers were removed, all the water in the Thames would run clean off, and leave a dry gully in its place. What was to become of the coal-barges—of the trade of Scotland-yard—of the very existence of its population? The tailor shook his head more sagely than usual, and grimly pointing to a knife on the table, bid them wait and see what happened. He said nothing—not he; but if the Lord Mayor didn't fall a victim to popular indignation, why he would be rather astonished; that was all.

They did wait; barge after barge arrived, and still no tidings of the assassination of the Lord Mayor. The first stone was laid: it was done by a Duke—the King's brother. Years passed away, and the bridge was opened by the King himself. In course of time, the piers were removed; and

77

when the people in Scotland-yard got up next morning in the confident expectation of being able to step over to Pedlar's Acre without wetting the soles of their shoes, they found to their unspeakable astonishment that the water was just where it used to be.

A result so different from that which they had anticipated from this first improvement, produced its full effect upon the inhabitants of Scotland-yard. One of the eating-house keepers began to court public opinion, and to look for customers among a new class of people. He covered his little dining-tables with white cloths, and got a painter's apprentice to inscribe something about hot joints from twelve to two, in one of the little panes of his shop-window. Improvement began to march with rapid strides to the very threshold of Scotland-yard. A new market sprung up at Hungerford, and the Police Commissioners established their office in Whitehall-place. The traffic in Scotland-yard increased; fresh Members were added to the House of Commons, the Metropolitan Representatives found it a near cut, and many other foot passengers followed their example.

We marked the advance of civilisation, and beheld it with a sigh. The eating-house keeper who manfully resisted the innovation of table-cloths, was losing ground every day, as his opponent gained it, and a deadly feud sprung up between them. The genteel one no longer took his evening's pint in Scotland-yard, but drank gin and water at a "parlour" in Parliament-street. The fruit-pie maker still continued to visit the old room, but he took to smoking cigars, and began to call himself a pastrycook, and to read the papers. The old heavers still assembled round the ancient fireplace, but their talk was mournful: and the loud song and the joyous shout were heard no more.

And what is Scotland-yard now? How have its old customs changed; and how has the ancient simplicity of its inhabitants faded away! The old tottering public-house is converted into a spacious and lofty "wine-vaults;" gold leaf has been used in the construction of the letters which emblazon its exterior, and the poet's art has been called into requisition, to intimate that if you drink a certain description of ale, you must hold fast by the rail. The tailor exhibits in his window the pattern of a foreign-looking brown surtout, with silk buttons, a fur collar, and fur cuffs. He wears a stripe down the outside of each leg of his trousers: and we have detected his assistants (for he has assistants now) in the act of sitting on the shop-board in the same uniform.

At the other end of the little row of houses a boot-maker has established himself in a brick box, with the additional innovation of a first floor; and here he exposes for sale, boots—real Wellington boots—an article which a few years ago, none of the original inhabitants had ever seen or heard of. It was but the other day, that a dress-maker opened another little box in the middle of the row; and, when we thought that the spirit of change could produce no alteration beyond that, a jeweller appeared, and not content with exposing gilt rings and copper bracelets out of number, put up an announcement, which still sticks in his window, that "ladies' ears may be pierced within." The dress-maker employs a young lady who wears pockets in her apron; and the tailor informs the public that gentlemen may have their own materials made up.

Amidst all this change, and restlessness, and innovation, there remains but one old man, who seems to mourn the downfall of this ancient place. He holds no converse with human kind, but, seated on a wooden bench at the angle of the wall which fronts the crossing from Whitehall-place, watches in silence the gambols of his sleek and well-fed dogs. He is the presiding genius of Scotland-yard. Years and years have rolled over his head; but, in fine weather or in foul, hot or cold, wet or dry, hail, rain, or snow, he is still in his accustomed spot. Misery and want are depicted in his countenance; his form is bent by age, his head is grey with length of trial, but there he sits from day to day, brooding over the past; and thither he will continue to drag his feeble limbs, until his eyes have closed upon Scotland-yard, and upon the world together.

A few years hence, and the antiquary of another generation looking into some mouldy record of the strife and passions that agitated the world in these times, may glance his eye over the pages we have just filled: and not all his knowledge of the history of the past, not all his black-letter lore, or his skill in book-collecting, not all the dry studies of a long life, or the dusty volumes that have cost him a fortune, may help him to the whereabouts, either of Scotland-yard, or of any one of the landmarks we have mentioned in describing it.

CHAPTER V

SEVEN DIALS

We have always been of opinion that if Tom King and the Frenchman had not immortalised Seven Dials, Seven Dials would have immortalised itself. Seven Dials! the region of song and poetry—first effusions, and last dying speeches: hallowed by the names of Catnach and of Pitts—names that will entwine themselves with costermongers, and barrel-organs, when penny magazines shall have superseded penny yards of song, and capital punishment be unknown!

Look at the construction of the place. The Gordian knot was all very well in its way: so was the maze of Hampton Court: so is the maze at the Beulah Spa: so were the ties of stiff white neckcloths, when the difficulty of getting one on, was only to be equalled by the apparent impossibility of ever getting it off again. But what involutions can compare with those of Seven Dials? Where is there such another maze of streets, courts, lanes, and alleys? Where such a pure mixture of Englishmen and Irishmen, as in this complicated part of London? We boldly aver that we doubt the veracity of the legend to which we have adverted. We *can* suppose a man rash enough to inquire at random—at a house with lodgers too—for a Mr. Thompson, with all but the certainty before his eyes, of finding at least two or three Thompsons in any house of moderate dimensions; but a Frenchman—a Frenchman in Seven Dials! Pooh! He was an Irishman. Tom King's education had been neglected in his infancy, and as he couldn't understand half the man said, he took it for granted he was talking French.

The stranger who finds himself in "The Dials" for the first time, and stands Belzoni-like, at the entrance of seven obscure passages, uncertain which to take, will see enough around him to keep his curiosity and attention awake for no inconsiderable time. From the irregular square into which he has plunged, the streets and courts dart in all directions, until they are lost in the unwholesome vapour which hangs over the house-tops, and renders the dirty perspective uncertain and confined; and lounging at every corner, as if they came there to take a few gasps of such fresh air as has found its way so far, but is too much exhausted already, to be enabled to force itself into the narrow alleys around, are groups of people, whose appearance and dwellings would fill any mind but a regular Londoner's with astonishment.

On one side, a little crowd has collected round a couple of ladies, who having imbibed the contents of various "three-outs" of gin and bitters in the course of the morning, have at length differed on some point of domestic arrangement, and are on the eve of settling the quarrel satisfactorily, by an appeal to blows, greatly to the interest of other ladies who live in the same house, and tenements adjoining, and who are all partisans on one side or other.

"Vy don't you pitch into her, Sarah?" exclaims one half-dressed matron, by way of encouragement. "Vy don't you? if *my* 'usband had treated her with a drain last night, unbe-known to me, I'd tear her precious eyes out—a wixen!"

"What's the matter, ma'am?" inquires another old woman, who has just bustled up to the spot.

"Matter!" replies the first speaker, talking *at* the obnoxious combatant, "matter! Here's poor dear Mrs. Sulliwin, as has five blessed children of her own, can't go out a charing for one arternoon, but what hussies must be a comin', and 'ticing avay her oun' 'usband, as she's been married to twelve year

82

Seven Dials

come next Easter Monday, for I see the certificate ven I vas a drinkin' a cup o' tea vith her, only the werry last blessed Ven'sday as ever was sent. I 'appen'd to say promiscuously, ' Mrs. Sulliwin,' says I—— "

" What do you mean by hussies? " interrupts a champion of the other party, who has evinced a strong inclination throughout to get up a branch fight on her own account (" Hooroar," ejaculates a pot-boy in parenthesis, " put the kye-bosk on her, Mary ! "), " What do you mean by hussies? " reiterates the champion.

" Niver mind," replies the opposition expressively, " niver mind ; *you* go home, and, ven you're quite sober, mend your stockings."

This somewhat personal allusion, not only to the lady's habits of intemperance, but also to the state of her wardrobe, rouses her utmost ire, and she accordingly complies with the urgent request of the bystanders to " pitch in," with consider-able alacrity. The scuffle became general, and terminates, in minor play-bill phraseology, with " arrival of the policemen, interior of the station-house, and impressive *dénouement*."

In addition to the numerous groups who are idling about the gin-shops and squabbling in the centre of the road, every post in the open space has its occupant, who leans against it for hours, with listless perseverance. It is odd enough that one class of men in London appear to have no enjoyment beyond leaning against posts. We never saw a regular brick-layer's labourer take any other recreation, fighting excepted. Pass through St. Giles's in the evening of a week-day, there they are in their fustian dresses, spotted with brick-dust and whitewash, leaning against posts. Walk through Seven Dials on Sunday morning : there they are again, drab or light corduroy trousers, Blucher boots, blue coats, and great yellow waistcoats, leaning against posts. The idea of a man dressing himself in his best clothes, to lean against a post all day !

The peculiar character of these streets, and the close resemblance each one bears to its neighbour, by no means tends to decrease the bewilderment in which the unexperienced wayfarer through "the Dials" finds himself involved. He traverses streets of dirty, straggling houses, with now and then an unexpected court composed of buildings as ill-proportioned and deformed as the half-naked children that wallow in the kennels. Here and there, a little dark chandler's shop, with a cracked bell hung up behind the door to announce the entrance of a customer, or betray the presence of some young gentleman in whom a passion for shop tills has developed itself at an early age : others, as if for support, against some handsome lofty building, which usurps the place of a low dingy public-house ; long rows of broken and patched windows expose plants that may have flourished when "the Dials" were built, in vessels as dirty as "the Dials" themselves ; and shops for the purchase of rags, bones, old iron, and kitchen-stuff, vie in cleanliness with the bird-fanciers and rabbit-dealers, which one might fancy so many arks, but for the irresistible conviction that no bird in its proper senses, who was permitted to leave one of them, would ever come back again. Brokers' shops, which would seem to have been established by humane individuals, as refuges for destitute bugs, interspersed with announcements of day-schools, penny theatres, petition-writers, mangles, and music for balls or routs, complete the "still life" of the subject ; and dirty men, filthy women, squalid children, fluttering shuttlecocks, noisy battledores, reeking pipes, bad fruit, more than doubtful oysters, attenuated cats, depressed dogs, and anatomical fowls, are its cheerful accompaniments.

If the external appearance of the houses, or a glance at their inhabitants, present but few attractions, a closer acquaintance with either is little calculated to alter one's first impression. Every room has its separate tenant, and every tenant is, by the same mysterious dispensation which causes a country curate to "increase and multiply" most marvellously, generally the head of a numerous family.

The man in the shop, perhaps, is in the baked "jemmy"

THE SHABBY-GENTEEL MAN

line, or the fire-wood and hearth-stone line, or any other line which requires a floating capital of eighteen-pence or thereabouts: and he and his family live in the shop, and the small back parlour behind it. Then there is an Irish labourer and *his* family in the back kitchen, and a jobbing man—carpet-beater and so forth—with *his* family in the front one. In the front one-pair, there's another man with another wife and family, and in the back one-pair, there's "a young 'oman as takes in tambour-work, and dresses quite genteel," who talks a good deal about "my friend," and can't "a-bear anything low." The second floor front, and the rest of the lodgers, are just a second edition of the people below, except a shabby-genteel man in the back attic, who has his half-pint of coffee every morning from the coffee-shop next door but one, which boasts a little front den called a coffee-room, with a fireplace, over which is an inscription, politely requesting that, "to prevent mistakes," customers will "please to pay on delivery." The shabby-genteel man is an object of some mystery, but as he leads a life of seclusion, and never was known to buy anything beyond an occasional pen, except half-pints of coffee, penny loaves, and ha'porths of ink, his fellow-lodgers very naturally suppose him to be an author; and rumours are current in the Dials, that he writes poems for Mr. Warren.

Now anybody who passed through the Dials on a hot summer's evening, and saw the different women of the house gossiping on the steps, would be apt to think that all was harmony among them, and that a more primitive set of people than the native Diallers could not be imagined. Alas! the man in the shop ill-treats his family; the carpet-beater extends his professional pursuits to his wife; the one-pair front has an undying feud with the two-pair front, in consequence of the two-pair front persisting in dancing over his (the one-pair front's) head, when he and his family have retired for the night; the two-pair back *will* interfere with the front kitchen's children; the Irishman comes home drunk every other night, and attacks everybody; and the one-pair back screams at everything. Animosities spring up between floor and floor; the very cellar asserts his equality. Mrs. A. "smacks" Mrs. B.'s child for "making faces." Mrs. B. forthwith throws cold water over Mrs. A.'s child for "calling names." The husbands are embroiled—the quarrel becomes general—an assault is the consequence, and a police-officer the result.

CHAPTER VI

WE have always entertained a particular attachment towards Monmouth-street, as the only true and real emporium for second-hand wearing apparel. Monmouth-street is venerable from its antiquity, and respectable from its usefulness. Holywell-street we despise; the red-headed and red-whiskered Jews who forcibly haul you into their squalid houses, and thrust you into a suit of clothes, whether you will or not, we detest.

The inhabitants of Monmouth-street are a distinct class; a peaceable and retiring race, who immure themselves for the most part in deep cellars, or small back parlours, and who seldom come forth into the world, except in the dusk and coolness of the evening, when they may be seen seated, in chairs on the pavement, smoking their pipes, or watching the gambols of their engaging children as they revel in the gutter, a happy troop of infantine scavengers. Their countenances bear a thoughtful and a dirty cast, certain indications of their love of traffic; and their habitations are distinguished by that disregard of outward appearance and neglect of personal comfort, so common among people who are constantly immersed in profound speculations, and deeply engaged in sedentary pursuits.

We have hinted at the antiquity of our favourite spot. " A Monmouth-street laced coat" was a by-word a century ago; and still we find Monmouth-street the same. Pilot great-coats with wooden buttons, have usurped the place of the ponderous laced coats with full skirts; embroidered waistcoats with large flaps, have yielded to double-breasted checks with roll-collars; and three-cornered hats of quaint appearance, have given place to the low crowns and broad brims of the coachman school; but it is the times that have changed, not Monmouth-street. Through every alteration and every change, Monmouth-street has still remained the burial-place of the fashions; and such, to judge from all present appearances, it will remain until there are no more fashions to bury.

We love to walk among these extensive groves of the illustrious dead, and to indulge in the speculations to which they give rise; now fitting a deceased coat, then a dead pair of trousers, and anon the mortal remains of a gaudy waistcoat, upon some being of our own conjuring up, and endeavouring, from the shape and fashion of the garment itself, to bring its former owner before our mind's eye. We have gone on speculating in this way, until whole rows of coats have started from their pegs, and buttoned up, of their own accord, round the waists of imaginary wearers; lines of trousers have jumped down to meet them; waistcoats have almost burst with anxiety to put themselves on; and half an acre of shoes have suddenly found feet to fit them, and gone stumping down the street with a noise which has fairly awakened us from our pleasant reverie, and driven us slowly away, with a bewildered stare, an object of astonishment to the good people of Monmouth-street, and of no slight suspicion to the policemen at the opposite street corner.

We were occupied in this manner the other day, endeavouring to fit a pair of lace-up half-boots on an ideal personage, for whom, to say the truth, they were full a couple of sizes too small, when our eyes happened to alight on a few suits of clothes ranged outside a shop-window, which it immediately struck us, must at different periods have all belonged

Monmouth-Street

to, and been worn by, the same individual, and had now, by one of those strange conjunctions of circumstances which will occur sometimes, come to be exposed together for sale in the same shop. The idea seemed a fantastic one, and we looked at the clothes again with a firm determination not to be easily led away. No, we were right; the more we looked, the more we were convinced of the accuracy of our previous impression. There was the man's whole life written as legibly on those clothes, as if we had his autobiography engrossed on parchment before us.

The first was a patched and much-soiled skeleton suit; one of those straight blue cloth cases in which small boys used to be confined, before belts and tunics had come in, and old notions had gone out: an ingenious contrivance for displaying the full symmetry of a boy's figure, by fastening him into a very tight jacket, with an ornamental row of buttons over each shoulder, and then buttoning his trousers over it, so as to give his legs the appearance of being hooked on, just under the armpits. This was the boy's dress. It had belonged to a town boy, we could see ; there was a shortness about the legs and arms of the suit; and a bagging at the knees, peculiar to the rising youth of London streets. A small day-school he had been at, evidently. If it had been a regular boys' school they wouldn't have let him play on the floor so much, and rub his knees so white. He had an indulgent mother too, and plenty of halfpence, as the numerous smears of some sticky substance about the pockets, and just below the chin, which even the salesman's skill could not succeed in disguising, sufficiently betokened. They were decent people, but not overburdened with riches, or he would not have so far outgrown the suit when he passed into those corduroys with the round jacket; in which he went to a boys' school, however, and learnt to write—and in ink of pretty tolerable blackness, too, if the place where he used to wipe his pen might be taken as evidence.

A black suit and the jacket changed into a diminutive

coat. His father had died, and the mother had got the boy a message-lad's place in some office. A long-worn suit that one; rusty and threadbare before it was laid aside, but clean and free from soil to the last. Poor woman! We could imagine her assumed cheerfulness over the scanty meal, and the refusal of her own small portion, that her hungry boy might have enough. Her constant anxiety for his welfare, her pride in his growth mingled sometimes with the thought, almost too acute to bear, that as he grew to be a man his old affection might cool, old kindnesses fade from his mind, and old promises be forgotten—the sharp pain that even then a careless word or a cold look would give her—all crowded on our thoughts as vividly as if the very scene were passing before us.

These things happen every hour, and we all know it; and yet we felt as much sorrow when we saw, or fancied we saw—it makes no difference which—the change that began to take place now, as if we had just conceived the bare possibility of such a thing for the first time. The next suit, smart but slovenly; meant to be gay, and yet not half so decent as the threadbare apparel; redolent of the idle lounge, and the blackguard companions, told us, we thought, that the widow's comfort had rapidly faded away. We could imagine that coat—imagine! we could see it; we *had* seen it a hundred times—sauntering in company with three or four other coats of the same cut, about some place of profligate resort at night.

We dressed, from the same shop-window in an instant, half a dozen boys of from fifteen to twenty; and putting cigars into their mouths, and their hands into their pockets, watched them as they sauntered down the street, and lingered at the corner, with the obscene jest, and the oft-repeated oath. We never lost sight of them, till they had cocked their hats a little more on one side, and swaggered into the public-house; and then we entered the desolate home, where the mother sat late in the night, alone; we watched her, as

A MELANCHOLY HISTORY

she paced the room in feverish anxiety, and every now and then opened the door, looked wistfully into the dark and empty street, and again returned, to be again and again disappointed. We beheld the look of patience with which she bore the brutish threat, nay, even the drunken blow; and we heard the agony of tears that gushed from her very heart, as she sank upon her knees in her solitary and wretched apartment.

A long period had elapsed, and a greater change had taken place, by the time of casting off the suit that hung above. It was that of a stout, broad-shouldered, sturdy-chested man; and we knew at once, as anybody would, who glanced at that broad-skirted green coat, with the large metal buttons, that its wearer seldom walked forth without a dog at his heels, and some idle ruffian, the very counterpart of himself, at his side. The vices of the boy had grown with the man, and we fancied his home then—if such a place deserve the name.

We saw the bare and miserable room, destitute of furniture, crowded with his wife and children, pale, hungry, and emaciated; the man cursing their lamentations, staggering to the tap-room, from whence he had just returned, followed by his wife and a sickly infant, clamouring for bread; and heard the street-wrangle and noisy recrimination that his striking her occasioned. And then imagination led us to some metropolitan workhouse, situated in the midst of crowded streets and alleys, filled with noxious vapours, and ringing with boisterous cries, where an old and feeble woman, imploring pardon for her son, lay dying in a close dark room, with no child to clasp her hand, and no pure air from heaven to fan her brow. A stranger closed the eyes that settled into a cold unmeaning glare, and strange ears received the words that murmured from the white and half-closed lips.

A coarse round frock, with a worn cotton neckerchief, and other articles of clothing of the commonest description completed the history. A prison, and the sentence—banish-ment or the gallows. What would the man have given then, to be once again the contented humble drudge of his boyish years; to have been restored to life, but for a week, a day, an hour, a minute, only for so long a time as would enable him to say one word of passionate regret to, and hear one sound of heartfelt forgiveness from, the cold and ghastly form that lay rotting in the pauper's grave! The children wild in the streets, the mother a destitute widow; both deeply tainted with the deep disgrace of the husband and father's name, and impelled by sheer necessity, down the precipice that had led him to a lingering death, possibly of many years' duration, thousands of miles away. We had no clue to the end of the tale; but it was easy to guess its termination.

We took a step or two further on, and by way of restoring the naturally cheerful tone of our thoughts, began fitting visionary feet and legs into a cellar-board full of boots and shoes, with a speed and accuracy that would have astonished the most expert artist in leather, living. There was one pair of boots in particular—a jolly, good-tempered, hearty-looking pair of tops, that excited our warmest regard; and we had got a fine, red-faced, jovial fellow of a market-gardener into them, before we had made their acquaintance half a minute. They were just the very thing for him. There were his huge fat legs bulging over the tops, and fitting them too tight to admit of his tucking in the loops he had pulled them on by; and his knee-cords with an interval of stocking; and his blue apron tucked up round his waist; and his red neckerchief and blue coat, and a white hat stuck on one side of his head; and there he stood with a broad grin on his great red face, whistling away, as if any other idea but that of being happy and comfortable had never entered his brain.

This was the very man after our own heart; we knew all about him; we had seen him coming up to Covent-garden in his green chaise-cart, with the fat, tubby little horse, half a thousand times; and even while we cast an affectionate look upon his boots, at that instant, the form of a coquettish servant-maid suddenly sprung into a pair of Denmark satin shoes that stood beside them, and we at once recognised the very girl who accepted his offer of a ride, just on this side the Hammersmith suspension-bridge, the very last Tuesday morning we rode into town from Richmond.

A very smart female, in a showy bonnet, stepped into a pair of grey cloth boots, with black fringe and binding, that were studiously pointing out their toes on the other side of the top-boots, and seemed very anxious to engage his attention, but we didn't observe that our friend the market-gardener appeared at all captivated with these blandishments; for beyond giving a knowing wink when they first began, as if to imply that he quite understood their end and object, he took no further notice of them. His indifference, however, was amply recompensed by the excessive gallantry of a very old gentleman with a silver-headed stick, who tottered into a pair of large list shoes, that were standing in one corner of the board, and indulged in a variety of gestures expressive of his admiration of the lady in the cloth boots, to the immeasurable amusement of a young fellow we put into a pair of long-quartered pumps, who we thought would have split the coat that slid down to meet him, with laughing.

We had been looking on at this little pantomime with great satisfaction for some time, when, to our unspeakable astonishment, we perceived that the whole of the characters, including a numerous *corps de ballet* of boots and shoes in the background, into which we had been hastily thrusting as many feet as we could press into the service, were arranging themselves in order for dancing; and some music striking up at the moment, to it they went without delay. It was perfectly delightful to witness the agility of the market-gardener. Out went the boots, first on one side, then on the other, then cutting, then shuffling, then setting to the Denmark satins, then advancing, then retreating, then going round, and then repeating the whole of the evolutions again, without appearing to suffer in the least from the violence of the exercise.

Nor were the Denmark satins a bit behindhand, for they jumped and bounded about, in all directions; and though they were neither so regular, nor so true to the time as the cloth boots, still, as they seemed to do it from the heart, and to enjoy it more, we candidly confess that we preferred their style of dancing to the other. But the old gentleman in the list shoes was the most amusing object in the whole party; for, besides his grotesque attempts to appear youthful, and amorous, which were sufficiently entertaining in themselves, the young fellow in the pumps managed so artfully that every time the old gentleman advanced to salute the lady in the cloth boots, he trod with his whole weight on the old fellow's toes, which made him roar with anguish, and rendered all the others like to die of laughing.

We were in the full enjoyment of these festivities when we heard a shrill, and by no means musical voice, exclaim, "Hope you'll know me agin, imperence!" and on looking intently forward to see from whence the sound came, we found that it proceeded, not from the young lady in the cloth boots, as we had at first been inclined to suppose, but from a bulky lady of elderly appearance who was seated in a chair at the head of the cellar-steps, apparently for the purpose of superintending the sale of the articles arranged there.

A barrel-organ, which had been in full force close behind us, ceased playing; the people we had been fitting into the shoes and boots took to flight at the interruption; and as we were conscious that in the depth of our meditations we might have been rudely staring at the old lady for half an hour without knowing it, we took to flight too, and were soon immersed in the deepest obscurity of the adjacent "Dials."

CHAPTER VII

WE maintain that hackney-coaches, properly so called, belong solely to the metropolis. We may be told, that there are hackney-coach stands in Edinburgh; and not to go quite so far for a contradiction to our position, we may be reminded that Liverpool, Manchester, "and other large towns" (as the Parlimentary phrase goes), have *their* hackney-coach stands. We readily concede to these places the possession of certain vehicles, which may look almost as dirty, and even go almost as slowly, as London hackney-coaches : but that they have the slightest claim to compete with the metropolis, either in point of stands, drivers, or cattle, we indignantly deny.

Take a regular, ponderous, rickety, London hackney-coach of the old school, and let any man have the boldness to assert, if he can, that he ever beheld any object on the face of the earth which at all resembles it, unless, indeed, it were another hackney-coach of the same date. We have recently observed on certain stands, and we say it with deep regret, rather dapper green chariots, and coaches of polished yellow, with four wheels of the same colour as the coach, whereas it is perfectly notorious to every one who has studied the subject, that every wheel ought to be of a different colour, and a different size. These are innovations, and, like other mis-called improvements, awful signs of the restlessness of the public mind, and the little respect paid to our time-honoured

95

institutions. Why should hackney-coaches be clean ? Our ancestors found them dirty, and left them so. Why should we, with a feverish wish to "keep moving," desire to roll along at the rate of six miles an hour, while they were content to rumble over the stones at four? These are solemn considerations. Hackney-coaches are part and parcel of the law of the land; they were settled by the Legislature; plated and numbered by the wisdom of Parliament.

Then why have they been swamped by cabs and omnibuses? Or why should people be allowed to ride quickly for eightpence a mile, after Parliament had come to the solemn decision that they should pay a shilling a mile for riding slowly? We pause for a reply;—and, having no chance of getting one, begin a fresh paragraph.

Our acquaintance with hackney-coach stands is of long standing. We are a walking book of fares, feeling ourselves, half bound, as it were, to be always in the right on contested points. We know all the regular watermen within three miles of Covent-garden by sight, and should be almost tempted to believe that all the hackney-coach horses in that district knew us by sight too, if one-half of them were not blind. We take great interest in hackney-coaches, but we seldom drive, having a knack of turning ourselves over when we attempt to do so. We are as great friends to horses, hackney-coach and otherwise, as the renowned Mr. Martin, of costermonger notoriety, and yet we never ride. We keep no horse, but a clotheshorse; enjoy no saddle so much as a saddle of mutton; and, following our own inclinations, have never followed the hounds. Leaving these fleeter means of getting over the ground, or of depositing oneself upon it, to those who like them, by hackneycoach stands we take our stand.

There is a hackney-coach stand under the very window at which we are writing; there is only one coach on it now, but it is a fair specimen of the class of vehicles to which we have alluded—a great, lumbering, square concern of a dingy yellow colour (like a bilious brunette), with very small glasses, but

Hackney-Coach Stands

very large frames; the panels are ornamented with a faded coat of arms, in shape something like a dissected bat, the axletree is red, and the majority of the wheels are green. The box is partially covered by an old great-coat, with a multiplicity of capes, and some extraordinary-looking clothes; and the straw, with which the canvas cushion is stuffed, is sticking up in several places, as if in rivalry of the hay, which is peeping through the chinks in the boot. The horses, with drooping heads, and each with a mane and tail as scanty and straggling as those of a worn-out rocking-horse, are standing patiently on some damp straw, occasionally wincing, and rattling the harness; and now and then, one of them lifts his mouth to the ear of his companion, as if he were saying, in a whisper, that he should like to assassinate the coachman. The coachman himself is in the watering-house; and the waterman, with his hands forced into his pockets as far as they can possibly go, is dancing the "double shuffle," in front of the pump, to keep his feet warm.

The servant-girl, with the pink ribbons, at No. 5, opposite, suddenly opens the street-door, and four small children forthwith rush out, and scream "Coach!" with all their might and main. The waterman darts from the pump, seizes the horses by their respective bridles, and drags them, and the coach too, round to the house, shouting all the time for the coachman at the very top, or rather very bottom of his voice, for it is a deep bass growl. A response is heard from the tap-room; the coachman, in his wooden-soled shoes, makes the street echo again as he runs across it; and then there is such a struggling, and backing, and grating of the kennel, to get the coach-door opposite the house-door, that the children are in perfect ecstasies of delight. What a commotion! The old lady, who has been stopping there for the last month, is going back to the country. Out comes box after box, and one side of the vehicle is filled with luggage in no time; the children get into everybody's way, and the youngest, who has upset himself in his attempts to carry an

97

umbrella, is borne off wounded and kicking. The youngsters disappear, and a short pause ensues, during which the old lady is, no doubt, kissing them all round in the back parlour. She appears at last, followed by her married daughter, all the children, and both the servants, who, with the joint assistance of the coachman and waterman, manage to get her safely into the coach. A cloak is handed in, and a little basket, which we could almost swear contains a small black bottle, and a paper of sandwiches. Up go the steps, bangs goes the door, "Golden-cross, Charing-cross, Tom," says the waterman; "Good-bye, grandma," cry the children, off jingles the coach at the rate of three miles an hour, and the mamma and children retire into the house, with the exception of one little villain, who runs up the street at the top of his speed, pursued by the servant; not ill-pleased to have such an opportunity of displaying her attractions. She brings him back, and, after casting two or three gracious glances across the way, which are either intended for us or the potboy (we are not quite certain which), shuts the door, and the hackney-coach stand is again at a standstill.

We have been frequently amused with the intense delight with which " a servant of all work," who is sent for a coach, deposits herself inside; and the unspeakable gratification which boys, who have been despatched on a similar errand, appear to derive from mounting the box. But we never recollect to have been more amused with a hackney-coach party, than one we saw early the other morning in Tottenham-court-road. It was a wedding-party, and emerged from one of the inferior streets near Fitzroy-square. There were the bride, with a thin white dress, and a great red face; and the bridesmaid, a little, dumpy, good-humoured young woman, dressed, of course, in the same appropriate costume; and the bridegroom and his chosen friend, in blue coats, yellow waistcoats, white trousers, and Berlin gloves to match. They stopped at the corner of the street, and called a coach with an air of indescribable dignity. The moment they were in, the bridesmaid threw a red shawl, which she had, no doubt, brought on purpose, negligently over the number on the door, evidently to delude pedestrians into the belief that the hackney-coach was a private carriage; and away they went, perfectly satisfied that the imposition was successful, and quite unconscious that there was a great staring number stuck up behind, on a plate as large as a schoolboy's slate. A shilling a mile!—the ride was worth five, at least, to them.

What an interesting book a hackney-coach might produce, if it could carry as much in its head as it does in its body! The autobiography of a broken-down hackney-coach, would surely be as amusing as the autobiography of a broken-down hackneyed dramatist; and it might tell as much of its travels *with* the pole, as others have of their expeditions *to* it. How many stories might be related of the different people it had conveyed on matters of business or profit—pleasure or pain! And how many melancholy tales of the same people at different periods! The country-girl—the showy, over-dressed woman—the drunken prostitute! The raw apprentice—the dissipated spendthrift—the thief!

Talk of cabs! Cabs are all very well in cases of expedition, when it's a matter of neck or nothing, life or death, your temporary home or your long one. But, besides a cab's lacking that gravity of deportment which so peculiarly distinguishes a hackney-coach, let it never be forgotten that a cab is a thing of yesterday, and that he never was anything better. A hackney-cab has always been a hackney-cab, from his first entry into life; whereas a hackney-coach is a remnant of past gentility, a victim to fashion, a hanger-on of an old English family, wearing their arms, and, in days of yore, escorted by men wearing their livery, stripped of his finery, and thrown upon the world, like a once-smart footman when he is no longer sufficiently juvenile for his office, progressing lower and lower in the scale of four-wheeled degradation, until at last it comes to—*a stand!*

CHAPTER VIII

DOCTORS' COMMONS

WALKING without any definite object through St. Paul's Churchyard, a little while ago, we happened to turn down a street entitled "Paul's-chain," and keeping straight forward for a few hundred yards, found ourself, as a natural consequence, in Doctors' Commons. Now Doctors' Commons being familiar by name to everybody, as the place where they grant marriage-licenses to love-sick couples, and divorces to unfaithful ones; register the wills of people who have any property to leave, and punish hasty gentlemen who call ladies by unpleasant names, we no sooner discovered that we were really within its precincts, than we felt a laudable desire to become better acquainted therewith; and as the first object of our curiosity was the Court, whose decrees can even unloose the bonds of matrimony, we procured a direction to it; and bent our steps thither without delay.

Crossing a quiet and shady court-yard, paved with stone, and frowned upon by old red brick houses, on the doors of which were painted the names of sundry learned civilians, we paused before a small, green-baized, brass-headed-nailed door, which yielding to our gentle push, at once admitted us into an old quaint-looking apartment, with sunken windows, and black carved wainscoting, at the upper end of which, seated on a raised platform, of semicircular shape, were about a dozen solemn-looking gentlemen, in crimson gowns and wigs.

100

THE ARCHES COURT

At a more elevated desk in the centre, sat a very fat and red-faced gentleman, in tortoise-shell spectacles, whose dignified appearance announced the judge; and round a long green-baized table below, something like a billiard-table without the cushions and pockets, were a number of very self-important-looking personages, in stiff neckcloths, and black gowns with white fur collars, whom we at once set down as proctors. At the lower end of the billiard-table was an individual in an arm-chair, and a wig, whom we afterwards discovered to be the registrar; and seated behind a little desk, near the door, were a respectable-looking man in black, of about twenty-stone weight or thereabouts, and a fat-faced, smirking, civil-looking body, in a black gown, black kid gloves, knee shorts, and silks, with a shirt-frill in his bosom, curls on his head, and a silver staff in his hand, whom we had no difficulty in recognising as the officer of the Court. The latter, indeed, speedily set our mind at rest upon this point, for, advancing to our elbow, and opening a conversation forthwith, he had communicated to us, in less than five minutes, that he was the apparitor, and the other the court-keeper; that this was the Arches Court, and therefore the counsel wore red gowns, and the proctors fur collars; and that when the other Courts sat there, they didn't wear red gowns or fur collars either; with many other scraps of intelligence equally interesting. Besides these two officers, there was a little thin old man, with long grizzly hair, crouched in a remote corner, whose duty, our communicative friend informed us, was to ring a large hand-bell when the Court opened in the morning, and who, for aught his appearance betokened to the contrary, might have been similarly employed for the last two centuries at least.

The red-faced gentleman in the tortoise-shell spectacles had got all the talk to himself just then, and very well he was doing it, too, only he spoke very fast, but that was habit; and rather thick, but that was good living. So we had plenty of time to look about us. There was one individual who amused us mightily. This was one of the bewigged gentlemen in the red robes, who was straddling before the fire in the centre of the Court, in the attitude of the brazen Colossus, to the complete exclusion of everybody else. He had gathered up his robe behind, in much the same manner as a slovenly woman would her petticoats on a very dirty day, in order that he might feel the full warmth of the fire. His wig was put on all awry, with the tail straggling about his neck; his scanty grey trousers and short black gaiters, made in the worst possible style, imparted an additional inelegant appearance to his uncouth person; and his limp, badly-starched shirt-collar almost obscured his eyes. We shall never be able to claim any credit as a physiognomist again, for, after a careful scrutiny of this gentleman's countenance, we had come to the conclusion that it bespoke nothing but conceit and silliness, when our friend with the silver staff whispered in our ear that he was no other than a doctor of civil law, and heaven knows what besides. So of course we were mistaken, and he must be a very talented man. He conceals it so well though—perhaps with the merciful view of not astonishing ordinary people too much— that you would suppose him to be one of the stupidest dogs alive.

The gentleman in the spectacles having concluded his judgment, and a few minutes having been allowed to elapse, to afford time for the buzz in the Court to subside, the registrar called on the next cause, which was " the office of the Judge promoted by Bumple against Sludberry." A general movement was visible in the Court, at this announcement, and the obliging functionary with silver staff whispered us that "there would be some fun now, for this was a brawling case."

We were not rendered much the wiser by this piece of information, till we found by the opening speech of the counsel for the promoter, that, under a half-obsolete statute of one of the Edwards, the court was empowered to visit with the

102

penalty of excommunication, any person who should be proved guilty of the crime of "brawling," or "smiting," in any church, or vestry adjoining thereto; and it appeared, by some eight-and-twenty affidavits, which were duly referred to, that on a certain night, at a certain vestry-meeting, in a certain parish particularly set forth, Thomas Sludberry, the party appeared against in that suit, had made use of, and applied to Michael Bumple, the promoter, the words "You be blowed;" and that, on the said Michael Bumple and others remonstrating with the said Thomas Sludberry, on the impropriety of his conduct, the said Thomas Sludberry repeated the aforesaid expression, "You be blowed;" and furthermore desired and requested to know, whether the said Michael Bumple "wanted anything for himself;" adding, "that if the said Michael Bumple did want anything for himself, he, the said Thomas Sludberry, was the man to give it him;" at the same time making use of other heinous and sinful expressions, all of which, Bumple submitted, came within the intent and meaning of the Act; and therefore he, for the soul's health and chastening of Sludberry, prayed for sentence of excommunication against him accordingly."

Upon these facts a long argument was entered into, on both sides, to the great edification of a number of persons interested in the parochial squabbles, who crowded the court; and when some very long and grave speeches had been made *pro* and *con*, the red-faced gentleman in the tortoise-shell spectacles took a review of the case, which occupied half an hour more, and then pronounced upon Sludberry the awful sentence of excommunication for a fortnight, and payment of the costs of the suit. Upon this, Sludberry, who was a little, red-faced, sly-looking, ginger-beer seller, addressed the court, and said, if they'd be good enough to take off the costs, and excommunicate him for the term of his natural life instead, it would be much more convenient to him, for he never went to church at all. To this appeal the gentleman in the spectacles made no other reply than a look of virtuous indignation; and Sludberry and his friends retired. As the man with the silver staff informed us that the court was on the point of rising, we retired too—pondering, as we walked away, upon the beautiful spirit of these ancient ecclesiastical laws, the kind and neighbourly feelings they are calculated to awaken, and the strong attachment to religious institutions which they cannot fail to engender.

We were so lost in these meditations, that we had turned into the street, and run up against a door-post, before we recollected where we were walking. On looking upwards to see what house we had stumbled upon, the words "Prerogative-Office," written in large characters, met our eye; and as we were in a sight-seeing humour and the place was a public one, we walked in.

The room into which we walked, was a long, busy-looking place, partitioned off, on either side, into a variety of little boxes, in which a few clerks were engaged in copying or examining deeds. Down the centre of the room were several desks nearly breast high, at each of which, three or four people were standing, poring over large volumes. As we knew that they were searching for wills, they attracted our attention at once.

It was curious to contrast the lazy indifference of the attorneys' clerks who were making a search for some legal purpose, with the air of earnestness and interest which distinguished the strangers to the place, who were looking up the will of some deceased relative; the former pausing every now and then with an impatient yawn, or raising their heads to look at the people who passed up and down the room; the latter stooping over the book, and running down column after column of names in the deepest abstraction.

There was one little dirty-faced man in a blue apron, who after a whole morning's search, extending some fifty years back, had just found the will to which he wished to refer, which one of the officials was reading to him in a low hurried voice from a thick vellum book with large clasps. It was

WILLS

perfectly evident that the more the clerk read, the less the man with the blue apron understood about the matter. When the volume was first brought down, he took off his hat, smoothed down his hair, smiled with great self-satisfaction, and looked up in the reader's face with the air of a man who had made up his mind to recollect every word he heard. The first two or three lines were intelligible enough; but then the technicalities began, and the little man began to look rather dubious. Then came a whole string of complicated trusts, and he was regularly at sea. As the reader proceeded, it was quite apparent that it was a hopeless case, and the little man, with his mouth open and his eyes fixed upon his face, looked on with an expression of bewilderment and perplexity irresistibly ludicrous.

A little further on, a hard-featured old man with a deeply-wrinkled face, was intently perusing a lengthy will with the aid of a pair of horn spectacles: occasionally pausing from his task, and slily noting down some brief memorandum of the bequests contained in it. Every wrinkle about his toothless mouth, and sharp keen eyes, told of avarice and cunning. His clothes were nearly threadbare, but it was easy to see that he wore them from choice and not from necessity; all his looks and gestures down to the very small pinches of snuff which he every now and then took from a little tin canister, told of wealth, and penury, and avarice.

As he leisurely closed the register, put up his spectacles, and folded his scraps of paper in a large leathern pocket-book, we thought what a nice hard bargain he was driving with some poverty-stricken legatee, who, tired of waiting year after year, until some life-interest should fall in, was selling his chance, just as it began to grow most valuable, for a twelfth part of its worth. It was a good speculation—a very safe one. The old man stowed his pocket-book carefully in the breast of his great-coat, and hobbled away with a leer of triumph. That will had made him ten years younger at the lowest computation.

Having commenced our observations, we should certainly have extended them to another dozen of people at least, had not a sudden shutting up and putting away of the worm-eaten old books, warned us that the time for closing the office had arrived; and thus deprived us of a pleasure, and spared our readers an infliction.

We naturally fell into a train of reflection as we walked homewards, upon the curious old records of likings and dis-likings; of jealousies and revenges; of affection defying the power of death, and hatred pursued beyond the grave, which these depositories contain; silent but striking tokens, some of them, of excellence of heart, and nobleness of soul; melancholy examples, others, of the worst passions of human nature. How many men as they lay speechless and helpless on the bed of death, would have given worlds but for the strength and power to blot out the silent evidence of animosity and bitterness, which now stands registered against them in Doctors' Commons!

CHAPTER IX

THE wish of persons in the humbler classes of life, to ape the manners and customs of those whom fortune has placed above them, is often the subject of remark, and not unfrequently of complaint. The inclination may, and no doubt does, exist to a great extent, among the small gentility —the would-be aristocrats—of the middle classes. Tradesmen and clerks, with fashionable novel-reading families, and circulating-library-subscribing daughters, get up small assemblies in humble imitation of Almack's, and promenade the dingy "large room" of some second-rate hotel with as much complacency as the enviable few who are privileged to exhibit their magnificence in that exclusive haunt of fashion and foolery. Aspiring young ladies, who read flaming accounts of some "fancy fair in high life," suddenly grow desperately charitable; visions of admiration and matrimony float before their eyes; some wonderfully meritorious institution, which, by the strangest accident in the world, has never been heard of before, is discovered to be in a languishing condition: Thomson's great room, or Johnson's nursery-ground, is forthwith engaged, and the aforesaid young ladies, from mere charity, exhibit themselves for three days, from twelve to four, for the small charge of one shilling per head! With the exception of these classes of society, however, and a few weak and insignificant persons, we do not think the attempt

107

at imitation to which we have alluded, prevails in any great degree. The different character of the recreations of different classes, has often afforded us amusement; and we have chosen it for the subject of our present sketch, in the hope that it may possess some amusement for our readers.

If the regular City man, who leaves Lloyd's at five o'clock, and drives home to Hackney, Clapton, Stamford-hill, or elsewhere, can be said to have any daily recreation beyond his dinner, it is his garden. He never does anything to it with his own hands; but he takes great pride in it notwithstanding; and if you are desirous of paying your addresses to the youngest daughter, be sure to be in raptures with every flower and shrub it contains. If your poverty of expression compel you to make any distinction between the two, we would certainly recommend your bestowing more admiration on his garden than his wine. He always takes a walk round it, before he starts for town in the morning, and is particularly anxious that the fish-pond should be kept specially neat. If you call on him on Sunday in summer-time, about an hour before dinner, you will find him sitting in an arm-chair, on the lawn behind the house, with a straw hat on, reading a Sunday paper. A short distance from him you will most likely observe a handsome paroquet in a large brass-wire cage; ten to one but the two eldest girls are loitering in one of the side walks accompanied by a couple of young gentlemen, who are holding parasols over them—of course only to keep the sun off—while the younger children, with the under nursery-maid, are strolling listlessly about, in the shade. Beyond these occasions, his delight in his garden appears to arise more from the consciousness of possession than actual enjoyment of it. When he drives you down to dinner on a week-day, he is rather fatigued with the occupations of the morning, and tolerably cross into the bargain; but when the cloth is removed, and he has drank three or four glasses of his favourite port, he orders the French windows of his dining-room (which of course look into the

George Cruikshank

London Recreations

THE GARDEN

garden) to be opened, and throwing a silk handkerchief over
his head, and leaning back in his arm-chair, descants at
considerable length upon its beauty, and the cost of main-
taining it. This is to impress you—who are a young friend
of the family—with a due sense of the excellence of the
garden, and the wealth of its owner; and when he has
exhausted the subject, he goes to sleep.

There is another and a very different class of men, whose
recreation is their garden. An individual of this class,
resides some short distance from town — say in the Hamp-
stead-road, or the Kilburn-road, or any other road where
the houses are small and neat, and have little slips of back
garden. He and his wife—who is as clean and compact a
little body as himself—have occupied the same house ever
since he retired from business twenty years ago. They have
no family. They once had a son, who died at about five
years old. The child's portrait hangs over the mantelpiece
in the best sitting-room, and a little cart he used to draw
about, is carefully preserved as a relic.

In fine weather the old gentleman is almost constantly in
the garden; and when it is too wet to go into it, he will
look out of the window at it, by the hour together. He has
always something to do there, and you will see him digging,
and sweeping, and cutting, and planting, with manifest
delight. In spring-time, there is no end to the sowing of
seeds, and sticking little bits of wood over them, with labels,
which look like epitaphs to their memory; and in the
evening, when the sun has gone down, the perseverance with
which he lugs a great watering-pot about is perfectly
astonishing. The only other recreation he has, is the newspaper, which he peruses every day, from beginning to end,
generally reading the most interesting pieces of intelligence
to his wife, during breakfast. The old lady is very fond of
flowers, as the hyacinth-glasses in the parlour-window, and
geranium-pots in the little front court, testify. She takes
great pride in the garden too: and when one of the four

109

fruit-trees produces rather a larger gooseberry than usual, it is carefully preserved under a wine-glass on the sideboard, for the edification of visitors, who are duly informed that Mr. So-and-so planted the tree which produced it, with his own hands. On a summer's evening, when the large watering-pot has been filled and emptied some fourteen times, and the old couple have quite exhausted themselves by trotting about, you will see them sitting happily together in the little summer-house, enjoying the calm and peace of the twilight, and watching the shadows as they fall upon the garden, and gradually growing thicker and more sombre, obscure the tints of their gayest flowers—no bad emblem of the years that have silently rolled over their heads, deadening in their course the brightest hues of early hopes and feelings which have long since faded away. These are their only recreations, and they require no more. They have within themselves, the materials of comfort and content; and the only anxiety of each, is to die before the other.

This is no ideal sketch. There *used* to be many old people of this description; their numbers may have diminished, and may decrease still more. Whether the course female education has taken of late days—whether the pursuit of giddy frivolities, and empty nothings, has tended to unfit women for that quiet domestic life, in which they show far more beautifully than in the most crowded assembly, is a question we should feel little gratification in discussing: we hope not.

Let us turn now, to another portion of the London population, whose recreations present about as strong a contrast as can well be conceived—we mean the Sunday pleasurers; and let us beg our readers to imagine themselves stationed by our side in some well-known rural "Tea-gardens."

The heat is intense this afternoon, and the people, of whom there are additional parties arriving every moment, look as warm as the tables which have been recently painted, and have the appearance of being red-hot. What a dust and noise! Men and women—boys and girls—sweethearts and

married people—babies in arms, and children in chaises—
pipes and shrimps—cigars and periwinkles—tea and tobacco.
Gentlemen, in alarming waistcoats, and steel watch-guards,
promenading about, three abreast, with surprising dignity
(or as the gentleman in the next box facetiously observes,
"cutting it uncommon fat!")—ladies, with great, long, white
pocket-handkerchiefs like small table-cloths, in their hands,
chasing one another on the grass in the most playful and
interesting manner, with the view of attracting the attention
of the aforesaid gentlemen—husbands in perspective ordering
bottles of ginger-beer for the objects of their affections, with
a lavish disregard of expense; and the said objects washing
down huge quantities of "shrimps" and "winkles," with an
equal disregard of their own bodily health and subsequent
comfort—boys, with great silk hats just balanced on the top
of their heads, smoking cigars, and trying to look as if they
liked them—gentlemen in pink shirts and blue waistcoats,
occasionally upsetting either themselves, or somebody else,
with their own canes.

Some of the finery of these people provokes a smile, but
they are all clean, and happy, and disposed to be good-
natured and sociable. Those two motherly-looking women in
the smart pelisses, who are chatting so confidentially, inserting a "ma'am" at every fourth word, scraped an acquaintance about a quarter of an hour ago: it originated in
admiration of the little boy who belongs to one of them—
that diminutive specimen of mortality in the three-cornered
pink satin hat with black feathers. The two men in the blue
coats and drab trousers, who are walking up and down,
smoking their pipes, are their husbands. The party in the
opposite box are a pretty fair specimen of the generality of
the visitors. These are the father and mother, and old grandmother: a young man and woman, and an individual
addressed by the euphonious title of "Uncle Bill," who is
evidently the wit of the party. They have some half-dozen
children with them, but it is scarcely necessary to notice the

111

fact, for that is a matter of course here. Every woman in " the gardens," who has been married for any length of time, must have had twins on two or three occasions; it is impossible to account for the extent of juvenile population in any other way.

Observe the inexpressible delight of the old grandmother, at Uncle Bill's splendid joke of "tea for four: bread-and-butter for forty;" and the loud explosion of mirth which follows his wafering a paper "pigtail" on the waiter's collar. The young man is evidently "keeping company" with Uncle Bill's niece: and Uncle Bill's hints—such as "Don't forget me at the dinner, you know," "I shall look out for the cake, Sally," "I'll be godfather to your first—wager it's a boy," and so forth, are equally embarrassing to the young people, and delightful to the elder ones. As to the old grandmother, she is in perfect ecstasies, and does nothing but laugh herself into fits of coughing, until they have finished the "gin-and-water warm with," of which Uncle Bill ordered "glasses round" after tea, "just to keep the night air out, and do it up comfortable and riglar arter sitch an as-tonishing hot day!"

It is getting dark, and the people begin to move. The field leading to town is quite full of them; the little hand-chaises are dragged wearily along, the children are tired, and amuse themselves and the company generally by crying, or resort to the much more pleasant expedient of going to sleep —the mothers begin to wish they were at home again—sweethearts grow more sentimental than ever, as the time for parting arrives—the gardens look mournful enough, by the light of the two lanterns which hang against the trees for the convenience of smokers—and the waiters who have been running about incessantly for the last six hours, think they feel a little tired, as they count their glasses and their gains.

CHAPTER X

"ARE you fond of the water?" is a question very frequently asked, in hot summer weather, by amphibious-looking young men. "Very," is the general reply. "An't you?"—"Hardly ever off it," is the response, accompanied by sundry adjectives, expressive of the speaker's heartfelt admiration of that element. Now, with all respect for the opinion of society in general, and cutter clubs in particular, we humbly suggest that some of the most painful reminiscences in the mind of every individual who has occasionally disported himself on the Thames, must be connected with his aquatic recreations. Who ever heard of a successful water-party ?—or to put the question in a still more intelligible form, who ever saw one? We have been on water excursions out of number, but we solemnly declare that we cannot call to mind one single occasion of the kind, which was not marked by more miseries than any one would suppose could be reasonably crowded into the space of some eight or nine hours. Something has always gone wrong. Either the cork of the salad-dressing has come out, or the most anxiously expected member of the party has not come out, or the most disagreeable man in company would come out, or a child or two have fallen into the water, or the gentleman who undertook to steer has endangered everybody's life all the way, or the gentlemen who volunteered to row have been "out of practice," and performed very

113

alarming evolutions, putting their oars down into the water and not being able to get them up again, or taking terrific pulls without putting them in at all; in either case, pitching over on the backs of their heads with startling violence, and exhibiting the soles of their pumps to the "sitters" in the boat, in a very humiliating manner.

We grant that the banks of the Thames are very beautiful at Richmond and Twickenham, and other distant havens, often sought though seldom reached; but from the "Red-us" back to Blackfriars-bridge, the scene is wonderfully changed. The Penitentiary is a noble building, no doubt, and the sportive youths who "go in" at that particular part of the river, on a summer's evening, may be all very well in perspective; but when you are obliged to keep in shore coming home, and the young ladies will colour up, and look perseveringly the other way, while the married dittos cough slightly, and stare very hard at the water, you feel awkward—especially if you happen to have been attempting the most distant approach to sentimentality, for an hour or two previously.

Although experience and suffering have produced in our minds the result we have just stated, we are by no means blind to a proper sense of the fun which a looker-on may extract from the amateurs of boating. What can be more amusing than Searle's yard on a fine Sunday morning? It's a Richmond tide, and some dozen boats are preparing for the reception of the parties who have engaged them. Two or three fellows in great rough trousers and Guernsey shirts, are getting them ready by easy stages; now coming down the yard with a pair of sculls and a cushion—then having a chat with the "jack," who, like all his tribe, seems to be wholly incapable of doing anything but lounging about—then going back again, and returning with a rudder-line and a stretcher—then solacing themselves with another chat—and then wondering, with their hands in their capacious pockets, "where them gentlemen's got to as ordered the six." One

of these, the head man, with the legs of his trousers carefully
tucked up at the bottom, to admit the water, we presume—
for it is an element in which he is infinitely more at home
than on land—is quite a character, and shares with the
defunct oyster-swallower the celebrated name of "Dando."
Watch him, as taking a few minutes' respite from his toils,
he negligently seats himself on the edge of a boat, and fans
his broad bushy chest with a cap scarcely half so furry.
Look at his magnificent, though reddish whiskers, and mark
the somewhat native humour with which he "chaffs" the
boys and 'prentices, or cunningly gammons the gen'lm'n into
the gift of a glass of gin, of which we verily believe he
swallows in one day as much as any six ordinary men, without ever being one atom the worse for it.

But the party arrives, and Dando, relieved from his state
of uncertainty, starts up into activity. They approach in
full aquatic costume, with round blue jackets, striped shirts,
and caps of all sizes and patterns, from the velvet skull-cap
of French manufacture, to the easy head-dress familiar to the
students of the old spelling-books, as having, on the authority
of the portrait, formed part of the costume of the Reverend
Mr. Dilworth.

This is the most amusing time to observe a regular Sunday
water-party. There has evidently been up to this period no
inconsiderable degree of boasting on everybody's part relative
to his knowledge of navigation ; the sight of the water rapidly
cools their courage, and the air of self-denial with which
each of them insists on somebody else's taking an oar, is perfectly delightful. At length, after a great deal of changing
and fidgeting, consequent upon the election of a stroke-oar :
the inability of one gentleman to pull on this side, of another
to pull on that, and of a third to pull at all, the boat's crew
are seated. " Shove her off ! " cries the cockswain, who looks
as easy and comfortable as if he were steering in the Bay of
Biscay. The order is obeyed ; the boat is immediately turned
completely round, and proceeds towards Westminster-bridge,

amidst such a splashing and struggling as never was seen before, except when the Royal George went down. "Back wa'ater, sir," shouts Dando, "Back wa'ater, you sir, aft;" upon which everybody thinking he must be the individual referred to, they all back water, and back comes the boat, stern first, to the spot whence it started. "Back water, you sir, aft; pull round, you sir, for'ad, can't you?" shouts Dando, in a frenzy of excitement. "Pull round, Tom, can't you?" re-echoes one of the party. "Tom an't for'ad," replies another. "Yes, he is," cries a third; and the unfortunate young man, at the imminent risk of breaking a blood-vessel, pulls and pulls, until the head of the boat fairly lies in the direction of Vauxhall-bridge. "That's right—now pull all on you!" shouts Dando again, adding, in an under-tone, to somebody by him, "Blowed if hever I see sich a set of muffs!" and away jogs the boat in a zigzag direction, every one of the six oars dipping into the water at a different time; and the yard is once more clear, until the arrival of the next party.

A well-contested rowing-match on the Thames, is a very lively and interesting scene. The water is studded with boats of all sorts, kinds, and descriptions; places in the coal-barges at the different wharfs are let to crowds of spectators, beer and tobacco flow freely about; men, women, and children wait for the start in breathless expectation; cutters of six and eight oars glide gently up and down, waiting to accompany their *protégés* during the race; bands of music add to the animation, if not to the harmony of the scene; groups of watermen are assembled at the different stairs, discussing the merits of the respective candidates; and the prize wherry, which is rowed slowly about by a pair of sculls, is an object of general interest.

Two o'clock strikes, and everybody looks anxiously in the direction of the bridge through which the candidates for the prize will come—half-past two, and the general attention which has been preserved so long begins to flag, when suddenly a gun is heard, and a noise of distant hurra'ing along each bank of the river—every head is bent forward—the noise draws nearer and nearer—the boats which have been waiting at the bridge start briskly up the river, and a well-manned galley shoots through the arch, the sitters cheering on the boats behind them, which are not yet visible.

"Here they are," is the general cry—and through darts the first boat, the men in her, stripped to the skin, and exerting every muscle to preserve the advantage they have gained—four other boats follow close astern; there are not two boats' length between them—the shouting is tremendous, and the interest intense. "Go on, Pink"—"Give it her, Red"—"Sulliwin for ever"—"Bravo! George"—"Now, Tom, now—now—now—why don't your partner stretch out?"—"Two pots to a pint on Yellow," &c., &c. Every little public-house fires its gun, and hoists its flag; and the men who win the heat, come in, amidst a splashing and shouting, and banging and confusion, which no one can imagine who has not witnessed it, and of which any description would convey a very faint idea.

One of the most amusing places we know is the steam-wharf of the London Bridge, or St. Katharine's Dock Company, on a Saturday morning in summer, when the Gravesend and Margate steamers are usually crowded to excess; and as we have just taken a glance at the river above bridge, we hope our readers will not object to accompany us on board a Gravesend packet.

Coaches are every moment setting down at the entrance to the wharf, and the stare of bewildered astonishment with which the "fares" resign themselves and their luggage into the hands of the porters, who seize all the packages at once as a matter of course, and run away with them, heaven knows where, is laughable in the extreme. A Margate boat lies alongside the wharf, the Gravesend boat (which starts first) lies alongside that again; and as a temporary communication is formed between the two, by means of a plank and handrail, the natural confusion of the scene is by no means diminished.

" Gravesend ? " inquires a stout father of a stout family, who follow him, under the guidance of their mother, and a servant, at the no small risk of two or three of them being left behind in the confusion. " Gravesend ? "

" Pass on, if you please, sir," replies the attendant—" other boat, sir."

Hereupon the stout father, being rather mystified, and the stout mother rather distracted by maternal anxiety, the whole party deposit themselves in the Margate boat, and after having congratulated himself on having secured very comfortable seats, the stout father sallies to the chimney to look for his luggage, which he has a faint recollection of having given some man, something, to take somewhere. No luggage, however, bearing the most remote resemblance to his own, in shape or form, is to be discovered; on which the stout father calls very loudly for an officer, to whom he states the case, in the presence of another father of another family—a little thin man—who entirely concurs with him (the stout father) in thinking that it's high time something was done with these steam companies, and that as the Corporation Bill failed to do it, something else must; for really people's property is not to be sacrificed in this way; and that if the luggage isn't restored without delay, he will take care it shall be put in the papers, for the public is not to be the victim of these great monopolies. To this, the officer, in his turn, replies, that that company, ever since it has been St. Kat'rine's Dock Company, has protected life and property; that if it had been the London Bridge Wharf Company, indeed, he shouldn't have wondered, seeing that the morality of that company (they being the opposition) can't be answered for, by no one; but as it is, he's convinced there must be some mistake, and he wouldn't mind making a solemn oath afore a magistrate that the gentleman'll find his luggage afore he gets to Margate.

Here the stout father, thinking he is making a capital point, replies, that as it happens, he is not going to Margate at all, and that "Passenger to Gravesend" was on the luggage, in letters of full two inches long; on which the officer rapidly explains the mistake, and the stout mother, and the stout children, and the servant, are hurried with all possible despatch on board the Gravesend boat, which they reached just in time to discover that their luggage is there, and that their comfortable seats are not. Then the bell, which is the signal for the Gravesend boat starting, begins to ring most furiously: and people keep time to the bell, by running in and out of our boat at a double-quick pace. The bell stops; the boat starts: people who have been taking leave of their friends on board, are carried away against their will; and people who have been taking leave of their friends on shore, find that they have performed a very needless ceremony, in consequence of their not being carried away at all. The regular passengers, who have season tickets, go below to breakfast; people who have purchased morning papers, compose themselves to read them; and people who have not been down the river before, think that both the shipping and the water, look a great deal better at a distance.

When we get down about as far as Blackwall, and begin to move at a quicker rate, the spirits of the passengers appear to rise in proportion. Old women who have brought large wicker hand-baskets with them, set seriously to work at the demolition of heavy sandwiches, and pass round a wine-glass, which is frequently replenished from a flat bottle like a stomach-warmer, with considerable glee: handing it first to the gentleman in the foraging-cap, who plays the harp— partly as an expression of satisfaction with his previous exertions, and partly to induce him to play "Dumbledumb-deary," for "Alick" to dance to; which being done, Alick, who is a damp earthy child in red worsted socks, takes certain small jumps upon the deck, to the unspeakable satisfaction of his family circle. Girls who have brought the first volume of some new novel in their reticule, become extremely plaintive, and expatiate to Mr. Brown, or young Mr. O'Brien, who has been looking over them, on the blueness of the sky, and brightness of the water; on which Mr. Brown or Mr. O'Brien, as the case may be, remarks in a low voice that he has been quite insensible of late to the beauties of nature—that his whole thoughts and wishes have centred in one object alone—whereupon the young lady looks up, and failing in her attempt to appear unconscious, looks down again; and turns over the next leaf with great difficulty, in order to afford opportunity for a lengthened pressure of the hand.

Telescopes, sandwiches, and glasses of brandy-and-water cold without, begin to be in great requisition; and bashful men who have been looking down the hatchway at the engine, find, to their great relief, a subject on which they can converse with one another—and a copious one too—Steam.

"Wonderful thing steam, sir." "Ah! (a deep-drawn sigh) it is indeed, sir." "Great power, sir." "Immense—immense!" "Great deal done by steam, sir." "Ah! (another sigh at the immensity of the subject, and a knowing shake of the head) you may say that, sir." "Still in its infancy, they say, sir." Novel remarks of this kind, are generally the commencement of a conversation which is prolonged until the conclusion of the trip, and, perhaps, lays the foundation of a speaking acquaintance between half-a-dozen gentlemen, who, having their families at Gravesend, take season tickets for the boat, and dine on board regularly every afternoon.

CHAPTER XI

WE never see any very large, staring, black Roman capitals, in a book, or shop-window, or placarded on a wall, without their immediately recalling to our mind an indistinct and confused recollection of the time when we were first initiated in the mysteries of the alphabet. We almost fancy we see the pin's point following the letter, to impress its form more strongly on our bewildered imagination; and wince involuntarily, as we remember the hard knuckles with which the reverend old lady who instilled into our mind the first principles of education for ninepence per week, or ten and sixpence per quarter, was wont to poke our juvenile head occasionally, by way of adjusting the confusion of ideas in which we were generally involved. The same kind of feeling pursues us in many other instances, but there is no place which recalls so strongly our recollections of childhood as Astley's. It was not a "Royal Amphitheatre" in those days, nor had Ducrow arisen to shed the light of classic taste and portable gas over the sawdust of the circus; but the whole character of the place was the same, the pieces were the same, the clown's jokes were the same, the riding-masters were equally grand, the comic performers equally witty, the tragedians equally hoarse, and the "highly-trained chargers" equally spirited. Astley's has altered for the better—we have changed for the worse. Our histrionic taste is gone, and with shame we

121

confess, that we are far more delighted and amused with the audience, than with the pageantry we once so highly appreciated.

We like to watch a regular Astley's party in the Easter or Midsummer holidays—pa and ma, and nine or ten children, varying from five foot six to two foot eleven: from fourteen years of age to four. We had just taken our seat in one of the boxes, in the centre of the house, the other night, when the next was occupied by just such a party as we should have attempted to describe, had we depicted our *beau idéal* of a group of Astley's visitors.

First of all, there came three little boys and a little girl, who, in pursuance of pa's directions, issued in a very audible voice from the box-door, occupied the front row; then two more little girls were ushered in by a young lady, evidently the governess. Then came three more little boys, dressed like the first, in blue jackets and trousers, with lay-down shirt-collars: then a child in a braided frock and high state of astonishment, with very large round eyes, opened to their utmost width, was lifted over the seats—a process which occasioned a considerable display of little pink legs—then came ma and pa, and then the eldest son, a boy of fourteen years old, who was evidently trying to look as if he did not belong to the family.

The first five minutes were occupied in taking the shawls off the little girls, and adjusting the bows which ornamented their hair; then it was providentially discovered that one of the little boys was seated behind a pillar and could not see, so the governess was stuck behind the pillar, and the boy lifted into her place. Then pa drilled the boys, and directed the stowing away of their pocket-handkerchiefs, and ma having first nodded and winked to the governess to pull the girls' frocks a little more off their shoulders, stood up to review the little troop—an inspection which appeared to terminate much to her own satisfaction, for she looked with a complacent air at pa, who was standing up at the further end of the seat. Pa returned the glance, and blew his nose very emphatically; and the poor governess peeped out from behind the pillar, and timidly tried to catch ma's eye, with a look expressive of her high admiration of the whole family. Then two of the little boys who had been discussing the point whether Astley's was more than twice as large as Drury Lane, agreed to refer it to "George" for his decision; at which "George," who was no other than the young gentleman before noticed, waxed indignant, and remonstrated in no very gentle terms on the gross impropriety of having his name repeated in so loud a voice at a public place, on which all the children laughed very heartily, and one of the little boys wound up by expressing his opinion, that "George began to think himself quite a man now," whereupon both pa and ma laughed too; and George (who carried a dress cane and was cultivating whiskers) muttered that "William always was encouraged in his impertinence;" and assumed a look of profound contempt, which lasted the whole evening.

The play began, and the interest of the little boys knew no bounds. Pa was clearly interested too, although he very unsuccessfully endeavoured to look as if he wasn't. As for ma, she was perfectly overcome by the drollery of the principal comedian, and laughed till every one of the immense bows on her ample cap trembled, at which the governess peeped out from behind the pillar again, and whenever she could catch ma's eye, put her handkerchief to her mouth, and appeared, as in duty bound, to be in convulsions of laughter also. Then when the man in the splendid armour vowed to rescue the lady or perish in the attempt, the little boys applauded vehemently, especially one little fellow who was apparently on a visit to the family, and had been carrying on a child's flirtation, the whole evening, with a small coquette of twelve years old, who looked like a model of her mamma on a reduced scale; and who, in common with the other little girls (who generally speaking have even more coquettish-ness about them than much older ones), looked very properly shocked, when the knight's squire kissed the princess's confidential chambermaid.

When the scenes in the circle commenced, the children were more delighted than ever; and the wish to see what was going forward, completely conquering pa's dignity, he stood up in the box, and applauded as loudly as any of them. Between each feat of horsemanship, the governess leant across to ma, and retailed the clever remarks of the children on that which had preceded: and ma, in the openness of her heart, offered the governess an acidulated drop, and the governess, gratified to be taken notice of, retired behind her pillar again with a brighter countenance: and the whole party seemed quite happy, except the exquisite in the back of the box, who, being too grand to take any interest in the children, and too insignificant to be taken notice of by anybody else, occupied himself, from time to time, in rubbing the place where the whiskers ought to be, and was completely alone in his glory.

We defy any one who has been to Astley's two or three times, and is consequently capable of appreciating the perseverance with which precisely the same jokes are repeated night after night, and season after season, not to be amused with one part of the performances at least—we mean the scenes in the circle. For ourself, we know that when the hoop, composed of jets of gas, is let down, the curtain drawn up for the convenience of the half-price on their ejectment from the ring, the orange-peel cleared away, and the sawdust shaken, with mathematical precision, into a complete circle, we feel as much enlivened as the youngest child present; and actually join in the laugh which follows the clown's shrill shout of " Here we are ! " just for old acquaintance' sake. Nor can we quite divest ourself of our old feeling of reverence for the riding-master, who follows the clown with a long whip in his hand, and bows to the audience with graceful dignity. He is none of your second-rate riding-masters in nankeen dressing-gowns, with brown frogs, but the regular gentleman-attendant on the principal riders, who always wears a military uniform with a table-cloth inside the breast of the coat, in which costume he forcibly reminds one of a fowl trussed for roasting. He is—but why should we attempt to describe that of which no description can convey an adequate idea? Everybody knows the man, and everybody remembers his polished boots, his graceful demeanour, stiff, as some misjudging persons have in their jealousy considered it, and the splendid head of black hair, parted high on the forehead, to impart to the countenance an appearance of deep thought and poetic melancholy. His soft and pleasing voice, too, is in perfect unison with his noble bearing, as he humours the clown by indulging in a little badinage; and the striking recollection of his own dignity, with which he exclaims, " Now, sir, if you please, inquire for Miss Woolford, sir," can never be forgotten. The graceful air, too, with which he introduces Miss Woolford into the arena, and, after assisting her to the saddle, follows her fairy courser round the circle, can never fail to create a deep impression in the bosom of every female servant present.

When Miss Woolford, and the horse, and the orchestra, all stop together to take breath, he urbanely takes part in some such dialogue as the following (commenced by the clown): " I say, sir!"—" Well, sir?" (it's always conducted in the politest manner.)—" Did you ever happen to hear I was in the army, sir?"—" No, sir."—" Oh, yes, sir—I can go through my exercise, sir."—" Indeed, sir!"—" Shall I do it now, sir?" —" If you please, sir; come, sir—make haste" (a cut with the long whip, and "Ha' done now—I don't like it," from the clown). Here the clown throws himself on the ground, and goes through a variety of gymnastic convulsions, doubling himself up, and untying himself again, and making himself look very like a man in the most hopeless extreme of human agony, to the vociferous delight of the gallery, until he is interrupted by a second cut from the long whip, and a request to see " what Miss Woolford's stopping for?" On which, to the inexpressible mirth of the gallery, he exclaims, " Now, Miss Woolford, what can I come for to go, for to fetch, for to bring, for to carry, for to do, for you, ma'am ? " On the lady's announcing with a sweet smile that she wants the two flags, they are, with sundry grimaces, procured and handed up ; the clown facetiously observing after the performance of the latter ceremony—" He, he, oh ! I say, sir, Miss Woolford knows me ; she smiled at me." Another cut from the whip, a burst from the orchestra, a start from the horse, and round goes Miss Woolford again on her graceful performance, to the delight of every member of the audience, young or old. The next pause affords an opportunity for similar witticisms, the only additional fun being that of the clown making ludicrous grimaces at the riding-master every time his back is turned ; and finally quitting the circle by jumping over his head, having previously directed his attention another way.

Did any of our readers ever notice the class of people, who hang about the stage-doors of our minor theatres in the day-time ? You will rarely pass one of these entrances without seeing a group of three or four men conversing on the pavement, with an indescribable public-house-parlour swagger, and a kind of conscious air, peculiar to people of this description. They always seem to think they are exhibiting ; the lamps are ever before them. That young fellow in the faded brown coat, and very full light green trousers, pulls down the wristbands of his check shirt, as ostentatiously as if it were of the finest linen, and cocks the white hat of the summer-before-last as knowingly over his right eye, as if it were a purchase of yesterday. Look at the dirty white Berlin gloves, and the cheap silk handkerchief stuck in the bosom of his threadbare coat. Is it possible to see him for an instant, and not come to the conclusion that he is the walking gentleman who wears a blue surtout, clean collar, and white trousers, for half an hour, and then shrinks into his worn-out scanty clothes : who has to boast night after night of his splendid fortune, with the painful consciousness of a pound a-week and his boots to find; to talk of his father's mansion in the country, with a dreary recollection of his own two-pair back, in the New Cut; and to be envied and flattered as the favoured lover of a rich heiress, remembering all the while that the ex-dancer at home is in the family way, and out of an engagement?

Next to him, perhaps, you will see a thin pale man, with a very long face, in a suit of shining black, thoughtfully knocking that part of his boot which once had a heel, with an ash stick. He is the man who does the heavy business, such as prosy fathers, virtuous servants, curates, landlords, and so forth.

By the way, talking of fathers, we should very much like to see some piece in which all the dramatis personæ were orphans. Fathers are invariably great nuisances on the stage, and always have to give the hero or heroine a long explanation of what was done before the curtain rose, usually commencing with "It is now nineteen years, my dear child, since your blessed mother (here the old villain's voice falters) confided you to my charge. You were then an infant," &c., &c. Or else they have to discover, all of a sudden, that somebody whom they have been in constant communication with, during three long acts, without the slightest suspicion, is their own child: in which case they exclaim, "Ah! what do I see? This bracelet! That smile! These documents! Those eyes! Can I believe my senses?—It must be!—Yes—it is, it is my child!"—"My father!" exclaims the child; and they fall into each other's arms, and look over each other's shoulders, and the audience give three rounds of applause.

To return from this digression, we were about to say, that these are the sort of people whom you see talking, and atti-tudinising, outside the stage-doors of our minor theatres. At Astley's they are always more numerous than at any other place. There is generally a groom or two, sitting on the window-sill, and two or three dirty shabby-genteel men in checked neckerchiefs, and sallow linen, lounging about, and carrying, perhaps, under one arm, a pair of stage shoes badly wrapped up in a piece of old newspaper. Some years ago we used to stand looking, open-mouthed, at these men, with a feeling of mysterious curiosity, the very recollection of which provokes a smile at the moment we are writing. We could not believe that the beings of light and elegance, in milk-white tunics, salmon-coloured legs, and blue scarfs, who flitted on sleek cream-coloured horses before our eyes at night, with all the aid of lights, music, and artificial flowers, could be the pale, dissipated-looking creatures we beheld by day.

We can hardly believe it now. Of the lower class of actors we have seen something, and it requires no great exercise of imagination to identify the walking gentleman with the "dirty swell," the comic singer with the public-house chair-man, or the leading tragedian with drunkenness and distress; but these other men are mysterious beings, never seen out of the ring, never beheld but in the costume of gods and sylphs. With the exception of Ducrow, who can scarcely be classed among them, who ever knew a rider at Astley's, or saw him but on horseback? Can our friend in the military uniform ever appear in threadbare attire, or descend to the compara-tively un-wadded costume of every-day life? Impossible! We cannot—we will not—believe it.

CHAPTER XII

IF the Parks be "the lungs of London," we wonder what Greenwich Fair is—a periodical breaking out, we suppose, a sort of spring-rash : a three days' fever, which cools the blood for six months afterwards, and at the expiration of which London is restored to its old habits of plodding industry, as suddenly and completely as if nothing had ever happened to disturb them.

In our earlier days, we were a constant frequenter of Greenwich Fair, for years. We have proceeded to, and returned from it, in almost every description of vehicle. We cannot conscientiously deny the charge of having once made the passage in a spring-van, accompanied by thirteen gentlemen, fourteen ladies, an unlimited number of children, and a barrel of beer ; and we have a vague recollection of having, in later days, found ourself the eighth outside, on the top of a hackney-coach, at something past four o'clock in the morning, with a rather confused idea of our own name, or place of residence. We have grown older since then, and quiet, and steady : liking nothing better than to spend our Easter, and all our other holidays, in some quiet nook, with people of whom we shall never tire ; but we think we still remember something of Greenwich Fair, and of those who resort to it. At all events we will try.

The road to Greenwich during the whole of Easter Monday,

is in a state of perpetual bustle and noise. Cabs, hackney-coaches, "shay" carts, coal-waggons, stages, omnibuses, sociables, gigs, donkey-chaises—all crammed with people (for the question never is, what the horse can draw, but what the vehicle will hold), roll along at their utmost speed; the dust flies in clouds, ginger-beer corks go off in volleys, the balcony of every public-house is crowded with people, smoking and drinking, half the private houses are turned into tea-shops, fiddles are in great request, every little fruit-shop displays its stall of gilt gingerbread and penny toys; turnpike men are in despair; horses won't go on, and wheels will come off; ladies in "carawans" scream with fright at every fresh con-cussion, and their admirers find it necessary to sit remarkably close to them, by way of encouragement; servants-of-all-work, who are not allowed to have followers, and have got a holiday for the day, make the most of their time with the faithful admirer who waits for a stolen interview at the corner of the street every night, when they go to fetch the beer—apprentices grow sentimental, and straw-bonnet makers kind. Everybody is anxious to get on, and actuated by the common wish to be at the fair, or in the park, as soon as possible.

Pedestrians linger in groups at the roadside, unable to resist the allurements of the stout proprietress of the "Jack-in-the-box, three shies a penny," or the more splendid offers of the man with three thimbles and a pea on a little round board, who astonishes the bewildered crowd with some such address as, "Here's the sort o' game to make you laugh seven years arter you're dead, and turn ev'ry air on your ed gray vith delight! Three thimbles and vun little pea—with a vun, two, three, and a two, three, vun: catch him who can, look on, keep your eyes open, and niver say die! niver mind the change, and the expense: all fair and above board: them as don't play can't vin, and luck attend the ryal sportsman! Bet any gen'lm'n any sum of money, from harf-a-crown up to a suverin, as he doesn't name the thimble as kivers the

George Cruikshank

Greenwich Fair

pea!" Here some greenhorn whispers his friend that he distinctly saw the pea roll under the middle thimble—an impression which is immediately confirmed by a gentleman in top-boots, who is standing by, and who, in a low tone, regrets his own inability to bet, in consequence of having unfortunately left his purse at home, but strongly urges the stranger not to neglect such a golden opportunity. The "plant" is successful, the bet is made, the stranger of course loses: and the gentleman with the thimbles consoles him, as he pockets the money, with an assurance that it's "all the fortin of war! this time I vin, next time you vin: niver mind the loss of two bob and a bender! Do it up in a small parcel, and break out in a fresh place. Here's the sort o' game," &c. —and the eloquent harangue, with such variations as the speaker's exuberant fancy suggests, is again repeated to the gaping crowd, reinforced by the accession of several new-comers.

The chief place of resort in the daytime, after the public-houses, is the park, in which the principal amusement is to drag young ladies up the steep hill which leads to the Observatory, and then drag them down again, at the very top of their speed, greatly to the derangement of their curls and bonnet-caps, and much to the edification of lookers-on from below. "Kiss in the Ring," and "Threading my Grandmother's Needle," too, are sports which receive their full share of patronage. Love-sick swains, under the influence of gin-and-water, and the tender passion, become violently affectionate: and the fair objects of their regard enhance the value of stolen kisses, by a vast deal of struggling, and holding down of heads, and cries of "Oh! Ha' done, then, George—Oh, do tickle him for me, Mary—Well, I never!" and similar Lucretian ejaculations. Little old men and women, with a small basket under one arm, and a wine-glass, without a foot, in the other hand, tender "a drop o' the right sort" to the different groups; and young ladies, who are persuaded to indulge in a drop of the aforesaid right sort, display a pleasing degree of reluctance to taste it, and cough afterwards with great propriety.

The old pensioners, who, for the moderate charge of a penny, exhibit the mast-house, the Thames and shipping, the place where the men used to hang in chains, and other interesting sights, through a telescope, are asked questions about objects within the range of the glass, which it would puzzle a Solomon to answer; and requested to find out particular houses in particular streets, which it would have been a task of some difficulty for Mr. Horner (not the young gentleman who ate mince-pies with his thumb, but the man of Colosseum notoriety) to discover. Here and there, where some three or four couple are sitting on the grass together, you will see a sun-burnt woman in a red cloak "telling fortunes" and prophesying husbands, which it requires no extraordinary observation to describe, for the originals are before her. Thereupon, the lady concerned laughs and blushes, and ultimately buries her face in an imitation cambric hand-kerchief, and the gentleman described looks extremely foolish, and squeezes her hand, and fees the gipsy liberally; and the gipsy goes away, perfectly satisfied herself, and leaving those behind her perfectly satisfied also: and the prophecy, like many other prophecies of greater importance, fulfils itself in time.

But it grows dark: the crowd has gradually dispersed, and only a few stragglers are left behind. The light in the direction of the church shows that the fair is illuminated; and the distant noise proves it to be filling fast. The spot, which half an hour ago was ringing with the shouts of boisterous mirth, is as calm and quiet as if nothing could ever disturb its serenity; the fine old trees, the majestic building at their feet, with the noble river beyond, glistening in the moonlight, appear in all their beauty, and under their most favourable aspect; the voices of the boys, singing their evening hymn, are borne gently on the air; and the humblest mechanic who has been lingering on the grass so pleasant to the feet that beat the same dull round from week to week in the paved streets of London, feels proud to think as he surveys the scene before him, that he belongs to the country which has selected such a spot as a retreat for its oldest and best defenders in the decline of their lives.

Five minutes' walking brings you to the fair; a scene calculated to awaken very different feelings. The entrance is occupied on either side by the vendors of gingerbread and toys: the stalls are gaily lighted up, the most attractive goods profusely disposed, and unbonneted young ladies, in their zeal for the interest of their employers, seize you by the coat, and use all the blandishments of "Do, dear"—"There's a love"—"Don't be cross, now," &c., to induce you to purchase half a pound of the real spice nuts, of which the majority of the regular fair-goers carry a pound or two as a present supply, tied up in a cotton pocket-handkerchief. Occasionally you pass a deal table, on which are exposed pen'orths of pickled salmon (fennel included), in little white saucers : oysters, with shells as large as cheese-plates, and divers specimens of a species of snail (*wilks*, we think they are called), floating in a somewhat bilious-looking green liquid. Cigars, too, are in great demand ; gentlemen must smoke, of course, and here they are, two a penny, in a regular authentic cigar-box, with a lighted tallow candle in the centre.

Imagine yourself in an extremely dense crowd, which swings you to and fro, and in and out, and every way but the right one ; add to this the screams of women, the shouts of boys, the clanging of gongs, the firing of pistols, the ringing of bells, the bellowings of speaking-trumpets, the squeaking of penny dittos, the noise of a dozen bands, with three drums in each, all playing different tunes at the same time, the hallooing of showmen, and an occasional roar from the wild-beast shows ; and you are in the very centre and heart of the fair.

This immense booth, with the large stage in front, so brightly illuminated with variegated lamps, and pots of

SKETCHES BY BOZ

burning fat, is "Richardson's," where you have a melo-drama
(with three murders and a ghost), a pantomime, a comic song,
an overture, and some incidental music, all done in five-and-
twenty minutes.

The company are now promenading outside in all the
dignity of wigs, spangles, red-ochre, and whitening. See with
what a ferocious air the gentleman who personates the Mexican
chief, paces up and down, and with what an eye of calm
dignity the principal tragedian gazes on the crowd below, or
converses confidentially with the harlequin! The four clowns,
who are engaged in a mock broadsword combat, may be all
very well for the low-minded holiday-makers; but these are
the people for the reflective portion of the community. They
look so noble in those Roman dresses, with their yellow legs
and arms, long black curly heads, bushy eyebrows, and scowl
expressive of assassination, and vengeance, and everything else
that is grand and solemn. Then, the ladies—were there ever
such innocent and awful-looking beings; as they walk up and
down the platform in twos and threes, with their arms round
each other's waists, or leaning for support on one of those
majestic men! Their spangled muslin dresses and blue satin
shoes and sandals (a *leetle* the worse for wear) are the admiration of all beholders; and the playful manner in which they
check the advances of the clown, is perfectly enchanting.

"Just a-going to begin! Pray come for'erd, come for'erd,"
exclaims the man in the countryman's dress, for the seventieth
time: and people force their way up the steps in crowds.
The band suddenly strikes up, the harlequin and columbine
set the example, reels are formed in less than no time, the
Roman heroes place their arms a-kimbo, and dance with
considerable agility; and the leading tragic actress, and the
gentleman who enacts the "swell" in the pantomime, foot it
to perfection. "All in to begin," shouts the manager, when
no more people can be induced to "come for'erd," and away
rush the leading members of the company to do the dreadful
in the first piece.

134

RICHARDSON'S BOOTH

A change of performance takes place every day during the fair, but the story of the tragedy is always pretty much the same. There is a rightful heir, who loves a young lady, and is beloved by her; and a wrongful heir, who loves her too, and isn't beloved by her; and the wrongful heir gets hold of the rightful heir, and throws him into a dungeon, just to kill him off when convenient, for which purpose he hires a couple of assassins—a good one and a bad one—who, the moment they are left alone, get up a little murder on their own account, the good one killing the bad one, and the bad one wounding the good one. Then the rightful heir is discovered in prison, carefully holding a long chain in his hands, and seated despondingly in a large arm-chair; and the young lady comes in to two bars of soft music, and embraces the rightful heir; and then the wrongful heir comes in to two bars of quick music (technically called "a hurry"), and goes on in the most shocking manner, throwing the young lady about as if she was nobody, and calling the rightful heir "Ar-recreant—ar-wretch!" in a very loud voice, which answers the double purpose of displaying his passion, and preventing the sound being deadened by the sawdust. The interest becomes intense; the wrongful heir draws his sword, and rushes on the rightful heir; a blue smoke is seen, a gong is heard, and a tall white figure (who has been all this time, behind the arm-chair, covered over with a table-cloth), slowly rises to the tune of "Oft in the stilly night." This is no other than the ghost of the rightful heir's father, who was killed by the wrongful heir's father, at sight of which the wrongful heir becomes apoplectic, and is literally "struck all of a heap," the stage not being large enough to admit of his falling down at full length. Then the good assassin staggers in, and says he was hired in conjunction with the bad assassin, by the wrongful heir, to kill the rightful heir; and he's killed a good many people in his time, but he's very sorry for it, and won't do so any more—a promise which he immediately redeems, by dying off hand without any nonsense about it. Then the rightful heir throws down his chain; and then two men, a sailor, and a young woman (the tenantry of the rightful heir) come in, and the ghost makes dumb motions to them, which they, by supernatural interference, understand—for no one else can; and the ghost (who can't do anything without blue fire) blesses the rightful heir and the young lady, by half suffocating them with smoke: and then a muffin-bell rings, and the curtain drops.

The exhibitions next in popularity to these itinerant theatres are the travelling menageries, or, to speak more intelligibly, the "Wild-beast shows," where a military band in beef-eater's costume, with leopard-skin caps, play incessantly; and where large highly-coloured representations of tigers tearing men's heads open, and a lion being burnt with red-hot irons to induce him to drop his victim, are hung up outside, by way of attracting visitors.

The principal officer at these places is generally a very tall, hoarse man, in a scarlet coat, with a cane in his hand, with which he occasionally raps the pictures we have just noticed, by way of illustrating his description—something in this way. "Here, here, here; the lion, the lion (tap), exactly as he is represented on the canvas outside (three taps): no waiting, remember; no deception. The fe-ro-cious lion (tap, tap) who bit off the gentleman's head last Cambervel vos a twelvemonth, and has killed on the awerage three keepers a-year ever since he arrived at matoority. No extra charge on this account recollect; the price of admission is only sixpence." This address never fails to produce a considerable sensation, and sixpences flow into the treasury with wonderful rapidity.

The dwarfs are also objects of great curiosity, and as a dwarf, a giantess, a living skeleton, a wild Indian, "a young lady of singular beauty, with perfectly white hair and pink eyes," and two or three other natural curiosities, are usually exhibited together for the small charge of a penny, they attract very numerous audiences. The best thing about a dwarf is, that he has always a little box, about two feet six inches high, into which, by long practice, he can just manage to get, by doubling himself up like a boot-jack; this box is painted outside like a six-roomed house, and as the crowd see him ring a bell, or fire a pistol out of the first-floor window, they verily believe that it is his ordinary town residence, divided like other mansions into drawing-rooms, dining-parlour, and bedchambers. Shut up in this case, the unfortunate little object is brought out to delight the throng by holding a facetious dialogue with the proprietor: in the course of which, the dwarf (who is always particularly drunk) pledges himself to sing a comic song inside, and pays various compliments to the ladies, which induce them to "come for'erd" with great alacrity. As a giant is not so easily moved, a pair of indescribables of most capacious dimensions, and a huge shoe, are usually brought out, into which two or three stout men get all at once, to the enthusiastic delight of the crowd, who are quite satisfied with the solemn assurance that these habiliments form part of the giant's everyday costume.

The grandest and most numerously-frequented booth in the whole fair, however, is "The Crown and Anchor"—a temporary ball-room—we forget how many hundred feet long, the price of admission to which is one shilling. Immediately on your right hand as you enter, after paying your money, is a refreshment place, at which cold beef, roast and boiled, French rolls, stout, wine, tongue, ham, even fowls, if we recollect right, are displayed in tempting array. There is a raised orchestra, and the place is boarded all the way down, in patches, just wide enough for a country dance.

There is no master of the ceremonies in this artificial Eden —all is primitive, unreserved, and unstudied. The dust is blinding, the heat insupportable, the company somewhat noisy, and in the highest spirits possible: the ladies, in the height of their innocent animation, dancing in the gentlemen's hats, and the gentlemen promenading "the gay and festive scene" in the ladies' bonnets, or with the more expensive ornaments of false noses, and low-crowned, tinder-box-looking hats: playing children's drums, and accompanied by ladies on the penny trumpet.

The noise of these various instruments, the orchestra, the shouting, the "scratchers," and the dancing, is perfectly bewildering. The dancing, itself, beggars description—every figure lasts about an hour, and the ladies bounce up and down the middle, with a degree of spirit which is quite indescribable. As to the gentlemen, they stamp their feet against the ground, every time "hands four round" begins, go down the middle and up again, with cigars in their mouths, and silk handkerchiefs in their hands, and whirl their partners round, nothing loth, scrambling and falling, and embracing, and knocking up against the other couples, until they are fairly tired out, and can move no longer. The same scene is repeated again and again (slightly varied by an occasional "row") until a late hour at night: and a great many clerks and 'prentices find themselves next morning with aching heads, empty pockets, damaged hats, and a very imperfect recollection of how it was they did *not* get home.

CHAPTER XIII

PRIVATE THEATRES

"RICHARD THE THIRD.—DUKE OF GLO'STER, 2*l.*; EARL OF RICHMOND, 1*l.*; DUKE OF BUCKINGHAM, 15*s.*; CATESBY, 12*s.*; TRESSEL, 10*s.* 6*d.*; LORD STANLEY, 5*s.*; LORD MAYOR OF LONDON, 2*s.* 6*d.*"

Such are the written placards wafered up in the gentlemen's dressing-room, or the green-room (where there is any), at a private theatre; and such are the sums extracted from the shop-till, or overcharged in the office expenditure, by the donkeys who are prevailed upon to pay for permission to exhibit their lamentable ignorance and boobyism on the stage of a private theatre. This they do, in proportion to the scope afforded by the character for the display of their imbecility. For instance, the Duke of Glo'ster is well worth two pounds, because he has it all to himself; he must wear a real sword, and what is better still, he must draw it, several times in the course of the piece. The soliloquies alone are well worth fifteen shillings; then there is the stabbing King Henry—decidedly cheap at three-and-sixpence, that's eighteen-and-sixpence; bullying the coffin-bearers—say eighteen-pence, though it's worth much more—that's a pound. Then the love scene with Lady Ann, and the bustle of the fourth act can't be dear at ten shillings more—that's only one pound ten, including the "off with his head!"—which is sure to bring down the applause, and it is very easy to

139

do—"Orf with his ed" (very quick and loud;—then slow and sneeringly)—"So much for Bu-u-u-uckingham!" Lay the emphasis on the "uck;" get yourself gradually into a corner, and work with your right hand, while you're saying it, as if you were feeling your way, and it's sure to do. The tent scene is confessedly worth half-a-sovereign, and so you have the fight in, gratis, and everybody knows what an effect may be produced by a good combat. One—two—three—four—over; then, one—two—three—four—under; then thrust; then dodge and slide about; then fall down on one knee; then fight upon it, and then get up again and stagger. You may keep on doing this, as long as it seems to take —say ten minutes—and then fall down (backwards, if you can manage it without hurting yourself), and die game: nothing like it for producing an effect. They always do it at Astley's and Sadler's Wells, and if they don't know how to do this sort of thing, who in the world does? A small child, or a female in white, increases the interest of a combat materially—indeed, we are not aware that a regular legitimate terrific broadsword combat could be done without; but it would be rather difficult, and somewhat unusual, to introduce this effect in the last scene of Richard the Third, so the only thing to be done, is, just to make the best of a bad bargain, and be as long as possible fighting it out.

The principal patrons of private theatres are dirty boys, low copying-clerks in attorneys' offices, capacious-headed youths from city counting-houses, Jews whose business, as lenders of fancy dresses, is a sure passport to the amateur stage, shop-boys who now and then mistake their masters' money for their own; and a choice miscellany of idle vagabonds. The proprietor of a private theatre may be an ex-scene-painter, a low coffee-house-keeper, a disappointed eighth-rate actor, a retired smuggler, or uncertificated bankrupt. The theatre itself may be in Catherine-street, Strand, the purlieus of the city, the neighbourhood of Gray's-inn-lane, or the vicinity of Sadler's Wells; or it may, perhaps, form

Private Theatres

the chief nuisance of some shabby street, on the Surrey side of Waterloo-bridge.

The lady performers pay nothing for their characters, and it is needless to add, are usually selected from one class of society; the audiences are necessarily of much the same character as the performers, who receive, in return for their contributions to the management, tickets to the amount of the money they pay.

All the minor theatres in London, especially the lowest, constitute the centre of a little stage-struck neighbourhood. Each of them has an audience exclusively its own; and at any you will see dropping into the pit at half-price, or swaggering into the back of a box, if the price of admission be a reduced one, divers boys of from fifteen to twenty-one years of age, who throw back their coat and turn up their wristbands, after the portraits of Count D'Orsay, hum tunes and whistle when the curtain is down, by way of persuading the people near them, that they are not at all anxious to have it up again, and speak familiarly of the inferior performers as Bill Such-a-one, and Ned So-and-so, or tell each other how a new piece called *The Unknown Bandit of the Invisible Cavern*, is in rehearsal; how Mister Palmer is to play *The Unknown Bandit*; how Charley Scarton is to take the part of an English sailor, and fight a broadsword combat with six unknown bandits, at one and the same time (one theatrical sailor is always equal to half a dozen men at least); how Mister Palmer and Charley Scarton are to go through a double hornpipe in fetters in the second act; how the interior of the invisible cavern is to occupy the whole extent of the stage; and other town-surprising theatrical announcements. These gentlemen are the amateurs— the *Richards, Shylocks, Beverleys,* and *Othellos*—the *Young Dorntons, Rovers, Captain Absolutes,* and *Charles Surfaces*—of a private theatre.

See them at the neighbouring public-house or the theatrical coffee-shop! They are the kings of the place, supposing no real performers to be present; and roll about, hats on one side, and arms a-kimbo, as if they had actually come into possession of eighteen shillings a-week, and a share of a ticket night. If one of them does but know an Astley's super-numerary he is a happy fellow. The mingled air of envy and admiration with which his companions will regard him, as he converses familiarly with some mouldy-looking man in a fancy neckerchief, whose partially corked eyebrows, and half-rouged face, testify to the fact of his having just left the stage or the circle, sufficiently shows in what high admiration these public characters are held.

With the double view of guarding against the discovery of friends or employers, and enhancing the interest of an assumed character, by attaching a high-sounding name to its representative, these geniuses assume fictitious names, which are not the least amusing part of the play-bill of a private theatre. Belville, Melville, Treville, Berkeley, Randolph, Byron, St. Clair, and so forth, are among the humblest; and the less imposing titles of Jenkins, Walker, Thomson, Barker, Solomons, &c., are completely laid aside. There is something imposing in this, and it is an excellent apology for shabbiness into the bargain. A shrunken, faded coat, a decayed hat, a patched and soiled pair of trousers—nay, even a very dirty shirt (and none of these appearances are very uncommon among the members of the *corps dramatique*), may be worn for the purpose of disguise, and to prevent the remotest chance of recognition. Then it prevents any troublesome inquiries or explanations about employment and pursuits; everybody is a gentleman at large, for the occasion, and there are none of those unpleasant and unnecessary distinctions to which even genius must occasionally succumb elsewhere. As to the ladies (God bless them), they are quite above any formal absurdities; the mere circumstance of your being behind the scenes is a sufficient introduction to their society —for of course they know that none but strictly respectable persons would be admitted into that close fellowship with them, which acting engenders. They place implicit reliance on the manager, no doubt; and as to the manager, he is all affability when he knows you well,—or, in other words, when he has pocketed your money once, and entertains confident hopes of doing so again.

A quarter before eight—there will be a full house to-night—six parties in the boxes, already; four little boys and a woman in the pit; and two fiddles and a flute in the orchestra, who have got through five overtures since seven o'clock (the hour fixed for the commencement of the per-formances), and have just begun the sixth. There will be plenty of it, though, when it does begin, for there is enough in the bill to last six hours at least.

That gentleman in the white hat and checked shirt, brown coat and brass buttons, lounging behind the stage-box on the O. P. side, is Mr. Horatio St. Julien, alias Jem Larkins. His line is genteel comedy—his father's, coal and potato. He *does* Alfred Highflier in the last piece, and very well he'll do it —at the price. The party of gentlemen in the opposite box, to whom he has just nodded, are friends and supporters of Mr. Beverley (otherwise Loggins), the *Macbeth* of the night. You observe their attempts to appear easy and gentlemanly, each member of the party, with his feet cocked upon the cushion in front of the box ! They let them do these things here, upon the same humane principle which permits poor people's children to knock double knocks at the door of an empty house—because they can't do it anywhere else. The two stout men in the centre box, with an opera-glass osten-tatiously placed before them, are friends of the proprietor— opulent country managers, as he confidentially informs every individual among the crew behind the curtain—opulent country managers looking out for recruits; a representation which Mr. Nathan, the dresser, who is in the manager's interest, and has just arrived with the costumes, offers to confirm upon oath if required—corroborative evidence, how-ever, is quite unnecessary, for the gulls believe it at once.

The stout Jewess who has just entered, is the mother of

the pale, bony little girl, with the necklace of blue glass beads, sitting by her; she is being brought up to "the profession." Pantomime is to be her line, and she is coming out to-night, in a hornpipe after the tragedy. The short thin man beside Mr. St. Julien, whose white face is so deeply seared with the small-pox, and whose dirty shirt-front is inlaid with open-work, and embossed with coral studs like ladybirds, is the low comedian and comic singer of the establishment. The remainder of the audience—a tolerably numerous one by this time—are a motley group of dupes and blackguards.

The foot-lights have just made their appearance: the wicks of the six little oil lamps round the only tier of boxes, are being turned up, and the additional light thus afforded serves to show the presence of dirt, and absence of paint, which forms a prominent feature in the audience part of the house. As these preparations, however, announce the speedy commencement of the play, let us take a peep "behind," previous to the ringing-up.

The little narrow passages beneath the stage are neither especially clean nor too brilliantly lighted; and the absence of any flooring, together with the damp mildewy smell which pervades the place, does not conduce in any great degree to their comfortable appearance. Don't fall over this plate basket—it's one of the "properties"—the caldron for the witches' cave; and the three uncouth-looking figures, with broken clothes-props in their hands, who are drinking gin-and-water out of a pint pot, are the weird sisters. This miserable room, lighted by candles in sconces placed at lengthened intervals round the wall, is the dressing-room, common to the gentlemen performers, and the square hole in the ceiling is *the* trap-door of the stage above. You will observe that the ceiling is ornamented with the beams that support the boards, and tastefully hung with cobwebs.

The characters in the tragedy are all dressed, and their own clothes are scattered in hurried confusion over the wooden dresser which surrounds the room. That snuff-shop-looking figure, in front of the glass, is *Banquo:* and the young lady with the liberal display of legs, who is kindly painting his face with a hare's foot, is dressed for *Fleance.* The large woman, who is consulting the stage directions in Cumberland's edition of *Macbeth*, is the *Lady Macbeth* of the night; she is always selected to play the part, because she is tall and stout, and *looks* a little like Mrs. Siddons—at a considerable distance. That stupid-looking milksop, with light hair and bow legs—a kind of man whom you can warrant town-made—is fresh caught; he plays *Malcolm* to-night, just to accustom himself to an audience. He will get on better by degrees; he will play *Othello* in a month, and in a month more, will very probably be apprehended on a charge of embezzlement. The black-eyed female with whom he is talking so earnestly, is dressed for the " gentlewoman." It is *her* first appearance, too—in that character. The boy of fourteen who is having his eyebrows smeared with soap and whitening, is *Duncan*, King of Scotland; and the two dirty men with the corked countenances, in very old green tunics, and dirty drab boots, are the " army."

" Look sharp below there, gents," exclaims the dresser, a red-headed and red-whiskered Jew, calling through the trap, " they're a-going to ring up. The flute says he'll be blowed if he plays any more, and they're getting precious noisy in front." A general rush immediately takes place to the half-dozen little steep steps leading to the stage, and the heterogeneous group are soon assembled at the side scenes, in breathless anxiety and motley confusion.

" Now," cries the manager, consulting the written list which hangs behind the first P. S. wing, " Scene 1, open country—lamps down—thunder and lightning—all ready, White?" [This is addressed to one of the army.] " All ready."—" Very well. Scene 2, front chamber. Is the front chamber down?"—" Yes."—" Very well."—" Jones " [to the other army who is up in the flies]. " Hallo!"—" Wind up the open country when we ring up."—" I'll take care."—

"Scene 3, back perspective with practical bridge. Bridge ready, White? Got the tressels there?"—"All right."

"Very well. Clear the stage," cries the manager, hastily packing every member of the company into the little space there is between the wings and the wall, and one wing and another. "Places, places. Now then, Witches—Duncan—Malcolm—bleeding officer—where's the bleeding officer?"—"Here!" replies the officer, who has been rose-pinking for the character. "Get ready, then; now, White, ring the second music-bell." The actors who are to be discovered, are hastily arranged, and the actors who are not to be discovered place themselves, in their anxiety to peep at the house, just where the audience can see them. The bell rings, and the orchestra, in acknowledgment of the call, play three distinct chords. The bell rings—the tragedy (!) opens—and our description closes.

CHAPTER XIV

THERE was a time when if a man ventured to wonder how Vauxhall-gardens would look by day, he was hailed with a shout of derision at the absurdity of the idea. Vauxhall by daylight! A porter-pot without porter, the House of Commons without the Speaker, a gas-lamp without the gas— pooh, nonsense, the thing was not to be thought of. It was rumoured, too, in those times, that Vauxhall-gardens by day, were the scene of secret and hidden experiments; that there, carvers were exercised in the mystic art of cutting a moderate-sized ham into slices thin enough to pave the whole of the grounds; that beneath the shade of the tall trees, studious men were constantly engaged in chemical experiments, with the view of discovering how much water a bowl of negus could possibly bear; and that in some retired nooks, appropriated to the study of ornithology, other sage and learned men were, by a process known only to themselves, incessantly employed in reducing fowls to a mere combination of skin and bone.

Vague rumours of this kind, together with many others of a similar nature, cast over Vauxhall-gardens an air of deep mystery; and as there is a great deal in the mysterious, there is no doubt that to a good many people, at all events, the pleasure they afforded was not a little enhanced by this very circumstance.

Of this class of people we confess to having made one. We loved to wander among these illuminated groves, thinking of the patient and laborious researches which had been carried on there during the day, and witnessing their results in the suppers which were served up beneath the light of lamps and to the sound of music at night. The temples and saloons and cosmoramas and fountains glittered and sparkled before our eyes; the beauty of the lady singers and the elegant deportment of the gentlemen, captivated our hearts; a few hundred thousand of additional lamps dazzled our senses; a bowl or two of punch bewildered our brains; and we were happy.

In an evil hour, the proprietors of Vauxhall-gardens took to opening them by day. We regretted this, as rudely and harshly disturbing that veil of mystery which had hung about the property for many years, and which none but the noonday sun, and the late Mr. Simpson, had ever penetrated. We shrunk from going; at this moment we scarcely know why. Perhaps a morbid consciousness of approaching disappointment—perhaps a fatal presentiment—perhaps the weather; whatever it was, we did *not* go until the second or third announcement of a race between two balloons tempted us, and we went.

We paid our shilling at the gate, and then we saw for the first time, that the entrance, if there had been any magic about it at all, was now decidedly disenchanted, being, in fact, nothing more nor less than a combination of very roughly-painted boards and sawdust. We glanced at the orchestra and supper-room as we hurried past—we just recognised them, and that was all. We bent our steps to the firework-ground; there, at least, we should not be disappointed. We reached it, and stood rooted to the spot with mortification and astonishment. *That* the Moorish tower—that wooden shed with a door in the centre, and daubs of crimson and yellow all round, like a gigantic watch-case! *That* the place where night after night we had beheld

148

Vauxhall-Gardens by Day

DISENCHANTMENT

the undaunted Mr. Blackmore make his terrific ascent, surrounded by flames of fire, and peals of artillery, and where the white garments of Madame Somebody (we forget even her name now), who nobly devoted her life to the manufacture of fireworks, had so often been seen fluttering in the wind, as she called up a red, blue, or party-coloured light to illumine her temple! *That* the——but at this moment the bell rung; the people scampered away, pell-mell, to the spot from whence the sound proceeded; and we, from the mere force of habit, found ourself running among the first, as if for very life.

It was for the concert in the orchestra. A small party of dismal men in cocked hats were "executing" the overture to *Tancredi*, and a numerous assemblage of ladies and gentlemen, with their families, had rushed from their half-emptied stout mugs in the supper boxes, and crowded to the spot. Intense was the low murmur of admiration when a particularly small gentleman, in a dress coat, led on a particularly tall lady in a blue sarcenet pelisse and bonnet of the same, ornamented with large white feathers, and forthwith commenced a plaintive duet.

We knew the small gentleman well; we had seen a lithographed semblance of him, on many a piece of music, with his mouth wide open as if in the act of singing; a wine-glass in his hand; and a table with two decanters and four pineapples on it in the background. The tall lady, too, we had gazed on, lost in raptures of admiration, many and many a time—how different people *do* look by daylight, and without punch, to be sure! It was a beautiful duet: first the small gentleman asked a question, and then the tall lady answered it; then the small gentleman and the tall lady sang together most melodiously; then the small gentleman went through a little piece of vehemence by himself, and got very tenor indeed, in the excitement of his feelings, to which the tall lady responded in a similar manner; then the small gentleman had a shake or two, after which the tall lady had the same, and then they both merged imperceptibly into the original

149

air : and the band wound themselves up to a pitch of fury, and the small gentleman handed the tall lady out, and the applause was rapturous.

The comic singer, however, was the especial favourite ; we really thought that a gentleman, with his dinner in a pocket-handkerchief, who stood near us, would have fainted with excess of joy. A marvellously facetious gentleman that comic singer is ; his distinguishing characteristics are, a wig approaching to the flaxen, and an aged countenance, and he bears the name of one of the English counties, if we recollect right. He sang a very good song about the seven ages, the first half-hour of which afforded the assembly the purest delight ; of the rest we can make no report, as we did not stay to hear any more.

We walked about, and met with a disappointment at every turn ; our favourite views were mere patches of paint ; the fountain that had sparkled so showily by lamp-light, presented very much the appearance of a water-pipe that had burst ; all the ornaments were dingy, and all the walks gloomy. There was a spectral attempt at rope-dancing in the little open theatre. The sun shone upon the spangled dresses of the performers, and their evolutions were about as inspiriting and appropriate as a country-dance in a family vault. So we retraced our steps to the firework-ground, and mingled with the little crowd of people who were contemplating Mr. Green.

Some half-dozen men were restraining the impetuosity of one of the balloons, which was completely filled, and had the car already attached ; and as rumours had gone abroad that a Lord was " going up," the crowd were more than usually anxious and talkative. There was one little man in faded black, with a dirty face and a rusty black neckerchief with a red border, tied in a narrow wisp round his neck, who entered into conversation with everybody, and had something to say upon every remark that was made within his hearing. He was standing with his arms folded, staring up at the balloon, and every now and then vented his feelings of reverence for the aëronaut, by saying, as he looked round to catch some-body's eye, " He's a rum 'un is Green; think o' this here being up'ards of his two hundredth ascent; ecod, the man as is ekal to Green never had the toothache yet, nor won't have within this hundred year, and that's all about it. When you meets with real talent, and native, too, encourage it, that's what I say; " and when he had delivered himself to this effect, he would fold his arms with more determination than ever, and stare at the balloon with a sort of admiring defiance of any other man alive, beyond himself and Green, that impressed the crowd with the opinion that he was an oracle.

" Ah, you're very right, sir," said another gentleman, with his wife, and children, and mother, and wife's sister, and a host of female friends, in all the gentility of white pocket-handkerchiefs, frills, and spencers, " Mr. Green is a steady hand, sir, and there's no fear about him."

" Fear ! " said the little man : " isn't it a lovely thing to see him and his wife a going up in one balloon, and his own son and *his* wife a jostling up against them in another, and all of them going twenty or thirty mile in three hours or so, and then coming back in pochayses? I don't know where this here science is to stop, mind you; that's what bothers me."

Here there was a considerable talking among the females in the spencers.

" What's the ladies a laughing at, sir ? " inquired the little man, condescendingly.

" It's only my sister Mary," said one of the girls, " as says she hopes his lordship won't be frightened when he's in the car, and want to come out again."

" Make yourself easy about that there, my dear," replied the little man. " If he was so much as to move a inch without leave, Green would jist fetch him a crack over the head with the telescope, as would send him into the bottom of the basket in no time, and stun him till they come down again."

"Would he, though?" inquired the other man.

"Yes, would he," replied the little one, "and think nothing of it, neither, if he was the king himself. Green's presence of mind is wonderful."

Just at this moment all eyes were directed to the preparations which were being made for starting. The car was attached to the second balloon, the two were brought pretty close together, and a military band commenced playing, with a zeal and fervour which would render the most timid man in existence but too happy to accept any means of quitting that particular spot of earth on which they were stationed. Then Mr. Green, sen., and his noble companion entered one car, and Mr. Green, jun., and *his* companion the other; and then the balloons went up, and the aërial travellers stood up, and the crowd outside roared with delight, and the two gentlemen who had never ascended before, tried to wave their flags, as if they were not nervous, but held on very fast all the while; and the balloons were wafted gently away, our little friend solemnly protesting, long after they were reduced to mere specks in the air, that he could still distinguish the white hat of Mr. Green. The gardens disgorged their multitudes, boys ran up and down screaming "bal-loon;" and in all the crowded thoroughfares people rushed out of their shops into the middle of the road, and having stared up in the air at two little black objects till they almost dislocated their necks, walked slowly in again, perfectly satisfied.

The next day there was a grand account of the ascent in the morning papers, and the public were informed how it was the finest day but four in Mr. Green's remembrance; how they retained sight of the earth till they lost it behind the clouds; and how the reflection of the balloon on the undulating masses of vapour was gorgeously picturesque; together with a little science about the refraction of the sun's rays, and some mysterious hints respecting atmospheric heat and eddying currents of air.

ACCOUNT IN THE MORNING PAPERS

There was also an interesting account how a man in a boat was distinctly heard by Mr. Green, jun., to exclaim, "My eye!" which Mr. Green, jun., attributed to his voice rising to the balloon, and the sound being thrown back from its surface into the car; and the whole concluded with a slight allusion to another ascent next Wednesday, all of which was very instructive and very amusing, as our readers will see if they look to the papers. If we have forgotten to mention the date, they have only to wait till next summer, and take the account of the first ascent, and it will answer the purpose equally well.

CHAPTER XV

We have often wondered how many months' incessant travelling in a post-chaise it would take to kill a man; and wondering by analogy, we should very much like to know how many months of constant travelling in a succession of early coaches, an unfortunate mortal could endure. Breaking a man alive upon the wheel, would be nothing to breaking his rest, his peace, his heart—everything but his fast—upon four; and the punishment of Ixion (the only practical person, by-the-bye, who has discovered the secret of the perpetual motion) would sink into utter insignificance before the one we have suggested. If we had been a powerful churchman in those good times when blood was shed as freely as water, and men were mowed down like grass, in the sacred cause of religion, we would have lain by very quietly till we got hold of some especially obstinate miscreant, who positively refused to be converted to our faith, and then we would have booked him for an inside place in a small coach, which travelled day and night: and securing the remainder of the places for stout men with a slight tendency to coughing and spitting, we would have started him forth on his last travels: leaving him mercilessly to all the tortures which the waiters, landlords, coachmen, guards, boots, chambermaids, and other familiars on his line of road, might think proper to inflict.

Who has not experienced the miseries inevitably consequent

154

upon a summons to undertake a hasty journey? You receive an intimation from your place of business—wherever that may be, or whatever you may be—that it will be necessary to leave town without delay. You and your family are forthwith thrown into a state of tremendous excitement; an express is immediately dispatched to the washerwoman's; everybody is in a bustle; and you, yourself, with a feeling of dignity which you cannot altogether conceal, sally forth to the booking-office to secure your place. Here a painful consciousness of your own unimportance first rushes on your mind—the people are as cool and collected as if nobody were going out of town, or as if a journey of a hundred odd miles were a mere nothing. You enter a mouldy-looking room, ornamented with large posting-bills; the greater part of the place enclosed behind a huge, lumbering, rough counter, and fitted up with recesses that look like the dens of the smaller animals in a travelling menagerie, without the bars. Some half-dozen people are " booking " brown-paper parcels, which one of the clerks flings into the aforesaid recesses with an air of recklessness which you, remembering the new carpet-bag you bought in the morning, feel considerably annoyed at; porters, looking like so many Atlases, keep rushing in and out, with large packages on their shoulders; and while you are waiting to make the necessary inquiries, you wonder what on earth the booking-office clerks can have been before they were booking-office clerks; one of them with his pen behind his ear, and his hands behind him, is standing in front of the fire, like a full-length portrait of Napoleon; the other with his hat half off his head, enters the passengers' names in the books with a coolness which is inexpressibly provoking; and the villain whistles—actually whistles—while a man asks him what the fare is outside, all the way to Holyhead !—in frosty weather, too ! They are clearly an isolated race, evidently possessing no sympathies or feelings in common with the rest of mankind. Your turn comes at last, and having paid the fare, you tremblingly inquire—" What time will it be necessary

for me to be here in the morning?"—"Six o'clock," replies
the whistler, carelessly pitching the sovereign you have just
parted with, into a wooden bowl on the desk. "Rather
before than arter," adds the man with the semi-roasted
unmentionables, with just as much ease and complacency as
if the whole world got out of bed at five. You turn into
the street, ruminating as you bend your steps homewards
on the extent to which men become hardened in cruelty,
by custom.

If there be one thing in existence more miserable than
another, it most unquestionably is the being compelled to
rise by candle-light. If you ever doubted the fact, you are
painfully convinced of your error, on the morning of your
departure. You left strict orders, overnight, to be called at
half-past four, and you have done nothing all night but doze
for five minutes at a time, and start up suddenly from a
terrific dream of a large church-clock with the small hand
running round, with astonishing rapidity, to every figure on the
dial-plate. At last, completely exhausted, you fall gradually
into a refreshing sleep—your thoughts grow confused—the
stage-coaches, which have been "going off" before your eyes
all night, become less and less distinct, until they go off
altogether; one moment you are driving with all the skill
and smartness of an experienced whip—the next you are
exhibiting à la Ducrow, on the off-leader; anon you are
closely muffled up, inside, and have just recognised in the
person of the guard an old schoolfellow, whose funeral, even
in your dream, you remember to have attended eighteen years
ago. At last you fall into a state of complete oblivion, from
which you are aroused, as if into a new state of existence, by
a singular illusion. You are apprenticed to a trunk-maker;
how, or why, or when, or wherefore, you don't take the trouble
to inquire; but there you are, pasting the lining in the lid
of a portmanteau. Confound that other apprentice in the
back shop, how he is hammering!—rap, rap, rap—what an
industrious fellow he must be! you have heard him at work

A THAW

for half an hour past, and he has been hammering incessantly
the whole time. Rap, rap, rap, again—he's talking now—
what's that he said? Five o'clock! You make a violent
exertion, and start up in bed. The vision is at once dispelled ;
the trunk-maker's shop is your own bedroom, and the other
apprentice your shivering servant, who has been vainly
endeavouring to wake you for the last quarter of an hour,
at the imminent risk of breaking either his own knuckles or
the panels of the door.

You proceed to dress yourself, with all possible dispatch.
The flaring flat candle with the long snuff, gives light enough
to show that the things you want, are not where they ought
to be, and you undergo a trifling delay in consequence of
having carefully packed up one of your boots in your over-
anxiety of the preceding night. You soon complete your
toilet, however, for you are not particular on such an occasion,
and you shaved yesterday evening ; so mounting your Peter-
sham great-coat, and green travelling shawl, and grasping
your carpet-bag in your right hand, you walk lightly down-
stairs, lest you should awaken any of the family, and after
pausing in the common sitting-room for one moment, just to
have a cup of coffee (the said common sitting-room looking
remarkably comfortable, with everything out of its place,
and strewed with the crumbs of last night's supper), you undo
the chain and bolts of the street-door, and find yourself fairly
in the street.

A thaw, by all that is miserable ! The frost is completely
broken up. You look down the long perspective of Oxford-
street, the gas-lights mournfully reflected on the wet pavement,
and can discern no speck in the road to encourage the belief
that there is a cab or a coach to be had—the very coachmen
have gone home in despair. The cold sleet is drizzling down
with that gentle regularity, which betokens a duration of
four-and-twenty hours at least; the damp hangs upon the
house-tops and lamp-posts, and clings to you like an invisible
cloak. The water is "coming in" in every area, the pipes

157

have burst, the water-butts are running over; the kennels seem to be doing matches against time, pump-handles descend of their own accord, horses in market-carts fall down, and there's no one to help them up again, policemen look as if they had been carefully sprinkled with powdered glass; here and there a milk-woman trudges slowly along, with a bit of list round each foot to keep her from slipping; boys who "don't sleep in the house," and are not allowed much sleep out of it, can't wake their masters by thundering at the shop-door, and cry with the cold—the compound of ice, snow, and water on the pavement, is a couple of inches thick—nobody ventures to walk fast to keep himself warm, and nobody could succeed in keeping himself warm if he did.

It strikes a quarter past five as you trudge down Waterloo-place on your way to the Golden Cross, and you discover, for the first time, that you were called about an hour too early. You have not time to go back; there is no place open to go into, and you have, therefore, no resource but to go forward, which you do, feeling remarkably satisfied with yourself, and everything about you. You arrive at the office, and look wistfully up the yard for the Birmingham High-flier, which, for aught you can see, may have flown away altogether, for no preparations appear to be on foot for the departure of any vehicle in the shape of a coach. You wander into the booking-office, which with the gas-lights and blazing fire, looks quite comfortable by contrast—that is to say, if any place *can* look comfortable at half-past five on a winter's morning. There stands the identical book-keeper in the same position as if he had not moved since you saw him yesterday. As he informs you, that the coach is up the yard, and will be brought round in about a quarter of an hour, you leave your bag, and repair to "The Tap" —not with any absurd idea of warming yourself, because you feel such a result to be utterly hopeless, but for the purpose of procuring some hot brandy-and-water, which you do, —when the kettle boils! an event which occurs exactly two minutes and a half before the time fixed for the starting of the coach.

The first stroke of six, peals from St. Martin's church steeple, just as you take the first sip of the boiling liquid. You find yourself at the booking-office in two seconds, and the tap-waiter finds himself much comforted by your brandy-and-water, in about the same period. The coach is out; the horses are in, and the guard and two or three porters, are stowing the luggage away, and running up the steps of the booking-office, and down the steps of the booking-office, with breathless rapidity. The place, which a few minutes ago was so still and quiet, is now all bustle; the early vendors of the morning papers have arrived, and you are assailed on all sides with shouts of " *Times*, gen'lm'n, *Times*," " Here's *Chron—Chron—Chron*," " *Herald*, ma'am," " Highly interesting murder, gen'lm'n," "Curious case o' breach o' promise, ladies." The inside passengers are already in their dens, and the outsides, with the exception of yourself, are pacing up and down the pavement to keep themselves warm; they consist of two young men with very long hair, to which the sleet has communicated the appearance of crystallised rats' tails; one thin young woman cold and peevish, one old gentleman ditto ditto, and something in a cloak and cap, intended to represent a military officer; every member of the party, with a large stiff shawl over his chin, looking exactly as if he were playing a set of Pan's pipes.

"Take off the cloths, Bob," says the coachman, who now appears for the first time, in a rough blue great-coat, of which the buttons behind are so far apart, that you can't see them both at the same time. " Now, gen'lm'n," cries the guard, with the waybill in his hand. "Five minutes behind time already!" Up jump the passengers—the two young men smoking like lime-kilns, and the old gentleman grumbling audibly. The thin young woman is got upon the roof, by dint of a great deal of pulling, and pushing, and helping and trouble, and she repays it by expressing her solemn conviction that she will never be able to get down again.

"All right," sings out the guard at last, jumping up as the coach starts, and blowing his horn directly afterwards, in proof of the soundness of his wind. "Let 'em go, Harry, give 'em their heads," cries the coachman—and off we start as briskly as if the morning were "all right," as well as the coach : and looking forward as anxiously to the termination of our journey, as we fear our readers will have done, long since, to the conclusion of our paper.

CHAPTER XVI

It is very generally allowed that public conveyances afford an extensive field for amusement and observation. Of all the public conveyances that have been constructed since the days of the Ark—we think that is the earliest on record—to the present time, commend us to an omnibus. A long stage is not to be despised, but there you have only six insides, and the chances are, that the same people go all the way with you— there is no change, no variety. Besides, after the first twelve hours or so, people get cross and sleepy, and when you have seen a man in his nightcap, you lose all respect for him; at least, that is the case with us. Then on smooth roads people frequently get prosy, and tell long stories, and even those who don't talk, may have very unpleasant predilections. We once travelled four hundred miles, inside a stage-coach, with a stout man, who had a glass of rum-and-water, warm, handed in at the window at every place where we changed horses. This was decidedly unpleasant. We have also travelled occasionally, with a small boy of a pale aspect, with light hair, and no perceptible neck, coming up to town from school under the protection of the guard, and directed to be left at the Cross Keys till called for. This is, perhaps, even worse than rum-and-water in a close atmosphere. Then there is the whole train of evils consequent on a change of the coachman; and the misery of the discovery—which the guard is sure to

161

make the moment you begin to doze—that he wants a brown-paper parcel, which he distinctly remembers to have deposited under the seat on which you are reposing. A great deal of bustle and groping takes place, and when you are thoroughly awakened, and severely cramped, by holding your legs up by an almost supernatural exertion, while he is looking behind them, it suddenly occurs to him that he put it in the fore-boot. Bang goes the door; the parcel is immediately found; off starts the coach again; and the guard plays the key-bugle as loud as he can play it, as if in mockery of your wretchedness.

Now, you meet with none of these afflictions in an omnibus; sameness there can never be. The passengers change as often in the course of one journey as the figures in a kaleidoscope, and though not so glittering, are far more amusing. We believe there is no instance on record, of a man's having gone to sleep in one of these vehicles. As to long stories, would any man venture to tell a long story in an omnibus? and even if he did, where would be the harm? nobody could possibly hear what he was talking about. Again; children, though occasionally, are not often to be found in an omnibus; and even when they are, if the vehicle be full, as is generally the case, somebody sits upon them, and we are unconscious of their presence. Yes, after mature reflection, and considerable experience, we are decidedly of opinion, that of all known vehicles, from the glass-coach in which we were taken to be christened, to that sombre caravan in which we must one day make our last earthly journey, there is nothing like an omnibus.

We will back the machine in which we make our daily peregrination from the top of Oxford-street to the city, against any "buss" on the road, whether it be for the gaudiness of its exterior, the perfect simplicity of its interior, or the native coolness of its cad. This young gentleman is a singular instance of self-devotion; his somewhat intemperate zeal on behalf of his employers, is constantly getting him into trouble, and occasionally into the house of correction.

A MODEL OMNIBUS CAD

He is no sooner emancipated, however, than he resumes the duties of his profession with unabated ardour. His principal distinction is his activity. His great boast is, "that he can chuck an old gen'lm'n into the buss, shut him in, and rattle off, afore he knows where it's a-going to"—a feat which he frequently performs, to the infinite amusement of every one but the old gentleman concerned, who, somehow or other, never can see the joke of the thing.

We are not aware that it has ever been precisely ascertained, how many passengers our omnibus will contain. The impression on the cad's mind evidently is, that it is amply sufficient for the accommodation of any number of persons that can be enticed into it. "Any room?" cries a very hot pedestrian. "Plenty o' room, sir," replies the conductor, gradually opening the door, and not disclosing the real state of the case, until the wretched man is on the steps. "Where?" inquires the entrapped individual, with an attempt to back out again. "Either side, sir," rejoins the cad, shoving him in, and slamming the door. "All right, Bill." Retreat is impossible; the new-comer rolls about, till he falls down somewhere, and there he stops.

As we get into the city a little before ten, four or five of our party are regular passengers. We always take them up at the same places, and they generally occupy the same seats; they are always dressed in the same manner, and invariably discuss the same topics—the increasing rapidity of cabs, and the disregard of moral obligations evinced by omnibus men. There is a little testy old man, with a powdered head, who always sits on the right-hand side of the door as you enter, with his hands folded on the top of his umbrella. He is extremely impatient, and sits there for the purpose of keeping a sharp eye on the cad, with whom he generally holds a running dialogue. He is very officious in helping people in and out, and always volunteers to give the cad a poke with his umbrella, when any one wants to alight. He usually recommends ladies to have sixpence ready, to prevent delay;

163

and if anybody puts a window down, that he can reach, he immediately puts it up again.

"Now, what are you stopping for?" says the little man every morning, the moment there is the slightest indication of "pulling up" at the corner of Regent-street, when some such dialogue as the following takes place between him and the cad:

"What are you stopping for?"

Here the cad whistles, and affects not to hear the question.

"I say [a poke], what are you stopping for?"

"For passengers, sir. Ba—nk.—Ty."

"I know you're stopping for passengers; but you've no business to do so. *Why* are you stopping?"

"Vy, sir, that's a difficult question. I think it is because we perfer stopping here to going on."

"Now mind," exclaims the little old man, with great vehemence, "I'll pull you up to-morrow; I've often threatened to do it; now I will."

"Thankee, sir," replies the cad, touching his hat with a mock expression of gratitude;—"werry much obliged to you indeed, sir." Here the young men in the omnibus laugh very heartily, and the old gentleman gets very red in the face, and seems highly exasperated.

The stout gentleman in the white neckcloth, at the other end of the vehicle, looks very prophetic, and says that something must shortly be done with these fellows, or there's no saying where all this will end; and the shabby-genteel man with the green bag, expresses his entire concurrence in the opinion, as he has done regularly every morning for the last six months.

A second omnibus now comes up, and stops immediately behind us. Another old gentleman elevates his cane in the air, and runs with all his might towards our omnibus; we watch his progress with great interest; the door is opened to receive him, he suddenly disappears—he has been spirited away by the opposition. Hereupon the driver of the opposition taunts our people with his having "regularly done 'em out of that old swell," and the voice of the " old swell " is heard, vainly protesting against this unlawful detention. We rattle off, the other omnibus rattles after us, and every time we stop to take up a passenger, they stop to take him too; sometimes we get him; sometimes they get him ; but whoever don't get him, say they ought to have had him, and the cads of the respective vehicles abuse one another accordingly.

As we arrive in the vicinity of Lincoln's-inn-fields, Bedford-row, and other legal haunts, we drop a great many of our original passengers, and take up fresh ones, who meet with a very sulky reception. It is rather remarkable, that the people already in an omnibus, always look at new-comers, as if they entertained some undefined idea that they have no business to come in at all. We are quite persuaded the little old man has some notion of this kind, and that he considers their entry as a sort of negative impertinence.

Conversation is now entirely dropped; each person gazes vacantly through the window in front of him, and everybody thinks that his opposite neighbour is staring at him. If one man gets out at Shoe-lane, and another at the corner of Farringdon-street, the little old gentleman grumbles, and suggests to the latter, that if he had got out at Shoe-lane too, he would have saved them the delay of another stoppage ; whereupon the young men laugh again, and the old gentle-man looks very solemn, and says nothing more till he gets to the Bank, when he trots off as fast as he can, leaving us to do the same, and to wish, as we walk away, that we could impart to others any portion of the amusement we have gained for ourselves.

CHAPTER XVII

OF all the cabriolet-drivers whom we have ever had the honour and gratification of knowing by sight—and our acquaintance in this way has been most extensive—there is one who made an impression on our mind which can never be effaced, and who awakened in our bosom a feeling of admiration and respect, which we entertain a fatal presentiment will never be called forth again by any human being. He was a man of most simple and prepossessing appearance. He was a brown-whiskered, white-hatted, no-coated cabman; his nose was generally red, and his bright blue eye not unfrequently stood out in bold relief against a black border of artificial workmanship; his boots were of the Wellington form, pulled up to meet his corduroy knee-smalls, or at least to approach as near them as their dimensions would admit of; and his neck was usually garnished with a bright yellow handkerchief. In summer he carried in his mouth a flower; in winter, a straw—slight, but, to a contemplative mind, certain indications of a love of nature, and a taste for botany.

His cabriolet was gorgeously painted—a bright red; and wherever we went, City or West End, Paddington or Holloway, North, East, West, or South, there was the red cab, bumping up against the posts at the street corners, and turning in and out, among hackney-coaches, and drays, and carts, and waggons, and omnibuses, and contriving by some

166

The Last Cab-Driver

strange means or other, to get out of places which no other
vehicle but the red cab could ever by any possibility have
contrived to get into at all. Our fondness for that red cab
was unbounded. How we should have liked to have seen it
in the circle at Astley's! Our life upon it, that it should
have performed such evolutions as would have put the whole
company to shame—Indian chiefs, knights, Swiss peasants,
and all.

Some people object to the exertion of getting into cabs,
and others object to the difficulty of getting out of them;
we think both these are objections which take their rise in
perverse and ill-conditioned minds. The getting into a cab
is a very pretty and graceful process, which, when well performed, is essentially melo-dramatic. First, there is the expressive pantomime of every one of the eighteen cabmen on the
stand, the moment you raise your eyes from the ground. Then
there is your own pantomime in reply—quite a little ballet.
Four cabs immediately leave the stand, for your especial
accommodation; and the evolutions of the animals who draw
them, are beautiful in the extreme, as they grate the wheels
of the cabs against the curb-stones, and sport playfully in
the kennel. You single out a particular cab, and dart
swiftly towards it. One bound, and you are on the first
step; turn your body lightly round to the right, and you are
on the second; bend gracefully beneath the reins, working
round to the left at the same time, and you are in the cab.
There is no difficulty in finding a seat: the apron knocks
you comfortably into it at once, and off you go.

The getting out of a cab is, perhaps, rather more complicated in its theory, and a shade more difficult in its execution.
We have studied the subject a great deal, and we think the
best way is, to throw yourself out, and trust to chance for
alighting on your feet. If you make the driver alight first,
and then throw yourself upon him, you will find that he
breaks your fall materially. In the event of your contemplating an offer of eightpence, on no account make

the tender, or show the money, until you are safely on the pavement. It is very bad policy attempting to save the fourpence. You are very much in the power of a cabman, and he considers it a kind of fee not to do you any wilful damage. Any instruction, however, in the art of getting out of a cab, is wholly unnecessary if you are going any distance, because the probability is, that you will be shot lightly out before you have completed the third mile.

We are not aware of any instance on record in which a cab-horse has performed three consecutive miles without going down once. What of that? It is all excitement. And in these days of derangement of the nervous system and universal lassitude, people are content to pay handsomely for excitement; where can it be procured at a cheaper rate?

But to return to the red cab; it was omnipresent. You had but to walk down Holborn, or Fleet-street, or any of the principal thoroughfares in which there is a great deal of traffic, and judge for yourself. You had hardly turned into the street, when you saw a trunk or two, lying on the ground: an uprooted post, a hat-box, a portmanteau, and a carpet-bag, strewed about in a very picturesque manner: a horse in a cab standing by, looking about him with great unconcern; and a crowd, shouting and screaming with delight, cooling their flushed faces against the glass windows of a chemist's shop.—" What's the matter here, can you tell me?"—" O'ny a cab, sir."—" Anybody hurt, do you know?"—" O'ny the fare, sir. I see him a turnin' the corner, and I ses to another gen'lm'n 'that's a reg'lar little oss that, and he's a comin' along rayther sweet, an't he?'—' He just is,' ses the other gen'lm'n, ven bump they cums agin the post, and out flies the fare like bricks." Need we say it was the red cab; or that the gentleman with the straw in his mouth, who emerged so coolly from the chemist's shop and philosophically climbing into the little dickey, started off at full gallop, was the red cab's licensed driver?

The ubiquity of this red cab, and the influence it exercised

over the risible muscles of justice itself, was perfectly astonishing. You walked into the justice-room of the Mansion-
house; the whole court resounded with merriment. The
Lord Mayor threw himself back in his chair, in a state of
frantic delight at his own joke; every vein in Mr. Hobler's
countenance was swollen with laughter, partly at the Lord
Mayor's facetiousness, but more at his own; the constables
and police-officers were (as in duty bound) in ecstasies at Mr.
Hobler and the Lord Mayor combined; and the very paupers,
glancing respectfully at the beadle's countenance, tried to
smile, as even he relaxed. A tall, weazen-faced man, with an
impediment in his speech, would be endeavouring to state a
case of imposition against the red cab's driver; and the red
cab's driver, and the Lord Mayor, and Mr. Hobler, would
be having a little fun among themselves, to the inordinate
delight of everybody but the complainant. In the end, justice
would be so tickled with the red cab-driver's native humour,
that the fine would be mitigated, and he would go away full
gallop, in the red cab, to impose on somebody else without
loss of time.

The driver of the red cab, confident in the strength of his
own moral principles, like many other philosophers, was wont
to set the feelings and opinions of society at complete defiance.
Generally speaking, perhaps, he would as soon carry a fare
safely to his destination, as he would upset him—sooner,
perhaps, because in that case he not only got the money, but
had the additional amusement of running a longer heat
against some smart rival. But society made war upon him
in the shape of penalties, and he must make war upon society
in his own way. This was the reasoning of the red cab-
driver. So, he bestowed a searching look upon the fare, as
he put his hand in his waistcoat pocket, when he had gone
half the mile, to get the money ready; and if he brought
forth eightpence, out he went.

The last time we saw our friend was one wet evening in
Tottenham-court-road, when he was engaged in a very warm

and somewhat personal altercation with a loquacious little gentleman in a green coat. Poor fellow! there were great excuses to be made for him: he had not received above eighteenpence more than his fare, and consequently laboured under a great deal of very natural indignation. The dispute had attained a pretty considerable height, when at last the loquacious little gentleman, making a mental calculation of the distance, and finding that he had already paid more than he ought, avowed his unalterable determination to "pull up" the cabman in the morning.

"Now, just mark this, young man," said the little gentleman, "I'll pull you up to-morrow morning."

"No! will you though?" said our friend, with a sneer.

"I will," replied the little gentleman, "mark my words, that's all. If I live till to-morrow morning, you shall repent this."

There was a steadiness of purpose, and indignation of speech, about the little gentleman, as he took an angry pinch of snuff, after this last declaration, which made a visible impression on the mind of the red cab-driver. He appeared to hesitate for an instant. It was only for an instant; his resolve was soon taken.

"You'll pull me up, will you?" said our friend.

"I will," rejoined the little gentleman, with even greater vehemence than before.

"Very well," said our friend, tucking up his shirt sleeves very calmly. "There'll be three veeks for that. Wery good; that'll bring me up to the middle o' next month. Three veeks more would carry me on to my birthday, and then I've got ten pound to draw. I may as well get board, lodgin', and washin', till then, out of the county, as pay for it myself; consequently here goes!"

So, without more ado, the red cab-driver knocked the little gentleman down, and then called the police to take himself into custody, with all the civility in the world.

A story is nothing without the sequel; and therefore, we

may state, that to our certain knowledge, the board, lodging, and washing, were all provided in due course. We happen to know the fact, for it came to our knowledge thus: We went over the House of Correction for the county of Middlesex shortly after, to witness the operation of the silent system; and looked on all the "wheels" with the greatest anxiety, in search of our long-lost friend. He was nowhere to be seen, however, and we began to think that the little gentleman in the green coat must have relented, when, as we were traversing the kitchen-garden, which lies in a sequestered part of the prison, we were startled by hearing a voice, which apparently proceeded from the wall, pouring forth its soul in the plaintive air of "All round my hat," which was then just beginning to form a recognised portion of our national music.

We started.—"What voice is that?" said we.

The Governor shook his head.

"Sad fellow," he replied, "very sad. He positively refused to work on the wheel; so, after many trials, I was compelled to order him into solitary confinement. He says he likes it very much though, and I am afraid he does, for he lies on his back on the floor, and sings comic songs all day!"

Shall we add, that our heart had not deceived us; and that the comic singer was no other than our eagerly-sought friend, the red cab-driver?

We have never seen him since, but we have strong reason to suspect that this noble individual was a distant relative of a waterman of our acquaintance, who, on one occasion, when we were passing the coach-stand over which he presides, after standing very quietly to see a tall man struggle into a cab, ran up very briskly when it was all over (as his brethren invariably do), and, touching his hat, asked, as a matter of course, for "a copper for the waterman." Now, the fare was by no means a handsome man; and, waxing very indignant at the demand, he replied—"Money! What for? Coming up and looking at me, I suppose!"—"Vell, sir," rejoined the waterman, with a smile of immovable complacency, "*that's* worth twopence."

The identical waterman afterwards attained a very prominent station in society; and as we know something of his life, and have often thought of telling what we *do* know, perhaps we shall never have a better opportunity than the present.

Mr. William Barker, then, for that was the gentleman's name, Mr. William Barker was born——— but why need we relate where Mr. William Barker was born, or when? Why scrutinise the entries in parochial ledgers, or seek to penetrate the Lucinian mysteries of lying-in hospitals? Mr. William Barker *was* born, or he had never been. There is a son—there was a father. There is an effect—there was a cause. Surely this is sufficient information for the most Fatima-like curiosity; and, if it be not, we regret our inability to supply any further evidence on the point. Can there be a more satisfactory, or more strictly parliamentary course? Impossible.

We at once avow a similar inability to record at what precise period, or by what particular process, this gentleman's patronymic, of William Barker, became corrupted into "Bill Boorker." Mr. Barker acquired a high standing, and no inconsiderable reputation, among the members of that profession to which he more peculiarly devoted his energies; and to them he was generally known, either by the familiar appellation of "Bill Boorker," or the flattering designation of "Aggerawatin Bill," the latter being a playful and expressive *sobriquet*, illustrative of Mr. Barker's great talent in "aggerawatin" and rendering wild such subjects of her Majesty as are conveyed from place to place, through the instrumentality of omnibuses. Of the early life of Mr. Barker little is known, and even that little is involved in considerable doubt and obscurity. A want of application, a restlessness of purpose, a thirsting after porter, a love of all that is roving and cadger-like in nature, shared in common with many other great geniuses, appear to have been his leading characteristics. The busy hum of a parochial free-school, and the shady repose of a county gaol, were alike inefficacious in producing the slightest alteration in Mr. Barker's disposition. His feverish attachment to change and variety nothing could repress; his native daring no punishment could subdue.

If Mr. Barker can be fairly said to have had any weakness in his earlier years, it was an amiable one—love; love in its most comprehensive form—a love of ladies, liquids, and pocket-handkerchiefs. It was no selfish feeling; it was not confined to his own possessions, which but too many men regard with exclusive complacency. No; it was a nobler love—a general principle. It extended itself with equal force to the property of other people.

There is something very affecting in this. It is still more affecting to know, that such philanthropy is but imperfectly rewarded. Bow-street, Newgate, and Millbank, are a poor return for general benevolence, evincing itself in an irrepressible love for all created objects. Mr. Barker felt it so. After a lengthened interview with the highest legal authorities, he quitted his ungrateful country, with the consent, and at the expense, of its Government; proceeded to a distant shore; and there employed himself, like another Cincinnatus, in clearing and cultivating the soil—a peaceful pursuit, in which a term of seven years glided almost imperceptibly away.

Whether, at the expiration of the period we have just mentioned, the British Government required Mr. Barker's presence here, or did not require his residence abroad, we have no distinct means of ascertaining. We should be inclined, however, to favour the latter position, inasmuch as we do not find that he was advanced to any other public post on his return, than the post at the corner of the Haymarket, where he officiated as assistant-waterman to the hackney-coach stand. Seated, in this capacity, on a couple of tubs near the curb-stone, with a brass plate and number suspended round his neck by a massive chain, and his ankles curiously enveloped in haybands, he is supposed to have made those observations

173

on human nature which exercised so material an influence over all his proceedings in later life.

Mr. Barker had not officiated for many months in this capacity, when the appearance of the first omnibus caused the public mind to go in a new direction, and prevented a great many hackney-coaches from going in any direction at all. The genius of Mr. Barker at once perceived the whole extent of the injury that would be eventually inflicted on cab and coach stands, and, by consequence, on watermen also, by the progress of the system of which the first omnibus was a part. He saw, too, the necessity of adopting some more profitable profession; and his active mind at once perceived how much might be done in the way of enticing the youthful and unwary, and shoving the old and helpless, into the wrong buss, and carrying them off, until, reduced to despair, they ransomed themselves by the payment of sixpence a-head, or, to adopt his own figurative expression in all its native beauty, "till they was rig'larly done over, and forked out the stumpy."

An opportunity for realising his fondest anticipations, soon presented itself. Rumours were rife on the hackney-coach stands, that a buss was building, to run from Lisson-grove to the Bank, down Oxford-street and Holborn; and the rapid increase of busses on the Paddington-road, encouraged the idea. Mr. Barker secretly and cautiously inquired in the proper quarters. The report was correct; the "Royal William" was to make its first journey on the following Monday. It was a crack affair altogether. An enterprising young cab-man, of established reputation as a dashing whip—for he had compromised with the parents of three scrunched children, and just "worked out" his fine for knocking down an old lady—was the driver; and the spirited proprietor, knowing Mr. Barker's qualifications, appointed him to the vacant office of cad on the very first application. The buss began to run, and Mr. Barker entered into a new suit of clothes, and on a new sphere of action.

A RIVAL GENIUS

To recapitulate all the improvements introduced by this extraordinary man into the omnibus system—gradually, indeed, but surely—would occupy a far greater space than we are enabled to devote to this imperfect memoir. To him is universally assigned the original suggestion of the practice which afterwards became so general—of the driver of a second buss keeping constantly behind the first one, and driving the pole of his vehicle either into the door of the other, every time it was opened, or through the body of any lady or gentleman who might make an attempt to get into it; a humorous and pleasant invention, exhibiting all that originality of idea, and fine, bold flow of spirits, so conspicuous in every action of this great man.

Mr. Barker had opponents of course; what man in public life has not? But even his worst enemies cannot deny that he has taken more old ladies and gentlemen to Paddington who wanted to go to the Bank, and more old ladies and gentlemen to the Bank who wanted to go to Paddington, than any six men on the road; and however much malevolent spirits may pretend to doubt the accuracy of the statement, they well know it to be an established fact, that he has forcibly conveyed a variety of ancient persons of either sex, to both places, who had not the slightest or most distant intention of going anywhere at all.

Mr. Barker was the identical cad who nobly distinguished himself, some time since, by keeping a tradesman on the step —the omnibus going at full speed all the time—till he had thrashed him to his entire satisfaction, and finally throwing him away, when he had quite done with him. Mr. Barker it *ought* to have been, who honestly indignant at being ignominiously ejected from a house of public entertainment, kicked the landlord in the knee, and thereby caused his death. We say it *ought* to have been Mr. Barker, because the action was not a common one, and could have emanated from no ordinary mind.

It has now become matter of history; it is recorded in

the Newgate Calendar; and we wish we could attribute this piece of daring heroism to Mr. Barker. We regret being compelled to state that it was not performed by him. Would, for the family credit we could add, that it was achieved by his brother!

It was in the exercise of the nicer details of his profession, that Mr. Barker's knowledge of human nature was beautifully displayed. He could tell at a glance where a passenger wanted to go to, and would shout the name of the place accordingly, without the slightest reference to the real destination of the vehicle. He knew exactly the kind of old lady that would be too much flurried by the process of pushing in and pulling out of the caravan, to discover where she had been put down, until too late; had an intuitive perception of what was passing in a passenger's mind when he inwardly resolved to "pull that cad up to-morrow morning;" and never failed to make himself agreeable to female servants, whom he would place next the door, and talk to all the way.

Human judgment is never infallible, and it would occasionally happen that Mr. Barker experimentalised with the timidity or forbearance of the wrong person, in which case a summons to a Police-office, was, on more than one occasion, followed by a committal to prison. It was not in the power of trifles such as these, however, to subdue the freedom of his spirit. As soon as they passed away, he resumed the duties of his profession with unabated ardour.

We have spoken of Mr. Barker and of the red cab-driver, in the past tense. Alas! Mr. Barker has again become an absentee; and the class of men to which they both belonged is fast disappearing. Improvement has peered beneath the aprons of our cabs, and penetrated to the very innermost recesses of our omnibuses. Dirt and fustian will vanish before cleanliness and livery. Slang will be forgotten when civility becomes general: and that enlightened, eloquent, sage, and profound body, the Magistracy of London, will be deprived of half their amusement, and half their occupation.

CHAPTER XVIII

A PARLIAMENTARY SKETCH

WE hope our readers will not be alarmed at this rather ominous title. We assure them that we are not about to become political, neither have we the slightest intention of being more prosy than usual—if we can help it. It has occurred to us that a slight sketch of the general aspect of "the House," and the crowds that resort to it on the night of an important debate, would be productive of some amusement: and as we have made some few calls at the aforesaid house in our time—have visited it quite often enough for our purpose, and a great deal too often for our personal peace and comfort—we have determined to attempt the description. Dismissing from our minds, therefore, all that feeling of awe, which vague ideas of breaches of privilege, Serjeant-at-Arms, heavy denunciations, and still heavier fees, are calculated to awaken, we enter at once into the building, and upon our subject.

Half-past four o'clock—and at five the mover of the Address will be "on his legs," as the newspapers announce sometimes by way of novelty, as if speakers were occasionally in the habit of standing on their heads. The members are pouring in, one after the other, in shoals. The few spectators who can obtain standing-room in the passages, scrutinise them as they pass, with the utmost interest, and the man who can identify a member occasionally, becomes a person of great importance. Every now and then you hear earnest whispers of "That's Sir John Thomson." "Which? him with the gilt order round his neck?" "No, no; that's one of the messengers—that other with the yellow gloves, is Sir John Thomson." "Here's Mr. Smith." "Lor!" "Yes, how d'ye do, sir?—(He is our new member)—How do you do, sir?" Mr. Smith stops: turns round with an air of enchanting urbanity (for the rumour of an intended dissolution has been very extensively circulated this morning); seizes both the hands of his gratified constituent, and, after greeting him with the most enthusiastic warmth, darts into the lobby with an extraordinary display of ardour in the public cause, leaving an immense impression in his favour on the mind of his "fellow-townsman."

The arrivals increase in number, and the heat and noise increase in very unpleasant proportion. The livery servants form a complete lane on either side of the passage, and you reduce yourself into the smallest possible space to avoid being turned out. You see that stout man with the hoarse voice, in the blue coat, queer-crowned, broad-brimmed hat, white corduroy breeches, and great boots, who has been talking incessantly for half an hour past, and whose importance has occasioned no small quantity of mirth among the strangers. That is the great conservator of the peace of Westminster. You cannot fail to have remarked the grace with which he saluted the noble Lord who passed just now, or the excessive dignity of his air, as he expostulates with the crowd. He is rather out of temper now, in consequence of the very irreverent behaviour of those two young fellows behind him, who have done nothing but laugh all the time they have been here.

"Will they divide to-night, do you think, Mr. —— ?" timidly inquires a little thin man in the crowd, hoping to conciliate the man of office.

"How *can* you ask such questions, sir?" replies the functionary, in an incredibly loud key, and pettishly grasping the thick stick he carries in his right hand. "Pray do not,

178

sir. I beg of you; pray do not, sir." The little man looks remarkably out of his element, and the uninitiated part of the throng are in positive convulsions of laughter.

Just at this moment some unfortunate individual appears, with a very smirking air, at the bottom of the long passage. He has managed to elude the vigilance of the special constable down-stairs, and is evidently congratulating himself on having made his way so far.

"Go back, sir—you must *not* come here," shouts the hoarse one, with tremendous emphasis of voice and gesture, the moment the offender catches his eye.

The stranger pauses.

"Do you hear, sir—will you go back ? " continues the official dignitary, gently pushing the intruder some half-dozen yards.

"Come, don't push me," replies the stranger, turning angrily round.

"I will, sir."

"You won't, sir."

"Go out, sir."

"Take your hands off me, sir."

"Go out of the passage, sir."

"You're a Jack-in-office, sir."

"A what ? " ejaculates he of the boots.

"A Jack-in-office, sir, and a very insolent fellow," reiterates the stranger, now completely in a passion.

"Pray do not force me to put you out, sir," retorts the other—"pray do not—my instructions are to keep this passage clear—it's the Speaker's orders, sir."

"D—n the Speaker, sir ! " shouts the intruder.

"Here, Wilson !—Collins ! " gasps the officer, actually paralysed at this insulting expression, which in his mind is all but high treason ; "take this man out—take him out, I say ! How dare you, sir ? " and down goes the unfortunate man five stairs at a time, turning round at every stoppage, to come back again, and denouncing bitter vengeance against the commander-in-chief, and all his supernumeraries.

"Make way, gentlemen,—pray make way for the Members, I beg of you!" shouts the zealous officer, turning back, and preceding a whole string of the liberal and independent.

You see this ferocious-looking gentleman, with a complexion almost as sallow as his linen, and whose large black moustache would give him the appearance of a figure in a hairdresser's window, if his countenance possessed the thought which is communicated to those waxen caricatures of the human face divine. He is a militia-officer, and the most amusing person in the House. Can anything be more exquisitely absurd than the burlesque grandeur of his air, as he strides up to the lobby, his eyes rolling like those of a Turk's head in a cheap Dutch clock? He never appears without that bundle of dirty papers which he carries under his left arm, and which are generally supposed to be the miscellaneous estimates for 1804, or some equally important documents. He is very punctual in his attendance at the House, and his self-satisfied "He-ar-He-ar," is not unfrequently the signal for a general titter.

This is the gentleman who once actually sent a messenger up to the Strangers' gallery in the old House of Commons, to inquire the name of an individual who was using an eyeglass, in order that he might complain to the Speaker that the person in question was quizzing him! On another occasion, he is reported to have repaired to Bellamy's kitchen —a refreshment-room, where persons who are not Members are admitted on sufferance, as it were—and perceiving two or three gentlemen at supper, who, he was aware, were not Members, and could not, in that place, very well resent his behaviour, he indulged in the pleasantry of sitting with his booted leg on the table at which they were supping! He is generally harmless, though, and always amusing.

By dint of patience, and some little interest with our friend the constable, we have contrived to make our way to the Lobby, and you can just manage to catch an occasional glimpse of the House, as the door is opened for the admission of Members. It is tolerably full already, and little groups of Members are congregated together here, discussing the interesting topics of the day.

That smart-looking fellow in the black coat with velvet facings and cuffs, who wears his *D'Orsay* hat so rakishly, is "Honest Tom," a metropolitan representative; and the large man in the cloak with the white lining—not the man by the pillar; the other with the light hair hanging over his coat collar behind—is his colleague. The quiet gentlemanly-looking man in the blue surtout, gray trousers, white neckerchief, and gloves, whose closely-buttoned coat displays his manly figure and broad chest to great advantage, is a very well-known character. He has fought a great many battles in his time, and conquered like the heroes of old, with no other arms than those the gods gave him. The old hard-featured man who is standing near him, is really a good specimen of a class of men, now nearly extinct. He is a county Member, and has been from time whereof the memory of man is not to the contrary. Look at his loose, wide, brown coat, with capacious pockets on each side; the knee-breeches and boots, the immensely long waistcoat, and silver watch-chain dangling below it, the wide-brimmed brown hat, and the white handkerchief tied in a great bow, with straggling ends sticking out beyond his shirt-frill. It is a costume one seldom sees nowadays, and when the few who wear it have died off, it will be quite extinct. He can tell you long stories of Fox, Pitt, Sheridan, and Canning, and how much better the House was managed in those times, when they used to get up at eight or nine o'clock, except on regular field-days, of which everybody was apprised beforehand. He has a great contempt for all young Members of Parliament, and thinks it quite impossible that a man can say anything worth hearing, unless he has sat in the House for fifteen years at least, without saying anything at all. He is of opinion that "that young Macaulay" was a regular impostor; he allows, that Lord Stanley may do something one of these days, but "he's too young, sir—too young." He is an excellent authority on points of precedent, and when he grows talkative, after his wine, will tell you how Sir Somebody Something, when he was whipper-in for the Government, brought four men out of their beds to vote in the majority, three of whom died on their way home again ; how the House once divided on the question, that fresh candles be now brought in ; how the Speaker was once upon a time left in the chair by accident, at the conclusion of business, and was obliged to sit in the House by himself for three hours, till some Member could be knocked up and brought back again, to move the adjournment ; and a great many other anecdotes of a similar description.

There he stands, leaning on his stick ; looking at the throng of Exquisites around him with most profound contempt ; and conjuring up, before his mind's eye, the scenes he beheld in the old House, in days gone by, when his own feelings were fresher and brighter, and when, as he imagines, wit, talent, and patriotism flourished more brightly too.

You are curious to know who that young man in the rough great-coat is, who has accosted every Member who has entered the House since we have been standing here. He is not a Member ; he is only an "hereditary bondsman," or, in other words, an Irish correspondent of an Irish newspaper, who has just procured his forty-second frank from a Member whom he never saw in his life before. There he goes again —another ! Bless the man, he has his hat and pockets full already.

We will try our fortune at the Strangers' gallery, though the nature of the debate encourages very little hope of success. What on earth are you about? Holding up your order as if it were a talisman at whose command the wicket would fly open ? Nonsense. Just preserve the order for an autograph, if it be worth keeping at all, and make your appearance at the door with your thumb and forefinger expressively inserted in your waistcoat-pocket. This tall stout man in black is the door-keeper. "Any room?" "Not an inch—two or three dozen gentlemen waiting down-stairs on the chance of somebody's going out." Pull out your purse—" Are you *quite* sure there's no room?"—"I'll go and look," replies the door-keeper, with a wistful glance at your purse, " but I'm afraid there's not." He returns, and with real feeling assures you that it is morally impossible to get near the gallery. It is of no use waiting. When you are refused admission into the Strangers' gallery at the House of Commons, under such circumstances, you may return home thoroughly satisfied that the place must be remarkably full indeed.*

Retracing our steps through the long passage, descending the stairs, and crossing Palace-yard, we halt at a small temporary door-way adjoining the King's entrance to the House of Lords. The order of the serjeant-at-arms will admit you into the Reporters' gallery, from whence you can obtain a tolerably good view of the House. Take care of the stairs, they are none of the best; through this little wicket—there. As soon as your eyes become a little used to the mist of the place, and the glare of the chandeliers below you, you will see that some unimportant personage on the Ministerial side of the House (to your right hand) is speaking, amidst a hum of voices and confusion which would rival Babel, but for the circumstance of its being all in one language.

The " hear, hear," which occasioned that laugh, proceeded from our warlike friend with the moustache; he is sitting on the back seat against the wall, behind the Member who is speaking, looking as ferocious and intellectual as usual. Take one look around you, and retire! The body of the House and the side galleries are full of Members; some, with their legs on the back of the opposite seat; some, with theirs stretched out to their utmost length on the floor; some going out, others coming in; all talking, laughing, lounging,

---

* This paper was written before the practice of exhibiting Members of Parliament, like other curiosities, for the small charge of half-a-crown, was abolished.

coughing, oh-ing, questioning, or groaning; presenting a conglomeration of noise and confusion, to be met with in no other place in existence, not even excepting Smithfield on a market-day, or a cock-pit in its glory.

But let us not omit to notice Bellamy's kitchen, or, in other words, the refreshment-room, common to both Houses of Parliament, where Ministerialists and Oppositionists, Whigs and Tories, Radicals, Peers, and Destructives, strangers from the gallery, and the more favoured strangers from below the bar, are alike at liberty to resort; where divers honourable members prove their perfect independence by remaining during the whole of a heavy debate, solacing themselves with the creature comforts; and whence they are summoned by whippers-in, when the House is on the point of dividing; either to give their "conscientious votes" on questions of which they are conscientiously innocent of knowing anything whatever, or to find a vent for the playful exuberance of their wine-inspired fancies, in boisterous shouts of "Divide," occasionally varied with a little howling, barking, crowing, or other ebullitions of senatorial pleasantry.

When you have ascended the narrow staircase which, in the present temporary House of Commons, leads to the place we are describing, you will probably observe a couple of rooms on your right hand, with tables spread for dining. Neither of these is the kitchen, although they are both devoted to the same purpose; the kitchen is further on to our left, up these half-dozen stairs. Before we ascend the staircase, however, we must request you to pause in front of this little bar-place with the sash-windows; and beg your particular attention to the steady, honest-looking old fellow in black, who is its sole occupant. Nicholas (we do not mind mentioning the old fellow's name, for if Nicholas be not a public man, who is?—and public men's names are public property)—Nicholas is the butler of Bellamy's, and has held the same place, dressed exactly in the same manner, and said precisely the same things, ever since the oldest of

184

its present visitors can remember. An excellent servant Nicholas is—an unrivalled compounder of salad-dressing—an admirable preparer of soda-water and lemon—a special mixer of cold grog and punch—and, above all, an unequalled judge of cheese. If the old man have such a thing as vanity in his composition, this is certainly his pride; and if it be possible to imagine that anything in this world could disturb his impenetrable calmness, we should say it would be the doubting his judgment on this important point.

We needn't tell you all this, however, for if you have an atom of observation, one glance at his sleek, knowing-looking head and face—his prim white neckerchief, with the wooden tie into which it has been regularly folded for twenty years past, merging by imperceptible degrees into a small-plaited shirt-frill—and his comfortable-looking form encased in a well-brushed suit of black—would give you a better idea of his real character than a column of our poor description could convey.

Nicholas is rather out of his element now; he cannot see the kitchen as he used to in the old House; there, one window of his glass-case opened into the room, and then, for the edification and behoof of more juvenile questioners, he would stand for an hour together, answering deferential questions about Sheridan, and Percival, and Castlereagh, and Heaven knows who beside, with manifest delight, always inserting a "Mister" before every commoner's name.

Nicholas, like all men of his age and standing, has a great idea of the degeneracy of the times. He seldom expresses any political opinions, but we managed to ascertain, just before the passing of the Reform Bill, that Nicholas was a thorough Reformer. What was our astonishment to discover shortly after the meeting of the first reformed Parliament, that he was a most inveterate and decided Tory! It was very odd: some men change their opinions from necessity, others from expediency, others from inspiration; but that Nicholas should undergo any change in any respect, was an event we had never contemplated, and should have considered impossible. His strong opinion against the clause which empowered the metropolitan districts to return Members to Parliament, too, was perfectly unaccountable.

We discovered the secret at last; the metropolitan Members always dined at home. The rascals! As for giving additional Members to Ireland, it was even worse—decidedly unconstitutional. Why, sir, an Irish Member would go up there, and eat more dinner than three English Members put together. He took no wine; drank table-beer by the half-gallon; and went home to Manchester-buildings, or Millbank-street, for his whiskey-and-water. And what was the consequence? Why, the concern lost—actually lost, sir—by his patronage. A queer old fellow is Nicholas, and as completely a part of the building as the house itself. We wonder he ever left the old place, and fully expected to see in the papers, the morning after the fire, a pathetic account of an old gentleman in black, of decent appearance, who was seen at one of the upper windows when the flames were at their height, and declared his resolute intention of falling with the floor. He must have been got out by force. However, he was got out—here he is again, looking as he always does, as if he had been in a bandbox ever since the last session. There he is, at his old post every night, just as we have described him : and, as characters are scarce, and faithful servants scarcer, long may he be there, say we!

Now, when you have taken your seat in the kitchen, and duly noticed the large fire and roasting-jack at one end of the room—the little table for washing glasses and draining jugs at the other—the clock over the window opposite St. Margaret's Church—the deal tables and wax candles—the damask table-cloths and bare floor—the plate and china on the tables, and the gridiron on the fire; and a few other anomalies peculiar to the place—we will point out to your notice two or three of the people present, whose station or absurdities render them the most worthy of remark.

SOME NOTABLE PERSONAGES.

It is half-past twelve o'clock, and as the division is not expected for an hour or two, a few Members are lounging away the time here in preference to standing at the bar of the House, or sleeping in one of the side galleries. That singularly awkward and ungainly-looking man, in the brownish-white hat, with the straggling black trousers which reach about half-way down the leg of his boots, who is leaning against the meat-screen, apparently deluding himself into the belief that he is thinking about something, is a splendid sample of a Member of the House of Commons concentrating in his own person the wisdom of a constituency. Observe the wig, of a dark hue but indescribable colour, for if it be naturally brown, it has acquired a black tint by long service, and if it be naturally black, the same cause has imparted to it a tinge of rusty brown; and remark how very materially the great blinker-like spectacles assist the expression of that most intelligent face. Seriously speaking, did you ever see a countenance so expressive of the most hopeless extreme of heavy dulness, or behold a form so strangely put together? He is no great speaker: but when he *does* address the House, the effect is absolutely irresistible.

The small gentleman with the sharp nose, who has just saluted him, is a Member of Parliament, an ex-Alderman, and a sort of amateur fireman. He, and the celebrated fireman's dog, were observed to be remarkably active at the conflagration of the two Houses of Parliament—they both ran up and down, and in and out, getting under people's feet, and into everybody's way, fully impressed with the belief that they were doing a great deal of good, and barking tremendously. The dog went quietly back to his kennel with the engine, but the gentleman kept up such an incessant noise for some weeks after the occurrence, that he became a positive nuisance. As no more parliamentary fires have occurred, however, and as he has consequently had no more opportunities of writing to the newspapers to relate how, by way of preserving pictures he cut them out of their frames, and

187

performed other great national services, he has gradually relapsed into his old state of calmness.

That female in black—not the one whom the Lord's-Day-Bill Baronet has just chucked under the chin; the shorter of the two—is "Jane:" the Hebe of Bellamy's. Jane is as great a character as Nicholas, in her way. Her leading features are a thorough contempt for the great majority of her visitors; her predominant quality, love of admiration, as you cannot fail to observe, if you mark the glee with which she listens to something the young Member near her mutters somewhat unintelligibly in her ear (for his speech is rather thick from some cause or other), and how playfully she digs the handle of a fork into the arm with which he detains her, by way of reply.

Jane is no bad hand at repartees, and showers them about, with a degree of liberality and total absence of reserve or constraint, which occasionally excites no small amazement in the minds of strangers. She cuts jokes with Nicholas, too, but looks up to him with a great deal of respect; the immovable stolidity with which Nicholas receives the aforesaid jokes, and looks on, at certain pastoral friskings and rompings (Jane's only recreations, and they are very innocent too) which occasionally take place in the passage, is not the least amusing part of his character.

The two persons who are seated at the table in the corner, at the farther end of the room, have been constant guests here, for many years past; and one of them has feasted within these walls, many a time, with the most brilliant characters of a brilliant period. He has gone up to the other House since then; the greater part of his boon companions have shared Yorick's fate, and his visits to Bellamy's are comparatively few.

If he really be eating his supper now, at what hour can he possibly have dined! A second solid mass of rump-steak has disappeared, and he eat the first in four minutes and three quarters, by the clock over the window. Was there ever such a personification of Falstaff! Mark the air with which he gloats over that Stilton, as he removes the napkin which has been placed beneath his chin to catch the superfluous gravy of the steak, and with what gusto he imbibes the porter which has been fetched, expressly for him, in the pewter pot. Listen to the hoarse sound of that voice, kept down as it is by layers of solids, and deep draughts of rich wine, and tell us if you ever saw such a perfect picture of a regular *gourmand*; and whether he is not exactly the man whom you would pitch upon as having been the partner of Sheridan's parliamentary carouses, the volunteer driver of the hackney-coach that took him home, and the involuntary upsetter of the whole party?

What an amusing contrast between his voice and appearance, and that of the spare, squeaking old man, who sits at the same table, and who, elevating a little cracked bantam sort of voice to its highest pitch, invokes damnation upon his own eyes or somebody else's at the commencement of every sentence he utters. "The Captain," as they call him, is a very old frequenter of Bellamy's; much addicted to stopping "after the House is up" (an inexpiable crime in Jane's eyes), and a complete walking reservoir of spirits and water.

The old Peer—or rather, the old man—for his peerage is of comparatively recent date—has a huge tumbler of hot punch brought him; and the other damns and drinks, and drinks and damns, and smokes. Members arrive every moment in a great bustle to report that "The Chancellor of the Exchequer's up," and to get glasses of brandy-and-water to sustain them during the division; people who have ordered supper, countermand it, and prepare to go down-stairs, when suddenly a bell is heard to ring with tremendous violence, and a cry of "Di-vi-sion!" is heard in the passage. This is enough; away rush the members pell-mell. The room is cleared in an instant; the noise rapidly dies away; you hear the creaking of the last boot on the last stair, and are left alone with the leviathan of rump-steaks.

CHAPTER XIX

ALL public dinners in London, from the Lord Mayor's annual banquet at Guildhall, to the Chimney-sweepers' anniversary at White Conduit House; from the Goldsmiths' to the Butchers', from the Sheriffs' to the Licensed Victuallers'; are amusing scenes. Of all entertainments of this description, however, we think the annual dinner of some public charity is the most amusing. At a Company's dinner, the people are nearly all alike—regular old stagers, who make it a matter of business, and a thing not to be laughed at. At a political dinner, everybody is disagreeable, and inclined to speechify— much the same thing, by-the-bye; but at a charity dinner you see people of all sorts, kinds, and descriptions. The wine may not be remarkably special, to be sure, and we have heard some hard-hearted monsters grumble at the collection; but we really think the amusement to be derived from the occasion, sufficient to counterbalance even these disadvantages.

Let us suppose you are induced to attend a dinner of this description—" Indigent Orphans' Friends' Benevolent Institution," we think it is. The name of the charity is a line or two longer, but never mind the rest. You have a distinct recollection, however, that you purchased a ticket at the solicitation of some charitable friend: and you deposit yourself in a hackney-coach, the driver of which—no doubt that you may do the thing in style—turns a deaf ear to your

190

earnest entreaties to be set down at the corner of Great Queen-street, and persists in carrying you to the very door of the Freemasons', round which a crowd of people are assembled to witness the entrance of the indigent orphans' friends. You hear great speculations as you pay the fare, on the possibility of your being the noble Lord who is announced to fill the chair on the occasion, and are highly gratified to hear it eventually decided that you are only a " wocalist."

The first thing that strikes you, on your entrance, is the astonishing importance of the committee. You observe a door on the first landing, carefully guarded by two waiters, in and out of which stout gentlemen with very red faces keep running, with a degree of speed highly unbecoming the gravity of persons of their years and corpulency. You pause, quite alarmed at the bustle, and thinking, in your innocence, that two or three people must have been carried out of the dining-room in fits, at least. You are immediately undeceived by the waiter—" Up-stairs, if you please, sir; this is the committee-room." Up-stairs you go, accordingly ; wondering, as you mount, what the duties of the committee can be, and whether they ever do anything beyond confusing each other, and running over the waiters.

Having deposited your hat and cloak, and received a remarkably small scrap of pasteboard in exchange (which, as a matter of course, you lose, before you require it again), you enter the hall, down which there are three long tables for the less distinguished guests, with a cross table on a raised platform at the upper end for the reception of the very particular friends of the indigent orphans. Being fortunate enough to find a plate without anybody's card in it, you wisely seat yourelf at once, and have a little leisure to look about you. Waiters, with wine-baskets in their hands, are placing decanters of sherry down the tables, at very respect-able distances ; melancholy-looking salt-cellars, and decayed vinegar-cruets, which might have belonged to the parents of the indigent orphans in their time, are scattered at distant intervals on the cloth; and the knives and forks look as if they had done duty at every public dinner in London since the accession of George the First. The musicians are scraping and grating and screwing tremendously—playing no notes but notes of preparation; and several gentlemen are gliding along the sides of the tables, looking into plate after plate with frantic eagerness, the expression of their countenances growing more and more dismal as they meet with everybody's card but their own.

You turn round to take a look at the table behind you, and—not being in the habit of attending public dinners—are somewhat struck by the appearance of the party on which your eyes rest. One of its principal members appears to be a little man, with a long and rather inflamed face, and gray hair brushed bolt upright in front; he wears a wisp of black silk round his neck, without any stiffener, as an apology for a neckerchief, and is addressed by his companions by the familiar appellation of " Fitz," or some such monosyllable. Near him is a stout man in a white neckerchief and buff waistcoat, with shining dark hair, cut very short in front, and a great, round, healthy-looking face, on which he studiously preserves a half sentimental simper. Next him, again, is a large-headed man, with black hair and bushy whiskers; and opposite them are two or three others, one of whom is a little round-faced person, in a dress-stock aud blue under-waistcoat. There is something peculiar in their air and manner, though you could hardly describe what it is; you cannot divest yourself of the idea that they have come for some other purpose than mere eating and drinking. You have no time to debate the matter, however, for the waiters (who have been arranged in lines down the room, placing the dishes on table) retire to the lower end; the dark man in the blue coat and bright buttons, who has the direction of the music, looks up to the gallery, and calls out "band" in a very loud voice; out burst the orchestra, up rise the visitors, in march fourteen stewards, each with a long wand in his

hand, like the evil genius in a pantomime; then the chairman, then the titled visitors; they all make their way up the
room, as fast as they can, bowing, and smiling, and smirking,
and looking remarkably amiable. The applause ceases, grace
is said, the clatter of plates and dishes begins; and every
one appears highly gratified, either with the presence of the
distinguished visitors, or the commencement of the anxiously-
expected dinner.

As to the dinner itself—the mere dinner—it goes off much
the same everywhere. Tureens of soup are emptied with
awful rapidity—waiters take plates of turbot away, to get
lobster-sauce, and bring back plates of lobster-sauce without
turbot; people who can carve poultry, are great fools if they
own it, and people who can't have no wish to learn. The
knives and forks form a pleasing accompaniment to Auber's
music, and Auber's music would form a pleasing accompaniment to the dinner, if you could hear anything besides the
cymbals. The substantials disappear—moulds of jelly vanish
like lightning—hearty eaters wipe their foreheads, and appear
rather overcome by their recent exertions—people who have
looked very cross hitherto, become remarkably bland, and ask
you to take wine in the most friendly manner possible—old
gentlemen direct your attention to the ladies' gallery, and
take great pains to impress you with the fact that the charity
is always peculiarly favoured in this respect—every one
appears disposed to become talkative—and the hum of conversation is loud and general.

"Pray, silence, gentlemen, if you please, for *Non nobis!*"
shouts the toast-master with stentorian lungs—a toast-master's
shirt-front, waistcoat, and neckerchief, by-the-bye, always
exhibit three distinct shades of cloudy-white.—"Pray, silence,
gentlemen, for *Non nobis!*" The singers, whom you discover
to be no other than the very party that excited your curiosity
at first, after "pitching" their voices immediately begin *too-
too*ing most dismally, on which the regular old stagers burst
into occasional cries of—"Sh—Sh—waiters!—Silence, waiters

—stand still, waiters—keep back, waiters," and other exor-
cisms, delivered in a tone of indignant remonstrance. The
grace is soon concluded, and the company resume their seats.
The uninitiated portion of the guests applaud *Non nobis*
as vehemently as if it were a capital comic song, greatly to
the scandal and indignation of the regular diners, who immediately attempt to quell this sacrilegious approbation, by cries
of " Hush, hush ! " whereupon the others, mistaking these
sounds for hisses, applaud more tumultuously than before,
and, by way of placing their approval beyond the possibility
of doubt, shout " *Encore !* " most vociferously.

The moment the noise ceases, up starts the toast-master :
—" Gentlemen, charge your glasses, if you please ! " Decanters
having been handed about, and glasses filled, the toast-master
proceeds, in a regular ascending scale :—" Gentlemen—*air*
—you—all charged ? Pray—silence—gentlemen—for—the
cha—i—r ! " The chairman rises, and, after stating that he
feels it quite unnecessary to preface the toast he is about
to propose, with any observations whatever, wanders into
a maze of sentences, and flounders about in the most
extraordinary manner, presenting a lamentable spectacle of
mystified humanity, until he arrives at the words, " con-
stitutional sovereign of these realms," at which elderly gentlemen exclaim " Bravo ! " and hammer the table tremendously
with their knife-handles. " Under any circumstances, it
would give him the greatest pride, it would give him the
greatest pleasure—he might almost say, it would afford him
satisfaction [cheers] to propose that toast. What must be his
feelings, then, when he has the gratification of announcing,
that he has received her Majesty's commands to apply to the
Treasurer of her Majesty's Household, for her Majesty's
annual donation of 25*l.* in aid of the funds of this charity ! "
This announcement (which has been regularly made by every
chairman, since the first foundation of the charity, forty-two
years ago) calls forth the most vociferous applause ; the toast
is drunk with a great deal of cheering and knocking ; and

"God save the Queen" is sung by the "professional gentle-men;" the unprofessional gentlemen joining in the chorus, and giving the national anthem an effect which the news-papers, with great justice, describe as "perfectly electrical."

The other "loyal and patriotic" toasts having been drunk with all due enthusiasm, a comic song having been well sung by the gentleman with the small neckerchief, and a sentimental one by the second of the party, we come to the most important toast of the evening—"Prosperity to the charity." Here again we are compelled to adopt newspaper phraseology, and to express our regret at being "precluded from giving even the substance of the noble lord's observations." Suffice it to say, that the speech, which is somewhat of the longest, is rapturously received; and the toast having been drunk, the stewards (looking more important than ever) leave the room, and presently return, heading a procession of indigent orphans, boys and girls, who walk round the room, curtseying, and bowing, and treading on each other's heels, and looking very much as if they would like a glass of wine apiece, to the high gratification of the company generally, and especially of the lady patronesses in the gallery. *Exeunt* children, and re-enter stewards, each with a blue plate in his hand. The band plays a lively air; the majority of the company put their hands in their pockets and look rather serious; and the noise of sovereigns, rattling on crockery, is heard from all parts of the room.

After a short interval, occupied in singing and toasting, the secretary puts on his spectacles, and proceeds to read the report and list of subscriptions, the latter being listened to with great attention. "Mr. Smith, one guinea — Mr. Tompkins, one guinea—Mr. Wilson, one guinea—Mr. Hickson, one guinea—Mr. Nixon, one guinea—Mr. Charles Nixon, one guinea—[hear, hear!]—Mr. James Nixon, one guinea—Mr. Thomas Nixon, one pound one [tremendous applause]. Lord Fitz Binkle, the chairman of the day, in addition to an annual donation of fifteen pounds—thirty guineas [prolonged knocking: several gentlemen knock the stems off their wine-glasses, in the vehemence of their approbation]. Lady Fitz Binkle, in addition to an annual donation of ten pound—twenty pound " [¡ rotracted knocking and shouts of " Bravo ! "] The list being at length concluded, the chairman rises, and proposes the health of the secretary, than whom he knows no more zealous or estimable individual. The secretary, in returning thanks, observes that *he* knows no more excellent individual than the chairman—except the senior officer of the charity, whose health *he* begs to propose. The senior officer, in returning thanks, observes that *he* knows no more worthy man than the secretary—except Mr. Walker, the auditor, whose health *he* begs to propose. Mr. Walker, in returning thanks, discovers some other estimable individual, to whom alone the senior officer is inferior—and so they go on toasting and lauding and thanking: the only other toast of importance being " The Lady Patronesses now present ! " on which all the gentlemen turn their faces towards the ladies' gallery, shouting tremendously ; and little priggish men, who have imbibed more wine than usual, kiss their hands and exhibit distressing contortions of visage.

We have protracted our dinner to so great a length, that we have hardly time to add one word by way of grace. We can only entreat our readers not to imagine, because we have attempted to extract some amusement from a charity dinner, that we are at all disposed to underrate, either the excellence of the benevolent institutions with which London abounds, or the estimable motives of those who support them.

CHAPTER XX

THE FIRST OF MAY

"Now ladies, up in the sky-parlour : only once a year, if you please!"
YOUNG LADY WITH BRASS LADLE.

" Sweep—sweep—sw-e-ep!"
ILLEGAL WATCHWORD.

THE first of May! There is a merry freshness in the sound,
calling to our minds a thousand thoughts of all that is
pleasant in nature and beautiful in her most delightful
form. What man is there, over whose mind a bright spring
morning does not exercise a magic influence—carrying him
back to the days of his childish sports, and conjuring up before
him the old green field with its gently-waving trees, where
the birds sang as he has never heard them since—where the
butterfly fluttered far more gaily than he ever sees him now,
in all his ramblings—where the sky seemed bluer, and the
sun shone more brightly—where the air blew more freshly
over greener grass, and sweeter-smelling flowers — where
everything wore a richer and more brilliant hue than it is
ever dressed in now! Such are the deep feelings of childhood, and such are the impressions which every lovely object
stamps upon its heart! The hardy traveller wanders through
the maze of thick and pathless woods, where the sun's rays
never shone, and heaven's pure air never played; he stands on
the brink of the roaring waterfall, and, giddy and bewildered,
watches the foaming mass as it leaps from stone to stone, and
from crag to crag; he lingers in the fertile plains of a land

of perpetual sunshine, and revels in the luxury of their balmy breath. But what are the deep forests, or the thundering waters, or the richest landscapes that bounteous nature ever spread, to charm the eyes, and captivate the senses of man, compared with the recollection of the old scenes of his early youth ? Magic scenes indeed ; for the fancies of childhood dressed them in colours brighter than the rainbow, and almost as fleeting !

In former times, spring brought with it not only such associations as these, connected with the past, but sports and games for the present—merry dances round rustic pillars, adorned with emblems of the season, and reared in honour of its coming. Where are they now ! Pillars we have, but they are no longer rustic ones ; and as to dancers, they are used to rooms, and lights, and would not show well in the open air. Think of the immorality, too ! What would your sabbath enthusiasts say, to an aristocratic ring encircling the Duke of York's column in Carlton-terrace—a grand *poussette* of the middle classes, round Alderman Waithman's monument in Fleet-street,—or a general hands-four-round of ten-pound householders, at the foot of the Obelisk in St. George's-fields ? Alas ! romance can make no head against the riot act ; and pastoral simplicity is not understood by the police.

Well ; many years ago we began to be a steady and matter-of-fact sort of people, and dancing in spring being beneath our dignity, we gave it up, and in course of time it descended to the sweeps—a fall certainly, because, though sweeps are very good fellows in their way, and moreover very useful in a civilised community, they are not exactly the sort of people to give the tone to the little elegances of society. The sweeps, however, got the dancing to themselves, and they kept it up, and handed it down. This was a severe blow to the romance of spring-time, but, it did not entirely destroy it, either ; for a portion of it descended to the sweeps with the dancing, and rendered them objects of great interest. A mystery hung over the sweeps in those days. Legends were

The First of May

in existence of wealthy gentlemen who had lost children, and who, after many years of sorrow and suffering, had found them in the character of sweeps. Stories were related of a young boy who, having been stolen from his parents in his infancy, and devoted to the occupation of chimney-sweeping, was sent, in the course of his professional career, to sweep the chimney of his mother's bedroom; and how, being hot and tired when he came out of the chimney, he got into the bed he had so often slept in as an infant, and was discovered and recognised therein by his mother, who once every year of her life, thereafter, requested the pleasure of the company of every London sweep, at half-past one o'clock, to roast beef, plum-pudding, porter, and sixpence.

Such stories as these, and there were many such, threw an air of mystery round the sweeps, and produced for them some of those good effects which animals derive from the doctrine of the transmigration of souls. No one (except the masters) thought of ill-treating a sweep, because no one knew who he might be, or what nobleman's or gentleman's son he might turn out. Chimney-sweeping was, by many believers in the marvellous, considered as a sort of probationary term, at an earlier or later period of which, divers young noblemen were to come into possession of their rank and titles: and the profession was held by them in great respect accordingly.

We remember, in our young days, a little sweep about our own age, with curly hair and white teeth, whom we devoutly and sincerely believed to be the lost son and heir of some illustrious personage—an impression which was resolved into an unchangeable conviction on our infant mind, by the subject of our speculations informing us, one day, in reply to our question, propounded a few moments before his ascent to the summit of the kitchen chimney, " that he believed he'd been born in the vurkis, but he'd never know'd his father." We felt certain, from that time forth, that he would one day be owned by a lord; and we never heard the church-bells ring, or saw a flag hoisted in the neighbourhood, without thinking that the happy event had at last occurred, and that his long-lost parent had arrived in a coach and six, to take him home to Grosvenor-square. He never came, however; and, at the present moment, the young gentleman in question is settled down as a master sweep in the neighbourhood of Battle-bridge, his distinguishing characteristics being a decided antipathy to washing himself, and the possession of a pair of legs very inadequate to the support of his unwieldy and corpulent body.

The romance of spring having gone out before our time, we were fain to console ourselves as we best could with the uncertainty that enveloped the birth and parentage of its attendant dancers, the sweeps; and we *did* console ourselves with it, for many years. But, even this wretched source of comfort received a shock from which it has never recovered— a shock which has been in reality its death-blow. We could not disguise from ourselves the fact that whole families of sweeps were regularly born of sweeps, in the rural districts of Somers Town and Camden Town—that the eldest son succeeded to the father's business, that the other branches assisted him therein, and commenced on their own account; that their children again, were educated to the profession; and that about their identity there could be no mistake whatever. We could not be blind, we say, to this melancholy truth, but we could not bring ourselves to admit it, neverthe- less, and we lived on for some years in a state of voluntary ignorance. We were roused from our pleasant slumber by certain dark insinuations thrown out by a friend of ours, to the effect that children in the lower ranks of life were beginning to *choose* chimney-sweeping as their particular walk; that applications had been made by various boys to the constituted authorities, to allow them to pursue the object of their ambition with the full concurrence and sanction of the law; that the affair, in short, was becoming one of mere legal contract. We turned a deaf ear to these rumours at first, but slowly and surely they stole upon us.

A COMING CHANGE

Month after month, week after week, nay, day after day, at last, did we meet with accounts of similar applications. The veil was removed, all mystery was at an end, and chimney-sweeping had become a favourite and chosen pursuit. There is no longer any occasion to steal boys; for boys flock in crowds to bind themselves. The romance of the trade has fled, and the chimney-sweeper of the present day, is no more like unto him of thirty years ago, than is a Fleet-street pickpocket to a Spanish brigand, or Paul Pry to Caleb Williams.

This gradual decay and disuse of the practice of leading noble youths into captivity, and compelling them to ascend chimneys, was a severe blow, if we may so speak, to the romance of chimney-sweeping, and to the romance of spring at the same time. But even this was not all, for some few years ago the dancing on May-day began to decline; small sweeps were observed to congregate in twos or threes, unsupported by a "green," with no "My Lord" to act as master of the ceremonies, and no "My Lady" to preside over the exchequer. Even in companies where there was a "green" it was an absolute nothing—a mere sprout—and the instrumental accompaniments rarely extended beyond the shovels and a set of Pan-pipes, better known to the many, as a "mouth-organ."

These were signs of the times, portentous omens of a coming change; and what was the result which they shadowed forth? Why, the master sweeps, influenced by a restless spirit of innovation, actually interposed their authority, in opposition to the dancing, and substituted a dinner—an anniversary dinner at White Conduit House—where clean faces appeared in lieu of black ones smeared with rose pink; and knee cords and tops superseded nankeen drawers and rosetted shoes.

Gentlemen who were in the habit of riding shy horses; and steady-going people who have no vagrancy in their souls, lauded this alteration to the skies, and the conduct of the

201

master sweeps was described as beyond the reach of praise. But how stands the real fact? Let any man deny, if he can, that when the cloth had been removed, fresh pots and pipes laid upon the table, and the customary loyal and patriotic toasts proposed, the celebrated Mr. Sluffen, of Adam-and-Eve-court, whose authority not the most malignant of our opponents can call in question, expressed himself in a manner following: "That now he'd cotcht the cheerman's hi, he vished he might be jolly vell blessed, if he worn't a goin' to have his innings, vich he vould say these here obserwashuns—that how some mischeevus coves as know'd nuffin about the consarn, had tried to sit people agin the mas'r swips, and take the shine out o' their bis'nes, and the bread out o' the traps o' their preshus kids, by a makin' o' this here remark, as chimblies could be as vell svept by 'sheenery as by boys; and that the makin' use o' boys for that there purpuss vos barbareous; vereas, he 'ad been a chummy—he begged the cheerman's parding for usin' such a wulgar hexpression—more nor thirty year—he might say he'd been born in a chimbley—and he know'd uncommon vell as 'sheenery vos vus nor o' no use: and as to kerhewelty to the boys, everybody in the chimbley line know'd as vell as he did, that they liked the climbin' better nor nuffin as vos." From this day, we date the total fall of the last lingering remnant of May-day dancing, among the *élite* of the profession: and from this period we commence a new era in that portion of our spring associations which relates to the 1st of May.

We are aware that the unthinking part of the population will meet us here, with the assertion, that dancing on May-day still continues—that "greens" are annually seen to roll along the streets—that youths in the garb of clowns, precede them, giving vent to the ebullitions of their sportive fancies; and that lords and ladies follow in their wake.

Granted. We are ready to acknowledge that in outward show, these processions have greatly improved: we do not deny the introduction of solos on the drum; we will even go so far as to admit an occasional fantasia on the triangle, but here our admissions end. We positively deny that the sweeps have art or part in these proceedings. We distinctly charge the dustmen with throwing what they ought to clear away, into the eyes of the public. We accuse scavengers, brick-makers, and gentlemen who devote their energies to the costermongering line, with obtaining money once a-year, under false pretences. We cling with peculiar fondness to the custom of days gone by, and have shut out conviction as long as we could, but it has forced itself upon us ; and we now proclaim to a deluded public, that the May-day dancers are *not* sweeps. The size of them, alone, is sufficient to repudiate the idea. It is a notorious fact that the widely-spread taste for register-stoves has materially increased the demand for small boys; whereas the men, who, under a fictitious character, dance about the streets on the first of May nowadays, would be a tight fit in a kitchen flue, to say nothing of the parlour. This is strong presumptive evidence, but we have positive proof—the evidence of our own senses. And here is our testimony.

Upon the morning of the second of the merry month of May, in the year of our Lord one thousand eight hundred and thirty-six, we went out for a stroll, with a kind of forlorn hope of seeing something or other which might induce us to believe that it was really spring, and not Christmas. After wandering as far as Copenhagen House, without meet-ing anything calculated to dispel our impression that there was a mistake in the almanacks, we turned back down Maiden-lane, with the intention of passing through the extensive colony lying between it and Battle-bridge, which is inhabited by proprietors of donkey-carts, boilers of horse-flesh, makers of tiles, and sifters of cinders; through which colony we should have passed, without stoppage or inter-ruption, if a little crowd gathered round a shed had not attracted our attention, and induced us to pause.

When we say a "shed," we do not mean the conservatory

sort of building, which, according to the old song, Love
tenanted when he was a young man, but a wooden house
with windows stuffed with rags and paper, and a small yard
at the side, with one dust-cart, two baskets, a few shovels,
and little heaps of cinders, and fragments of china and tiles,
scattered about it. Before this inviting spot we paused; and
the longer we looked, the more we wondered what exciting
circumstance it could be, that induced the foremost members
of the crowd to flatten their noses against the parlour
window, in the vain hope of catching a glimpse of what was
going on inside. After staring vacantly about us for some
minutes, we appealed, touching the cause of this assemblage,
to a gentleman in a suit of tarpaulin, who was smoking his
pipe on our right hand; but as the only answer we obtained
was a playful inquiry whether our mother had disposed of
her mangle, we determined to await the issue in silence.

Judge of our virtuous indignation, when the street-door
of the shed opened, and a party emerged therefrom, clad in
the costume and emulating the appearance, of May-day
sweeps!

The first person who appeared was "my lord," habited in
a blue coat and bright buttons, with gilt paper tacked over
the seams, yellow knee-breeches, pink cotton stockings, and
shoes; a cocked hat, ornamented with shreds of various-
coloured paper, on his head, a *bouquet* the size of a prize
cauliflower in his button-hole, a long Belcher handkerchief
in his right hand, and a thin cane in his left. A murmur of
applause ran through the crowd (which was chiefly composed
of his lordship's personal friends), when this graceful figure
made his appearance, which swelled into a burst of applause
as his fair partner in the dance bounded forth to join him.
Her ladyship was attired in pink crape over bed-furniture,
with a low body and short sleeves. The symmetry of her
ankles was partially concealed by a very perceptible pair
of frilled trousers; and the inconvenience which might have
resulted from the circumstance of her white satin shoes being

THE DECAY OF MAY-DAY

a few sizes too large, was obviated by their being firmly attached to her legs with strong tape sandals.

Her head was ornamented with a profusion of artificial flowers; and in her hand she bore a large brass ladle, wherein to receive what she figuratively denominated " the tin." The other characters were a young gentleman in girl's clothes and a widow's cap; two clowns who walked upon their hands in the mud, to the immeasurable delight of all the spectators; a man with a drum; another man with a flageolet; a dirty woman in a large shawl, with a box under her arm for the money,—and last, though not least, the " green," animated by no less a personage than our identical friend in the tarpaulin suit.

The man hammered away at the drum, the flageolet squeaked, the shovels rattled, the " green" rolled about, pitching first on one side and then on the other; my lady threw her right foot over her left ankle, and her left foot over her right ankle, alternately; my lord ran a few paces forward, and butted at the " green," and then a few paces backward upon the toes of the crowd, and then went to the right, and then to the left, and then dodged my lady round the " green; " and finally drew her arm through his, and called upon the boys to shout, which they did lustily—for this was the dancing.

We passed the same group, accidentally, in the evening. We never saw a " green" so drunk, a lord so quarrelsome (no: not even in the house of peers after dinner), a pair of clowns so melancholy, a lady so muddy, or a party so miserable.

How has May-day decayed!

CHAPTER XXI

BROKERS' AND MARINE-STORE SHOPS

WHEN we affirm that brokers' shops are strange places, and that if an authentic history of their contents could be procured, it would furnish many a page of amusement, and many a melancholy tale, it is necessary to explain the class of shops to which we allude. Perhaps when we make use of the term "Brokers' Shop," the minds of our readers will at once picture large, handsome warehouses, exhibiting a long perspective of French-polished dining-tables, rosewood chiffoniers, and mahogany wash-hand-stands, with an occasional vista of a four-post bedstead and hangings, and an appropriate foreground of dining-room chairs. Perhaps they will imagine that we mean an humble class of second-hand furniture repositories. Their imagination will then naturally lead them to that street at the back of Long-acre, which is composed almost entirely of brokers' shops; where you walk through groves of deceitful, showy-looking furniture, and where the prospect is occasionally enlivened by a bright red, blue, and yellow hearth-rug, embellished with the pleasing device of a mail-coach at full speed, or a strange animal, supposed to have been originally intended for a dog, with a mass of worsted-work in his mouth, which conjecture has likened to a basket of flowers.

This, by-the-bye, is a tempting article to young wives in the humbler ranks of life, who have a first-floor front to furnish—they are lost in admiration, and hardly know which to admire most. The dog is very beautiful, but they have a dog already on the best tea-tray, and two more on the mantel-piece. Then, there is something so genteel about that mail-coach; and the passengers outside (who are all hat) give it such an air of reality!

The goods here are adapted to the taste, or rather to the means, of cheap purchasers. There are some of the most beautiful *looking* Pembroke tables that were ever beheld: the wood as green as the trees in the Park, and the leaves almost as certain to fall off in the course of a year. There is also a most extensive assortment of tent and turn-up bedsteads, made of stained wood, and innumerable specimens of that base imposition on society—a sofa bedstead.

A turn-up bedstead is a blunt, honest piece of furniture; it may be slightly disguised with a sham drawer; and sometimes a mad attempt is even made to pass it off for a book-case; ornament it as you will, however, the turn-up bedstead seems to defy disguise, and to insist on having it distinctly understood that he is a turn-up bedstead, and nothing else— that he is indispensably necessary, and that being so useful, he disdains to be ornamental.

How different is the demeanour of a sofa bedstead! Ashamed of its real use, it strives to appear an article of luxury and gentility—an attempt in which it miserably fails. It has neither the respectability of a sofa, nor the virtues of a bed; every man who keeps a sofa bedstead in his house, becomes a party to a wilful and designing fraud—we question whether you could insult him more, than by insinuating that you entertain the least suspicion of its real use.

To return from this digression, we beg to say, that neither of these classes of brokers' shops, forms the subject of this sketch. The shops to which we advert, are immeasurably inferior to those on whose outward appearance we have slightly touched. Our readers must often have observed in some by-street, in a poor neighbourhood, a small dirty shop, exposing for sale the most extraordinary and confused jumble of old, worn-out, wretched articles, that can well be imagined. Our wonder at their ever having been bought, is only to be equalled by our astonishment at the idea of their ever being sold again. On a board, at the side of the door, are placed about twenty books—all odd volumes; and as many wine-glasses—all different patterns; several locks, an old earthen-ware pan, full of rusty keys; two or three gaudy chimney-ornaments—cracked, of course; the remains of a lustre, without any drops; a round frame like a capital O, which has once held a mirror; a flute, complete with the exception of the middle joint; a pair of curling-irons; and a tinder-box. In front of the shop-window, are ranged some half-dozen high-backed chairs, with spinal complaints and wasted legs; a corner cupboard; two or three very dark mahogany tables with flaps like mathematical problems; some pickle-jars, some surgeons' ditto, with gilt labels and without stoppers; an unframed portrait of some lady who flourished about the beginning of the thirteenth century, by an artist who never flourished at all; an incalculable host of miscellanies of every description, including bottles and cabinets, rags and bones, fenders and street-door knockers, fire-irons, wearing apparel and bedding, a hall-lamp, and a room-door. Imagine, in addition to this incongruous mass, a black doll in a white frock, with two faces—one looking up the street, and the other looking down, swinging over the door; a board with the squeezed-up inscription "Dealer in marine stores," in lanky white letters, whose height is strangely out of pro-portion to their width; and you have before you precisely the kind of shop to which we wish to direct your attention.

Although the same heterogeneous mixture of things will be found at all these places, it is curious to observe how truly and accurately some of the minor articles which are exposed for sale—articles of wearing apparel, for instance— mark the character of the neighbourhood. Take Drury-lane and Covent-garden for example.

DRAMATIC FINERY

This is essentially a theatrical neighbourhood. There is not a potboy in the vicinity who is not, to a greater or less extent, a dramatic character. The errand-boys and chandler's-shop-keepers' sons, are all stage-struck : they "gets up" plays in back kitchens hired for the purpose, and will stand before a shop-window for hours, contemplating a great staring portrait of Mr. Somebody or other, of the Royal Coburg Theatre, "as he appeared in the character of Tongo the Denounced." The consequence is, that there is not a marine-store shop in the neighbourhood, which does not exhibit for sale some faded articles of dramatic finery, such as three or four pairs of soiled buff boots with turn-over red tops, heretofore worn by a "fourth robber," or "fifth mob;" a pair of rusty broadswords, a few gauntlets, and certain resplendent ornaments, which, if they were yellow instead of white, might be taken for insurance plates of the Sun Fire-office. There are several of these shops in the narrow streets and dirty courts, of which there are so many near the national theatres, and they all have tempting goods of this description, with the addition, perhaps, of a lady's pink dress covered with spangles ; white wreaths, stage shoes, and a tiara like a tin lamp reflector. They have been purchased of some wretched supernumeraries, or sixth-rate actors, and are now offered for the benefit of the rising generation, who, on condition of making certain weekly payments, amounting in the whole to about ten times their value, may avail themselves of such desirable bargains.

Let us take a very different quarter, and apply it to the same test. Look at a marine-store dealer's, in that reservoir of dirt, drunkenness, and drabs : thieves, oysters, baked potatoes, and pickled salmon—Ratcliff-highway. Here, the wearing apparel is all nautical. Rough blue jackets, with mother-of-pearl buttons, oil-skin hats, coarse checked shirts, and large canvas trousers that look as if they were made for a pair of bodies instead of a pair of legs, are the staple commodities. Then, there are large bunches of cotton pocket-handkerchiefs, in colour and pattern unlike any one ever

209

saw before, with the exception of those on the backs of the three young ladies without bonnets who passed just now. The furniture is much the same as elsewhere, with the addition of one or two models of ships, and some old prints of naval engagements in still older frames. In the window, are a few compasses, a small tray containing silver watches in clumsy thick cases; and tobacco-boxes, the lid of each ornamented with a ship, or an anchor, or some such trophy. A sailor generally pawns or sells ail he .has before he has been long ashore, and if he does not, some favoured companion kindly saves him the trouble. In either case, it is an even chance that he afterwards unconsciously repurchases the same things at a higher price than he gave for them at first.

Again: pay a visit with a similar object, to a part of London, as unlike both of these as they are to each other. Cross over to the Surrey side, and look at such shops of this description as are to be found near the King's Bench prison, and in "the Rules." How different, and how strikingly illustrative of the decay of some of the unfortunate residents in this part of the metropolis! Imprisonment and neglect have done their work. There is contamination in the profligate denizens of a debtor's prison; old friends have fallen off; the recollection of former prosperity has passed away; and with it all thoughts for the past, all care for the future. First, watches and rings, then cloaks, coats, and all the more expensive articles of dress, have found their way to the pawnbroker's. That miserable resource has failed at last, and the sale of some trifling article at one of these shops, has been the only mode left of raising a shilling or two, to meet the urgent demands of the moment. Dressing-cases and writing-desks, too old to pawn but too good to keep; guns, fishing-rods, musical instruments, all in the same condition; have first been sold, and the sacrifice has been but slightly felt. But hunger must be allayed, and what has already become a habit, is easily resorted to, when an emergency arises. Light articles of clothing, first of the ruined man, then of his wife, at last of their children, even of the youngest, have been parted with, piecemeal. There they are, thrown carelessly together until a purchaser presents himself, old, and patched and repaired, it is true; but the make and materials tell of better days; and the older they are, the greater the misery and destitution of those whom they once adorned.

CHAPTER XXII

IT is a remarkable circumstance, that different trades appear to partake of the disease to which elephants and dogs are especially liable, and to run stark, staring, raving mad, periodically. The great distinction between the animals and the trades, is, that the former run mad with a certain degree of propriety—they are very regular in their irregularities. We know the period at which the emergency will arise, and provide against it accordingly. If an elephant run mad, we are all ready for him—kill or cure—pills or bullets, calomel in conserve of roses, or lead in a musket-barrel. If a dog happen to look unpleasantly warm in the summer months, and to trot about the shady side of the streets with a quarter of a yard of tongue hanging out of his mouth, a thick leather muzzle, which has been previously prepared in compliance with the thoughtful injunctions of the Legislature, is instantly clapped over his head, by way of making him cooler, and he either looks remarkably unhappy for the next six weeks, or becomes legally insane, and goes mad, as it were, by Act of Parliament. But these trades are as eccentric as comets; nay, worse, for no one can calculate on the recurrence of the strange appearances which betoken the disease. Moreover, the contagion is general, and the quickness with which it diffuses itself, almost incredible.

We will cite two or three cases in illustration of our

212

meaning. Six or eight years ago, the epidemic began to display itself among the linen-drapers and haberdashers. The primary symptoms were an inordinate love of plate-glass, and a passion for gas-lights and gilding. The disease gradually progressed, and at last attained a fearful height. Quiet, dusty old shops in different parts of town, were pulled down; spacious premises with stuccoed fronts and gold letters, were erected instead; floors were covered with Turkey carpets; roofs supported by massive pillars; doors knocked into windows; a dozen squares of glass into one; one shopman into a dozen; and there is no knowing what would have been done, if it had not been fortunately discovered, just in time, that the Commissioners of Bankruptcy were as competent to decide such cases as the Commissioners of Lunacy, and that a little confinement and gentle examination did wonders. The disease abated. It died away. A year or two of comparative tranquillity ensued. Suddenly it burst out again amongst the chemists; the symptoms were the same, with the addition of a strong desire to stick the royal arms over the shop-door, and a great rage for mahogany, varnish, and expensive floor-cloth. Then, the hosiers were infected, and began to pull down their shop-fronts with frantic recklessness. The mania again died away, and the public began to congratulate themselves on its entire disappearance, when it burst forth with tenfold violence among the publicans, and keepers of " wine vaults." From that moment it has spread among them with unprecedented rapidity, exhibiting a concatenation of all the previous symptoms; onward it has rushed to every part of town, knocking down all the old public-houses, and depositing splendid mansions, stone balustrades, rosewood fittings, immense lamps, and illuminated clocks, at the corner of every street.

The extensive scale on which these places are established, and the ostentatious manner in which the business of even the smallest among them is divided into branches, is amusing. A handsome plate of ground glass in one door directs you

"To the Counting-house;" another to the "Bottle Department;" a third to the "Wholesale Department;" a fourth, to "The Wine Promenade;" and so forth, until we are in daily expectation of meeting with a "Brandy Bell," or a "Whiskey Entrance." Then, ingenuity is exhausted in devising attractive titles for the different descriptions of gin ; and the dram-drinking portion of the community as they gaze upon the gigantic black and white announcements, which are only to be equalled in size by the figures beneath them, are left in a state of pleasing hesitation between " The Cream of the Valley," " The Out and Out," "The No Mistake," "The Good for Mixing," " The real Knock-me-down," " The celebrated Butter Gin," " The regular Flare-up," and a dozen other, equally inviting and wholesome *liqueurs*. Although places of this description are to be met with in every second street, they are invariably numerous and splendid in precise proportion to the dirt and poverty of the surrounding neighbourhood. The gin-shops in and near Drury-lane, Holborn, St. Giles's, Covent-garden, and Clare-market, are the handsomest in London. There is more of filth and squalid misery near those great thoroughfares than in any part of this mighty city.

We will endeavour to sketch the bar of a large gin-shop, and its ordinary customers, for the edification of such of our readers as may not have had opportunities of observing such scenes ; and on the chance of finding one well suited to our purpose, we will make for Drury-lane, through the narrow streets and dirty courts which divide it from Oxford-street, and that classical spot adjoining the brewery at the bottom of Tottenham-court-road, best known to the initiated as the "Rookery."

The filthy and miserable appearance of this part of London can hardly be imagined by those (and there are many such) who have not witnessed it. Wretched houses with broken windows patched with rags and paper : every room let out to a different family, and in many instances to two or even three

—fruit and "sweet-stuff" manufacturers in the cellars, barbers and red-herring vendors in the front parlours, cobblers in the back ; a bird-fancier in the first floor, three families on the second, starvation in the attics, Irishmen in the passage, a "musician" in the front kitchen, and a charwoman and five hungry children in the back one—filth everywhere—a gutter before the houses and a drain behind—clothes drying and slops emptying, from the windows; girls of fourteen or fifteen, with matted hair, walking about barefoot, and in white great-coats, almost their only covering; boys of all ages, in coats of all sizes and no coats at all ; men and women, in every variety of scanty and dirty apparel, lounging, scolding, drinking, smoking, squabbling, fighting, and swearing.

You turn the corner. What a change ! All is light and brilliancy. The hum of many voices issues from that splendid gin-shop which forms the commencement of the two streets opposite; and the gay building with the fantastically orna-mented parapet, the illuminated clock, the plate-glass windows surrounded by stucco rosettes, and its profusion of gas-lights in richly-gilt burners, is perfectly dazzling when contrasted with the darkness and dirt we have just left. The interior is even gayer than the exterior. A bar of French-polished mahogany, elegantly carved, extends the whole width of the place ; and there are two side-aisles of great casks, painted green and gold, enclosed within a light brass rail, and bearing such inscriptions, as "Old Tom, 549 ;" "Young Tom, 360 ;" "Samson, 1421"—the figures agreeing, we presume, with "gallons," understood. Beyond the bar is a lofty and spacious saloon, full of the same enticing vessels, with a gallery running round it, equally well furnished. On the counter, in addition to the usual spirit apparatus, are two or three little baskets of cakes and biscuits, which are carefully secured at top with wicker-work, to prevent their contents being unlawfully abstracted. Behind it, are two showily-dressed damsels with large necklaces, dispensing the spirits and "com-pounds." They are assisted by the ostensible proprietor of the concern, a stout, coarse fellow in a fur cap, put on very much on one side to give him a knowing air, and to display his sandy whiskers to the best advantage.

The two old washerwomen, who are seated on the little bench to the left of the bar, are rather overcome by the head-dresses and haughty demeanour of the young ladies who officiate. They receive their half-quartern of gin and pepper-mint, with considerable deference, prefacing a request for "one of them soft biscuits," with a "Jist be good enough, ma'am." They are quite astonished at the impudent air of the young fellow in a brown coat and bright buttons, who, ushering in his two companions, and walking up to the bar in as careless a manner as if he had been used to green and gold ornaments all his life, winks at one of the young ladies with singular coolness, and calls for a "kervorten and a three-out-glass," just as if the place were his own. "Gin for you, sir?" says the young lady when she has drawn it: care-fully looking every way but the right one, to show that the wink had no effect upon her. "For me, Mary, my dear," replies the gentleman in brown. "My name an't Mary as it happens," says the young girl, rather relaxing as she delivers the change. "Well, if it an't, it ought to be," responds the irresistible one; "all the Marys as ever I see, was handsome gals." Here the young lady, not precisely remembering how blushes are managed in such cases, abruptly ends the flirtation by addressing the female in the faded feathers who has just entered, and who, after stating explicitly, to prevent any subsequent misunderstanding, that "this gentleman pays," calls for "a glass of port wine and a bit of sugar."

Those two old men who came in "just to have a drain," finished their third quartern a few seconds ago: they have made themselves crying drunk; and the fat comfortable-looking elderly women, who had "a glass of rum-srub" each, having chimed in with their complaints on the hardness of the times, one of the women has agreed to stand a glass round, jocularly observing that "grief never mended no broken bones, and as good people's wery scarce, what I says is, make the most on 'em, and that's all about it!" a sentiment which appears to afford unlimited satisfaction to those who have nothing to pay.

It is growing late, and the throng of men, women, and children, who have been constantly going in and out, dwindles down to two or three occasional stragglers—cold, wretched-looking creatures, in the last stage of emaciation and disease. The knot of Irish labourers at the lower end of the place, who have been alternately shaking hands with, and threatening the life of each other, for the last hour, become furious in their disputes, and finding it impossible to silence one man, who is particularly anxious to adjust the difference, they resort to the expedient of knocking him down and jumping on him afterwards. The man in the fur cap, and the potboy rush out; a scene of riot and confusion ensues; half the Irishmen get shut out, and the other half get shut in; the potboy is knocked among the tubs in no time; the landlord hits everybody, and everybody hits the landlord; the barmaids scream; the police come in; the rest is a confused mixture of arms, legs, staves, torn coats, shouting, and struggling. Some of the party are borne off to the station-house, and the remainder slink home to beat their wives for complaining, and kick the children for daring to be hungry.

We have sketched this subject very slightly, not only because our limits compel us to do so, but because, if it were pursued farther, it would be painful and repulsive. Well-disposed gentlemen, and charitable ladies, would alike turn with coldness and disgust from a description of the drunken besotted men, and wretched broken-down miserable women, who form no inconsiderable portion of the frequenters of these haunts; forgetting, in the pleasant consciousness of their own rectitude, the poverty of the one, and the temptation of the other. Gin-drinking is a great vice in England, but wretchedness and dirt are a greater; and until you improve

217

the homes of the poor, or persuade a half-famished wretch not to seek relief in the temporary oblivion of his own misery, with the pittance which, divided among his family, would furnish a morsel of bread for each, gin-shops will increase in number and splendour. If Temperance Societies would suggest an antidote against hunger, filth, and foul air, or could establish dispensaries for the gratuitous distribution of bottles of Lethe-water, gin-palaces would be numbered among the things that were.

CHAPTER XXIII

OF the numerous receptacles for misery and distress with which the streets of London unhappily abound, there are, perhaps, none which present such striking scenes as the pawnbrokers' shops. The very nature and description of these places occasions their being but little known, except to the unfortunate beings whose profligacy or misfortune drives them to seek the temporary relief they offer. The subject may appear, at first sight, to be anything but an inviting one, but we venture on it nevertheless, in the hope that, as far as the limits of our present paper are concerned, it will present nothing to disgust even the most fastidious reader.

There are some pawnbrokers' shops of a very superior description. There are grades in pawning as in everything else, and distinctions must be observed even in poverty. The aristocratic Spanish cloak and the plebeian calico shirt, the silver fork and the flat iron, the muslin cravat and the Belcher neckerchief, would but ill assort together; so, the better sort of pawnbroker calls himself a silversmith, and decorates his shop with handsome trinkets and expensive jewellery, while the more humble money-lender boldly advertises his calling, and invites observation. It is with pawnbrokers' shops of the latter class, that we have to do. We have selected one for our purpose, and will endeavour to describe it.

The pawnbroker's shop is situated near Drury-lane, at the

219

corner of a court, which affords a side entrance for the accommodation of such customers as may be desirous of avoiding the observation of the passers-by, or the chance of recognition in the public street. It is a low, dirty-looking, dusty shop, the door of which stands always doubtfully, a little way open: half inviting, half repelling the hesitating visitor, who, if he be as yet uninitiated, examines one of the old garnet brooches in the window for a minute or two with affected eagerness, as if he contemplated making a purchase; and then looking cautiously round to ascertain that no one watches him, hastily slinks in: the door closing of itself after him, to just its former width. The shop front and the window-frames bear evident marks of having been once painted; but, what the colour was originally, or at what date it was probably laid on, are at this remote period questions which may be asked, but cannot be answered. Tradition states that the transparency in the front door, which displays at night three red balls on a blue ground, once bore also, inscribed in graceful waves, the words "Money advanced on plate, jewels, wearing apparel, and every description of property," but a few illegible hieroglyphics are all that now remain to attest the fact. The plate and jewels would seem to have disappeared, together with the announcement, for the articles of stock, which are displayed in some profusion in the window, do not include any very valuable luxuries of either kind. A few old china cups; some modern vases, adorned with paltry paintings of three Spanish cavaliers playing three Spanish guitars; or a party of boors carousing: each boor with one leg painfully elevated in the air, by way of expressing his perfect freedom and gaiety; several sets of chessmen, two or three flutes, a few fiddles, a round-eyed portrait staring in astonishment from a very dark ground; some gaudily-bound prayer-books and testaments, two rows of silver watches quite as clumsy and almost as large as Ferguson's first; numerous old-fashioned table and tea spoons, displayed, fan-like, in half-dozens; strings of coral with great broad gilt snaps; cards of

The Pawnbroker's Shop

rings and brooches, fastened and labelled separately, like the insects in the British Museum; cheap silver penholders and snuff-boxes, with a masonic star, complete the jewellery department; while five or six beds in smeary clouded ticks, strings of blankets and sheets, silk and cotton handkerchiefs, and wearing apparel of every description, form the more useful, though even less ornamental, part, of the articles exposed for sale. An extensive collection of planes, chisels, saws, and other carpenters' tools, which have been pledged, and never redeemed, form the foreground of the picture; while the large frames full of ticketed bundles, which are dimly seen through the dirty casement up-stairs—the squalid neighbourhood—the adjoining houses, straggling, shrunken, and rotten, with one or two filthy, unwholesome-looking heads thrust out of every window, and old red pans and stunted plants exposed on the tottering parapets, to the manifest hazard of the heads of the passers-by—the noisy men loitering under the archway at the corner of the court, or about the gin-shop next door—and their wives patiently standing on the curb-stone, with large baskets of cheap vegetables slung round them for sale, are its immediate auxiliaries.

If the outside of the pawnbroker's shop be calculated to attract the attention, or excite the interest, of the speculative pedestrian, its interior cannot fail to produce the same effect in an increased degree. The front door, which we have before noticed, opens into the common shop, which is the resort of all those customers whose habitual acquaintance with such scenes renders them indifferent to the observation of their companions in poverty. The side door opens into a small passage from which some half-dozen doors (which may be secured on the inside by bolts) open into a corresponding number of little dens, or closets, which face the counter. Here, the more timid or respectable portion of the crowd shroud themselves from the notice of the remainder, and patiently wait until the gentleman behind the counter, with the curly black hair, diamond ring, and double silver watch-guard, shall feel disposed to favour them with his notice—a consummation which depends considerably on the temper of the aforesaid gentleman for the time being.

At the present moment, this elegantly-attired individual is in the act of entering the duplicate he has just made out, in a thick book : a process from which he is diverted occasionally, by a conversation he is carrying on with another young man similarly employed at a little distance from him, whose allusions to "that last bottle of soda-water last night," and "how regularly round my hat he felt himself when the young 'ooman gave 'em in charge," would appear to refer to the consequences of some stolen joviality of the preceding evening. The customers generally, however, seem unable to participate in the amusement derivable from this source, for an old sallow-looking woman, who has been leaning with both arms on the counter with a small bundle before her, for half an hour previously, suddenly interrupts the conversation by addressing the jewelled shopman—"Now, Mr. Henry, do make haste, there's a good soul, for my two grandchildren's locked up at home, and I'm afeer'd of the fire." The shopman slightly raises his head, with an air of deep abstraction, and resumes his entry with as much deliberation as if he were engraving. "You're in a hurry, Mrs. Tatham, this ev'nin', an't you?" is the only notice he deigns to take, after the lapse of five minutes or so. "Yes, I am indeed, Mr. Henry; now, do serve me next, there's a good creetur. I wouldn't worry you, only it's all along o' them botherin' children." "What have you got here?" inquires the shopman, unpinning the bundle—"old concern, I suppose—pair o' stays and a petticut. You must look up somethin' else, old 'ooman; I can't lend you anything more upon them; they're completely worn out by this time, if it's only by putting in, and taking out again, three times a week." "Oh! you're a rum un, you are," replies the old woman, laughing extremely, as in duty bound; "I wish I'd got the gift of the gab like you; see if I'd be up the spout so often then! No, no; it an't the petticut; it's a child's frock and a beautiful silk ankecher, as belongs to my husband. He gave four shillin' for it, the werry same blessed day as he broke his arm."—"What do you want upon these?" inquires Mr. Henry, slightly glancing at the articles, which in all probability are old acquaintances. "What do you want upon these?—"Eighteenpence."—"Lend you ninepence."—"Oh, make it a shillin'; there's a dear—do now?"—"Not another farden."—"Well, I suppose I must take it. The duplicate is made out, one ticket pinned on the parcel, the other given to the old woman; the parcel is flung carelessly down into a corner, and some other customer prefers his claim to be served without further delay.

The choice falls on an unshaven, dirty, sottish-looking fellow, whose tarnished paper-cap, stuck negligently over one eye, communicates an additionally repulsive expression to his very uninviting countenance. He was enjoying a little relaxation from his sedentary pursuits a quarter of an hour ago, in kicking his wife up the court. He has come to redeem some tools:—probably to complete a job with, on account of which he has already received some money, if his inflamed countenance and drunken stagger, may be taken as evidence of the fact. Having waited some little time, he makes his presence known by venting his ill-humour on a ragged urchin, who, being unable to bring his face on a level with the counter by any other process, has employed himself in climbing up, and then hooking himself on with his elbows —an uneasy perch, from which he has fallen at intervals, generally alighting on the toes of the person in his immediate vicinity. In the present case, the unfortunate little wretch has received a cuff which sends him reeling to the door; and the donor of the blow is immediately the object of general indignation.

"What do you strike the boy for, you brute?" exclaims a slipshod woman, with two flat irons in a little basket. "Do you think he's your wife, you willin?" "Go and hang yourself!" replies the gentleman addressed, with a drunken look of savage stupidity, aiming at the same time a blow at the woman which fortunately misses its object. " Go and hang yourself; and wait till I come and cut you down."—" Cut you down," rejoins the woman, " I wish I had the cutting of you up, you wagabond ! (loud.) Oh ! you precious wagabond ! (rather louder.) Where's your wife, you willin ? (louder still ; women of this class are always sympathetic, and work them- selves into a tremendous passion on the shortest notice.) Your poor dear wife as you uses worser nor a dog—strike a woman—you a man ! (very shrill ;) I wish I had you—I'd murder you, I would, if I died for it !"—"Now be civil," retorts the man fiercely. " Be civil, you wiper !" ejaculates the woman contemptuously.   " An't it shocking ? " she continues, turning round, and appealing to an old woman who is peeping out of one of the little closets we have before described, and who has not the slightest objection to join in the attack, possessing, as she does, the comfortable conviction that she is bolted in. " Ain't it shocking, ma'am ? (Dreadful ! says the old woman in a parenthesis, not exactly knowing what the question refers to.) He's got a wife, ma'am, as takes in mangling, and is as 'dustrious and hard-working a young 'ooman as can be, (very fast) as lives in the back parlour of our 'ous, which my husband and me lives in the front one (with great rapidity)—and we hears him a beaten' on her sometimes when he comes home drunk, the whole night through, and not only a beaten' her, but beaten' his own child too, to make her more miserable—ugh, you beast ! and she, poor creater, won't swear the peace agin him, nor do nothin', because she likes the wretch arter all—worse luck !" Here, as the woman has completely run herself out of breath, the pawnbroker himself, who has just appeared behind the counter in a gray dressing-gown, embraces the favourable opportunity of putting in a word :—"Now I won't have none of this sort of thing on my premises !" he inter- poses with an air of authority. " Mrs. Mackin, keep yourself to yourself, or you don't get fourpence for a flat iron here ;

and Jinkins, you leave your ticket here till you're sober, and send your wife for them two planes, for I won't have you in my shop at no price; so make yourself scarce, before I make you scarcer."

This eloquent address produces anything but the effect desired; the women rail in concert; the man hits about him in all directions, and is in the act of establishing an indisputable claim to gratuitous lodgings for the night, when the entrance of his wife, a wretched, worn-out woman, apparently in the last stage of consumption, whose face bears evident marks of recent ill-usage, and whose strength seems hardly equal to the burden—light enough, God knows!—of the thin, sickly child she carries in her arms, turns his cowardly rage in a safer direction. "Come home, dear," cries the miserable creature, in an imploring tone; " *do* come home, there's a good fellow, and go to bed."—"Go home yourself," rejoins the furious ruffian. "Do come home quietly," repeats the wife, bursting into tears. "Go home yourself," retorts the husband again, enforcing his argument by a blow which sends the poor creature flying out of the shop. Her "natural protector" follows her up the court, alternately venting his rage in accelerating her progress, and in knocking the little scanty blue bonnet of the unfortunate child over its still more scanty and faded-looking face.

In the last box, which is situated in the darkest and most obscure corner of the shop, considerably removed from either of the gas-lights, are a young delicate girl of about twenty, and an elderly female, evidently her mother from the resemblance between them, who stand at some distance back, as if to avoid the observation even of the shopman. It is not their first visit to a pawnbroker's shop, for they answer without a moment's hesitation the usual questions, put in a rather respectful manner, and in a much lower tone than usual, of "What name shall I say?—Your own property, of course?—Where do you live?—Housekeeper or lodger?" They bargain, too, for a higher loan than the shopman is at first inclined to offer, which a perfect stranger would be little disposed to do; and the elder female urges her daughter on, in scarcely audible whispers, to exert her utmost powers of persuasion to obtain an advance of the sum, and expatiate on the value of the articles they have brought to raise a present supply upon. They are a small gold chain and a " Forget me not" ring: the girl's property, for they are both too small for the mother; given her in better times; prized, perhaps, once, for the giver's sake, but parted with now without a struggle; for want has hardened the mother, and her example has hardened the girl, and the prospect of receiving money, coupled with a recollection of the misery they have both endured from the want of it—the coldness of old friends —the stern refusal of some, and the still more galling compassion of others—appears to have obliterated the consciousness of self-humiliation, which the idea of their present situation would once have aroused.

In the next box, is a young female, whose attire, miserably poor, but extremely gaudy, wretchedly cold, but extravagantly fine, too plainly bespeaks her station. The rich satin gown with its faded trimmings, the worn-out thin shoes, and pink silk stockings, the summer bonnet in winter, and the sunken face, where a daub of rouge only serves as an index to the ravages of squandered health never to be regained, and lost happiness never to be restored, and where the practised smile is a wretched mockery of the misery of the heart, cannot be mistaken. There is something in the glimpse she has just caught of her young neighbour, and in the sight of the little trinkets she has offered in pawn, that seems to have awakened in this woman's mind some slumbering recollection, and to have changed, for an instant, her whole demeanour. Her first hasty impulse was to bend forward as if to scan more minutely the appearance of her half-concealed companions; her next, on seeing them involuntarily shrink from her, to retreat to the back of the box, cover her face with her hands, and burst into tears.

226

FEELINGS OF SYMPATHY

There are strange chords in the human heart, which will lie dormant through years of depravity and wickedness, but which will vibrate at last to some slight circumstance apparently trivial in itself, but connected by some undefined and indistinct association, with past days that can never be recalled, and with bitter recollections from which the most degraded creature in existence cannot escape.

There has been another spectator, in the person of a woman in the common shop; the lowest of the low; dirty, unbonneted, flaunting, and slovenly. Her curiosity was at first attracted by the little she could see of the group; then her attention. The half-intoxicated leer changed to an expression of something like interest, and a feeling similar to that we have described, appeared for a moment, and only a moment, to extend itself even to her bosom.

Who shall say how soon these women may change places? The last has but two more stages—the hospital and the grave. How many females situated as her two companions are, and as she may have been once, have terminated the same wretched course, in the same wretched manner! One is already tracing her footsteps with frightful rapidity. How soon may the other follow her example! How many have done the same!

CHAPTER XXIV

CRIMINAL COURTS

WE shall never forget the mingled feelings of awe and respect with which we used to gaze on the exterior of Newgate in our schoolboy days. How dreadful its rough heavy walls, and low massive doors, appeared to us—the latter looking as if they were made for the express purpose of letting people in, and never letting them out again. Then the fetters over the debtors' door, which we used to think were a *bonâ fide* set of irons, just hung up there, for convenience' sake, ready to be taken down at a moment's notice, and riveted on the limbs of some refractory felon! We were never tired of wondering how the hackney-coachmen on the opposite stand could cut jokes in the presence of such horrors, and drink pots of half-and-half so near the last drop.

Often have we strayed here, in sessions time, to catch a glimpse of the whipping-place, and that dark building on one side of the yard, in which is kept the gibbet with all its dreadful apparatus, and on the door of which we half expected to see a brass plate, with the inscription " Mr. Ketch ; " for we never imagined that the distinguished functionary could by possibility live anywhere else ! The days of these childish dreams have passed away, and with them many other boyish ideas of a gayer nature. But we still retain so much of our original feeling, that to this hour we never pass the building without something like a shudder.

JUST LET OUT

What London pedestrian is there who has not, at some time or other, cast a hurried glance through the wicket at which prisoners are admitted into this gloomy mansion, and surveyed the few objects he could discern, with an indescribable feeling of curiosity? The thick door, plated with iron and mounted with spikes, just low enough to enable you to see, leaning over them, an ill-looking fellow, in a broad-brimmed hat, Belcher handkerchief and top-boots: with a brown coat, something between a great-coat and a "sporting" jacket, on his back, and an immense key in his left hand. Perhaps you are lucky enough to pass, just as the gate is being opened; then, you see on the other side of the lodge, another gate, the image of its predecessor, and two or three more turnkeys, who look like multiplications of the first one, seated round a fire which just lights up the whitewashed apartment sufficiently to enable you to catch a hasty glimpse of these different objects. We have a great respect for Mrs. Fry, but she certainly ought to have written more romances than Mrs. Radcliffe.

We were walking leisurely down the Old Bailey, some time ago, when, as we passed this identical gate, it was opened by the officiating turnkey. We turned quickly round, as a matter of course, and saw two persons descending the steps. We could not help stopping and observing them.

They were an elderly woman, of decent appearance, though evidently poor, and a boy of about fourteen or fifteen. The woman was crying bitterly; she carried a small bundle in her hand, and the boy followed at a short distance behind her. Their little history was obvious. The boy was her son, to whose early comfort she had perhaps sacrificed her own—for whose sake she had borne misery without repining, and poverty without a murmur—looking steadily forward to the time, when he who had so long witnessed her struggles for himself, might be enabled to make some exertions for their joint support. He had formed dissolute connexions; idleness had led to crime; and he had been committed to take his trial for some petty theft. He had been long in prison, and, after receiving some trifling additional punishment, had been ordered to be discharged that morning. It was his first offence, and his poor old mother, still hoping to reclaim him, had been waiting at the gate to implore him to return home.

We cannot forget the boy; he descended the steps with a dogged look, shaking his head with an air of bravado and obstinate determination. They walked a few paces, and paused. The woman put her hand upon his shoulder in an agony of entreaty, and the boy sullenly raised his head as if in refusal. It was a brilliant morning, and every object looked fresh and happy in the broad, gay sunlight; he gazed round him for a few moments, bewildered with the brightness of the scene, for it was long since he had beheld anything save the gloomy walls of a prison. Perhaps the wretchedness of his mother made some impression on the boy's heart; perhaps some undefined recollection of the time when he was a happy child, and she his only friend, and best companion, crowded on him—he burst into tears; and covering his face with one hand, and hurriedly placing the other in his mother's, walked away with her.

Curiosity has occasionally led us into both Courts at the Old Bailey. Nothing is so likely to strike the person who enters them for the first time, as the calm indifference with which the proceedings are conducted; every trial seems a mere matter of business. There is a great deal of form, but no compassion; considerable interest, but no sympathy. Take the Old Court for example. There sit the Judges, with whose great dignity everybody is acquainted, and of whom therefore we need say no more. Then, there is the Lord Mayor in the centre, looking as cool as a Lord Mayor *can* look, with an immense *bouquet* before him, and habited in all the splendour of his office. Then, there are the Sheriffs, who are almost as dignified as the Lord Mayor himself; and the Barristers, who are quite dignified enough in their own opinion; and the spectators, who having paid for their admission, look upon the whole scene as if it were got up especially for their amusement. Look upon the whole group in the body of the Court—some wholly engrossed in the morning papers, others carelessly conversing in low whispers, and others, again, quietly dozing away an hour—and you can scarcely believe that the result of the trial is a matter of life or death to one wretched being present. But turn your eyes to the dock ; watch the prisoner attentively for a few moments ; and the fact is before you, in all its painful reality. Mark how restlessly he has been engaged for the last ten minutes, in forming all sorts of fantastic figures with the herbs which are strewed upon the ledge before him ; observe the ashy paleness of his face when a particular witness appears, and how he changes his position and wipes his clammy forehead, and feverish hands, when the case for the prosecution is closed, as if it were a relief to him to feel that the jury knew the worst.

The defence is concluded ; the judge proceeds to sum up the evidence ; and the prisoner watches the countenances of the jury, as a dying man, clinging to life to the very last, vainly looks in the face of his physician for a slight ray of hope. They turn round to consult ; you can almost hear the man's heart beat, as he bites the stalk of rosemary, with a desperate effort to appear composed. They resume their places—a dead silence prevails as the foreman delivers in the verdict—" Guilty ! " A shriek bursts from a female in the gallery ; the prisoner casts one look at the quarter from whence the noise proceeded ; and is immediately hurried from the dock by the gaoler. The clerk directs one of the officers of the Court to " take the woman out," and fresh business is proceeded with, as if nothing had occurred.

No imaginary contrast to a case like this, could be as complete as that which is constantly presented in the New Court, the gravity of which is frequently disturbed in no small degree, by the cunning and pertinacity of juvenile offenders. A boy of thirteen is tried, say for picking the pocket of some subject of her Majesty, and the offence is about as clearly proved as an offence can be. He is called upon for his defence, and contents himself with a little declamation about the jurymen and his country—asserts that all the witnesses have committed perjury, and hints that the police force generally have entered into a conspiracy "again" him. However probable this statement may be, it fails to convince the Court, and some such scene as the following then takes place:

Court: Have you any witnesses to speak to your character, boy?

Boy: Yes, my Lord; fifteen gen'lm'n is a vaten outside, and vos a vaten all day yesterday, vich they told me the night afore my trial vos a comin' on.

Court: Inquire for these witnesses.

Here, a stout beadle runs out, and vociferates for the witnesses at the very top of his voice; for you hear his cry grow fainter and fainter as he descends the steps into the court-yard below. After an absence of five minutes, he returns, very warm and hoarse, and informs the Court of what it knew perfectly well before—namely, that there are no such witnesses in attendance. Hereupon, the boy sets up a most awful howling; screws the lower part of the palms of his hands into the corners of his eyes; and endeavours to look the picture of injured innocence. The jury at once find him "guilty," and his endeavours to squeeze out a tear or two are redoubled. The governor of the gaol then states, in reply to an inquiry from the bench, that the prisoner has been under his care twice before. This the urchin resolutely denies in some such terms as—"S'elp me, gen'lm'n, I never vos in trouble afore—indeed, my Lord, I never vos. It's all a howen to my having a twin brother, vich has wrongfully got into trouble, and vich is so exactly like me, that no vun ever knows the difference atween us."

This representation, like the defence, fails in producing the desired effect, and the boy is sentenced, perhaps, to seven years' transportation. Finding it impossible to excite compassion, he gives vent to his feelings in an imprecation bearing reference to the eyes of "old big vig!" and as he declines to take the trouble of walking from the dock, is forthwith carried out, congratulating himself on having succeeded in giving everybody as much trouble as possible.

CHAPTER XXV.

"THE force of habit" is a trite phrase in everybody's mouth; and it is not a little remarkable that those who use it most as applied to others, unconsciously afford in their own persons singular examples of the power which habit and custom exercise over the minds of men, and of the little reflection they are apt to bestow on subjects with which every day's experience has rendered them familiar. If Bedlam could be suddenly removed like another Aladdin's palace, and set down on the space now occupied by Newgate, scarcely one man out of a hundred, whose road to business every morning lies through Newgate-street, or the Old Bailey, would pass the building without bestowing a hasty glance on its small, grated windows, and a transient thought upon the condition of the unhappy beings immured in its dismal cells; and yet these same men, day by day, and hour by hour, pass and repass this gloomy depository of the guilt and misery of London, in one perpetual stream of life and bustle, utterly unmindful of the throng of wretched creatures pent up within it—nay, not even knowing, or if they do, not heeding, the fact, that as they pass one particular angle of the massive wall with a light laugh or a merry whistle, they stand within one yard of a fellow-creature, bound and helpless, whose hours are numbered, from whom the last feeble ray of hope has fled for ever, and whose miserable career will shortly terminate

234

in a violent and shameful death. Contact with death even in its least terrible shape, is solemn and appalling. How much more awful is it to reflect on this near vicinity to the dying—to men in full health and vigour, in the flower of youth or the prime of life, with all their faculties and perceptions as acute and perfect as your own; but dying, nevertheless — dying as surely — with the hand of death imprinted upon them as indelibly—as if mortal disease had wasted their frames to shadows, and corruption had already begun!

It was with some such thoughts as these that we determined, not many weeks since, to visit the interior of Newgate —in an amateur capacity, of course; and, having carried our intention into effect, we proceed to lay its results before our readers, in the hope—founded more upon the nature of the subject, than on any presumptuous confidence in our own descriptive powers—that this paper may not be found wholly devoid of interest. We have only to premise, that we do not intend to fatigue the reader with any statistical accounts of the prison; they will be found at length in numerous reports of numerous committees, and a variety of authorities of equal weight. We took no notes, made no memoranda, measured none of the yards, ascertained the exact number of inches in no particular room: are unable even to report of how many apartments the gaol is composed.

We saw the prison, and saw the prisoners; and what we did see, and what we thought, we will tell at once in our own way.

Having delivered our credentials to the servant who answered our knock at the door of the governor's house, we were ushered into the " office;" a little room, on the right-hand side as you enter, with two windows looking into the Old Bailey: fitted up like an ordinary attorney's office, or merchant's counting-house, with the usual fixtures—a wainscoted partition, a shelf or two, a desk, a couple of stools, a pair of clerks, an almanack, a clock, and a few maps. After a little delay, occasioned by sending into the interior of the prison for the officer whose duty it was to conduct us, that functionary arrived; a respectable-looking man of about two or three and fifty, in a broad-brimmed hat, and full suit of black, who, but for his keys, would have looked quite as much like a clergyman as a turnkey. We were disappointed; he had not even top-boots on. Following our conductor by a door opposite to that at which we had entered, we arrived at a small room, without any other furniture than a little desk, with a book for visitors' autographs, and a shelf, on which were a few boxes for papers, and casts of the heads and faces of the two notorious murderers, Bishop and Williams; the former, in particular, exhibiting a style of head and set of features, which might have afforded sufficient moral grounds for his instant execution at any time, even had there been no other evidence against him. Leaving this room also, by an opposite door, we found ourself in the lodge which opens on the Old Bailey; one side of which is plentifully garnished with a choice collection of heavy sets of irons, including those worn by the redoubtable Jack Sheppard—genuine; and those *said* to have been graced by the sturdy limbs of the no less celebrated Dick Turpin—doubtful. From this lodge, a heavy oaken gate, bound with iron, studded with nails of the same material, and guarded by another turnkey, opens on a few steps, if we remember right, which terminate in a narrow and dismal stone passage, running parallel with the Old Bailey, and leading to the different yards, through a number of tortuous and intricate windings, guarded in their turn by huge gates and gratings, whose appearance is sufficient to dispel at once the slightest hope of escape that any new-comer may have entertained; and the very recollection of which, on eventually traversing the place again, involves one in a maze of confusion.

It is necessary to explain here, that the buildings in the prison, or in other words the different wards—form a square, of which the four sides abut respectively on the Old Bailey,

236

the old College of Physicians (now forming a part of New-gate-market), the Sessions-house, and Newgate-street. The intermediate space is divided into several paved yards, in which the prisoners take such air and exercise as can be had in such a place. These yards, with the exception of that in which prisoners under sentence of death are confined (of which we shall presently give a more detailed description), run parallel with Newgate-street, and consequently from the Old Bailey, as it were, to Newgate-market. The women's side is in the right wing of the prison nearest the Sessions-house. As we were introduced into this part of the building first, we will adopt the same order, and introduce our readers to it also.

Turning to the right, then, down the passage to which we just now adverted, omitting any mention of intervening gates —for if we noticed every gate that was unlocked for us to pass through, and locked again as soon as we had passed, we should require a gate at every comma—we came to a door composed of thick bars of wood, through which were discernible, passing to and fro in a narrow yard, some twenty women : the majority of whom, however, as soon as they were aware of the presence of strangers, retreated to their wards. One side of this yard is railed off at a considerable distance, and formed into a kind of iron cage, about five feet ten inches in height, roofed at the top, and defended in front by iron bars, from which the friends of the female prisoners communicate with them. In one corner of this singular-looking den, was a yellow, haggard, decrepit old woman, in a tattered gown that had once been black, and the remains of an old straw bonnet, with faded ribbon of the same hue, in earnest conversation with a young girl—a prisoner, of course—of about two-and-twenty. It is impossible to imagine a more poverty-stricken object, or a creature so borne down in soul and body, by excess of misery and destitution, as the old woman. The girl was a good-looking, robust female, with a profusion of hair streaming about in the wind—for she had no bonnet on—and a man's silk pocket-handkerchief loosely thrown over a most ample pair of shoulders. The old woman was talking in that low, stifled tone of voice which tells so forcibly of mental anguish; and every now and then burst into an irrepressible sharp, abrupt cry of grief, the most distressing sound that ears can hear. The girl was perfectly unmoved. Hardened beyond all hope of redemption, she listened doggedly to her mother's entreaties, whatever they were: and, beyond inquiring after "Jem," and eagerly catching at the few halfpence her miserable parent had brought her, took no more apparent interest in the conversation than the most unconcerned spectators. Heaven knows there were enough of them, in the persons of the other prisoners in the yard, who were no more concerned by what was passing before their eyes, and within their hearing, than if they were blind and deaf. Why should they be? Inside the prison, and out, such scenes were too familiar to them, to excite even a passing thought, unless of ridicule or contempt for feelings which they had long since forgotten.

A little farther on, a squalid-looking woman in a slovenly, thick-bordered cap, with her arms muffled in a large red shawl, the fringed ends of which straggled nearly to the bottom of a dirty white apron, was communicating some instructions to *her* visitor—her daughter evidently. The girl was thinly clad, and shaking with the cold. Some ordinary word of recognition passed between her and her mother when she appeared at the grating, but neither hope, condolence, regret, nor affection was expressed on either side. The mother whispered her instructions, and the girl received them with her pinched-up, half-starved features twisted into an expression of careful cunning. It was some scheme for the woman's defence that she was disclosing, perhaps; and a sullen smile came over the girl's face for an instant, as if she were pleased: not so much at the probability of her mother's liberation, as at the chance of her "getting off" in spite of her prosecutors. The dialogue was soon concluded; and with the same careless

238

indifference with which they had approached each other, the mother turned towards the inner end of the yard, and the girl to the gate at which she had entered.

The girl belonged to a class—unhappily but too extensive —the very existence of which, should make men's hearts bleed. Barely past her childhood, it required but a glance to discover that she was one of those children, born and bred in neglect and vice, who have never known what childhood is: who have never been taught to love and court a parent's smile, or to dread a parent's frown. The thousand nameless endearments of childhood, its gaiety and its innocence, are alike unknown to them. They have entered at once upon the stern realities and miseries of life, and to their better nature it is almost hopeless to appeal in after-times, by any of the references which will awaken, if it be only for a moment, some good feeling in ordinary bosoms, however corrupt they may have become. Talk to *them* of parental solicitude, the happy days of childhood, and the merry games of infancy! Tell them of hunger and the streets, beggary and stripes, the gin-shop, the station-house, and the pawnbroker's, and they will understand you.

Two or three women were standing at different parts of the grating, conversing with their friends, but a very large pro-portion of the prisoners appeared to have no friends at all, beyond such of their old companions as might happen to be within the walls. So, passing hastily down the yard, and pausing only for an instant to notice the little incidents we have just recorded, we were conducted up a clean and well-lighted flight of stone stairs to one of the wards. There are several in this part of the building, but a description of one is a description of the whole.

It was a spacious, bare, whitewashed apartment, lighted, of course, by windows looking into the interior of the prison, but far more light and airy than one could reasonably expect to find in such a situation. There was a large fire with a deal table before it, round which ten or a dozen women were seated on wooden forms at dinner. Along both sides of the room ran a shelf; below it, at regular intervals, a row of large hooks were fixed in the wall, on each of which was hung the sleeping mat of a prisoner: her rug and blanket being folded up, and placed on the shelf above. At night, these mats are placed on the floor, each beneath the hook on which it hangs during the day; and the ward is thus made to answer the purposes both of a day-room and sleeping apartment. Over the fireplace, was a large sheet of pasteboard, on which were displayed a variety of texts from Scripture, which were also scattered about the room in scraps about the size and shape of the copy-slips which are used in schools. On the table was a sufficient provision of a kind of stewed beef and brown bread, in pewter dishes, which are kept perfectly bright, and displayed on shelves in great order and regularity when they are not in use.

The women rose hastily, on our entrance, and retired in a hurried manner to either side of the fireplace. They were all cleanly—many of them decently—attired, and there was nothing peculiar, either in their appearance or demeanour. One or two resumed the needlework which they had probably laid aside at the commencement of their meal; others gazed at the visitors with listless curiosity; and a few retired behind their companions to the very end of the room, as if desirous to avoid even the casual observation of the strangers. Some old Irish women, both in this and other wards, to whom the thing was no novelty, appeared perfectly indifferent to our presence, and remained standing close to the seats from which they had just risen; but the general feeling among the females seemed to be one of uneasiness during the period of our stay among them: which was very brief. Not a word was uttered during the time of our remaining, unless, indeed, by the wardswoman in reply to some question which we put to the turnkey who accompanied us. In every ward on the female side, a wardswoman is appointed to preserve order, and a similar regulation is adopted among the males. The wardsmen and wardswomen are all prisoners, selected for good conduct. They alone are allowed the privilege of sleeping on bedsteads; a small stump bedstead being placed in every ward for that purpose. On both sides of the gaol, is a small receiving-room, to which prisoners are conducted on their first reception, and whence they cannot be removed until they have been examined by the surgeon of the prison.*

Retracing our steps to the dismal passage in which we found ourselves at first (and which, by-the-bye, contains three or four dark cells for the accommodation of refractory prisoners), we were led through a narrow yard to the "school" —a portion of the prison set apart for boys under fourteen years of age. In a tolerable-sized room, in which were writing-materials and some copy-books, was the schoolmaster, with a couple of his pupils; the remainder having been fetched from an adjoining apartment, the whole were drawn up in line for our inspection. There were fourteen of them in all, some with shoes, some without; some in pinafores without jackets, others in jackets without pinafores, and one in scarce anything at all. The whole number, without an exception we believe, had been committed for trial on charges of pocket-picking; and fourteen such terrible little faces we never beheld.—There was not one redeeming feature among them—not a glance of honesty—not a wink expressive of anything but the gallows and the hulks, in the whole collection. As to anything like shame or contrition, that was entirely out of the question. They were evidently quite gratified at being thought worth the trouble of looking at; their idea appeared to be, that we had come to see Newgate as a grand affair, and that they were an indispensable part of the show; and every boy as he "fell in" to the line, actually seemed as pleased and important as if he had done something excessively

* The regulations of the prison relative to the confinement of prisoners during the day, their sleeping at night, their taking their meals, and other matters of gaol economy, have been all altered—greatly for the better—since this sketch was first published. Even the construction of the prison itself has been changed.

241

meritorious in getting there at all. We never looked upon a more disagreeable sight, because we never saw fourteen such hopeless creatures of neglect, before.

On either side of the school-yard is a yard for men, in one of which—that towards Newgate-street—prisoners of the more respectable-class are confined. Of the other, we have little description to offer, as the different wards necessarily partake of the same character. They are provided, like the wards on the women's side, with mats and rugs, which are disposed of in the same manner during the day; the only very striking difference between their appearance and that of the wards inhabited by the females, is the utter absence of any employment. Huddled together on two opposite forms, by the fireside, sit twenty men perhaps; here, a boy in livery; there, a man in a rough great-coat and top-boots; farther on, a desperate-looking fellow in his shirt-sleeves, with an old Scotch cap upon his shaggy head; near him again, a tall ruffian, in a smock-frock; next to him, a miserable being of distressed appearance, with his head resting on his hand;— all alike in one respect, all idle and listless. When they do leave the fire, sauntering moodily about, lounging in the window, or leaning against the wall, vacantly swinging their bodies to and fro. With the exception of a man reading an old newspaper, in two or three instances, this was the case in every ward we entered.

The only communication these men have with their friends, is through two close iron gratings, with an intermediate space of about a yard in width between the two, so that nothing can be handed across, nor can the prisoner have any communication by touch with the person who visits him. The married men have a separate grating, at which to see their wives, but its construction is the same.

The prison chapel is situated at the back of the governor's house: the latter having no windows looking into the interior of the prison. Whether the associations connected with the place—the knowledge that here a portion of the burial service

242

is, on some dreadful occasions, performed over the quick and not upon the dead—cast over it a still more gloomy and sombre air than art has imparted to it, we know not, but its appearance is very striking. There is something in a silent and deserted place of worship, solemn and impressive at any time; and the very dissimilarity of this one from any we have been accustomed to, only enhances the impression. The meanness of its appointments—the bare and scanty pulpit, with the paltry painted pillars on either side—the women's gallery with its great heavy curtain—the men's with its unpainted benches and dingy front—the tottering little table at the altar, with the commandments on the wall above it, scarcely legible through lack of paint, and dust and damp— so unlike the velvet and gilding, the marble and wood, of a modern church—are strange and striking. There is one object, too, which rivets the attention and fascinates the gaze, and from which we may turn horror-stricken in vain, for the recollection of it will haunt us, waking and sleeping, for a long time afterwards. Immediately below the reading-desk, on the floor of the chapel, and forming the most conspicuous object in its little area, is *the condemned pew;* a huge black pen, in which the wretched people, who are singled out for death, are placed on the Sunday preceding their execution, in sight of all their fellow-prisoners, from many of whom they may have been separated but a week before, to hear prayers for their own souls, to join in the responses of their own burial service, and to listen to an address, warning their recent companions to take example by their fate, and urging them- selves, while there is yet time—nearly four-and-twenty hours —to "turn, and flee from the wrath to come!" Imagine what have been the feelings of the men whom that fearful pew has enclosed, and of whom, between the gallows and the knife, no mortal remnant may now remain! Think of the hopeless clinging to life to the last, and the wild despair, far exceeding in anguish the felon's death itself, by which they have heard the certainty of their speedy transmission to another world, with all their crimes upon their heads, rung into their ears by the officiating clergyman!

At one time—and at no distant period either—the coffins of the men about to be executed, were placed in that pew, upon the seat by their side, during the whole service. It may seem incredible, but it is true. Let us hope that the increased spirit of civilisation and humanity which abolished this frightful and degrading custom, may extend itself to other usages equally barbarous; usages which have not even the plea of utility in their defence, as every year's experience has shown them to be more and more inefficacious.

Leaving the chapel, descending to the passage so frequently alluded to, and crossing the yard before noticed as being allotted to prisoners of a more respectable description than the generality of men confined here, the visitor arrives at a thick iron gate of great size and strength. Having been admitted through it by the turnkey on duty, he turns sharp round to the left, and pauses before another gate; and, having passed this last barrier, he stands in the most terrible part of this gloomy building—the condemned ward.

The press-yard, well known by name to newspaper readers, from its frequent mention in accounts of executions, is at the corner of the building, and next to the ordinary's house, in Newgate-street: running from Newgate-street, towards the centre of the prison, parallel with Newgate-market. It is a long, narrow court, of which a portion of the wall in New-gate-street forms one end, and the gate the other. At the upper end, on the left hand—that is, adjoining the wall in Newgate-street—is a cistern of water, and at the bottom a double grating (of which the gate itself forms a part) similar to that before described. Through these grates the prisoners are allowed to see their friends; a turnkey always remaining in the vacant space between, during the whole interview. Immediately on the right as you enter, is a building containing the press-room, day-room, and cells; the yard is on every side surrounded by lofty walls guarded by *chevaux de frise*;

and the whole is under the constant inspection of vigilant and experienced turnkeys.

In the first apartment into which we were conducted— which was at the top of a staircase, and immediately over the press-room—were five-and-twenty or thirty prisoners, all under sentence of death, awaiting the result of the recorder's report—men of all ages and appearances, from a hardened old offender with swarthy face and grizzly beard of three days' growth, to a handsome boy, not fourteen years old, and of singularly youthful appearance even for that age, who had been condemned for burglary. There was nothing remarkable in the appearance of these prisoners. One or two decently-dressed men were brooding with a dejected air over the fire; several little groups of two or three had been engaged in conversation at the upper end of the room, or in the windows; and the remainder were crowded round a young man seated at a table, who appeared to be engaged in teaching the younger ones to write. The room was large, airy, and clean. There was very little anxiety or mental suffering depicted in the countenance of any of the men;—they had all been sentenced to death, it is true, and the recorder's report had not yet been made; but, we question whether there was a man among them, notwithstanding, who did not *know* that although he had undergone the ceremony, it never was intended that his life should be sacrificed. On the table lay a Testament, but there were no tokens of its having been in recent use.

In the press-room below, were three men, the nature of whose offence rendered it necessary to separate them, even from their companions in guilt. It is a long, sombre room, with two windows sunk into the stone wall, and here the wretched men are pinioned on the morning of their execution, before moving towards the scaffold. The fate of one of these prisoners was uncertain; some mitigatory circumstances having come to light since his trial, which had been humanely represented in the proper quarter. The other two had nothing to expect from the mercy of the crown; their doom was sealed; no plea could be urged in extenuation of their crime, and they well knew that for them there was no hope in this world. "The two short ones," the turnkey whispered, "were dead men."

The man to whom we have alluded as entertaining some hopes of escape, was lounging, at the greatest distance he could place between himself and his companions, in the window nearest to the door. He was probably aware of our approach, and had assumed an air of courageous indifference; his face was purposely averted towards the window, and he stirred not an inch while we were present. The other two men were at the upper end of the room. One of them, who was imperfectly seen in the dim light, had his back towards us, and was stooping over the fire, with his right arm on the mantel-piece, and his head sunk upon it. The other was leaning on the sill of the farthest window. The light fell full upon him, and communicated to his pale, haggard face, and disordered hair, an appearance which, at that distance, was ghastly. His cheek rested upon his hand; and, with his face a little raised, and his eyes wildly staring before him, he seemed to be unconsciously intent on counting the chinks in the opposite wall. We passed this room again afterwards. The first man was pacing up and down the court with a firm military step—he had been a soldier in the foot-guards—and a cloth cap jauntily thrown on one side of his head. He bowed respectfully to our conductor, and the salute was returned. The other two still remained in the positions we have described, and were as motionless as statues.*

A few paces up the yard, and forming a continuation of the building, in which are the two rooms we have just quitted, lie the condemned cells. The entrance is by a narrow and obscure staircase leading to a dark passage, in which a charcoal stove casts a lurid tint over the objects in its immediate

* These two men were executed shortly afterwards. The other was respited during his Majesty's pleasure.

vicinity, and diffuses something like warmth around. From the left-hand side of this passage, the massive door of every cell on the story opens; and from it alone can they be approached. There are three of these passages, and three of these ranges of cells, one above the other; but in size, furniture and appearance, they are all precisely alike. Prior to the recorder's report being made, all the prisoners under sentence of death are removed from the day-room at five o'clock in the afternoon, and locked up in these cells, where they are allowed a candle until ten o'clock; and here they remain until seven next morning. When the warrant for a prisoner's execution arrives, he is removed to the cells and confined in one of them until he leaves it for the scaffold. He is at liberty to walk in the yard; but, both in his walks and in his cell, he is constantly attended by a turnkey who never leaves him on any pretence.

We entered the first cell. It was a stone dungeon, eight feet long by six wide, with a bench at the upper end, under which were a common rug, a bible, and prayer-book. An iron candlestick was fixed into the wall at the side; and a small high window in the back admitted as much air and light as could struggle in between a double row of heavy, crossed iron bars. It contained no other furniture of any description.

Conceive the situation of a man, spending his last night on earth in this cell. Buoyed up with some vague and undefined hope of reprieve, he knew not why—indulging in some wild and visionary idea of escaping, he knew not how—hour after hour of the three preceding days allowed him for preparation, has fled with a speed which no man living would deem possible, for none but this dying man can know. He has wearied his friends with entreaties, exhausted the attendants with importunities, neglected in his feverish restlessness the timely warnings of his spiritual consoler; and, now that the illusion is at last dispelled, now that eternity is before him and guilt behind, now that his fears of death amount

247

almost to madness, and an overwhelming sense of his helpless, hopeless state rushes upon him, he is lost and stupefied,
and has neither thoughts to turn to, nor power to call
upon, the Almighty Being, from whom alone he can seek
mercy and forgiveness, and before whom his repentance can
alone avail.

Hours have glided by, and still he sits upon the same
stone bench with folded arms, heedless alike of the fast
decreasing time before him, and the urgent entreaties of the
good man at his side. The feeble light is wasting gradually,
and the deathlike stillness of the street without, broken
only by the rumbling of some passing vehicle which echoes
mournfully through the empty yards, warns him that the
night is waning fast away. The deep bell of St. Paul's
strikes—one! He heard it; it has roused him. Seven
hours left! He paces the narrow limits of his cell with
rapid strides, cold drops of terror starting on his forehead, and every muscle of his frame quivering with
agony. Seven hours! He suffers himself to be led to his
seat, mechanically takes the bible which is placed in his hand,
and tries to read and listen. No: his thoughts will wander.
The book is torn and soiled by use—and like the book he read
his lessons in, at school, just forty years ago! He has never
bestowed a thought upon it, perhaps, since he left it as a
child: and yet the place, the time, the room—nay, the very
boys he played with, crowd as vividly before him as if they
were scenes of yesterday; and some forgotten phrase, some
childish word, rings in his ears like the echo of one uttered
but a minute since. The voice of the clergyman recalls him
to himself. He is reading from the sacred book its solemn
promises of pardon for repentance, and its awful denunciation
of obdurate men. He falls upon his knees and clasps his
hands to pray. Hush! what sound was that? He starts
upon his feet. It cannot be two yet. Hark! Two quarters
have struck;—the third—the fourth. It is! Six hours
left. Tell him not of repentance! Six hours' repentance for

eight times six years of guilt and sin! He buries his face in his hands, and throws himself on the bench.

Worn with watching and excitement, he sleeps, and the same unsettled state of mind pursues him in his dreams. An insupportable load is taken from his breast; he is walking with his wife in a pleasant field, with the bright sky above them, and a fresh and boundless prospect on every side—how different from the stone walls of Newgate! She is looking —not as she did when he saw her for the last time in that dreadful place, but as she used when he loved her—long, long ago, before misery and ill-treatment had altered her looks, and vice had changed his nature, and she is leaning upon his arm, and looking up into his face with tenderness and affection —and he does *not* strike her now, nor rudely shake her from him. And oh! how glad he is to tell her all he had forgotten in that last hurried interview, and to fall on his knees before her and fervently beseech her pardon for all the unkindness and cruelty that wasted her form and broke her heart! The scene suddenly changes. He is on his trial again: there are the judge and jury, and prosecutors, and witnesses, just as they were before. How full the court is—what a sea of heads—with a gallows, too, and a scaffold—and how all those people stare at *him!* Verdict, "Guilty." No matter; he will escape.

The night is dark and cold, the gates have been left open, and in an instant he is in the street, flying from the scene of his imprisonment like the wind. The streets are cleared, the open fields are gained and the broad, wide country lies before him. Onward he dashes in the midst of darkness, over hedge and ditch, through mud and pool, bounding from spot to spot with a speed and lightness, astonishing even to himself. At length he pauses; he must be safe from pursuit now; he will stretch himself on that bank and sleep till sunrise.

A period of unconsciousness succeeds. He wakes, cold and wretched. The dull, gray light of morning is stealing into the cell, and falls upon the 'form of the attendant turnkey. Confused by his dreams, he starts from his uneasy bed in momentary uncertainty. It is but momentary. Every object in the narrow cell is too frightfully real to admit of doubt or mistake. He is the condemned felon again, guilty and despairing; and in two hours more will be dead.

CHARACTERS

CHAPTER I

THOUGHTS ABOUT PEOPLE.

IT is strange with how little notice, good, bad, or indifferent, a man may live and die in London.   He awakens no sympathy in the breast of any single person; his existence is a matter of interest to no one save himself; he cannot be said to be forgotten when he dies, for no one remembered him when he was alive.   There is a numerous class of people in this great metropolis who seem not to possess a single friend, and whom nobody appears to care for.   Urged by imperative necessity in the first instance, they have resorted to London in search of employment, and the means of subsistence.   It is hard, we know, to break the ties which bind us to our homes and friends, and harder still to efface the thousand recollections of happy days and old times, which have been slumbering in our bosoms for years, and only rush upon the mind, to bring before it associations connected with the friends we have left, the scenes we have beheld too probably for the last time, and the hopes we once cherished, but may entertain no more. These men, however, happily for themselves, have long forgotten such thoughts.   Old country friends have died or emigrated; former correspondents have become lost, like themselves, in the crowd and turmoil of some busy city; and they have gradually settled down into mere passive creatures of habit and endurance.

We were seated in the enclosure of St. James's Park the other day, when our attention was attracted by a man whom we immediately put down in our own mind as one of this class. He was a tall, thin, pale person, in a black coat, scanty gray trousers, little pinched-up gaiters, and brown beaver gloves. He had an umbrella in his hand—not for use, for the day was fine—but, evidently, because he always carried one to the office in the morning. He walked up and down before the little patch of grass on which the chairs are placed for hire, not as if he were doing it for pleasure or recreation, but as if it were a matter of compulsion, just as he would walk to the office every morning from the back settlements of Islington. It was Monday; he had escaped for four-and-twenty hours from the thraldom of the desk; and was walking here for exercise and amusement—perhaps for the first time in his life. We were inclined to think he had never had a holiday before, and that he did not know what to do with himself. Children were playing on the grass; groups of people were loitering about, chatting and laughing; but the man walked steadily up and down, unheeding and unheeded, his spare, pale face looking as if it were incapable of bearing the expression of curiosity or interest.

There was something in the man's manner and appearance which told us, we fancied, his whole life, or rather his whole day, for a man of this sort has no variety of days. We thought we almost saw the dingy little back office into which he walks every morning, hanging his hat on the same peg, and placing his legs beneath the same desk: first, taking off that black coat which lasts the year through, and putting on the one which did duty last year, and which he keeps in his desk to save the other. There he sits till five o'clock, working on, all day, as regularly as the dial over the mantel-piece, whose loud ticking is as monotonous as his whole existence: only raising his head when some one enters the counting-house, or

George Cruikshank

Thoughts about People

when, in the midst of some difficult calculation, he looks up to the ceiling as if there were inspiration in the dusty skylight with a green knot in the centre of every pane of glass. About five, or half-past, he slowly dismounts from his accustomed stool, and again changing his coat, proceeds to his usual dining-place, somewhere near Bucklersbury. The waiter recites the bill of fare in a rather confidential manner—for he is a regular customer—and after inquiring "What's in the best cut?" and "What was up last?" he orders a small plate of roast beef, with greens, and half-a-pint of porter. He has a small plate to-day, because greens are a penny more than potatoes, and he had "two breads" yesterday, with the additional enormity of "a cheese" the day before. This important point settled, he hangs up his hat—he took it off the moment he sat down—and bespeaks the paper after the next gentleman. If he can get it while he is at dinner, he eats with much greater zest; balancing it against the water-bottle, and eating a bit of beef, and reading a line or two, alternately. Exactly at five minutes before the hour is up, he produces a shilling, pays the reckoning, carefully deposits the change in his waistcoat-pocket (first deducting a penny for the waiter), and returns to the office, from which, if it is not foreign post night, he again sallies forth, in about half an hour. He then walks home, at his usual pace, to his little back room at Islington, where he has his tea; perhaps solacing himself during the meal with the conversation of his landlady's little boy, whom he occasionally rewards with a penny, for solving problems in simple addition. Sometimes, there is a letter or two to take up to his employer's, in Russell-square; and then, the wealthy man of business, hearing his voice, calls out from the dining-parlour,—"Come in, Mr. Smith:" and Mr. Smith, putting his hat at the feet of one of the hall chairs, walks timidly in, and being condescendingly desired to sit down, carefully tucks his legs under his chair, and sits at a considerable distance from the table while he drinks the glass of sherry which is poured out for him by the eldest boy, and after drinking which, he backs and slides out of the room, in a state of nervous agitation from which he does not perfectly recover, until he finds himself once more in the Islington-road. Poor, harmless creatures such men are; contented but not happy; broken-spirited and humbled, they may feel no pain, but they never know pleasure.

Compare these men with another class of beings who, like them, have neither friend nor companion, but whose position in society is the result of their own choice. These are generally old fellows with white heads and red faces, addicted to port wine and Hessian boots, who from some cause, real or imaginary—generally the former, the excellent reason being that they are rich, and their relations poor—grow suspicious of everybody, and do the misanthropical in chambers, taking great delight in thinking themselves unhappy, and making everybody they come near, miserable. You may see such men as these, anywhere; you will know them at coffee-houses by their discontented exclamations and the luxury of their dinners; at theatres, by their always sitting in the same place and looking with a jaundiced eye on all the young people near them; at church, by the pomposity with which they enter, and the loud tone in which they repeat the responses; at parties, by their getting cross at whist and hating music. An old fellow of this kind will have his chambers splendidly furnished, and collect books, plate, and pictures about him in profusion; not so much for his own gratification, as to be superior to those who have the desire, but not the means, to compete with him. He belongs to two or three clubs, and is envied, and flattered, and hated by the members of them all. Sometimes he will be appealed to by a poor relation—a married nephew perhaps—for some little assistance : and then he will declaim with honest indignation on the improvidence of young married people, the worthlessness of a wife, the insolence of having a family, the atrocity of getting into debt with a hundred and twenty-five pounds a year, and other unpardonable crimes; winding up his exhortations with a complacent review of his own conduct, and a delicate allusion to parochial relief. He dies, some day after dinner, of apoplexy, having bequeathed his property to a Public Society, and the Institution erects a tablet to his memory, expressive of their admiration of his Christian conduct in this world, and their comfortable conviction of his happiness in the next.

But, next to our very particular friends, hackney-coachmen, cabmen and cads, whom we admire in proportion to the extent of their cool impudence and perfect self-possession, there is no class of people who amuse us more than London apprentices. They are no longer an organised body, bound down by solemn compact to terrify his Majesty's subjects whenever it pleases them to take offence in their heads and staves in their hands. They are only bound, now, by indentures, and, as to their valour, it is easily restrained by the wholesome dread of the New Police, and a perspective view of a damp station-house, terminating in a police-office and a reprimand. They are still, however, a peculiar class, and not the less pleasant for being inoffensive. Can any one fail to have noticed them in the streets on Sunday? And were there ever such harmless efforts at the grand and magnificent as the young fellows display! We walked down the Strand, a Sunday or two ago, behind a little group; and they furnished food for our amusement the whole way. They had come out of some part of the city; it was between three and four o'clock in the afternoon; and they were on their way to the Park. There were four of them, all arm-in-arm, with white kid gloves like so many bridegrooms, light trousers of unprecedented patterns, and coats for which the English language has yet no name—a kind of cross between a great-coat and a surtout, with the collar of the one, the skirts of the other, and pockets peculiar to themselves.

Each of the gentlemen carried a thick stick, with a large tassel at the top, which he occasionally twirled gracefully round; and the whole four, by way of looking easy and un-concerned, were walking with a paralytic swagger irresistibly ludicrous. One of the party had a watch about the size and shape of a reasonable Ribstone pippin, jammed into his waistcoat-pocket, which he carefully compared with the clocks at St. Clement's and the New Church, the illuminated clock at Exeter 'Change, the clock of St. Martin's Church, and the clock of the Horse Guards. When they at last arrived in St. James's Park, the member of the party who had the best-made boots on, hired a second chair expressly for his feet, and flung himself on this two-pennyworth of sylvan luxury with an air which levelled all distinctions between Brookes's and Snooks's, Crockford's and Bagnigge Wells.

We may smile at such people, but they can never excite our anger. They are usually on the best terms with them-selves, and it follows almost as a matter of course, in good humour with every one about them. Besides, they are always the faint reflection of higher lights; and, if they do display a little occasional foolery in their own proper persons, it is surely more tolerable than precocious puppyism in the Quadrant, whiskered dandyism in Regent-street and Pall-mall, or gallantry in its dotage anywhere.

CHAPTER II

CHRISTMAS time! That man must be a misanthrope indeed, in whose breast something like a jovial feeling is not roused— in whose mind some pleasant associations are not awakened —by the recurrence of Christmas. There are people who will tell you that Christmas is not to them what it used to be; that each succeeding Christmas has found some cherished hope, or happy prospect, of the year before, dimmed or passed away; that the present only serves to remind them of reduced circumstances and straitened incomes—of the feasts they once bestowed on hollow friends, and of the cold looks that meet them now, in adversity and misfortune. Never heed such dismal reminiscences. There are few men who have lived long enough in the world, who cannot call up such thoughts any day in the year. Then do not select the merriest of the three hundred and sixty-five for your doleful recollections, but draw your chair nearer the blazing fire—fill the glass and send round the song—and if your room be smaller than it was a dozen years ago, or if your glass be filled with reeking punch, instead of sparkling wine, put a good face on the matter, and empty it off-hand, and fill another, and troll off the old ditty you used to sing, and thank God it's no worse. Look on the merry faces of your children (if you have any) as they sit round the fire. One little seat may be empty; one slight form that gladdened the father's heart, and roused

257

the mother's pride to look upon, may not be there. Dwell not upon the past; think not that one short year ago, the fair child now resolving into dust, sat before you, with the bloom of health upon its cheek, and the gaiety of infancy in its joyous eye. Reflect upon your present blessings—of which every man has many—not on your past misfortunes, of which all men have some. Fill your glass again, with a merry face and contented heart. Our life on it, but your Christmas shall be merry, and your new year a happy one!

Who can be insensible to the outpourings of good feeling, and the honest interchange of affectionate attachment, which abound at this season of the year? A Christmas family-party! We know nothing in nature more delightful! There seems a magic in the very name of Christmas. Petty jealousies and discords are forgotten; social feelings are awakened, in bosoms to which they have long been strangers; father and son, or brother and sister, who have met and passed with averted gaze, or a look of cold recognition, for months before, proffer and return the cordial embrace, and bury their past animosities in their present happiness. Kindly hearts that have yearned towards each other, but have been withheld by false notions of pride and self-dignity, are again reunited, and all is kindness and benevolence! Would that Christmas lasted the whole year through (as it ought), and that the prejudices and passions which deform our better nature, were never called into action among those to whom they should ever be strangers!

The Christmas family-party that we mean, is not a mere assemblage of relations, got up at a week or two's notice, originating this year, having no family precedent in the last, and not likely to be repeated in the next. No. It is an annual gathering of all the accessible members of the family, young or old, rich or poor; and all the children look forward to it, for two months beforehand, in a fever of anticipation. Formerly, it was held at grandpapa's; but grandpapa getting old, and grandmamma getting old too, and rather infirm, they have given up house-keeping, and domesticated themselves with uncle George ; so, the party always takes place at uncle George's house, but grandmamma sends in most of the good things, and grandpapa always *will* toddle down, all the way to Newgate-market, to buy the turkey, which he engages a porter to bring home behind him in triumph, always insisting on the man's being rewarded with a glass of spirits, over and above his hire, to drink " a merry Christmas and a happy new year" to aunt George. As to grandmamma, she is very secret and mysterious for two or three days beforehand, but not sufficiently so, to prevent rumours getting afloat that she has purchased a beautiful new cap with pink ribbons for each of the servants, together with sundry books, and pen-knives, and pencil-cases, for the younger branches ; to say nothing of divers secret additions to the order originally given by aunt George at the pastry-cook's, such as another dozen of mince-pies for the dinner, and a large plum-cake for the children.

On Christmas-eve, grandmamma is always in excellent spirits, and after employing all the children, during the day, in stoning the plums, and all that, insists, regularly every year, on uncle George coming down into the kitchen, taking off his coat, and stirring the pudding for half an hour or so, which uncle George good-humouredly does, to the vociferous delight of the children and servants. The evening concludes with a glorious game of blind-man's-buff, in an early stage of which grandpapa takes great care to be caught, in order that he may have an opportunity of displaying his dexterity.

On the following morning, the old couple, with as many of the children as the pew will hold, go to church in great state : leaving aunt George at home dusting decanters and filling casters, and uncle George carrying bottles into the dining-parlour, and calling for corkscrews, and getting into every-body's way.

When the church-party return to lunch, grandpapa produces a small sprig of mistletoe from his pocket, and tempts the boys to kiss their little cousins under it—a proceeding which

affords both the boys and the old gentleman unlimited satisfaction, but which rather outrages grandmamma's ideas of
decorum, until grandpapa says, that when he was just thirteen
years and three months old, *he* kissed grandmamma under a
mistletoe too, on which the children clap their hands, and
laugh very heartily, as do aunt George and uncle George;
and grandmamma looks pleased, and says, with a benevolent
smile, that grandpapa was an impudent young dog, on which
the children laugh very heartily again, and grandpapa more
heartily than any of them.

But all these diversions are nothing to the subsequent excitement when grandmamma in a high cap, and slate-coloured silk
gown; and grandpapa with a beautifully plaited shirt-frill, and
white neckerchief; seat themselves on one side of the drawing-
room fire, with uncle George's children and little cousins
innumerable, seated in the front, waiting the arrival of the
expected visitors. Suddenly a hackney-coach is heard to stop,
and uncle George, who has been looking out of the window,
exclaims " Here's Jane ! " on which the children rush to the
door, and helter-skelter down-stairs; and uncle Robert and
aunt Jane, and the dear little baby, and the nurse, and the
whole party, are ushered up-stairs amidst tumultuous shouts
of "Oh, my!" from the children, and frequently repeated
warnings not to hurt baby from the nurse. And grandpapa
takes the child, and grandmamma kisses her daughter, and the
confusion of this first entry has scarcely subsided, when some
other aunts and uncles with more cousins arrive, and the
grown-up cousins flirt with each other, and so do the little
cousins too, for that matter, and nothing is to be heard but
a confused din of talking, laughing, and merriment.

A hesitating double knock at the street-door, heard during
a momentary pause in the conversation, excites a general
inquiry of " Who's that ? " and two or three children, who
have been standing at the window, announce in a low voice,
that it's "poor aunt Margaret." Upon which, aunt George
leaves the room to welcome the new-comer; and grandmamma

draws herself up, rather stiff and stately; for Margaret married a poor man without her consent, and poverty not being a sufficiently weighty punishment for her offence, has been discarded by her friends, and debarred the society of her dearest relatives. But Christmas has come round, and the unkind feelings that have struggled against better dispositions during the year, have melted away before its genial influence, like half-formed ice beneath the morning sun. It is not difficult in a moment of angry feeling for a parent to denounce a disobedient child; but, to banish her at a period of general good-will and hilarity, from the hearth, round which she has sat on so many anniversaries of the same day, expanding by slow degrees from infancy to girlhood, and then bursting, almost imperceptibly, into a woman, is widely different. The air of conscious rectitude, and cold forgiveness, which the old lady has assumed, sits ill upon her; and when the poor girl is led in by her sister, pale in looks and broken in hope—not from poverty, for that she could bear, but from the consciousness of undeserved neglect, and unmerited unkindness —it is easy to see how much of it is assumed. A momentary pause succeeds; the girl breaks suddenly from her sister and throws herself, sobbing, on her mother's neck. The father steps hastily forward, and takes her husband's hand. Friends crowd round to offer their hearty congratulations, and happiness and harmony again prevail.

As to the dinner, it's perfectly delightful—nothing goes wrong, and everybody is in the very best of spirits, and disposed to please and be pleased. Grandpapa relates a circumstantial account of the purchase of the turkey, with a slight digression relative to the purchase of previous turkeys, on former Christmas-days, which grandmamma corroborates in the minutest particular. Uncle George tells stories, and carves poultry, and takes wine, and jokes with the children at the side-table, and winks at the cousins that are making love, or being made love to, and exhilarates everybody with his good humour and hospitality; and when, at last, a stout servant staggers in with a gigantic pudding, with a sprig of holly in the top, there is such a laughing, and shouting, and clapping of little chubby hands, and kicking up of fat dumpy legs, as can only be equalled by the applause with which the astonishing feat of pouring lighted brandy into mince-pies, is received by the younger visitors. Then the dessert!—and the wine!—and the fun! Such beautiful speeches, and *such* songs, from aunt Margaret's husband, who turns out to be such a nice man, and *so* attentive to grandmamma! Even grandpapa not only sings his annual song with unprecedented vigour, but on being honoured with an unanimous *encore*, according to annual custom, actually comes out with a new one which nobody but grandmamma ever heard before; and a young scape-grace of a cousin, who has been in some disgrace with the old people, for certain heinous sins of omission and commission—neglecting to call, and persisting in drinking Burton Ale—astonishes everybody into convulsions of laughter by volunteering the most extraordinary comic songs that ever were heard. And thus the evening passes, in a strain of rational good-will and cheerfulness, doing more to awaken the sympathies of every member of the party in behalf of his neighbour, and to perpetuate their good feeling during the ensuing year, than half the homilies that have ever been written, by half the Divines that have ever lived.

CHAPTER III

NEXT to Christmas-day, the most pleasant annual epoch in existence is the advent of the New Year. There are a lachrymose set of people who usher in the New Year with watching and fasting, as if they were bound to attend as chief mourners at the obsequies of the old one. Now, we cannot but think it a great deal more complimentary, both to the old year that has rolled away, and to the New Year that is just beginning to dawn upon us, to see the old fellow out, and the new one in, with gaiety and glee.

There must have been some few occurrences in the past year to which we can look back, with a smile of cheerful recollection, if not with a feeling of heartfelt thankfulness. And we are bound by every rule of justice and equity to give the New Year credit for being a good one, until he proves himself unworthy the confidence we repose in him.

This is our view of the matter ; and entertaining it, notwithstanding our respect for the old year, one of the few remaining moments of whose existence passes away with every word we write, here we are, seated by our fireside on this last night of the old year, one thousand eight hundred and thirty-six, penning this article with as jovial a face as if nothing extraordinary had happened, or was about to happen, to disturb our good humour.

Hackney-coaches and carriages keep rattling up the street

263

and down the street in rapid succession, conveying, doubtless, smartly-dressed coachfuls to crowded parties; loud and repeated double knocks at the house with green blinds, opposite, announce to the whole neighbourhood that there's one large party in the street at all events; and we saw through the window, and through the fog too, till it grew so thick that we rung for candles, and drew our curtains, pastrycooks' men with green boxes on their heads, and rout-furniture-warehouse-carts, with cane seats and French lamps, hurrying to the numerous houses where an annual festival is held in honour of the occasion.

We can fancy one of these parties, we think, as well as if we were duly dress-coated and pumped, and had just been announced at the drawing-room door.

Take the house with the green blinds for instance. We know it is a quadrille party, because we saw some men taking up the front drawing-room carpet while we sat at breakfast this morning, and if further evidence be required, and we must tell the truth, we just now saw one of the young ladies "doing" another of the young ladies' hair, near one of the bedroom windows, in an unusual style of splendour, which nothing else but a quadrille party could possibly justify.

The master of the house with the green blinds is in a public office; we know the fact by the cut of his coat, the tie of his neckcloth, and the self-satisfaction of his gait—the very green blinds themselves have a Somerset House air about them.

Hark!—a cab! That's a junior clerk in the same office; a tidy sort of young man, with a tendency to cold and corns, who comes in a pair of boots with black cloth fronts, and brings his shoes in his coat-pocket, which shoes he is at this very moment putting on in the hall. Now he is announced by the man in the passage to another man in a blue coat, who is a disguised messenger from the office.

The man on the first landing precedes him to the drawing-room door. "Mr. Tupple!" shouts the messenger. "How *are* you, Tupple?" says the master of the house, advancing

264

from the fire, before which he has been talking politics and airing himself. "My dear, this is Mr. Tupple (a courteous salute from the lady of the house); Tupple, my eldest daughter; Julia, my dear, Mr. Tupple; Tupple, my other daughters; my son, sir;" Tupple rubs his hands very hard, and smiles as if it were all capital fun, and keeps constantly bowing and turning himself round, till the whole family have been introduced, when he glides into a chair at the corner of the sofa, and opens a miscellaneous conversation with the young ladies upon the weather, and the theatres, and the old year, and the last new murder, and the balloon, and the ladies' sleeves, and the festivities of the season, and a great many other topics of small talk.

More double knocks! what an extensive party! what an incessant hum of conversation and general sipping of coffee! We see Tupple now, in our mind's eye, in the height of his glory. He has just handed that stout old lady's cup to the servant; and now, he dives among the crowd of young men by the door, to intercept the other servant, and secure the muffin-plate for the old lady's daughter, before he leaves the room; and now, as he passes the sofa on his way back, he bestows a glance of recognition and patronage upon the young ladies, as condescending and familiar as if he had known them from infancy.

Charming person Mr. Tupple—perfect ladies' man—such a delightful companion, too! Laugh!—nobody ever understood papa's jokes half so well as Mr. Tupple, who laughs himself into convulsions at every fresh burst of facetiousness. Most delightful partner! talks through the whole set! and although he does seem at first rather gay and frivolous, so romantic and with so *much* feeling! Quite a love. No great favourite with the young men, certainly, who sneer at, and affect to despise him; but everybody knows that's only envy, and they needn't give themselves the trouble to depreciate his merits at any rate, for Ma says he shall be asked to every future dinner-party, if it's only to talk to people between the courses, and distract their attention when there's any unexpected delay in the kitchen.

At supper, Mr. Tupple shows to still greater advantage than he has done throughout the evening, and when Pa requests every one to fill their glasses for the purpose of drinking happiness throughout the year, Mr. Tupple is *so* droll: insisting on all the young ladies having their glasses filled, notwithstanding their repeated assurances that they never can, by any possibility, think of emptying them: and subsequently begging permission to say a few words on the sentiment which has just been uttered by Pa—when he makes one of the most brilliant and poetical speeches that can possibly be imagined, about the old year and the new one. After the toast has been drunk, and when the ladies have retired, Mr. Tupple requests that every gentleman will do him the favour of filling his glass, for he has a toast to propose: on which all the gentlemen cry " Hear! hear!" and pass the decanters accordingly: and Mr. Tupple being informed by the master of the house that they are all charged, and waiting for his toast, rises, and begs to remind the gentlemen present, how much they have been delighted by the dazzling array of elegance and beauty which the drawing-room has exhibited that night, and how their senses have been charmed, and their hearts captivated, by the bewitching concentration of female loveliness which that very room has so recently displayed. (Loud cries of " Hear!") Much as he (Tupple) would be disposed to deplore the absence of the ladies, on other grounds, he cannot but derive some consolation from the reflection that the very circumstance of their not being present, enables him to propose a toast, which he would have otherwise been prevented from giving—that toast he begs to say is—" The Ladies!" (Great applause.) The Ladies! among whom the fascinating daughters of their excellent host, are alike conspicuous for their beauty, their accomplishments, and their elegance. He begs them to drain a bumper to " The Ladies, and a happy new year to them!" (Prolonged approbation; above which the noise of the ladies dancing the Spanish dance among themselves, overhead, is distinctly audible.)

The applause consequent on this toast, has scarcely subsided, when a young gentleman in a pink under-waistcoat, sitting towards the bottom of the table, is observed to grow very restless and fidgety, and to evince strong indications of some latent desire to give vent to his feelings in a speech, which the wary Tupple at once perceiving, determines to forestall by speaking himself. He, therefore, rises again, with an air of solemn importance, and trusts he may be permitted to propose another toast (unqualified approbation, and Mr. Tupple proceeds). He is sure they must all be deeply impressed with the hospitality—he may say the splendour— with which they have been that night received by their worthy host and hostess. (Unbounded applause.) Although this is the first occasion on which he has had the pleasure and delight of sitting at that board, he has known his friend Dobble long and intimately; he has been connected with him in business—he wishes everybody present knew Dobble as well as he does. (A cough from the host.) He (Tupple) can lay his hand upon his (Tupple's) heart, and declare his confident belief that a better man, a better husband, a better father, a better brother, a better son, a better relation in any relation of life, than Dobble, never existed. (Loud cries of "Hear!") They have seen him to-night in the peaceful bosom of his family; they should see him in the morning, in the trying duties of his office. Calm in the perusal of the morning papers, uncompromising in the signature of his name, dignified in his replies to the inquiries of stranger applicants, deferential in his behaviour to his superiors, majestic in his deportment to the messengers. (Cheers.) When he bears this merited testimony to the excellent qualities of his friend Dobble, what can he say in approaching such a subject as Mrs. Dobble? Is it requisite for him to expatiate on the qualities of that amiable woman? No; he will spare his friend Dobble's feelings; he will spare the feelings of his friend—if he will allow him to have the honour of calling him so—Mr. Dobble, junior. (Here Mr. Dobble, junior, who has been previously distending his mouth to a considerable width, by thrusting a particularly fine orange into that feature, suspends operations, and assumes a proper appearance of intense melancholy.) He will simply say—and he is quite certain it is a sentiment in which all who hear him will readily concur—that his friend Dobble is as superior to any man he ever knew, as Mrs. Dobble is far beyond any woman he ever saw (except her daughters); and he will conclude by proposing their worthy "Host and Hostess, and may they live to enjoy many more new years!"

The toast is drunk with acclamation; Dobble returns thanks, and the whole party rejoin the ladies in the drawing-room. Young men who were too bashful to dance before supper, find tongues and partners; the musicians exhibit unequivocal symptoms of having drunk the new year in, while the company were out; and dancing is kept up, until far in the first morning of the new year.

We have scarcely written the last word of the previous sentence, when the first stroke of twelve, peals from the neighbouring churches. There certainly—we must confess it now—is something awful in the sound. Strictly speaking, it may not be more impressive now, than at any other time; for the hours steal as swiftly on, at other periods, and their flight is little heeded. But, we measure man's life by years, and it is a solemn knell that warns us we have passed another of the landmarks which stand between us and the grave. Disguise it as we may, the reflection will force itself on our minds, that when the next bell announces the arrival of a new year, we may be insensible alike of the timely warning we have so often neglected, and of all the warm feelings that glow within us now.

CHAPTER IV

MISS EVANS AND THE EAGLE

MR. SAMUEL WILKINS was a carpenter, a journeyman carpenter of small dimensions, decidedly below the middle size—bordering, perhaps, upon the dwarfish. His face was round and shining, and his hair carefully twisted into the outer corner of each eye, till it formed a variety of that description of semi-curls, usually known as "aggerawators." His earnings were all-sufficient for his wants, varying from eighteen shillings to one pound five, weekly—his manner undeniable—his sabbath waistcoats dazzling. No wonder that, with these qualifications, Samuel Wilkins found favour in the eyes of the other sex: many women have been captivated by far less substantial qualifications. But, Samuel was proof against their blandishments, until at length his eyes rested on those of a Being for whom, from that time forth, he felt fate had destined him. He came, and conquered—proposed, and was accepted—loved, and was beloved. Mr. Wilkins "kept company" with Jemima Evans.

Miss Evans (or Ivins, to adopt the pronunciation most in vogue with her circle of acquaintance) had adopted in early life the useful pursuit of shoe-binding, to which she had afterwards superadded the occupation of a straw-bonnet maker. Herself, her maternal parent, and two sisters, formed an harmonious quartett in the most secluded portion of Camden-town; and here it was that Mr. Wilkins presented

269

himself, one Monday afternoon, in his best attire, with his face more shining and his waistcoat more bright than either had ever appeared before. The family were just going to tea, and were *so* glad to see him. It was quite a little feast; two ounces of seven-and-sixpenny green, and a quarter of a pound of the best fresh; and Mr. Wilkins had brought a pint of shrimps, neatly folded up in a clean belcher, to give a zest to the meal, and propitiate Mrs. Ivins. Jemima was "cleaning herself" up-stairs; so Mr. Samuel Wilkins sat down and talked domestic economy with Mrs. Ivins, whilst the two youngest Miss Ivinses poked bits of lighted brown paper between the bars under the kettle, to make the water boil for tea.

"I wos a thinking," said Mr. Samuel Wilkins, during a pause in the conversation—"I wos a thinking of taking J'mima to the Eagle to-night."—"O my!" exclaimed Mrs. Ivins. "Lor! how nice!" said the youngest Miss Ivins. "Well, I declare!" added the youngest Miss Ivins but one. "Tell J'mima to put on her white muslin, Tilly," screamed Mrs. Ivins, with motherly anxiety; and down came J'mima herself soon afterwards in a white muslin gown carefully hooked and eyed, a little red shawl, plentifully pinned, a white straw bonnet trimmed with red ribbons, a small necklace, a large pair of bracelets, Denmark satin shoes, and open-worked stockings; white cotton gloves on her fingers, and a cambric pocket-handkerchief, carefully folded up, in her hand—all quite genteel and ladylike. And away went Miss J'mima Ivins and Mr. Samuel Wilkins, and a dress-cane, with a gilt knob at the top, to the admiration and envy of the street in general, and to the high gratification of Mrs. Ivins, and the two youngest Miss Ivinses in particular. They had no sooner turned into the Pancras-road, than who should Miss J'mima Ivins stumble upon, by the most fortunate accident in the world, but a young lady as she knew, with *her* young man!—And it is so strange how things do turn out sometimes—they were actually going to the Eagle too. So

Jemima Evans

Mr. Samuel Wilkins was introduced to Miss J'mima Ivins's friend's young man, and they all walked on together, talking, and laughing, and joking away like anything; and when they got as far as Pentonville, Miss Ivins's friend's young man *would* have the ladies go into the Crown, to taste some shrub, which, after a great blushing and giggling, and hiding of faces in elaborate pocket-handkerchiefs, they consented to do. Having tasted it once, they were easily prevailed upon to taste it again; and they sat out in the garden tasting shrub, and looking at the Busses alternately, till it was just the proper time to go to the Eagle; and then they resumed their journey, and walked very fast, for fear they should lose the beginning of the concert in the Rotunda.

"How ev'nly!" said Miss J'mima Ivins, and Miss J'mima Ivins's friend, both at once, when they had passed the gate and were fairly inside the gardens. There were the walks, beautifully gravelled and planted—and the refreshment-boxes, painted and ornamented like so many snuff-boxes—and the variegated lamps shedding their rich light upon the company's heads—and the place for dancing ready chalked for the company's feet—and a Moorish band playing at one end of the gardens—and an opposition military band playing away at the other. Then, the waiters were rushing to and fro with glasses of negus, and glasses of brandy-and-water, and bottles of ale, and bottles of stout; and ginger-beer was going off in one place, and practical jokes were going on in another; and people were crowding to the door of the Rotunda; and in short the whole scene was, as Miss J'mima Ivins, inspired by the novelty, or the shrub, or both, observed—"one of dazzling excitement." As to the concert-room, never was anything half so splendid. There was an orchestra for the singers, all paint, gilding, and plate-glass; and such an organ! Miss J'mima Ivins's friend's young man whispered it had cost "four hundred pound," which Mr. Samuel Wilkins said was "not dear neither;" an opinion in which the ladies perfectly coincided. The audience were seated on elevated benches round the room, and crowded into every part of it; and everybody was eating and drinking as comfortably as possible. Just before the concert commenced, Mr. Samuel Wilkins ordered two glasses of rum-and-water "warm with—" and two slices of lemon, for himself and the other young man, together with "a pint o' sherry wine for the ladies, and some sweet carraway-seed biscuits;" and they would have been quite comfortable and happy, only a strange gentleman with large whiskers *would* stare at Miss J'mima Ivins, and another gentleman in a plaid waistcoat *would* wink at Miss J'mima Ivins's friend; on which Miss J'mima Ivins's friend's young man exhibited symptoms of boiling over, and began to mutter about "people's imperence," and "swells out o' luck;" and to intimate, in oblique terms, a vague intention of knocking somebody's head off; which he was only prevented from announcing more emphatically, by both Miss J'mima Ivins and her friend threatening to faint away on the spot if he said another word.

The concert commenced—overture on the organ. "How solemn!" exclaimed Miss J'mima Ivins, glancing, perhaps unconsciously, at the gentleman with the whiskers. Mr. Samuel Wilkins, who had been muttering apart for some time past, as if he were holding a confidential conversation with the gilt knob of the dress-cane, breathed hard—breathing vengeance, perhaps,—but said nothing. "The soldier tired," Miss Somebody in white satin. "Ancore!" cried Miss J'mima Ivins's friend. "Ancore!" shouted the gentleman in the plaid waistcoat immediately, hammering the table with a stout-bottle. Miss J'mima Ivins's friend's young man eyed the man behind the waistcoat from head to foot, and cast a look of interrogative contempt towards Mr. Samuel Wilkins. Comic song, accompanied on the organ. Miss J'mima Ivins was convulsed with laughter—so was the man with the whiskers. Everything the ladies did, the plaid waistcoat and whiskers did, by way of expressing unity of sentiment and congeniality of soul; and Miss J'mima Ivins, and Miss J'mima

272

Ivins's friend, grew lively and talkative, as Mr. Samuel Wilkins, and Miss J'mima Ivins's friend's young man, grew morose and surly in inverse proportion.

Now, if the matter had ended here, the little party might soon have recovered their former equanimity; but Mr. Samuel Wilkins and his friend began to throw looks of defiance upon the waistcoat and whiskers. And the waistcoat and whiskers, by way of intimating the slight degree in which they were affected by the looks aforesaid, bestowed glances of increased admiration upon Miss J'mima Ivins and friend. The concert and vaudeville concluded, they promenaded the gardens. The waistcoat and whiskers did the same: and made divers remarks complimentary to the ankles of Miss J'mima Ivins and friend, in an audible tone. At length, not satisfied with these numerous atrocities, they actually came up and asked Miss J'mima Ivins, and Miss J'mima Ivins's friend, to dance, without taking no more notice of Mr. Samuel Wilkins, and Miss J'mima Ivins's friend's young man, than if they was nobody!.

"What do you mean by that, scoundrel!" exclaimed Mr. Samuel Wilkins, grasping the gilt-knobbed dress-cane firmly in his right hand. "What's the matter with *you*, you little humbug?" replied the whiskers. "How dare you insult me and my friend?" inquired the friend's young man. "You and your friend be hanged!" responded the waistcoat. "Take that," exclaimed Mr. Samuel Wilkins. The ferrule of the gilt-knobbed dress-cane was visible for an instant, and then the light of the variegated lamps shone brightly upon it as it whirled into the air, cane and all: "Give it him," said the waistcoat. "Horficer!" screamed the ladies. Miss J'mima Ivins's beau, and the friend's young man, lay gasping on the gravel, and the waistcoat and whiskers were seen no more.

Miss J'mima Ivins and friend being conscious that the affray was in no slight degree attributable to themselves, of course went into hysterics forthwith; declared themselves the most injured of women; exclaimed, in incoherent ravings, that they had been suspected—wrongfully suspected—oh! that they should ever have lived to see the day—and so forth; suffered a relapse every time they opened their eyes and saw their unfortunate little admirers; and were carried to their respective abodes in a hackney-coach, and a state of insensibility, compounded of shrub, sherry, and excitement.

CHAPTER V

We had been lounging one evening, down Oxford-street, Holborn, Cheapside, Coleman-street, Finsbury-square, and so on, with the intention of returning westward, by Pentonville and the New-road, when we began to feel rather thirsty, and disposed to rest for five or ten minutes. So, we turned back towards an old, quiet, decent public-house, which we remembered to have passed but a moment before (it was not far from the City-road), for the purpose of solacing ourself with a glass of ale. The house was none of your stuccoed, French-polished, illuminated palaces, but a modest public-house of the old school, with a little old bar, and a little old landlord, who, with a wife and daughter of the same pattern, was comfortably seated in the bar aforesaid—a snug little room with a cheerful fire, protected by a large screen: from behind which the young lady emerged on our representing our inclination for a glass of ale.

"Won't you walk into the parlour, sir?" said the young lady, in seductive tones.

"You had better walk into the parlour, sir," said the little old landlord, throwing his chair back, and looking round one side of the screen, to survey our appearance.

"You had much better step into the parlour, sir," said the little old lady, popping out her head, on the other side of the screen.

275

We cast a slight glance around, as if to express our ignorance of the locality so much recommended. The little old landlord observed it; bustled out of the small door of the small bar; and forthwith ushered us into the parlour itself.

It was an ancient, dark-looking room, with oaken wainscoting, a sanded floor, and a high mantel-piece. The walls were ornamented with three or four old coloured prints in black frames, each print representing a naval engagement, with a couple of men-of-war banging away at each other most vigorously, while another vessel or two were blowing up in the distance, and the foreground presented a miscellaneous collection of broken masts and blue legs sticking up out of the water. Depending from the ceiling in the centre of the room, were a gas-light and bell-pull; on each side were three or four long narrow tables, behind which was a thickly-planted row of those slippery, shiny-looking wooden chairs, peculiar to hostelries of this description. The monotonous appearance of the sanded boards was relieved by an occasional spittoon; and a triangular pile of those useful articles adorned the two upper corners of the apartment.

At the furthest table, nearest the fire, with his face towards the door at the bottom of the room, sat a stoutish man of about forty, whose short, stiff, black hair curled closely round a broad high forehead, and a face to which something besides water and exercise had communicated a rather inflamed appearance. He was smoking a cigar, with his eyes fixed on the ceiling, and had that confident oracular air which marked him as the leading politician, general authority, and universal anecdote-relater, of the place. He had evidently just delivered himself of something very weighty; for the remainder of the company were puffing at their respective pipes and cigars in a kind of solemn abstraction, as if quite overwhelmed with the magnitude of the subject recently under discussion.

On his right hand sat an elderly gentleman with a white head, and broad-brimmed brown hat; on his left, a sharp-

nosed, light-haired man in a brown surtout reaching nearly
to his heels, who took a whiff at his pipe, and an admiring
glance at the red-faced man, alternately.

"Very extraordinary!" said the light-haired man after a
pause of five minutes. A murmur of assent ran through
the company.

"Not at all extraordinary—not at all," said the red-faced
man, awakening suddenly from his reverie, and turning upon
the light-haired man, the moment he had spoken.

"Why should it be extraordinary?—why is it extraordinary?—prove it to be extraordinary!"

"Oh, if you come to that—" said the light-haired man,
meekly.

"Come to that!" ejaculated the man with the red face;
"but we *must* come to that. We stand, in these times,
upon a calm elevation of intellectual attainment, and not in
the dark recess of mental deprivation. Proof, is what I
require—proof, and not assertions, in these stirring times.
Every gen'lem'n that knows me, knows what was the nature
and effect of my observations, when it was in the contemplation of the Old-street Suburban Representative Discovery
Society, to recommend a candidate for that place in Cornwall
there—I forget the name of it. 'Mr. Snobee,' said Mr.
Wilson, 'is a fit and proper person to represent the borough
in Parliament.' 'Prove it,' says I. 'He is a friend to
Reform,' says Mr. Wilson. 'Prove it,' says I. 'The
abolitionist of the national debt, the unflinching opponent
of pensions, the uncompromising advocate of the negro, the
reducer of sinecures and the duration of Parliaments; the
extender of nothing but the suffrages of the people,' says
Mr. Wilson. 'Prove it,' says I. 'His acts prove it,' says
he. 'Prove *them*,' says I.

"And he could not prove them," said the red-faced man,
looking round triumphantly; "and the borough didn't have
him; and if you carried this principle to the full extent,
you'd have no debt, no pensions, no sinecures, no negroes,

no nothing. And then, standing upon an elevation of intellectual attainment, and having reached the summit of popular prosperity, you might bid defiance to the nations of the earth, and erect yourselves in the proud confidence of wisdom and superiority. This is my argument—this always has been my argument—and if I was a Member of the House of Commons to-morrow, I'd make 'em shake in their shoes with it." And the red-faced man, having struck the table very hard with his clenched fist, to add weight to the declaration, smoked away like a brewery.

"Well !" said the sharp-nosed man, in a very slow and soft voice, addressing the company in general, "I always do say, that of all the gentlemen I have the pleasure of meeting in this room, there is not one whose conversation I like to hear so much as Mr. Rogers's, or who is such improving company."

"Improving company !" said Mr. Rogers, for that, it seemed, was the name of the red-faced man. "You may say I am improving company, for I've improved you all to some purpose; though as to my conversation being as my friend Mr. Ellis here describes it, that is not for me to say anything about. You, gentlemen, are the best judges on that point; but this I will say, when I came into this parish, and first used this room, ten years ago, I don't believe there was one man in it, who knew he was a slave—and now you all know it, and writhe under it. Inscribe that upon my tomb, and I am satisfied."

"Why, as to inscribing it on your tomb," said a little greengrocer with a chubby face, "of course you can have anything chalked up, as you likes to pay for, so far as it relates to yourself and your affairs; but, when you come to talk about slaves, and that there abuse, you'd better keep it in the family, 'cos I for one don't like to be called them names, night after night."

"You *are* a slave," said the red-faced man, "and the most pitiable of all slaves."

278

"Werry hard if I am," interrupted the greengrocer, "for I got no good out of the twenty million that was paid for 'mancipation, anyhow."

"A willing slave," ejaculated the red-faced man, getting more red with eloquence, and contradiction—"resigning the dearest birthright of your children—neglecting the sacred call of Liberty—who, standing imploringly before you, appeals to the warmest feelings of your heart, and points to your helpless infants, but in vain."

"Prove it," said the greengrocer.

"Prove it!" sneered the man with the red face. "What! bending beneath the yoke of an insolent and factious oligarchy; bowed down by the domination of cruel laws; groaning beneath tyranny and oppression on every hand, at every side, and in every corner. Prove it!—" The red-faced man abruptly broke off, sneered melo-dramatically, and buried his countenance and his indignation together, in a quart pot.

"Ah, to be sure, Mr. Rogers," said a stout broker in a large waistcoat, who had kept his eyes fixed on this luminary all the time he was speaking. "Ah, to be sure," said the broker with a sigh, "that's the point."

"Of course, of course," said divers members of the company, who understood almost as much about the matter as the broker himself.

"You had better let him alone, Tommy," said the broker, by way of advice to the little greengrocer; "he can tell what's o'clock by an eight-day, without looking at the minute hand, he can. Try it on, on some other suit; it won't do with him, Tommy."

"What is a man?" continued the red-faced specimen of the species, jerking his hat indignantly from its peg on the wall. "What is an Englishman? Is he to be trampled upon by every oppressor? Is he to be knocked down at everybody's bidding? What's freedom? Not a standing army. What's a standing army? Not freedom. What's general happiness?

279

Not universal misery. Liberty ain't the window-tax, is it? The Lords ain't the Commons, are they?" And the red-faced man, gradually bursting into a radiating sentence, in which such adjectives as "dastardly," "oppressive," "violent," and "sanguinary," formed the most conspicuous words, knocked his hat indignantly over his eyes, left the room, and slammed the door after him.

"Wonderful man!" said he of the sharp nose.

"Splendid speaker!" added the broker.

"Great power!" said everybody but the greengrocer. And as they said it, the whole party shook their heads mysteriously, and one by one retired, leaving us alone in the old parlour.

If we had followed the established precedent in all such instances, we should have fallen into a fit of musing, without delay. The ancient appearance of the room—the old panelling of the wall—the chimney blackened with smoke and age—would have carried us back a hundred years at least, and we should have gone dreaming on, until the pewter-pot on the table, or the little beer-chiller on the fire, had started into life, and addressed to us a long story of days gone by. But, by some means or other, we were not in a romantic humour; and although we tried very hard to invest the furniture with vitality, it remained perfectly unmoved, obstinate, and sullen. Being thus reduced to the unpleasant necessity of musing about ordinary matters, our thoughts reverted to the red-faced man, and his oratorical display.

A numerous race are these red-faced men; there is not a parlour, or club-room, or benefit society, or humble party of any kind, without its red-faced man. Weak-pated dolts they are, and a great deal of mischief they do to their cause, however good. So, just to hold a pattern one up, to know the others by, we took his likeness at once, and put him in here. And that is the reason why we have written this paper.

CHAPTER VI

THE HOSPITAL PATIENT.

In our rambles through the streets of London after evening
has set in, we often pause beneath the windows of some
public hospital, and picture to ourself the gloomy and mournful scenes that are passing within. The sudden moving of a
taper as its feeble ray shoots from window to window, until
its light gradually disappears, as if it were carried farther
back into the room to the bedside of some suffering patient,
is enough to awaken a whole crowd of reflections; the mere
glimmering of the low-burning lamps, which, when all other
habitations are wrapped in darkness and slumber, denote the
chamber where so many forms are writhing with pain, or
wasting with disease, is sufficient to check the most boisterous
merriment.

Who can tell the anguish of those weary hours, when the
only sound the sick man hears, is the disjointed wanderings
of some feverish slumberer near him, the low moan of pain,
or perhaps the muttered, long-forgotten prayer of a dying
man? Who, but they who have felt it, can imagine the
sense of loneliness and desolation which must be the portion
of those who in the hour of dangerous illness are left to be
tended by strangers; for what hands, be they ever so gentle,
can wipe the clammy brow, or smooth the restless bed, like
those of mother, wife, or child?

Impressed with these thoughts, we have turned away,

281

through the nearly-deserted streets; and the sight of the few miserable creatures still hovering about them, has not tended to lessen the pain which such meditations awaken. The hospital is a refuge and resting-place for hundreds, who but for such institutions must die in the streets and door-ways; but what can be the feelings of some outcasts when they are stretched on the bed of sickness with scarcely a hope of recovery? The wretched woman who lingers about the pavement, hours after midnight, and the miserable shadow of a man—the ghastly remnant that want and drunkenness have left—which crouches beneath a window-ledge, to sleep where there is some shelter from the rain, have little to bind them to life, but what have they to look back upon, in death? What are the unwonted comforts of a roof and a bed, to them, when the recollections of a whole life of debasement stalk before them; when repentance seems a mockery, and sorrow comes too late?

About a twelvemonth ago, as we were strolling through Covent-garden (we had been thinking about these things over-night), we were attracted by the very prepossessing appearance of a pickpocket, who having declined to take the trouble of walking to the Police-office, on the ground that he hadn't the slightest wish to go there at all, was being conveyed thither in a wheelbarrow, to the huge delight of a crowd.

Somehow, we never can resist joining a crowd, so we turned back with the mob, and entered the office, in company with our friend the pickpocket, a couple of policemen, and as many dirty-faced spectators as could squeeze their way in.

There was a powerful, ill-looking young fellow at the bar, who was undergoing an examination, on the very common charge of having, on the previous night, ill-treated a woman, with whom he lived in some court hard by. Several witnesses bore testimony to acts of the grossest brutality; and a cer-tificate was read from the house-surgeon of a neighbouring hospital, describing the nature of the injuries the woman had

282

A Pickpocket in Custody

received, and intimating that her recovery was extremely doubtful.

Some question appeared to have been raised about the identity of the prisoner; for when it was agreed that the two magistrates should visit the hospital at eight o'clock that evening, to take her deposition, it was settled that the man should be taken there also. He turned pale at this, and we saw him clench the bar very hard when the order was given. He was removed directly afterwards, and he spoke not a word.

We felt an irrepressible curiosity to witness this interview, although it is hard to tell why, at this instant, for we knew it must be a painful one. It was no very difficult matter for us to gain permission, and we obtained it.

The prisoner, and the officer who had him in custody, were already at the hospital when we reached it, and waiting the arrival of the magistrates in a small room below stairs. The man was handcuffed, and his hat was pulled forward over his eyes. It was easy to see, though, by the whiteness of his countenance, and the constant twitching of the muscles of his face, that he dreaded what was to come. After a short interval, the magistrates and clerk were bowed in by the house-surgeon and a couple of young men who smelt very strong of tobacco-smoke—they were introduced as "dressers"—and after one magistrate had complained bitterly of the cold, and the other of the absence of any news in the evening paper, it was announced that the patient was pre-pared; and we were conducted to the "casualty ward" in which she was lying.

The dim light which burnt in the spacious room, increased rather than diminished the ghastly appearance of the hapless creatures in the beds, which were ranged in two long rows on either side. In one bed, lay a child enveloped in bandages, with its body half-consumed by fire; in another, a female, rendered hideous by some dreadful accident, was wildly beat-ing her clenched fists on the coverlet, in pain; on a third, there lay stretched a young girl, apparently in the heavy stupor often the immediate precursor of death: her face was stained with blood, and her breast and arms were bound up in folds of linen. Two or three of the beds were empty, and their recent occupants were sitting beside them, but with faces so wan, and eyes so bright and glassy, that it was fearful to meet their gaze. On every face was stamped the expression of anguish and suffering.

The object of the visit was lying at the upper end of the room. She was a fine young woman of about two or three and twenty. Her long black hair, which had been hastily cut from near the wounds on her head, streamed over the pillow in jagged and matted locks. Her face bore deep marks of the ill-usage she had received: her hand was pressed upon her side, as if her chief pain were there; her breathing was short and heavy; and it was plain to see that she was dying fast. She murmured a few words in reply to the magistrate's inquiry whether she was in great pain; and, having been raised on the pillow by the nurse, looked vacantly upon the strange countenances that surrounded her bed. The magistrate nodded to the officer, to bring the man forward. He did so, and stationed him at the bedside. The girl looked on with a wild and troubled expression of face; but her sight was dim, and she did not know him.

"Take off his hat," said the magistrate. The officer did as he was desired, and the man's features were disclosed.

The girl started up, with an energy quite preternatural; the fire gleamed in her heavy eyes, and the blood rushed to her pale and sunken cheeks. It was a convulsive effort. She fell back upon her pillow, and covering her scarred and bruised face with her hands, burst into tears. The man cast an anxious look towards her, but otherwise appeared wholly unmoved. After a brief pause the nature of the errand was explained, and the oath tendered.

"Oh, no, gentlemen," said the girl, raising herself once more, and folding her hands together; "no, gentlemen, for

THE DYING GIRL

God's sake! I did it myself—it was nobody's fault—it was an accident. He didn't hurt me; he wouldn't for all the world. Jack, dear Jack, you know you wouldn't!"

Her sight was fast failing her, and her hand groped over the bedclothes in search of his. Brute as the man was, he was not prepared for this. He turned his face from the bed, and sobbed. The girl's colour changed, and her breathing grew more difficult. She was evidently dying.

"We respect the feelings which prompt you to this," said the gentleman who had spoken first, "but let me warn you, not to persist in what you know to be untrue, until it is too late. It cannot save him."

"Jack," murmured the girl, laying her hand upon his arm, "they shall not persuade me to swear your life away. He didn't do it, gentlemen. He never hurt me." She grasped his arm tightly, and added, in a broken whisper, "I hope God Almighty will forgive me all the wrong I have done, and the life I have led. God bless you, Jack. Some kind gentleman take my love to my poor old father. Five years ago, he said he wished I had died a child. Oh, I wish I had! I wish I had!"

The nurse bent over the girl for a few seconds, and then drew the sheet over her face. It covered a corpse.

CHAPTER VII

THE MISPLACED ATTACHMENT OF MR. JOHN DOUNCE

If we had to make a classification of society, there is a particular kind of men whom we should immediately set down under the head of " Old Boys ; " and a column of most extensive dimensions the old boys would require. To what precise causes the rapid advance of old-boy population is to be traced, we are unable to determine. It would be an interesting and curious speculation, but, as we have not sufficient space to devote to it here, we simply state the fact that the numbers of the old boys have been gradually augmenting within the last few years, and that they are at this moment alarmingly on the increase.

Upon a general review of the subject, and without considering it minutely in detail, we should be disposed to subdivide the old boys into two distinct classes—the gay old boys, and the steady old boys. The gay old boys, are paunchy old men in the disguise of young ones, who frequent the Quadrant and Regent-street in the day-time : the theatres (especially theatres under lady management) at night; and who assume all the foppishness and levity of boys, without the excuse of youth or inexperience. The steady old boys are certain stout old gentlemen of clean appearance, who are always to be seen in the same taverns, at the same hours every evening, smoking and drinking in the same company.

There was once a fine collection of old boys to be seen

286

Mr. John Dounce

round the circular table at Offley's every night, between the hours of half-past eight and half-past eleven. We have lost sight of them for some time. There were, and may be still, for aught we know, two splendid specimens in full blossom at the Rainbow Tavern in Fleet-street, who always used to sit in the box nearest the fireplace, and smoked long cherry-stick pipes which went under the table, with the bowls resting on the floor. Grand old boys they were—fat, red-faced, white-headed old fellows—always there—one on one side the table, and the other opposite—puffing and drinking away in great state. Everybody knew them, and it was supposed by some people that they were both immortal.

Mr. John Dounce was an old boy of the latter class (we don't mean immortal, but steady), a retired glove and braces maker, a widower, resident with three daughters—all grown up, and all unmarried—in Cursitor-street, Chancery-lane. He was a short, round, large-faced, tubbish sort of man, with a broad-brimmed hat, and a square coat; and had that grave, but confident, kind of roll, peculiar to old boys in general. Regular as clockwork—breakfast at nine—dress and tittivate a little—down to the Sir Somebody's Head—a glass of ale and the paper—come back again, and take daughters out for a walk—dinner at three—glass of grog and pipe—nap—tea—little walk—Sir Somebody's Head again—capital house—delightful evenings. There were Mr. Harris, the law-stationer, and Mr. Jennings, the robe-maker (two jolly young fellows like himself), and Jones, the barrister's clerk—rum fellow that Jones—capital company—full of anecdote!—and there they sat every night till just ten minutes before twelve, drinking their brandy-and-water, and smoking their pipes, and telling stories, and enjoying themselves with a kind of solemn joviality particularly edifying.

Sometimes Jones would propose a half-price visit to Drury Lane or Covent Garden, to see two acts of a five-act play, and a new farce, perhaps, or a ballet, on which occasions the whole four of them went together: none of your hurrying and nonsense, but having their brandy-and-water first, comfortably, and ordering a steak and some oysters for their supper against they came back, and then walking coolly into the pit, when the "rush" had gone in, as all sensible people do, and did when Mr. Dounce was a young man, except when the celebrated Master Betty was at the height of his popularity, and then, sir,—then—Mr. Dounce perfectly well remembered getting a holiday from business; and going to the pit doors at eleven o'clock in the forenoon, and waiting there, till six in the afternoon, with some sandwiches in a pocket-handkerchief and some wine in a phial; and fainting after all, with the heat and fatigue, before the play began; in which situation he was lifted out of the pit, into one of the dress boxes, sir, by five of the finest women of that day, sir, who compassionated his situation and administered restoratives, and sent a black servant, six foot high, in blue and silver livery, next morning with their compliments, and to know how he found himself, sir—by G— ! Between the acts Mr. Dounce and Mr. Harris, and Mr. Jennings, used to stand up, and look round the house, and Jones—knowing fellow that Jones—knew everybody—pointed out the fashionable and celebrated Lady So-and-So in the boxes, at the mention of whose name Mr. Dounce, after brushing up his hair, and adjusting his neckerchief, would inspect the aforesaid Lady So-and-So through an immense glass, and remark, either, that she was a "fine woman—very fine woman, indeed," or that "there might be a little more of her,—eh, Jones?" just as the case might happen to be. When the dancing began, John Dounce and the other old boys were particularly anxious to see what was going forward on the stage, and Jones— wicked dog that Jones — whispered little critical remarks into the ears of John Dounce, which John Dounce retailed to Mr. Harris and Mr. Harris to Mr. Jennings; and then they all four laughed, until the tears ran down out of their eyes.

When the curtain fell, they walked back together, two and

two, to the steaks and oysters; and when they came to the second glass of brandy-and-water, Jones—hoaxing scamp, that Jones—used to recount how he had observed a lady in white feathers, in one of the pit boxes, gazing intently on Mr. Dounce all the evening, and how he had caught Mr. Dounce, whenever he thought no one was looking at him, bestowing ardent looks of intense devotion on the lady in return; on which Mr. Harris and Mr. Jennings used to laugh very heartily, and John Dounce more heartily than either of them, acknowledging, however, that the time *had* been when he *might* have done such things; upon which Mr. Jones used to poke him in the ribs, and tell him he had been a sad dog in his time, which John Dounce with chuckles confessed. And after Mr. Harris and Mr. Jennings had preferred their claims to the character of having been sad dogs too, they separated harmoniously, and trotted home.

The decrees of Fate, and the means by which they are brought about, are mysterious and inscrutable. John Dounce had led this life for twenty years and upwards, without wish for change, or care for variety, when his whole social system was suddenly upset, and turned completely topsy-turvy—not by an earthquake, or some other dreadful convulsion of nature, as the reader would be inclined to suppose, but by the simple agency of an oyster; and thus it happened.

Mr. John Dounce was returning one night from the Sir Somebody's Head, to his residence in Cursitor-street—not tipsy, but rather excited, for it was Mr. Jennings's birthday, and they had had a brace of partridges for supper, and a brace of extra glasses afterwards, and Jones had been more than ordinarily amusing—when his eyes rested on a newly-opened oyster-shop, on a magnificent scale, with natives laid, one deep, in circular marble basins in the windows, together with little round barrels of oysters directed to Lords and Baronets, and Colonels and Captains, in every part of the habitable globe.

Behind the natives were the barrels, and behind the barrels

was a young lady of about five-and-twenty, all in blue, and all alone—splendid creature, charming face and lovely figure! It is difficult to say whether Mr. John Dounce s red countenance, illuminated as it was by the flickering gas-light in the window before which he paused, excited the lady's risibility, or whether a natural exuberance of animal spirits proved too much for that staidness of demeanour which the forms of society rather dictatorially prescribe. But certain it is, that the lady smiled; then put her finger upon her lip, with a striking recollection of what was due to herself; and finally retired, in oyster-like bashfulness, to the very back of the counter. The sad-dog sort of feeling came strongly upon John Dounce: he lingered—the lady in blue made no sign. He coughed—still she came not. He entered the shop.

"Can you open me an oyster, my dear?" said Mr. John Dounce.

"Dare say I can, sir," replied the lady in blue, with playfulness. And Mr. John Dounce eat one oyster, and then looked at the young lady, and then eat another, and then squeezed the young lady's hand as she was opening the third, and so forth, until he had devoured a dozen of those at eightpence in less than no time.

"Can you open me half-a-dozen more, my dear?" inquired Mr. John Dounce.

"I'll see what I can do for you, sir," replied the young lady in blue, even more bewitchingly than before; and Mr. John Dounce eat half-a-dozen more of those at eightpence.

"You couldn't manage to get me a glass of brandy-and-water, my dear, I suppose?" said Mr. John Dounce, when he had finished the oysters: in a tone which clearly implied his supposition that she could.

"I'll see, sir," said the young lady: and away she ran out of the shop, and down the street, her long auburn ringlets shaking in the wind in the most enchanting manner; and back she came again, tripping over the coal-cellar lids like a whipping-top, with a tumbler of brandy-and-water, which Mr.

THE YOUNG LADY IN BLUE

John Dounce insisted on her taking a share of, as it was regular ladies' grog—hot, strong, sweet, and plenty of it.

So, the young lady sat down with Mr. John Dounce, in a little red box with a green curtain, and took a small sip of the brandy-and-water, and a small look at Mr. John Dounce, and then turned her head away, and went through various other serio-pantomimic fascinations, which forcibly reminded Mr. John Dounce of the first time he courted his first wife, and which made him feel more affectionate than ever; in pursuance of which affection, and actuated by which feeling, Mr. John Dounce sounded the young lady on her matrimonial engagements, when the young lady denied having formed any such engagements at all—she couldn't abear the men, they were such deceivers: thereupon Mr. John Dounce inquired whether this sweeping condemnation was meant to include other than very young men; on which the young lady blushed deeply—at least she turned away her head, and said Mr. John Dounce had made her blush, so of course she *did* blush— and Mr. John Dounce was a long time drinking the brandy-and-water; and, at last, John Dounce went home to bed, and dreamed of his first wife, and his second wife, and the young lady, and partridges, and oysters, and brandy-and-water, and disinterested attachments.

The next morning, John Dounce was rather feverish with the extra brandy-and-water of the previous night; and, partly in the hope of cooling himself with an oyster, and partly with the view of ascertaining whether he owed the young lady anything, or not, went back to the oyster-shop. If the young lady had appeared beautiful by night, she was perfectly irresistible by day; and, from this time forward, a change came over the spirit of John Dounce's dream. He bought shirt-pins; wore a ring on his third finger; read poetry; bribed a cheap miniature-painter to perpetrate a faint resemblance to a youthful face, with a curtain over his head, six large books in the background, and an open country in the distance (this he called his portrait); "went on" altogether in such an uproarious manner, that the three Miss Dounces went off on small pensions, he having made the tenement in Cursitor-street too warm to contain them ; and in short, comported and demeaned himself in every respect like an unmitigated old Saracen, as he was.

As to his ancient friends, the other old boys, at the Sir Somebody's Head, he dropped off from them by gradual degrees ; for, even when he did go there, Jones—vulgar fellow that Jones—persisted in asking " when it was to be ? " and " whether he was to have any gloves ? " together with other inquiries of an equally offensive nature : at which not only Harris laughed, but Jennings also ; so, he cut the two, altogether, and attached himself solely to the blue young lady at the smart oyster-shop.

Now comes the moral of the story—for it has a moral after all. The last-mentioned young lady, having derived sufficient profit and emolument from John Dounce's attachment, not only refused, when matters came to a crisis, to take him for better for worse, but expressly declared, to use her own forcible words, that she " wouldn't have him at no price ; " and John Dounce, having lost his old friends, alienated his relations, and rendered himself ridiculous to everybody, made offers successively to a schoolmistress, a landlady, a feminine tobacconist, and a housekeeper ; and, being directly rejected by each and every of them, was accepted by his cook, with whom he now lives, a henpecked husband, a melancholy monument of antiquated misery, and a living warning to all uxorious old boys.

CHAPTER VIII

THE MISTAKEN MILLINER.   A TALE OF AMBITION

MISS AMELIA MARTIN was pale, tallish, thin, and two-and-thirty—what ill-natured people would call plain, and police reports interesting. She was a milliner and dressmaker, living on her business and not above it. If you had been a young lady in service, and had wanted Miss Martin, as a great many young ladies in service did, you would just have stepped up, in the evening, to number forty-seven, Drummond-street, George-street, Euston-square, and after casting your eye on a brass door-plate, one foot ten by one and a half, ornamented with a great brass knob at each of the four corners, and bearing the inscription "Miss Martin; millinery and dressmaking, in all its branches;" you'd just have knocked two loud knocks at the street-door; and down would have come Miss Martin herself, in a merino gown of the newest fashion, black velvet bracelets on the genteelest principle, and other little elegancies of the most approved description.

If Miss Martin knew the young lady who called, or if the young lady who called had been recommended by any other young lady whom Miss Martin knew, Miss Martin would forthwith show her up-stairs into the two-pair front, and chat she would—*so* kind, and *so* comfortable—it really wasn't like a matter of business, she was so friendly; and, then Miss Martin, after contemplating the figure and general appearance of the young lady in service with great apparent admiration, would say how well she would look, to be sure, in a low

293

dress with short sleeves; made very full in the skirts, with four tucks in the bottom; to which the young lady in service would reply in terms expressive of her entire concurrence in the notion, and of the virtuous indignation with which she reflected on the tyranny of "Missis," who wouldn't allow a young girl to wear a short sleeve of an arternoon— no, nor nothing smart, not even a pair of ear-rings; let alone hiding people's heads of hair under them frightful caps. At the termination of this complaint, Miss Amelia Martin would distantly suggest certain dark suspicions that some people were jealous on account of their own daughters, and were obliged to keep their servants' charms under, for fear they should get married first, which was no uncommon circumstance—leastways she had known two or three young ladies in service, who had married a great deal better than their missises, and *they* were not very good-looking either; and then the young lady would inform Miss Martin, in confidence, that how one of their young ladies was engaged to a young man and was a-going to be married, and Missis was so proud about it there was no bearing of her; but how she needn't hold her head quite so high neither, for, after all, he was only a clerk. And, after expressing due contempt for clerks in general, and the engaged clerk in particular, and the highest opinion possible of themselves and each other, Miss Martin and the young lady in service would bid each other good night, in a friendly but perfectly genteel manner: and the one went back to her "place," and the other, to her room on the second-floor front.

There is no saying how long Miss Amelia Martin might have continued this course of life; how extensive a connection she might have established among young ladies in service; or what amount her demands upon their quarterly receipts might have ultimately attained, had not an unforeseen train of circumstances directed her thoughts to a sphere of action very different from dressmaking or millinery.

A friend of Miss Martin's who had long been keeping

company with an ornamental painter and decorator's journeyman, at last consented (on being at last asked to do so) to
name the day which would make the aforesaid journeyman
a happy husband. It was a Monday that was appointed for
the celebration of the nuptials, and Miss Amelia Martin was
invited, among others, to honour the wedding-dinner with
her presence. It was a charming party; Somers-town the
locality, and a front parlour the apartment. The ornamental
painter and decorator's journeyman had taken a house—no
lodgings nor vulgarity of that kind, but a house—four
beautiful rooms, and a delightful little washhouse at the end
of the passage—which was the most convenient thing in the
world, for the bridesmaids could sit in the front parlour and
receive the company, and then run into the little washhouse
and see how the pudding and boiled pork were getting on
in the copper, and then pop back into the parlour again, as
snug and comfortable as possible. And such a parlour as it
was! Beautiful Kidderminster carpet—six bran-new cane-
bottomed stained chairs—three wine-glasses and a tumbler on
each sideboard—farmer's girl and farmer's boy on the mantel-
piece: girl tumbling over a stile, and boy spitting himself, on
the handle of a pitchfork—long white dimity curtains in the
window—and, in short, everything on the most genteel scale
imaginable.

Then, the dinner. There was baked leg of mutton at the
top, boiled leg of mutton at the bottom, pair of fowls and
leg of pork in the middle; porter-pots at the corners;
pepper, mustard, and vinegar in the centre; vegetables on
the floor; and plum-pudding and apple-pie and tartlets
without number: to say nothing of cheese, and celery, and
water-cresses, and all that sort of thing. As to the company!
Miss Amelia Martin herself declared, on a subsequent
occasion, that, much as she had heard of the ornamental
painter's journeyman's connexion, she never could have
supposed it was half so genteel. There was his father, such a
funny old gentleman—and his mother, such a dear old lady

—and his sister, such a charming girl—and his brother, such a manly-looking young man—with such a eye! But even all these were as nothing when compared with his musical friends, Mr. and Mrs. Jennings Rodolph, from White Conduit, with whom the ornamental painter's journeyman had been fortunate enough to contract an intimacy while engaged in decorating the concert-room of that noble institution. To hear them sing separately, was divine, but when they went through the tragic duet of " Red Ruffian, retire ! " it was, as Miss Martin afterwards remarked, " thrilling." And why (as Mr. Jennings Rodolph observed) why were they not engaged at one of the patent theatres ? If he was to be told that their voices were not powerful enough to fill the House, his only reply was, that he would back himself for any amount to fill Russell-square—a statement in which the company, after hearing the duet, expressed their full belief; so they all said it was shameful treatment ; and both Mr. and Mrs. Jennings Rodolph said it was shameful too ; and Mr. Jennings Rodolph looked very serious, and said he knew who his malignant opponents were, but they had better take care how far they went, for if they irritated him too much he had not quite made up his mind whether he wouldn't bring the subject before Parliament ; and they all agreed that it " 'ud serve 'em quite right, and it was very proper that such people should be made an example of." So Mr. Jennings Rodolph said he'd think of it.

When the conversation resumed its former tone, Mr. Jennings Rodolph claimed his right to call upon a lady, and the right being conceded, trusted Miss Martin would favour the company—a proposal which met with unanimous approbation, whereupon Miss Martin, after sundry hesitatings and coughings, with a preparatory choke or two, and an introductory declaration that she was frightened to death to attempt it before such great judges of the art, commenced a species of treble chirruping containing frequent allusions to some young gentleman of the name of Hen-e-ry, with an occasional reference to madness and broken hearts. Mr. Jennings Rodolph frequently interrupted the progress of the song, by ejaculating "Beautiful!" — "Charming!" — "Brilliant!"—"Oh! splendid," &c.; and at its close the admiration of himself, and his lady, knew no bounds.

"Did you ever hear so sweet a voice, my dear?" inquired Mr. Jennings Rodolph of Mrs. Jennings Rodolph.

"Never; indeed I never did, love," replied Mrs. Jennings Rodolph.

"Don't you think Miss Martin, with a little cultivation, would be very like Signora Marra Boni, my dear?" asked Mr. Jennings Rodolph.

"Just exactly the very thing that struck me, my love," answered Mrs. Jennings Rodolph.

And thus the time passed away; Mr. Jennings Rodolph played tunes on a walking-stick, and then went behind the parlour-door and gave his celebrated imitations of actors, edge-tools, and animals; Miss Martin sang several other songs with increased admiration every time; and even the funny old gentleman began singing. His song had properly seven verses, but as he couldn't recollect more than the first one, he sang that over seven times, apparently very much to his own personal gratification. And then all the company sang the national anthem with national independence—each for himself, without reference to the other—and finally separated: all declaring that they never had spent so pleasant an evening: and Miss Martin inwardly resolving to adopt the advice of Mr. Jennings Rodolph, and to "come out" without delay.

Now, "coming out," either in acting, or singing, or society, or facetiousness, or anything else, is all very well, and remarkably pleasant to the individual principally concerned, if he or she can but manage to come out with a burst, and being out, to keep out, and not go in again; but, it does unfortunately happen that both consummations are extremely difficult to accomplish, and that the difficulties, of getting out at all in the first instance, and if you surmount them, of keeping out in the second, are pretty much on a par, an no slight ones either—and so Miss Amelia Martin shortly discovered. It is a singular fact (there being ladies in the case) that Miss Amelia Martin's principal foible was vanity, and the leading characteristic of Mrs. Jennings Rodolph an attachment to dress. Dismal wailings were heard to issue from the second-floor front of number forty-seven, Drummond-street, George-street, Euston-square; it was Miss Martin practising. Half-suppressed murmurs disturbed the calm dignity of the White Conduit orchestra at the commencement of the season. It was the appearance of Mrs. Jennings Rodolph in full dress, that occasioned them. Miss Martin studied incessantly—the practising was the consequence. Mrs. Jennings Rodolph taught gratuitously now and then—the dresses were the result.

Weeks passed away; the White Conduit season had begun, and progressed, and was more than half over. The dress-making business had fallen off, from neglect; and its profits had dwindled away almost imperceptibly. A benefit-night approached; Mr. Jennings Rodolph yielded to the earnest solicitations of Miss Amelia Martin, and introduced her personally to the "comic gentleman" whose benefit it was. The comic gentleman was all smiles and blandness—he had composed a duet, expressly for the occasion, and Miss Martin should sing it with him. The night arrived; there was an immense room—ninety-seven sixpenn'orths of gin-and-water, thirty-two small glasses of brandy-and-water, five-and-twenty bottled ales, and forty-one neguses; and the ornamental painter's journeyman, with his wife and a select circle of acquaintance, were seated at one of the side-tables near the orchestra. The concert began. Song—sentimental—by a light-haired young gentleman in a blue coat, and bright basket buttons—[applause]. Another song, doubtful, by another gentleman in another blue coat and more bright basket buttons—[increased applause]. Duet, Mr. Jennings Rodolph, and Mrs. Jennings Rodolph, "Red Ruffian, retire!"

—[great applause]. Solo, Miss Julia Montague (positively on this occasion only)—" I am a Friar"—[enthusiasm]. Original duet, comic—Mr. H. Taplin (the comic gentleman) and Miss Martin—" The Time of Day." "Brayvo!—Brayvo!" cried the ornamental painter's journeyman's party, as Miss Martin was gracefully led in by the comic gentleman. "Go to work, Harry," cried the comic gentleman's personal friends. "Tap—tap—tap," went the leader's bow on the music-desk. The symphony began, and was soon afterwards followed by a faint kind of ventriloquial chirping, proceeding apparently from the deepest recesses of the interior of Miss Amelia Martin. "Sing out"—shouted one gentleman in a white great-coat. "Don't be afraid to put the steam on, old gal," exclaimed another, "S—s—s—s—s—s—s"—went the five-and-twenty bottled ales. "Shame, shame!" remonstrated the ornamental painter's journeyman's party—"S—s—s—s" went the bottled ales again, accompanied by all the gins, and a majority of the brandies.

"Turn them geese out," cried the ornamental painter's journeyman's party, with great indignation.

"Sing out," whispered Mr. Jennings Rodolph.

"So I do," responded Miss Amelia Martin.

"Sing louder," said Mrs. Jennings Rodolph.

"I can't," replied Miss Amelia Martin.

"Off, off, off," cried the rest of the audience.

"Bray-vo!" shouted the painter's party. It wouldn't do—Miss Amelia Martin left the orchestra, with much less cere-mony than she had entered it; and, as she couldn't sing out, never came out. The general good humour was not restored until Mr. Jennings Rodolph had become purple in the face, by imitating divers quadrupeds for half an hour, without being able to render himself audible; and, to this day, neither has Miss Amelia Martin's good humour been restored, nor the dresses made for and presented to Mrs. Jennings Rodolph, nor the local abilities which Mr. Jennings Rodolph once staked his professional reputation that Miss Martin possessed.

CHAPTER IX

Of all the dancing academies that ever were established,
there never was one more popular in its immediate vicinity
than Signor Billsmethi's, of the "King's Theatre." It was
not in Spring-gardens, or Newman-street, or Berners-street,
or Gower-street, or Charlotte-street, or Percy-street, or any
other of the numerous streets which have been devoted time
out of mind to professional people, dispensaries, and boarding-
houses; it was not in the West-end at all—it rather approxi-
mated to the eastern portion of London, being situated in the
populous and improving neighbourhood of Gray's-inn-lane.
It was not a dear dancing academy—four-and-sixpence a
quarter is decidedly cheap upon the whole. It was *very*
select, the number of pupils being strictly limited to seventy-
five, and a quarter's payment in advance being rigidly exacted.
There was public tuition and private tuition—an assembly-
room and a parlour. Signor Billsmethi's family were always
thrown in with the parlour, and included in parlour price;
that is to say, a private pupil had Signor Billsmethi's parlour
to dance *in*, and Signor Billsmethi's family to dance *with*;
and when he had been sufficiently broken in in the parlour,
he began to run in couples in the assembly-room.

Such was the dancing academy of Signor Billsmethi, when
Mr. Augustus Cooper, of Fetter-lane, first saw an unstamped
advertisement walking leisurely down Holborn-hill, announcing

300

The Dancing Academy

to the world that Signor Billsmethi, of the King's Theatre, intended opening for the season with a Grand Ball.

Now, Mr. Augustus Cooper was in the oil and colour line —just of age, with a little money, a little business, and a little mother, who, having managed her husband and *his* business in his lifetime, took to managing her son and *his* business after his decease; and so, somehow or other, he had been cooped up in the little back parlour behind the shop on week-days, and in a little deal box without a lid (called by courtesy a pew) at Bethel Chapel, on Sundays, and had seen no more of the world than if he had been an infant all his days; whereas Young White, at the gas-fitter's over the way, three years younger than him, had been flaring away like winkin'—going to the theatre—supping at harmonic meetings —eating oysters by the barrel—drinking stout by the gallon —even stopping out all night, and coming home as cool in the morning as if nothing had happened. So Mr. Augustus Cooper made up his mind that he would not stand it any longer, and had that very morning expressed to his mother a firm determination to be "blowed," in the event of his not being instantly provided with a street-door key. And he was walking down Holborn-hill, thinking about all these things, and wondering how he could manage to get intro- duced into genteel society for the first time, when his eyes rested on Signor Billsmethi's announcement, which it imme- diately struck him was just the very thing he wanted; for he should not only be able to select a genteel circle of acquaint- ance at once, out of the five-and-seventy pupils at four-and- sixpence a quarter, but should qualify himself at the same time to go through a hornpipe in private society, with perfect ease to himself and great delight to his friends. So, he stopped the unstamped advertisement—an animated sandwich, composed of a boy between two boards—and having procured a very small card with the Signor's address indented thereon, walked straight at once to the Signor's house—and very fast he walked too, for fear the list should be filled up, and the five-and-seventy completed, before he got there. The Signor was at home, and, what was still more gratifying, he was an Englishman! Such a nice man—and so polite! The list was not full, but it was a most extraordinary circumstance that there was only just one vacancy, and even that one would have been filled up, that very morning, only Signor Billsmethi was dissatisfied with the reference, and, being very much afraid that the lady wasn't select, wouldn't take her.

"And very much delighted I am, Mr. Cooper," said Signor Billsmethi, "that I did *not* take her. I assure you, Mr. Cooper—I don't say it to flatter you, for I know you're above it—that I consider myself extremely fortunate in having a gentleman of your manners and appearance, sir."

"I am very glad of it too, sir," said Augustus Cooper.

"And I hope we shall be better acquainted, sir," said Signor Billsmethi.

"And I'm sure I hope we shall too, sir," responded Augustus Cooper. Just then, the door opened, and in came a young lady, with her hair curled in a crop all over her head, and her shoes tied in sandals all over her ankles.

"Don't run away, my dear," said Signor Billsmethi; for the young lady didn't know Mr. Cooper was there when she ran in, and was going to run out again in her modesty, all in confusion-like. "Don't run away, my dear," said Signor Billsmethi, "this is Mr. Cooper—Mr. Cooper, of Fetter-lane. Mr. Cooper, my daughter, sir—Miss Billsmethi, sir, who I hope will have the pleasure of dancing many a quadrille, minuet, gavotte, country-dance, fandango, double-hornpipe, and farinagholkajingo with you, sir. She dances them all, sir; and so shall you, sir, before you're a quarter older, sir."

And Signor Billsmethi slapped Mr. Augustus Cooper on the back, as if he had known him a dozen years,—so friendly; —and Mr. Cooper bowed to the young lady, and the young lady curtseyed to him, and Signor Billsmethi said they were as handsome a pair as ever he'd wish to see; upon which the young lady exclaimed, "Lor, pa!" and blushed as red as Mr.

302

Cooper himself—you might have thought they were both standing under a red lamp at a chemist's shop; and before Mr. Cooper went away it was settled that he should join the family circle that very night—taking them just as they were —no ceremony nor nonsense of that kind—and learn his positions in order that he might lose no time, and be able to come out at the forthcoming ball.

Well; Mr. Augustus Cooper went away to one of the cheap shoemakers' shops in Holborn, where gentlemen's dress-pumps are seven-and-sixpence, and men's strong walking just nothing at all, and bought a pair of the regular seven-and-sixpenny, long-quartered, town-mades, in which he astonished himself quite as much as his mother, and sallied forth to Signor Billsmethi's. There were four other private pupils in the parlour: two ladies and two gentlemen. Such nice people! Not a bit of pride about them. One of the ladies in particular, who was in training for a Columbine, was remarkably affable; and she and Miss Billsmethi took such an interest in Mr. Augustus Cooper, and joked, and smiled, and looked so bewitching, that he got quite at home, and learnt his steps in no time. After the practising was over, Signor Billsmethi, and Miss Billsmethi, and Master Billsmethi, and a young lady, and the two ladies, and the two gentlemen, danced a quadrille—none of your slipping and sliding about, but regular warm work, flying into corners, and diving among chairs, and shooting out at the door,—something like dancing! Signor Billsmethi in particular, notwithstanding his having a little fiddle to play all the time, was out on the landing every figure, and Master Billsmethi, when everybody else was breathless, danced a hornpipe, with a cane in his hand, and a cheese-plate on his head, to the unqualified admiration of the whole company. Then, Signor Billsmethi insisted, as they were so happy, that they should all stay to supper, and proposed sending Master Billsmethi for the beer and spirits, whereupon the two gentlemen swore, "strike 'em wulgar if they'd stand that;" and were just going to quarrel who should pay for it, when Mr. Augustus Cooper said he would, if they'd have the kindness to allow him—and they *had* the kindness to allow him; and Master Billsmethi brought the beer in a can, and the rum in a quart pot. They had a regular night of it; and Miss Billsmethi squeezed Mr. Augustus Cooper's hand under the table; and Mr. Augustus Cooper returned the squeeze, and returned home too, at something to six o'clock in the morning, when he was put to bed by main force by the apprentice, after repeatedly expressing an uncontrollable desire to pitch his revered parent out of the second-floor window, and to throttle the apprentice with his own neck-handkerchief.

Weeks had worn on, and the seven-and-sixpenny town-mades had nearly worn out, when the night arrived for the grand dress-ball at which the whole of the five-and-seventy pupils were to meet together, for the first time that season, and to take out some portion of their respective four-and-sixpences in lamp-oil and fiddlers. Mr. Augustus Cooper had ordered a new coat for the occasion—a two-pound-tenner from Turnstile. It was his first appearance in public; and, after a grand Sicilian shawl-dance by fourteen young ladies in cha-racter, he was to open the quadrille department with Miss Billsmethi herself, with whom he had become quite intimate since his first introduction. It *was* a night! Everything was admirably arranged. The sandwich-boy took the hats and bonnets at the street-door; there was a turn-up bedstead in the back parlour, on which Miss Billsmethi made tea and coffee for such of the gentlemen as chose to pay for it, and such of the ladies as the gentlemen treated; red port-wine negus and lemonade were handed round at eighteen-pence a head; and in pursuance of a previous engagement with the public-house at the corner of the street, an extra potboy was laid on for the occasion. In short, nothing could exceed the arrangements, except the company. Such ladies! Such pink silk stockings! Such artificial flowers! Such a number of cabs! No sooner had one cab set down a couple of ladies,

than another cab drove up and set down another couple of
ladies, and they all knew : not only one another, but the
majority of the gentlemen into the bargain, which made it all
as pleasant and lively as could be. Signor Billsmethi, in
black tights, with a large blue bow in his buttonhole, introduced the ladies to such of the gentlemen as were strangers :
and the ladies talked away—and laughed they did—it was
delightful to see them.

As to the shawl-dance, it was the most exciting thing that
ever was beheld ; there was such a whisking, and rustling,
and fanning, and getting ladies into a tangle with artificial
flowers, and then disentangling them again ! And as to Mr.
Augustus Cooper's share in the quadrille, he got through it
admirably. He was missing from his partner, now and then,
certainly, and discovered on such occasions to be either
dancing with laudable perseverance in another set, or sliding
about in perspective, without any definite object ; but,
generally speaking, they managed to shove him through the
figure, until he turned up in the right place. Be this as it
may, when he had finished, a great many ladies and gentlemen came up and complimented him very much, and said
they had never seen a beginner do anything like it before ;
and Mr. Augustus Cooper was perfectly satisfied with himself,
and everybody else into the bargain ; and " stood " considerable quantities of spirits-and-water, negus, and compounds,
for the use and behoof of two or three dozen very particular
friends, selected from the select circle of five-and-seventy pupils.

Now, whether it was the strength of the compounds, or the
beauty of the ladies, or what not, it did so happen that Mr.
Augustus Cooper encouraged, rather than repelled, the very
flattering attentions of a young lady in brown gauze over white
calico who had appeared particularly struck with him from
the first ; and when the encouragements had been prolonged
for some time, Miss Billsmethi betrayed her spite and jealousy
thereat by calling the young lady in brown gauze a " creeter,"
which induced the young lady in brown gauze to retort, in

305

certain sentences containing a taunt founded on the payment of four-and-sixpence a quarter, which reference Mr. Augustus Cooper, being then and there in a state of considerable bewilderment, expressed his entire concurrence in. Miss Bill-smethi, thus renounced, forthwith began screaming in the loudest key of her voice, at the rate of fourteen screams a minute; and being unsuccessful, in an onslaught on the eyes and face, first of the lady in gauze and then of Mr. Augustus Cooper, called distractedly on the other three-and-seventy pupils to furnish her with oxalic acid for her own private drinking; and, the call not being honoured, made another rush at Mr. Cooper, and then had her stay-lace cut, and was carried off to bed. Mr. Augustus Cooper, not being remark-able for quickness of apprehension, was at a loss to under-stand what all this meant, until Signor Billsmethi explained it in a most satisfactory manner, by stating to the pupils, that Mr. Augustus Cooper had made and confirmed divers promises of marriage to his daughter on divers occasions, and had now basely deserted her; on which, the indignation of the pupils became universal; and as several chivalrous gentlemen inquired rather pressingly of Mr. Augustus Cooper, whether he required anything for his own use, or, in other words, whether he "wanted anything for himself," he deemed it prudent to make a precipitate retreat. And the upshot of the matter was, that a lawyer's letter came next day, and an action was commenced next week; and that Mr. Augustus Cooper, after walking twice to the Serpentine for the purpose of drowning himself, and coming twice back without doing it, made a confidante of his mother, who compromised the matter with twenty pounds from the till: which made twenty pounds four shillings and sixpence paid to Signor Billsmethi, exclusive of treats and pumps. And Mr. Augustus Cooper went back and lived with his mother, and there he lives to this day; and as he has lost his ambition for society, and never goes into the world, he will never see this account of himself, and will never be any the wiser.

CHAPTER X

SHABBY-GENTEEL PEOPLE

THERE are certain descriptions of people who, oddly enough, appear to appertain exclusively to the metropolis. You meet them, every day, in the streets of London, but no one ever encounters them elsewhere; they seem indigenous to the soil, and to belong as exclusively to London as its own smoke, or the dingy bricks and mortar. We could illustrate the remark by a variety of examples, but, in our present sketch, we will only advert to one class as a specimen—that class which is so aptly and expressively designated as "shabby-genteel."

Now, shabby people, God knows, may be found anywhere, and genteel people are not articles of greater scarcity out of London than in it; but this compound of the two—this shabby-gentility—is as purely local as the statue at Charing-cross, or the pump at Aldgate. It is worthy of remark, too, that only men are shabby-genteel; a woman is always either dirty and slovenly in the extreme, or neat and respectable, however poverty-stricken in appearance. A very poor man, "who has seen better days," as the phrase goes, is a strange compound of dirty-slovenliness and wretched attempts at faded smartness.

We will endeavour to explain our conception of the term which forms the title of this paper. If you meet a man, lounging up Drury-lane, or leaning with his back against a post in Long-acre, with his hands in the pockets of a pair of drab trousers plentifully besprinkled with grease-spots: the trousers made very full over the boots, and ornamented with two cords down the outside of each leg—wearing, also, what has been a brown coat with bright buttons, and a hat very much pinched up at the side, cocked over his right eye—don't pity him. He is not shabby-genteel. The "harmonic meetings" at some fourth-rate public-house, or the purlieus of a private theatre, are his chosen haunts; he entertains a rooted antipathy to any kind of work, and is on familiar terms with several pantomime men at the large houses. But, if you see hurrying along a by-street, keeping as close as he can to the area-railings, a man of about forty or fifty, clad in an old rusty suit of threadbare black cloth which shines with constant wear as if it had been bees-waxed—the trousers tightly strapped down, partly for the look of the thing and partly to keep his old shoes from slipping off at the heels,—if you observe, too, that his yellowish-white neckerchief is carefully pinned up, to conceal the tattered garment underneath, and that his hands are encased in the remains of an old pair of beaver gloves, you may set him down as a shabby-genteel man. A glance at that depressed face, and timorous air of conscious poverty, will make your heart ache—always supposing that you are neither a philosopher nor a political economist.

We were once haunted by a shabby-genteel man; he was bodily present to our senses all day, and he was in our mind's eye all night. The man of whom Sir Walter Scott speaks in his Demonology, did not suffer half the persecution from his imaginary gentleman-usher in black velvet, that we sustained from our friend in quondam black cloth. He first attracted our notice, by sitting opposite to us in the reading-room at the British Museum; and what made the man more remarkable was, that he always had before him a couple of shabby-genteel books—two old dog's-eared folios, in mouldy worm-eaten covers, which had once been smart. He was in his chair, every morning, just as the clock struck ten; he was always the last to leave the room in the afternoon; and when he did, he quitted it with the air of a man who knew not where else to go, for warmth and quiet. There he used to sit all day, as close to the table as possible, in order to conceal the lack of buttons on his coat: with his old hat carefully deposited at his feet, where he evidently flattered himself it escaped observation.

About two o'clock, you would see him munching a French roll or a penny loaf; not taking it boldly out of his pocket at once, like a man who knew he was only making a lunch; but breaking off little bits in his pocket, and eating them by stealth. He knew too well it was his dinner.

When we first saw this poor object, we thought it quite impossible that his attire could ever become worse. We even went so far, as to speculate on the possibility of his shortly appearing in a decent second-hand suit. We knew nothing about the matter; he grew more and more shabby-genteel every day. The buttons dropped off his waistcoat, one by one; then, he buttoned his coat; and when one side of the coat was reduced to the same condition as the waistcoat, he buttoned it over on the other side. He looked somewhat better at the beginning of the week than at the conclusion, because the neckerchief, though yellow, was not quite so dingy; and, in the midst of all this wretchedness, he never appeared without gloves and straps. He remained in this state for a week or two. At length, one of the buttons on the back of the coat fell off, and then the man himself disappeared, and we thought he was dead.

We were sitting at the same table about a week after his disappearance, and as our eyes rested on his vacant chair, we insensibly fell into a train of meditation on the subject of his retirement from public life. We were wondering whether he had hung himself, or thrown himself off a bridge—whether he really was dead or had only been arrested—when our conjectures were suddenly set at rest by the entry of the man himself. He had undergone some strange metamorphosis, and walked up the centre of the room with an air which showed he was fully conscious of the improvement in his appearance. It was very odd. His clothes were a fine, deep, glossy black; and yet they looked like the same suit; nay, there were the very darns with which old acquaintance had made us familiar. The hat, too—nobody could mistake the shape of that hat, with its high crown gradually increasing in circumference towards the top. Long service had imparted to it a reddish-brown tint; but, now, it was as black as the coat. The truth flashed suddenly upon us—they had been " revived." It is a deceitful liquid that black and blue reviver; we have watched its effects on many a shabby-genteel man. It betrays its victims into a temporary assumption of impor- tance: possibly into the purchase of a new pair of gloves, or a cheap stock, or some other trifling article of dress. It elevates their spirits for a week, only to depress them, if possible, below their original level. It was so in this case; the transient dignity of the unhappy man decreased, in exact proportion as the " reviver " wore off. The knees of the unmentionables, and the elbows of the coat, and the seams generally, soon began to get alarmingly white. The hat was once more deposited under the table, and its owner crept into his seat as quietly as ever.

There was a week of incessant small rain and mist. At its expiration the " reviver " had entirely vanished, and the shabby-genteel man never afterwards attempted to effect any improvement in his outward appearance.

It would be difficult to name any particular part of town as the principal resort of shabby-genteel men. We have met a great many persons of this description in the neigh- bourhood of the inns of court. They may be met with, in Holborn, between eight and ten any morning; and whoever has the curiosity to enter the Insolvent Debtors' Court will observe, both among spectators and practitioners, a great variety of them. We never went on 'Change, by any chance, without seeing some shabby-genteel men, and we have often

310

wondered what earthly business they can have there. They will sit there, for hours, leaning on great, dropsical, mildewed umbrellas, or eating Abernethy biscuits. Nobody speaks to them, nor they to any one. On consideration, we remember to have occasionally seen two shabby-genteel men conversing together on 'Change, but our experience assures us that this is an uncommon circumstance, occasioned by the offer of a pinch of snuff, or some such civility.

It would be a task of equal difficulty, either to assign any particular spot for the residence of these beings, or to endeavour to enumerate their general occupations. We were never engaged in business with more than one shabby-genteel man; and he was a drunken engraver, and lived in a damp back-parlour in a new row of houses at Camden-town, half street, half brick-field, somewhere near the canal. A shabby-genteel man may have no occupation, or he may be a corn agent, or a coal agent, or a wine merchant, or a collector of debts, or a broker's assistant, or a broken-down attorney. He may be a clerk of the lowest description, or a contributor to the press of the same grade. Whether our readers have noticed these men, in their walks, as often as we have, we know not; this we know—that the miserably poor man (no matter whether he owes his distresses to his own conduct, or that of others) who feels his poverty and vainly strives to conceal it, is one of the most pitiable objects in human nature. Such objects, with few exceptions, are shabby-genteel people.

CHAPTER XI

DAMON and Pythias were undoubtedly very good fellows in their way: the former for his extreme readiness to put in special bail for a friend : and the latter for a certain trump-like punctuality in turning up just in the very nick of time, scarcely less remarkable. Many points in their character have, however, grown obsolete. Damons are rather hard to find, in these days of imprisonment for debt (except the sham ones, and they cost half-a-crown); and, as to the Pythiases, the few that have existed in these degenerate times, have had an unfortunate knack of making themselves scarce, at the very moment when their appearance would have been strictly classical. If the actions of these heroes, however, can find no parallel in modern times, their friendship can. We have Damon and Pythias on the one hand. We have Potter and Smithers on the other; and, lest the two last-mentioned names should never have reached the ears of our unenlightened readers, we can do no better than make them acquainted with the owners thereof.

Mr. Thomas Potter, then, was a clerk in the city, and Mr. Robert Smithers was a ditto in the same ; their incomes were limited, but their friendship was unbounded. They lived in the same street, walked into town every morning at the same hour, dined at the same slap-bang every day, and revelled in each other's company every night. They were knit

312

together by the closest ties of intimacy and friendship, or, as Mr. Thomas Potter touchingly observed, they were "thick-and-thin pals, and nothing but it." There was a spice of romance in Mr. Smithers's disposition, a ray of poetry, a gleam of misery, a sort of consciousness of he didn't exactly know what, coming across him he didn't precisely know why—which stood out in fine relief against the off-hand, dashing, amateur-pickpocket-sort-of-manner, which distinguished Mr. Potter in an eminent degree.

The peculiarity of their respective dispositions, extended itself to their individual costume. Mr. Smithers generally appeared in public in a surtout and shoes, with a narrow black neckerchief and a brown hat, very much turned up at the sides—peculiarities which Mr. Potter wholly eschewed, for it was his ambition to do something in the celebrated "kiddy" or stage-coach way, and he had even gone so far as to invest capital in the purchase of a rough blue coat with wooden buttons, made upon the fireman's principle, in which, with the addition of a low-crowned, flower-pot-saucer-shaped hat, he had created no inconsiderable sensation at the Albion in Little Russell-street, and divers other places of public and fashionable resort.

Mr. Potter and Mr. Smithers had mutually agreed that, on the receipt of their quarter's salary, they would jointly and in company "spend the evening"—an evident misnomer—the spending applying, as everybody knows, not to the evening itself but to all the money the individual may chance to be possessed of, on the occasion to which reference is made; and they had likewise agreed that, on the evening aforesaid, they would "make a night of it"—an expressive term, implying the borrowing of several hours from to-morrow morning, adding them to the night before, and manufacturing a compound night of the whole.

The quarter-day arrived at last—we say at last, because quarter-days are as eccentric as comets: moving wonderfully quick when you have a good deal to pay, and marvellously

313

slow when you have a little to receive. Mr. Thomas Potter and Mr. Robert Smithers met by appointment to begin the evening with a dinner; and a nice, snug, comfortable dinner they had, consisting of a little procession of four chops and four kidneys, following each other, supported on either side by a pot of the real draught stout, and attended by divers cushions of bread, and wedges of cheese.

When the cloth was removed, Mr. Thomas Potter ordered the waiter to bring in, two goes of his best Scotch whiskey, with warm water and sugar, and a couple of his "very mildest" Havannahs, which the waiter did. Mr. Thomas Potter mixed his grog, and lighted his cigar; Mr. Robert Smithers did the same; and then, Mr. Thomas Potter jocularly proposed as the first toast, "the abolition of all offices whatever" (not sinecures, but counting-houses), which was immediately drunk by Mr. Robert Smithers, with enthusiastic applause. So they went on, talking politics, puffing cigars, and sipping whiskey-and-water, until the "goes"—most appropriately so called—were both gone, which Mr. Robert Smithers perceiving, immediately ordered in two more goes of the best Scotch whiskey, and two more of the very mildest Havannahs; and the goes kept coming in, and the mild Havannahs kept going out, until, what with the drinking, and lighting, and puffing, and the stale ashes on the table, and the tallow-grease on the cigars, Mr. Robert Smithers began to doubt the mildness of the Havannahs, and to feel very much as if he had been sitting in a hackney-coach with his back to the horses.

As to Mr. Thomas Potter, he *would* keep laughing out loud, and volunteering inarticulate declarations that he was "all right;" in proof of which, he feebly bespoke the evening paper after the next gentleman, but finding it a matter of some difficulty to discover any news in its columns, or to ascertain distinctly whether it had any columns at all, walked slowly out to look for the moon, and, after coming back quite pale with looking up at the sky so long, and attempting

314

to express mirth at Mr. Robert Smithers having fallen asleep, by various galvanic chuckles, laid his head on his arm, and went to sleep also. When he awoke again, Mr. Robert Smithers awoke too, and they both very gravely agreed that it was extremely unwise to eat so many pickled walnuts with the chops, as it was a notorious fact that they always made people queer and sleepy; indeed, if it had not been for the whiskey and cigars, there was no knowing what harm they mightn't have done 'em. So they took some coffee, and after paying the bill,—twelve and twopence the dinner, and the odd tenpence for the waiter—thirteen shillings in all—started out on their expedition to manufacture a night.

It was just half-past eight, so they thought they couldn't do better than go at half-price to the slips at the City Theatre, which they did accordingly. Mr. Robert Smithers, who had become extremely poetical after the settlement of the bill, enlivening the walk by informing Mr. Thomas Potter in confidence that he felt an inward presentiment of approaching dissolution, and subsequently embellishing the theatre, by falling asleep, with his head and both arms gracefully drooping over the front of the boxes.

Such was the quiet demeanour of the unassuming Smithers, and such were the happy effects of Scotch whiskey and Havannahs on that interesting person! But Mr. Thomas Potter, whose great aim it was to be considered as a "knowing card," a "fast-goer," and so forth, conducted himself in a very different manner, and commenced going very fast indeed —rather too fast at last, for the patience of the audience to keep pace with him. On his first entry, he contented himself by earnestly calling upon the gentlemen in the gallery to "flare up," accompanying the demand with another request, expressive of his wish that they would instantaneously "form a union," both which requisitions were responded to, in the manner most in vogue on such occasions.

" Give that dog a bone! " cried one gentleman in his shirt-sleeves.

315

"Where have you been a having half a pint of intermediate beer?" cried a second. "Tailor!" screamed a third.
"Barber's clerk!" shouted a fourth. "Throw him o—ver!"
roared a fifth; while numerous voices concurred in desiring
Mr. Thomas Potter to "go home to his mother!" All these
taunts Mr. Thomas Potter received with supreme contempt,
cocking the low-crowned hat a little more on one side,
whenever any reference was made to his personal appearance,
and, standing up with his arms a-kimbo, expressing defiance
melodramatically.

The overture—to which these various sounds had been
an *ad libitum* accompaniment—concluded, the second piece
began, and Mr. Thomas Potter, emboldened by impunity,
proceeded to behave in a most unprecedented and outrageous
manner. First of all, he imitated the shake of the principal
female singer; then, groaned at the blue fire; then, affected
to be frightened into convulsions of terror at the appearance
of the ghost; and, lastly, not only made a running com-
mentary, in an audible voice, upon the dialogue on the stage,
but actually awoke Mr. Robert Smithers, who, hearing his
companion making a noise, and having a very indistinct
notion where he was, or what was required of him, immediately, by way of imitating a good example, set up the most
unearthly, unremitting, and appalling howling that ever
audience heard. It was too much. "Turn them out!" was
the general cry. A noise, as of shuffling of feet, and men
being knocked up with violence against wainscoting, was
heard: a hurried dialogue of "Come out?"—"I won't!"—
"You shall!"—"I shan't!"—"Give me your card, Sir?"
—"You're a scoundrel, Sir!" and so forth, succeeded.
A round of applause betokened the approbation of the
audience, and Mr. Robert Smithers and Mr. Thomas Potter
found themselves shot with astonishing swiftness into the
road, without having had the trouble of once putting foot to
ground during the whole progress of their rapid descent.

Mr. Robert Smithers, being constitutionally one of the

slow-goers, and having had quite enough of fast-going, in the course of his recent expulsion, to last until the quarter-day then next ensuing at the very least, had no sooner emerged with his companion from the precincts of Milton-street, than he proceeded to indulge in circuitous references to the beauties of sleep, mingled with distant allusions to the propriety of returning to Islington, and testing the influence of their patent Bramahs over the street-door locks to which they respectively belonged. Mr. Thomas Potter, however, was valorous and peremptory. They had come out to make a night of it: and a night must be made. So Mr. Robert Smithers, who was three parts dull, and the other dismal, despairingly assented; and they went into a wine-vaults, to get materials for assisting them in making a night; where they found a good many young ladies, and various old gentlemen, and a plentiful sprinkling of hackney-coachmen and cab-drivers, all drinking and talking together; and Mr. Thomas Potter and Mr. Robert Smithers drank small glasses of brandy, and large glasses of soda, until they began to have a very confused idea, either of things in general, or of anything in particular; and, when they had done treating themselves they began to treat everybody else; and the rest of the entertainment was a confused mixture of heads and heels, black eyes and blue uniforms, mud and gas-lights, thick doors, and stone paving.

Then, as standard novelists expressively inform us—"all was a blank!" and in the morning the blank was filled up with the words "STATION-HOUSE," and the station-house was filled up with Mr. Thomas Potter, Mr. Robert Smithers, and the major part of their wine-vault companions of the pre-ceding night, with a comparatively small portion of clothing of any kind. And it was disclosed at the Police-office, to the indignation of the Bench, and the astonishment of the spectators, how one Robert Smithers, aided and abetted by one Thomas Potter, had knocked down and beaten, in divers streets, at different times, five men, four boys, and three

317

women; how the said Thomas Potter had feloniously obtained possession of five door-knockers, two bell-handles, and a bonnet; how Robert Smithers, his friend, had sworn, at least forty pounds' worth of oaths, at the rate of five shillings apiece; terrified whole streets full of Her Majesty's subjects with awful shrieks and alarms of fire; destroyed the uniforms of five policemen; and committed various other atrocities, too numerous to recapitulate. And the magistrate, after an appropriate reprimand, fined Mr. Thomas Potter and Mr. Robert Smithers five shillings each, for being, what the law vulgarly terms, drunk; and thirty-four pounds for seventeen assaults at forty shillings a-head, with liberty to speak to the prosecutors.

The prosecutors *were* spoken to, and Messrs. Potter and Smithers lived on credit, for a quarter, as best they might; and, although the prosecutors expressed their readiness to be assaulted twice a week, on the same terms, they have never since been detected in "making a night of it."

CHAPTER XII

WE were passing the corner of Bow-street, on our return from a lounging excursion the other afternoon, when a crowd, assembled round the door of the Police-office, attracted our attention. We turned up the street accordingly. There were thirty or forty people, standing on the pavement and half across the road; and a few stragglers were patiently stationed on the opposite side of the way—all evidently waiting in expectation of some arrival. We waited too, a few minutes, but nothing occurred; so, we turned round to an unshorn, sallow-looking cobbler, who was standing next us with his hands under the bib of his apron, and put the usual question of "What's the matter?" The cobbler eyed us from head to foot, with superlative contempt, and laconically replied "Nuffin."

Now, we were perfectly aware that if two men stop in the street to look at any given object, or even to gaze in the air, two hundred men will be assembled in no time; but, as we knew very well that no crowd of people could by possibility remain in a street for five minutes without getting up a little amusement among themselves, unless they had some absorbing object in view, the natural inquiry next in order was, "What are all these people waiting here for?"—"Her Majesty's carriage," replied the cobbler. This was still more extraordinary. We could not imagine what earthly business Her

319

Majesty's carriage could have at the Public Office, Bow-street. We were beginning to ruminate on the possible causes of such an uncommon appearance, when a general exclamation from all the boys in the crowd of " Here's the wan ! " caused us to raise our heads, and look up the street.

The covered vehicle, in which prisoners are conveyed from the police-offices to the different prisons, was coming along at full speed. It then occurred to us, for the first time, that Her Majesty's carriage was merely another name for the prisoners' van, conferred upon it, not only by reason of the superior gentility of the term, but because the aforesaid van is maintained at Her Majesty's expense : having been originally started for the exclusive accommodation of ladies and gentlemen under the necessity of visiting the various houses of call known by the general denomination of " Her Majesty's Gaols."

The van drew up at the office-door, and the people thronged round the steps, just leaving a little alley for the prisoners to pass through. Our friend the cobbler, and the other stragglers, crossed over, and we followed their example. The driver, and another man who had been seated by his side in front of the vehicle, dismounted, and were admitted into the office. The office-door was closed after them, and the crowd were on the tiptoe of expectation.

After a few minutes' delay, the door again opened, and the two first prisoners appeared. They were a couple of girls, of whom the elder could not be more than sixteen, and the younger of whom had certainly not attained her fourteenth year. That they were sisters, was evident, from the resemblance which still subsisted between them, though two additional years of depravity had fixed their brand upon the elder girl's features, as legibly as if a red-hot iron had seared them. They were both gaudily dressed, the younger one especially ; and, although there was a strong similarity between them in both respects, which was rendered the more obvious by their being handcuffed together, it is impossible to conceive a greater contrast than the demeanour of the two presented.

REAPING THE WHIRLWIND

The younger girl was weeping bitterly—not for display, or in the hope of producing effect, but for very shame: her face was buried in her handkerchief: and her whole manner was but too expressive of bitter and unavailing sorrow.

"How long are you for, Emily?" screamed a red-faced woman in the crowd. "Six weeks and labour," replied the elder girl with a flaunting laugh; "and that's better than the stone jug anyhow; the mill's a deal better than the Sessions, and here's Bella a-going too for the first time. Hold up your head, you chicken," she continued, boisterously tearing the other girl's handkerchief away; "Hold up your head, and show 'em your face. I an't jealous, but I'm blessed if I an't game!"—"That's right, old gal," exclaimed a man in a paper cap, who, in common with the greater part of the crowd, had been inexpressibly delighted with this little incident.—"Right!" replied the girl; "ah, to be sure; what's the odds, eh?"—"Come! In with you," interrupted the driver. "Don't you be in a hurry, coachman," replied the girl, "and recollect I want to be set down in Cold Bath Fields—large house with a high garden-wall in front; you can't mistake it. Hallo. Bella, where are you going to— you'll pull my precious arm off?" This was addressed to the younger girl, who, in her anxiety to hide herself in the caravan, had ascended the steps first, and forgotten the strain upon the handcuff. "Come down, and let's show you the way." And after jerking the miserable girl down with a force which made her stagger on the pavement, she got into the vehicle, and was followed by her wretched companion.

These two girls had been thrown upon London streets, their vices and debauchery, by a sordid and rapacious mother. What the younger girl was then, the elder had been once; and what the elder then was, the younger must soon become. A melancholy prospect, but how surely to be realised; a tragic drama, but how often acted! Turn to the prisons and police offices of London—nay, look into the very streets themselves. These things pass before our eyes, day after day, and hour after hour—they have ·become such matters of course, that they are utterly disregarded. The progress of these girls in crime will be as rapid as the flight of a pestilence, resembling it too in its baneful influence and wide-spreading infection. Step by step, how many wretched females, within the sphere of every man's observation, have become involved in a career of vice, frightful to contemplate; hopeless at its commencement, loathsome and repulsive in its course; friendless, forlorn, and unpitied, at its miserable conclusion!

There were other prisoners—boys of ten, as hardened in vice as men of fifty—a houseless vagrant, going joyfully to prison as a place of food and shelter, handcuffed to a man whose prospects were ruined, character lost, and family rendered destitute, by his first offence. Our curiosity, however, was satisfied. The first group had left an impression on our mind we would gladly have avoided, and would willingly have effaced.

The crowd dispersed; the vehicle rolled away with its load of guilt and misfortune; and we saw no more of the Prisoners' Van.

TALES

CHAPTER I

Mrs. Tibbs was, beyond all dispute, the most tidy, fidgety, thrifty little personage that ever inhaled the smoke of London ; and the house of Mrs. Tibbs was, decidedly, the neatest in all Great Coram-street. The area and the area-steps, and the street-door and the street-door steps, and the brass handle, and the door-plate, and the knocker, and the fan-light, were all as clean and bright, as indefatigable white-washing, and hearth-stoning, and scrubbing and rubbing, could make them. The wonder was, that the brass door-plate, with the interesting inscription "Mrs. Tibbs," had never caught fire from constant friction, so perseveringly was it polished. There were meat-safe-looking blinds in the parlour-windows, blue and gold curtains in the drawing-room, and spring-roller blinds, as Mrs. Tibbs was wont in the pride of her heart to boast, "all the way up." The bell-lamp in the passage looked as clear as a soap-bubble; you could see yourself in all the tables, and French-polish yourself on any one of the chairs. The banisters were bees-waxed; and the very stair-wires made your eyes wink, they were so glittering.

Mrs. Tibbs was somewhat short of stature, and Mr. Tibbs was by no means a large man. He had, moreover, very short legs, but, by way of indemnification, his face was peculiarly long. He was to his wife what the 0 is in 90—he was of some importance *with* her—he was nothing without her. Mrs. Tibbs was always talking. Mr. Tibbs rarely spoke; but, if it were at any time possible to put in a word, when he should have said nothing at all, he had that talent. Mrs. Tibbs detested long stories, and Mr. Tibbs had one, the conclusion of which had never been heard by his most intimate friends. It always began, "I recollect when I was in the volunteer corps, in eighteen hundred and six,"—but, as he spoke very slowly and softly, and his better half very quickly and loudly, he rarely got beyond the introductory sentence. He was a melancholy specimen of the story-teller. He was the wandering Jew of Joe Millerism.

Mr. Tibbs enjoyed a small independence from the pension-list—about 43*l*. 15*s*. 10*d*. a year. His father, mother, and five interesting scions from the same stock, drew a like sum from the revenue of a grateful country, though for what particular service was never known. But, as this said independence was not quite sufficient to furnish two people with *all* the luxuries of this life, it had occurred to the busy little spouse of Tibbs, that the best thing she could do with a legacy of 700*l*., would be to take and furnish a tolerable house—somewhere in that partially-explored tract of country which lies between the British Museum, and a remote village called Somers-town —for the reception of boarders. Great Coram-street was the spot pitched upon. The house had been furnished accordingly; two female servants and a boy engaged; and an advertisement inserted in the morning papers, informing the public that "Six individuals would meet with all the comforts of a cheerful musical home in a select private family, residing within ten minutes' walk of"—everywhere. Answers out of number were received, with all sorts of initials; all the letters of the alphabet seemed to be seized with a sudden wish to go out boarding and lodging; voluminous was the correspondence between Mrs. Tibbs and the applicants; and

The Boarding-House

most profound was the secrecy observed. "E." didn't like this; "I." couldn't think of putting up with that; "I. O. U." didn't think the terms would suit him; and "G. R." had never slept in a French bed. The result, however, was, that three gentlemen became inmates of Mrs. Tibbs's house, on terms which were "agreeable to all parties." In went the advertisement again, and a lady with her two daughters, proposed to increase—not their families, but Mrs. Tibbs's.

"Charming woman, that Mrs. Maplesone!" said Mrs. Tibbs, as she and her spouse were sitting by the fire after breakfast; the gentlemen having gone out on their several avocations. "Charming woman, indeed!" repeated little Mrs. Tibbs, more by way of soliloquy than anything else, for she never thought of consulting her husband. "And the two daughters are delightful. We must have some fish to-day; they'll join us at dinner for the first time."

Mr. Tibbs placed the poker at right angles with the fire shovel, and essayed to speak, but recollected he had nothing to say.

"The young ladies," continued Mrs. T., "have kindly volunteered to bring their own piano."

Tibbs thought of the volunteer story, but did not venture it. A bright thought struck him—

"It's very likely—— " said he.

"Pray don't lean your head against the paper," interrupted Mrs. Tibbs; "and don't put your feet on the steel fender; that's worse."

Tibbs took his head from the paper, and his feet from the fender, and proceeded. "It's very likely one of the young ladies may set her cap at young Mr. Simpson, and you know a marriage—— "

"A what!" shrieked Mrs. Tibbs. Tibbs modestly repeated his former suggestion.

"I beg you won't mention such a thing," said Mrs. T. "A marriage, indeed!—to rob me of my boarders—no, not for the world."

SKETCHES BY BOZ

Tibbs thought in his own mind that the event was by no means unlikely, but, as he never argued with his wife, he put a stop to the dialogue, by observing it was "time to go to business." He always went out at ten o'clock in the morning, and returned at five in the afternoon, with an exceedingly dirty face, and smelling mouldy. Nobody knew what he was, or where he went; but Mrs. Tibbs used to say with an air of great importance, that he was engaged in the City.

The Miss Maplesones and their accomplished parent arrived in the course of the afternoon in a hackney-coach, and accompanied by a most astonishing number of packages. Trunks, bonnet-boxes, muff-boxes and parasols, guitar-cases, and parcels of all imaginable shapes, done up in brown paper, and fastened with pins, filled the passage. Then, there was such a running up and down with the luggage, such scampering for warm water for the ladies to wash in, and such a bustle, and confusion, and heating of servants, and curling-irons, as had never been known in Great Coram-street before. Little Mrs. Tibbs was quite in her element, bustling about, talking incessantly, and distributing towels and soap, like a head nurse in a hospital. The house was not restored to its usual state of quiet repose, until the ladies were safely shut up in their respective bedrooms, engaged in the important occupation of dressing for dinner.

"Are these gals 'andsome?" inquired Mr. Simpson of Mr. Septimus Hicks, another of the boarders, as they were amusing themselves in the drawing-room, before dinner, by lolling on sofas, and contemplating their pumps.

"Don't know," replied Mr. Septimus Hicks, who was a tallish, white-faced young man, with spectacles, and a black ribbon round his neck instead of a neckerchief—a most interesting person; a poetical walker of the hospitals, and a "very talented young man." He was fond of "lugging" into conversation all sorts of quotations from Don Juan, without fettering himself by the propriety of their application; in which particular he was remarkably independent.

326

INTRODUCTIONS

The other, Mr. Simpson, was one of those young men, who are in society what walking gentlemen are on the stage, only infinitely worse skilled in his vocation than the most indifferent artist. He was as empty-headed as the great bell of St. Paul's; always dressed according to the caricatures published in the monthly fashion; and spelt Character with a K.

"I saw a devilish number of parcels in the passage when I came home," simpered Mr. Simpson.

"Materials for the toilet, no doubt," rejoined the Don Juan reader.

——— "Much linen, lace, and several pair
Of stockings, slippers, brushes, combs, complete;
With other articles of ladies fair,
To keep them beautiful, or leave them neat."

"Is that from Milton?" inquired Mr. Simpson.

"No—from Byron," returned Mr. Hicks, with a look of contempt. He was quite sure of his author, because he had never read any other. "Hush! Here come the gals," and they both commenced talking in a very loud key.

"Mrs. Maplesone and the Miss Maplesones, Mr. Hicks. Mr. Hicks—Mrs. Maplesone and the Miss Maplesones," said Mrs. Tibbs, with a very red face, for she had been superintending the cooking operations below stairs, and looked like a wax doll on a sunny day. "Mr. Simpson, I beg your pardon—Mr. Simpson—Mrs. Maplesone and the Miss Maplesones"—and *vice versâ*. The gentlemen immediately began to slide about with much politeness, and to look as if they wished their arms had been legs, so little did they know what to do with them. The ladies smiled, curtseyed, and glided into chairs, and dived for dropped pocket-handkerchiefs : the gentlemen leant against two of the curtain-pegs; Mrs. Tibbs went through an admirable bit of serious pantomime with a servant who had come up to ask some question about the fish-sauce ; and then the two young ladies looked at each other; and everybody else appeared to discover something very attractive in the pattern of the fender.

327

"Julia, my love," said Mrs. Maplesone to her youngest daughter, in a tone loud enough for the remainder of the company to hear—"Julia."

"Yes, Ma."

"Don't stoop."—This was said for the purpose of directing general attention to Miss Julia's figure, which was undeniable. Everybody looked at her, accordingly, and there was another pause.

"We had the most uncivil hackney-coachman to-day, you can imagine," said Mrs. Maplesone to Mrs. Tibbs, in a confidential tone.

"Dear me!" replied the hostess, with an air of great commiseration. She couldn't say more, for the servant again appeared at the door, and commenced telegraphing most earnestly to her "Missis."

"I think hackney-coachmen generally *are* uncivil," said Mr. Hicks in his most insinuating tone.

"Positively I think they are," replied Mrs. Maplesone, as if the idea had never struck her before.

"And cabmen, too," said Mr. Simpson. This remark was a failure, for no one intimated, by word or sign, the slightest knowledge of the manners and customs of cabmen.

"Robinson, what *do* you want?" said Mrs. Tibbs to the servant, who, by way of making her presence known to her mistress, had been giving sundry hems and sniffs outside the door during the preceding five minutes.

"Please, ma'am, master wants his clean things," replied the servant, taken off her guard. The two young men turned their faces to the window, and "went off" like a couple of bottles of ginger-beer; the ladies put their handkerchiefs to their mouths; and little Mrs. Tibbs bustled out of the room to give Tibbs his clean linen,—and the servant warning.

Mr. Calton, the remaining boarder, shortly afterwards made his appearance, and proved a surprising promoter of the conversation. Mr. Calton was a superannuated beau— an old boy. He used to say of himself that although his

328

features were not regularly handsome, they were striking.
They certainly were. It was impossible to look at his face
without being reminded of a chubby street-door knocker,
half-lion half-monkey; and the comparison might be extended
to his whole character and conversation. He had stood still,
while everything else had been moving. He never originated
a conversation, or started an idea; but if any commonplace
topic were broached, or, to pursue the comparison, if anybody *lifted him up*, he would hammer away with surprising
rapidity. He had the tic-douloureux occasionally, and then
he might be said to be muffled, because he did not make
quite as much noise as at other times, when he would go on
prosing, rat-tat-tat the same thing over and over again. He
had never been married; but he was still on the look-out
for a wife with money. He had a life interest worth about
300*l.* a year—he was exceedingly vain, and inordinately
selfish. He had acquired the reputation of being the very
pink of politeness, and he walked round the park, and up
Regent-street, every day.

This respectable personage had made up his mind to
render himself exceedingly agreeable to Mrs. Maplesone—
indeed, the desire of being as amiable as possible extended
itself to the whole party; Mrs. Tibbs having considered it
an admirable little bit of management to represent to the
gentlemen that she had *some* reason to believe the ladies
were fortunes, and to hint to the ladies, that all the gentlemen were "eligible." A little flirtation, she thought, might
keep her house full, without leading to any other result.

Mrs. Maplesone was an enterprising widow of about fifty:
shrewd, scheming, and good-looking. She was amiably
anxious on behalf of her daughters; in proof whereof she
used to remark, that she would have no objection to marry
again, if it would benefit her dear girls—she could have no
other motive. The "dear girls" themselves were not at all
insensible to the merits of "a good establishment." One of
them was twenty-five; the other, three years younger. They

had been at different watering-places, for four seasons; they had gambled at libraries, read books in balconies, sold at fancy fairs, danced at assemblies, talked sentiment—in short, they had done all that industrious girls could do—but, as yet, to no purpose.

"What a magnificent dresser Mr. Simpson is!" whispered Matilda Maplesone to her sister Julia.

"Splendid!" returned the youngest. The magnificent individual alluded to wore a maroon-coloured dress-coat, with a velvet collar and cuffs of the same tint—very like that which usually invests the form of the distinguished unknown who condescends to play the "swell" in the pantomime at "Richardson's Show."

"What whiskers!" said Miss Julia.

"Charming!" responded her sister; "and what hair!" His hair was like a wig, and distinguished by that insinuating wave which graces the shining locks of those *chef-d'œuvres* of art surmounting the waxen images in Bartellot's window in Regent-street; his whiskers meeting beneath his chin, seemed strings wherewith to tie it on, ere science had rendered them unnecessary by her patent invisible springs.

"Dinner's on the table, ma'am, if you please," said the boy, who now appeared for the first time, in a revived black coat of his master's.

"Oh! Mr. Calton, will you lead Mrs. Maplesone?—Thank you." Mr. Simpson offered his arm to Miss Julia; Mr. Septimus Hicks escorted the lovely Matilda; and the procession proceeded to the dining-room. Mr. Tibbs was introduced, and Mr. Tibbs bobbed up and down to the three ladies like a figure in a Dutch clock, with a powerful spring in the middle of his body, and then dived rapidly into his seat at the bottom of the table, delighted to screen himself behind a soup-tureen, which he could just see over, and that was all. The boarders were seated, a lady and gentleman alternately, like the layers of bread and meat in a plate of sandwiches; and then Mrs. Tibbs directed James to take off the covers. Salmon, lobster-sauce, giblet-soup, and the usual accompaniments were *dis*-covered: potatoes like petrifactions, and bits of toasted bread, the shape and size of blank dice.

"Soup for Mrs. Maplesone, my dear," said the bustling Mrs. Tibbs. She always called her husband "my dear" before company. Tibbs, who had been eating his bread, and calculating how long it would be before he should get any fish, helped the soup in a hurry, made a small island on the table-cloth, and put his glass upon it, to hide it from his wife.

"Miss Julia, shall I assist you to some fish?"

"If you please—very little—oh! plenty, thank you" (a bit about the size of a walnut put upon the plate).

"Julia is a *very* little eater," said Mrs. Maplesone to Mr. Calton.

The knocker gave a single rap. He was busy eating the fish with his eyes: so he only ejaculated, "Ah!"

"My dear," said Mrs. Tibbs to her spouse after every one else had been helped, "what do *you* take?" The inquiry was accompanied with a look intimating that he mustn't say fish, because there was not much left. Tibbs thought the frown referred to the island on the table-cloth; he therefore coolly replied, "Why—I'll take a little—fish, I think."

"Did you say fish, my dear?" (another frown).

"Yes, dear," replied the villain, with an expression of acute hunger depicted in his countenance. The tears almost started to Mrs. Tibbs's eyes, as she helped her "wretch of a husband," as she inwardly called him, to the last eatable bit of salmon on the dish.

"James, take this to your master, and take away your master's knife." This was deliberate revenge, as Tibbs never could eat fish without one. He was, however, constrained to chase small particles of salmon round and round his plate with a piece of bread and a fork, the number of successful attempts being about one in seventeen.

331

"Take away, James," said Mrs. Tibbs, as Tibbs swallowed the fourth mouthful—and away went the plates like lightning.

"I'll take a bit of bread, James," said the poor "master of the house," more hungry than ever.

"Never mind your master now, James," said Mrs. Tibbs, "see about the meat." This was conveyed in the tone in which ladies usually give admonitions to servants in company, that is to say, a low one; but which, like a stage whisper, from its peculiar emphasis, is most distinctly heard by everybody present.

A pause ensued, before the table was replenished—a sort of parenthesis in which Mr. Simpson, Mr. Calton, and Mr. Hicks, produced respectively a bottle of sauterne, bucellas, and sherry, and took wine with everybody—except Tibbs. No one ever thought of him.

Between the fish and an intimated sirloin, there was a prolonged interval.

Here was an opportunity for Mr. Hicks. He could not resist the singularly appropriate quotation—

> "But beef is rare within these oxless isles;
> Goats' flesh there is, no doubt, and kid, and mutton,
> And when a holiday upon them smiles,
> A joint upon their barbarous spits they put on."

"Very ungentlemanly behaviour," thought little Mrs. Tibbs, "to talk in that way."

"Ah," said Mr. Calton, filling his glass. "Tom Moore is my poet."

"And mine," said Mrs. Maplesone.

"And mine," said Miss Julia.

"And mine," added Mr. Simpson.

"Look at his compositions," resumed the knocker.

"To be sure," said Simpson, with confidence.

"Look at Don Juan," replied Mr. Septimus Hicks.

"Julia's letter," suggested Miss Matilda.

"Can anything be grander than the Fire Worshippers?" inquired Miss Julia.

"To be sure," said Simpson.

"Or Paradise and the Peri," said the old beau.

"Yes; or Paradise and the Peer," repeated Simpson, who thought he was getting through it capitally.

"It's all very well," replied Mr. Septimus Hicks, who, as we have before hinted, never had read anything but Don Juan. "Where will you find anything finer than the description of the siege, at the commencement of the seventh canto?"

"Talking of a siege," said Tibbs, with a mouthful of bread—"when I was in the volunteer corps, in eighteen hundred and six, our commanding officer was Sir Charles Rampart; and one day, when we were exercising on the ground on which the London University now stands, he says, says he, Tibbs (calling me from the ranks), Tibbs——"

"Tell your master, James," interrupted Mrs. Tibbs, in an awfully distinct tone, "tell your master if he *won't* carve those fowls, to send them to me." The discomfited volunteer instantly set to work, and carved the fowls almost as expeditiously as his wife operated on the haunch of mutton. Whether he ever finished the story is not known; but, if he did, nobody heard it.

As the ice was now broken, and the new inmates more at home, every member of the company felt more at ease. Tibbs himself most certainly did, because he went to sleep immediately after dinner. Mr. Hicks and the ladies discoursed most eloquently about poetry, and the theatres, and Lord Chesterfield's Letters; and Mr. Calton followed up what everybody said, with continuous double knocks. Mrs. Tibbs highly approved of every observation that fell from Mrs. Maplesone; and as Mr. Simpson sat with a smile upon his face and said "Yes," or "Certainly," at intervals of about four minutes each, he received full credit for understanding what was going forward. The gentlemen rejoined the ladies in the drawing-room very shortly after they had left the dining-parlour. Mrs. Maplesone and Mr. Calton played

333

cribbage, and the "young people" amused themselves with music and conversation. The Miss Maplesones sang the most fascinating duets, and accompanied themselves on guitars, ornamented with bits of ethereal blue ribbon. Mr. Simpson put on a pink waistcoat, and said he was in raptures; and Mr. Hicks felt in the seventh heaven of poetry or the seventh canto of Don Juan—it was the same thing to him. Mrs. Tibbs was quite charmed with the new-comers; and Mr. Tibbs spent the evening in his usual way—he went to sleep, and woke up, and went to sleep again, and woke at supper-time.

* * * * * *

We are not about to adopt the licence of novel-writers, and to let "years roll on;" but we will take the liberty of requesting the reader to suppose that six months have elapsed, since the dinner we have described, and that Mrs. Tibbs's boarders have, during that period, sang, and danced, and gone to theatres and exhibitions, together, as ladies and gentlemen, wherever they board, often do. And we will beg them, the period we have mentioned having elapsed, to imagine farther, that Mr. Septimus Hicks received, in his own bedroom (a front attic), at an early hour one morning, a note from Mr. Calton, requesting the favour of seeing him, as soon as convenient to himself, in his (Calton's) dressing-room on the second-floor back.

"Tell Mr. Calton I'll come down directly," said Mr. Septimus to the boy. "Stop—is Mr. Calton unwell?" inquired this excited walker of hospitals, as he put on a bed-furniture-looking dressing-gown.

"Not as I knows on, sir," replied the boy. "Please, sir, he looked rather rum, as it might be."

"Ah, that's no proof of his being ill," returned Hicks, unconsciously. "Very well: I'll be down directly." Downstairs ran the boy with the message, and down went the excited Hicks himself, almost as soon as the message was delivered. "Tap, tap." "Come in."—Door opens, and

334

discovers Mr. Calton sitting in an easy chair. Mutual shakes of the hand exchanged, and Mr. Septimus Hicks motioned to a seat. A short pause. Mr. Hicks coughed, and Mr. Calton took a pinch of snuff. It was one of those interviews where neither party knows what to say. Mr. Septimus Hicks broke silence.

" I received a note— " he said, very tremulously, in a voice like a Punch with a cold.

" Yes," returned the other, " you did."

" Exactly. "

" Yes. "

Now, although this dialogue must have been satisfactory, both gentlemen felt there was something more important to be said; therefore they did as most men in such a situation would have done—they looked at the table with a determined aspect. The conversation had been opened, however, and Mr. Calton had made up his mind to continue it with a regular double knock. He always spoke very pompously.

" Hicks," said he, " I have sent for you, in consequence of certain arrangements which are pending in this house, connected with a marriage."

" With a marriage ! " gasped Hicks, compared with whose expression of countenance, Hamlet's, when he sees his father's ghost, is pleasing and composed.

" With a marriage," returned the knocker. " I have sent for you to prove the great confidence I can repose in you."

" And will you betray me ? " eagerly inquired Hicks, who in his alarm had even forgotten to quote.

" *I* betray *you* ! Won't *you* betray *me* ? "

" Never : no one shall know, to my dying day, that you had a hand in the business," responded the agitated Hicks, with an inflamed countenance, and his hair standing on end as if he were on the stool of an electrifying machine in full operation.

" People must know that, some time or other—within a

year, I imagine," said Mr. Calton, with an air of great self-complacency. "We *may* have a family."

"*We!*—That won't affect you, surely?"

"The devil it won't!"

"No! how can it?" said the bewildered Hicks. Calton was too much inwrapped in the contemplation of his happiness to see the equivoque between Hicks and himself; and threw himself back in his chair. "Oh, Matilda!" sighed the antique beau, in a lack-a-daisical voice, and applying his right hand a little to the left of the fourth button of his waistcoat, counting from the bottom. "Oh, Matilda!"

"What Matilda?" inquired Hicks, starting up.

"Matilda Maplesone," responded the other, doing the same.

"I marry her to-morrow morning," said Hicks.

"It's false," rejoined his companion: "I marry her!"

"You marry her?"

"I marry her!"

"You marry Matilda Maplesone?"

"Matilda Maplesone."

"*Miss* Maplesone marry *you?*"

"Miss Maplesone! No: Mrs. Maplesone."

"Good Heaven!" said Hicks, falling into his chair: "You marry the mother, and I the daughter!"

"Most extraordinary circumstance!" replied Mr. Calton, "and rather inconvenient too; for the fact is, that owing to Matilda's wishing to keep her intention secret from her daughters until the ceremony had taken place, she doesn't like applying to any of her friends to give her away. I entertain an objection to making the affair known to my acquaintance just now; and the consequence is, that I sent to you to know whether you'd oblige me by acting as father."

"I should have been most happy, I assure you," said Hicks, in a tone of condolence; "but, you see, I shall be acting as bridegroom. One character is frequently a consequence of the other; but it is not usual to act in both at the same time. There's Simpson—I have no doubt he'll do it for you."

"I don't like to ask him," replied Calton, "he's such a donkey."

Mr. Septimus Hicks looked up at the ceiling, and down at the floor; at last an idea struck him. "Let the man of the house, Tibbs, be the father," he suggested; and then he quoted, as peculiarly applicable to Tibbs and the pair—

> "Oh Powers of Heaven! what dark eyes meets she there?
> 'Tis—'tis her father's—fixed upon the pair."

"The idea has struck me already," said Mr. Calton : "but, you see, Matilda, for what reason I know not, is very anxious that Mrs. Tibbs should know nothing about it, till it's all over. It's a natural delicacy, after all, you know."

"He's the best-natured little man in existence, if you manage him properly," said Mr. Septimus Hicks. "Tell him not to mention it to his wife, and assure him she won't mind it, and he'll do it directly. My marriage is to be a secret one, on account of the mother and *my* father; therefore he must be enjoined to secrecy."

A small double knock, like a presumptuous single one, was that instant heard at the street-door. It was Tibbs ; it could be no one else; for no one else occupied five minutes in rubbing his shoes. He had been out to pay the baker's bill.

"Mr. Tibbs," called Mr. Calton in a very bland tone, looking over the banisters.

"Sir!" replied he of the dirty face.

"Will you have the kindness to step up-stairs for a moment?"

"Certainly, sir," said Tibbs, delighted to be taken notice of. The bedroom-door was carefully closed, and Tibbs, having put his hat on the floor (as most timid men do), and been accommodated with a seat, looked as astounded as if he were suddenly summoned before the familiars of the Inquisition.

"A rather unpleasant occurrence, Mr. Tibbs," said Calton,

337

in a very portentous manner, "obliges me to consult you, and to beg you will not communicate what I am about to say, to your wife."

Tibbs acquiesced, wondering in his own mind what the deuce the other could have done, and imagining that at least he must have broken the best decanters.

Mr. Calton resumed; "I am placed, Mr. Tibbs, in rather an unpleasant situation."

Tibbs looked at Mr. Septimus Hicks, as if he thought Mr. H.'s being in the immediate vicinity of his fellow-boarder might constitute the unpleasantness of his situation; but as he did not exactly know what to say, he merely ejaculated the monosyllable "Lor!"

"Now," continued the knocker, "let me beg you will exhibit no manifestations of surprise, which may be overheard by the domestics, when I tell you—command your feelings of astonishment—that two inmates of this house intend to be married to-morrow morning." And he drew back his chair, several feet, to perceive the effect of the unlooked-for announcement.

If Tibbs had rushed from the room, staggered down-stairs, and fainted in the passage—if he had instantaneously jumped out of the window into the mews behind the house, in an agony of surprise—his behaviour would have been much less inexplicable to Mr. Calton than it was, when he put his hands into his inexpressible-pockets, and said with a half-chuckle, "Just so."

"You are not surprised, Mr. Tibbs?" inquired Mr. Calton.

"Bless you, no, sir," returned Tibbs; "after all, it's very natural. When two young people get together, you know—"

"Certainly, certainly," said Calton, with an indescribable air of self-satisfaction.

"You don't think it's at all an out-of-the-way affair then?" asked Mr. Septimus Hicks, who had watched the countenance of Tibbs in mute astonishment.

"No, sir," replied Tibbs; "I was just the same at his age." He actually smiled when he said this.

"How devilish well I must carry my years!" thought the delighted old beau, knowing he was at least ten years older than Tibbs at that moment.

"Well, then, to come to the point at once," he continued, "I have to ask you whether you will object to act as father on the occasion?"

"Certainly not," replied Tibbs; still without evincing an atom of surprise.

"You will not?"

"Decidedly not," reiterated Tibbs, still as calm as a pot of porter with the head off.

Mr. Calton seized the hand of the petticoat-governed little man, and vowed eternal friendship from that hour. Hicks, who was all admiration and surprise, did the same.

"Now, confess," asked Mr. Calton of Tibbs, as he picked up his hat, "were you not a little surprised?"

"I b'lieve you!" replied that illustrious person, holding up one hand; "I b'lieve you! When I first heard of it."

"So sudden," said Septimus Hicks.

"So strange to ask *me*, you know," said Tibbs.

"So odd altogether!" said the superannuated love-maker; and then all three laughed.

"I say," said Tibbs, shutting the door which he had previously opened, and giving full vent to a hitherto corked-up giggle, "what bothers me is, what *will* his father say?"

Mr. Septimus Hicks looked at Mr. Calton.

"Yes; but the best of it is," said the latter, giggling in his turn, "I haven't got a father—he! he! he!"

"*You* haven't got a father. No; but *he* has," said Tibbs.

"*Who* has?" inquired Septimus Hicks.

"Why, *him*."

"Him, who? Do you know my secret? Do you mean me?"

"You! No; you know who I mean," returned Tibbs with a knowing wink.

"For Heaven's sake, whom *do* you mean?" inquired Mr. Calton, who, like Septimus Hicks, was all but out of his senses at the strange confusion.

"Why Mr. Simpson, of course," replied Tibbs; "who else could I mean?"

"I see it all," said the Byron-quoter; "Simpson marries Julia Maplesone to-morrow morning!"

"Undoubtedly," replied Tibbs, thoroughly satisfied, "of course he does."

It would require the pencil of Hogarth to illustrate—our feeble pen is inadequate to describe—the expression which the countenances of Mr. Calton and Mr. Septimus Hicks respectively assumed, at this unexpected announcement. Equally impossible is it to describe, although perhaps it is easier for our lady readers to imagine, what arts the three ladies could have used, so completely to entangle their separate partners. Whatever they were, however, they were successful. The mother was perfectly aware of the intended marriage of both daughters; and the young ladies were equally acquainted with the intention of their estimable parent. They agreed, however, that it would have a much better appearance if each feigned ignorance of the other's engagement; and it was equally desirable that all the marriages should take place on the same day, to prevent the discovery of one clandestine alliance, operating prejudicially on the others. Hence, the mystification of Mr. Calton and Mr. Septimus Hicks, and the pre-engagement of the unwary Tibbs.

On the following morning, Mr. Septimus Hicks was united to Miss Matilda Maplesone. Mr. Simpson also entered into a "holy alliance" with Miss Julia; Tibbs acting as father, "his first appearance in that character." Mr. Calton, not being quite so eager as the two young men, was rather struck by the double discovery; and as he had found some difficulty in getting any one to give the lady away, it occurred to him that the best mode of obviating the inconvenience would be not to take her at all. The lady, however, "appealed," as her counsel said on the trial of the cause, *Maplesone* v. *Calton*, for a breach of promise, " with a broken heart, to the outraged laws of her country." She recovered damages to the amount of 1,000*l.* which the unfortunate knocker was compelled to pay. Mr. Septimus Hicks having walked the hospitals, took it into his head to walk off altogether. His injured wife is at present residing with her mother at Boulogne. Mr. Simpson, having the misfortune to lose his wife six weeks after marriage (by her eloping with an officer during his temporary sojourn in the Fleet Prison, in consequence of his inability to discharge her little mantua-maker's bill), and being disinherited by his father, who died soon afterwards, was fortunate enough to obtain a permanent engagement at a fashionable haircutter's; hairdressing being a science to which he had frequently directed his attention. In this situation he had necessarily many opportunities of making himself acquainted with the habits, and style of thinking, of the exclusive portion of the nobility of this kingdom. To this fortunate circumstance are we indebted for the production of those brilliant efforts of genius, his fashionable novels, which so long as good taste, unsullied by exaggeration, cant, and quackery, continues to exist, cannot fail to instruct and amuse the thinking portion of the community.

It only remains to add, that this complication of disorders completely deprived poor Mrs. Tibbs of all her inmates, except the one whom she could have best spared—her husband. That wretched little man returned home, on the day of the wedding, in a state of partial intoxication; and, under the influence of wine, excitement, and despair, actually dared to brave the anger of his wife. Since that ill-fated hour he has constantly taken his meals in the kitchen, to which apartment, it is understood, his witticisms will be in future confined: a turn-up bedstead having been conveyed there by Mrs. Tibbs's order for his exclusive accommodation. It is possible that he

341

will be enabled to finish, in that seclusion, his story of the volunteers.

The advertisement has again appeared in the morning papers. Results must be reserved for another chapter.

CHAPTER THE SECOND.

"WELL!" said little Mrs. Tibbs to herself, as she sat in the front parlour of the Coram-street mansion one morning, mending a piece of stair-carpet off the first landing;—"Things have not turned out so badly, either, and if I only get a favourable answer to the advertisement, we shall be full again."

Mrs. Tibbs resumed her occupation of making worsted lattice-work in the carpet, anxiously listening to the two-penny postman, who was hammering his way down the street, at the rate of a penny a knock. The house was as quiet as possible. There was only one low sound to be heard—it was the unhappy Tibbs cleaning the gentlemen's boots in the back kitchen, and accompanying himself with a buzzing noise, in wretched mockery of humming a tune.

The postman drew near the house. He paused—so did Mrs. Tibbs. A knock—a bustle—a letter—post-paid.

"T. I. presents compt. to I. T. and T. I. begs To say that i see the advertisement And she will Do Herself the pleasure of calling On you at 12 o'clock to-morrow morning.

"T. I. as To apologise to I. T. for the shortness Of the notice But i hope it will not unconvenience you.

"I remain yours Truly
"Wednesday evening.'

Little Mrs. Tibbs perused the document, over and over again; and the more she read it, the more was she confused by the mixture of the first and third person; the substitution of the "i" for the "T. I.;" and the transition from the "I. T." to the "you." The writing looked like a skein of thread in

342

a tangle, and the note was ingeniously folded into a perfect square, with the direction squeezed up into the right-hand corner, as if it were ashamed of itself. The back of the epistle was pleasingly ornamented with a large red wafer, which, with the addition of divers ink-stains, bore a marvellous resemblance to a black beetle trodden upon. One thing, however, was perfectly clear to the perplexed Mrs. Tibbs. Somebody was to call at twelve. The drawing-room was forthwith dusted for the third time that morning; three or four chairs were pulled out of their places, and a corresponding number of books carefully upset, in order that there might be a due absence of formality. Down went the piece of stair-carpet before noticed, and up ran Mrs. Tibbs "to make herself tidy."

The clock of New Saint Pancras Church struck twelve, and the Foundling, with laudable politeness, did the same ten minutes afterwards. Saint something else struck the quarter, and then there arrived a single lady with a double knock, in a pelisse the colour of the interior of a damson pie; a bonnet of the same, with a regular conservatory of artificial flowers; a white veil, and a green parasol, with a cobweb border.

The visitor (who was very fat and red-faced) was shown into the drawing-room; Mrs. Tibbs presented herself, and the negotiation commenced.

"I called in consequence of an advertisement," said the stranger, in a voice as if she had been playing a set of Pan's pipes for a fortnight without leaving off.

"Yes!" said Mrs. Tibbs, rubbing her hands very slowly, and looking the applicant full in the face—two things she always did on such occasions.

"Money isn't no object whatever to me," said the lady, "so much as living in a state of retirement and obtrusion."

Mrs. Tibbs, as a matter of course, acquiesced in such an exceedingly natural desire.

"I am constantly attended by a medical man," resumed the pelisse wearer; "I have been a shocking unitarian for

343

some time—I, indeed, have had very little peace since the death of Mr. Bloss."

Mrs. Tibbs looked at the relict of the departed Bloss, and thought he must have had very little peace in his time. Of course she could not say so ; so she looked very sympathising.

" I shall be a good deal of trouble to you," said Mrs. Bloss ; "but, for that trouble I am willing to pay. I am going through a course of treatment which renders attention necessary. I have one mutton-chop in bed at half-past eight, and another at ten, every morning."

Mrs. Tibbs, as in duty bound, expressed the pity she felt for anybody placed in such a distressing situation ; and the carnivorous Mrs. Bloss proceeded to arrange the various preliminaries with wonderful despatch. " Now mind," said that lady, after terms were arranged ; " I am to have the second-floor front, for my bedroom ? "

" Yes, ma'am."

" And you'll find room for my little servant Agnes ? "

" Oh ! certainly."

" And I can have one of the cellars in the area for my bottled porter."

" With the greatest pleasure ;—James shall get it ready for you by Saturday."

" And I'll join the company at the breakfast-table on Sunday morning," said Mrs. Bloss. " I shall get up on purpose."

" Very well," returned Mrs. Tibbs, in her most amiable tone ; for satisfactory references had " been given and required," and it was quite certain that the new-comer had plenty of money. " It's rather singular," continued Mrs. Tibbs, with what was meant for a most bewitching smile, " that we have a gentleman now with us, who is in a very delicate state of health—a Mr. Gobler.—His apartment is the back drawing-room."

" The next room ? " inquired Mrs. Bloss.

" The next room," repeated the hostess.

A GENTLEMAN WITHOUT A STOMACH

"How very promiscuous!" ejaculated the widow.

"He hardly ever gets up," said Mrs. Tibbs in a whisper.

"Lor!" cried Mrs. Bloss, in an equally low tone.

"And when he is up," said Mrs. Tibbs, "we never can persuade him to go to bed again."

"Dear me!" said the astonished Mrs. Bloss, drawing her chair nearer Mrs. Tibbs. "What is his complaint?"

"Why, the fact is," replied Mrs. Tibbs, with a most communicative air, "he has no stomach whatever."

"No what?" inquired Mrs. Bloss, with a look of the most indescribable alarm.

"No stomach," repeated Mrs. Tibbs, with a shake of the head.

"Lord bless us! what an extraordinary case!" gasped Mrs. Bloss, as if she understood the communication in its literal sense, and was astonished at a gentleman without a stomach finding it necessary to board anywhere.

"When I say he has no stomach," explained the chatty little Mrs. Tibbs, "I mean that his digestion is so much impaired, and his interior so deranged, that his stomach is not of the least use to him;—in fact, it's an inconvenience."

"Never heard such a case in my life!" exclaimed Mrs. Bloss. "Why, he's worse than I am."

"Oh, yes!" replied Mrs. Tibbs;—"certainly." She said this with great confidence, for the damson pelisse suggested that Mrs. Bloss, at all events, was not suffering under Mr. Gobler's complaint.

"You have quite incited my curiosity," said Mrs. Bloss, as she rose to depart. "How I long to see him!"

"He generally comes down, once a week," replied Mrs. Tibbs; "I dare say you'll see him on Sunday." With this consolatory promise Mrs. Bloss was obliged to be contented. She accordingly walked slowly down the stairs, detailing her complaints all the way; and Mrs. Tibbs followed her, uttering an exclamation of compassion at every step. James (who looked very gritty, for he was cleaning the knives) fell up the kitchen-stairs, and opened the street-door; and, after mutual farewells, Mrs. Bloss slowly departed, down the shady side of the street.

It is almost superfluous to say, that the lady whom we have just shown out at the street-door (and whom the two female servants are now inspecting from the second-floor windows) was exceedingly vulgar, ignorant, and selfish. Her deceased better-half had been an eminent cork-cutter, in which capacity he had amassed a decent fortune. He had no relative but his nephew, and no friend but his cook. The former had the insolence one morning to ask for the loan of fifteen pounds; and, by way of retaliation, he married the latter next day; he made a will immediately afterwards, containing a burst of honest indignation against his nephew (who supported himself and two sisters on 100*l.* a year), and a bequest of his whole property to his wife. He felt ill after breakfast, and died after dinner. There is a mantelpiece-looking tablet in a civic parish church, setting forth his virtues, and deploring his loss. He never dishonoured a bill, or gave away a halfpenny.

The relict and sole executrix of this noble-minded man was an odd mixture of shrewdness and simplicity, liberality and meanness. Bred up as she had been, she knew no mode of living so agreeable as a boarding-house; and having nothing to do, and nothing to wish for, she naturally imagined she must be very ill—an impression which was most assiduously promoted by her medical attendant, Dr. Wosky, and her handmaid Agnes: both of whom, doubtless for good reasons, encouraged all her extravagant notions.

Since the catastrophe recorded in the last chapter, Mrs. Tibbs had been very shy of young-lady boarders. Her present inmates were all lords of the creation, and she availed herself of the opportunity of their assemblage at the dinner-table, to announce the expected arrival of Mrs. Bloss. The gentlemen received the communication with stoical indifference, and Mrs. Tibbs devoted all her energies to prepare for the reception of the valetudinarian. The second-floor front was scrubbed, and washed, and flannelled, till the wet went through to the drawing-room ceiling. Clean white counterpanes, and curtains, and napkins, water-bottles as clear as crystal, blue jugs, and mahogany furniture, added to the splendour, and increased the comfort, of the apartment. The warming-pan was in constant requisition, and a fire lighted in the room every day. The chattels of Mrs. Bloss were forwarded by instalments. First, there came a large hamper of Guinness's stout, and an umbrella; then, a train of trunks; then, a pair of clogs and a bandbox; then, an easy chair with an air-cushion; then, a variety of suspicious-looking packages; and—"though last not least"—Mrs. Bloss and Agnes: the latter in a cherry-coloured merino dress, open-work stockings, and shoes with sandals: like a disguised Columbine.

The installation of the Duke of Wellington, as Chancellor of the University of Oxford, was nothing, in point of bustle and turmoil, to the installation of Mrs. Bloss in her new quarters. True, there was no bright doctor of civil law to deliver a classical address on the occasion; but there were several other old women present, who spoke quite as much to the purpose, and understood themselves equally well. The chop-eater was so fatigued with the process of removal that she declined leaving her room until the following morning; so a mutton-chop, pickle, a pill, a pint bottle of stout, and other medicines, were carried up-stairs for her consumption.

"Why, what *do* you think, ma'am?" inquired the inquisitive Agnes of her mistress, after they had been in the house some three hours; "what *do* you think, ma'am? the lady of the house is married."

"Married!" said Mrs. Bloss, taking the pill and a draught of Guinness—"married! Unpossible!"

"She is indeed, ma'am," returned the Columbine; "and her husband, ma'am, lives—he—he—he—lives in the kitchen, ma'am."

"In the kitchen!"

347

"Yes, ma'am: and he—he—he—the housemaid says, he never goes into the parlour except on Sundays; and that Mrs. Tibbs makes him clean the gentlemen's boots; and that he cleans the windows, too, sometimes; and that one morning early, when he was in the front balcony cleaning the drawing-room windows, he called out to a gentleman on the opposite side of the way, who used to live here—'Ah! Mr. Calton, sir, how are you?'" Here the attendant laughed till Mrs. Bloss was in serious apprehension of her chuckling herself into a fit.

"Well, I never!" said Mrs. Bloss.

"Yes. And please, ma'am, the servants gives him gin-and-water sometimes; and then he cries, and says he hates his wife and the boarders, and wants to tickle them."

"Tickle the boarders!" exclaimed Mrs. Bloss, seriously alarmed.

"No, ma'am, not the boarders, the servants."

"Oh, is that all!" said Mrs. Bloss, quite satisfied.

"He wanted to kiss me as I came up the kitchen-stairs, just now," said Agnes, indignantly; "but I gave it him—a little wretch!"

This intelligence was but too true. A long course of snubbing and neglect; his days spent in the kitchen, and his nights in the turn-up bedstead, had completely broken the little spirit that the unfortunate volunteer had ever possessed. He had no one to whom he could detail his injuries but the servants, and they were almost of necessity his chosen confidants. It is no less strange than true, however, that the little weaknesses which he had incurred, most probably during his military career, seemed to increase as his comforts diminished. He was actually a sort of journeyman Giovanni of the basement story.

The next morning, being Sunday, breakfast was laid in the front parlour at ten o'clock. Nine was the usual time, but the family always breakfasted an hour later on sabbath. Tibbs enrobed himself in his Sunday costume—a black coat, and exceedingly short, thin trousers; with a very large white waistcoat, white stockings and cravat, and Blucher boots—and mounted to the parlour aforesaid. Nobody had come down, and he amused himself by drinking the contents of the milkpot with a teaspoon.

A pair of slippers were heard descending the stairs. Tibbs flew to a chair; and a stern-looking man, of about fifty, with very little hair on his head, and a Sunday paper in his hand, entered the room.

"Good morning, Mr. Evenson," said Tibbs, very humbly, with something between a nod and a bow.

"How do you do, Mr. Tibbs?" replied he of the slippers, as he sat himself down, and began to read his paper without saying another word.

"Is Mr. Wisbottle in town to-day, do you know, sir?" inquired Tibbs, just for the sake of saying something.

"I should think he was," replied the stern gentleman. "He was whistling 'The Light Guitar,' in the next room to mine, at five o'clock this morning."

"He's very fond of whistling," said Tibbs, with a slight smirk.

"Yes—I ain't," was the laconic reply.

Mr. John Evenson was in the receipt of an independent income, arising chiefly from various houses he owned in the different suburbs. He was very morose and discontented. He was a thorough radical, and used to attend a great variety of public meetings, for the express purpose of finding fault with everything that was proposed. Mr. Wisbottle, on the other hand, was a high Tory. He was a clerk in the Woods and Forests Office, which he considered rather an aristocratic employment; he knew the peerage by heart, and could tell you, off-hand, where any illustrious personage lived. He had a good set of teeth, and a capital tailor. Mr. Evenson looked on all these qualifications with profound contempt; and the consequence was that the two were always disputing, much to the edification of the rest of the house. It should be added,

349

that, in addition to his partiality for whistling, Mr. Wisbottle had a great idea of his singing powers. There were two other boarders, besides the gentleman in the back drawing-room —Mr. Alfred Tomkins and Mr. Frederick O'Bleary. Mr. Tomkins was a clerk in a wine-house; he was a connoisseur in paintings, and had a wonderful eye for the picturesque. Mr. O'Bleary was an Irishman, recently imported; he was in a perfectly wild state; and had come over to England to be an apothecary, a clerk in a government office, an actor, a reporter, or anything else that turned up—he was not particular. He was on familiar terms with two small Irish members, and got franks for everybody in the house. He felt convinced that his intrinsic merits must procure him a high destiny. He wore shepherd's-plaid inexpressibles, and used to look under all the ladies' bonnets as he walked along the streets. His manners and appearance reminded one of Orson.

"Here comes Mr. Wisbottle," said Tibbs; and Mr. Wisbottle forthwith appeared in blue slippers, and a shawl dressing-gown, whistling "*Di piacer.*"

"Good morning, sir," said Tibbs again. It was almost the only thing he ever said to anybody.

"How are you, Tibbs?" condescendingly replied the amateur; and he walked to the window, and whistled louder than ever.

"Pretty air, that!" said Evenson, with a snarl, and without taking his eyes off the paper.

"Glad you like it," replied Wisbottle, highly gratified.

"Don't you think it would sound better, if you whistled it a little louder?" inquired the mastiff.

"No; I don't think it would," rejoined the unconscious Wisbottle.

"I'll tell you what, Wisbottle," said Evenson, who had been bottling up his anger for some hours—"the next time you feel disposed to whistle 'The Light Guitar' at five o'clock in the morning, I'll trouble you to whistle it with

350

your head out o' window. If you don't, I'll learn the triangle
—I will, by—— "

The entrance of Mrs. Tibbs (with the keys in a little basket)
interrupted the threat, and prevented its conclusion.

Mrs. Tibbs apologised for being down rather late; the
bell was rung; James brought up the urn, and received an
unlimited order for dry toast and bacon. Tibbs sat down at
the bottom of the table, and began eating water-cresses like
a Nebuchadnezzar. Mr. O'Bleary appeared, and Mr. Alfred
Tomkins. The compliments of the morning were exchanged,
and the tea was made.

" God bless me ! " exclaimed Tomkins, who had been
looking out at the window. " Here—Wisbottle—pray come
here—make haste."

Mr. Wisbottle started from the table, and every one
looked up.

" Do you see," said the connoisseur, placing Wisbottle in
the right position—" a little more this way : there—do you
see how splendidly the light falls upon the left side of that
broken chimney-pot at No. 48 ? "

" Dear me ! I see," replied Wisbottle, in a tone of
admiration.

" I never saw an object stand out so beautifully against the
clear sky in my life," ejaculated Alfred. Everybody (except
John Evenson) echoed the sentiment; for Mr. Tomkins had
a great character for finding out beauties which no one else
could discover—he certainly deserved it.

" I have frequently observed a chimney-pot in College-green,
Dublin, which has a much better effect," said the patriotic
O'Bleary, who never allowed Ireland to be outdone on any
point.

The assertion was received with obvious incredulity, for Mr.
Tomkins declared that no other chimney-pot in the United
Kingdom, broken or unbroken, could be so beautiful as the
one at No. 48.

The room-door was suddenly thrown open, and Agnes

appeared, leading in Mrs. Bloss, who was dressed in a geranium-coloured muslin gown, and displayed a gold watch of huge dimensions; a chain to match; and a splendid assortment of rings, with enormous stones. A general rush was made for a chair, and a regular introduction took place. Mr. John Evenson made a slight inclination of the head; Mr. Frederick O'Bleary, Mr. Alfred Tomkins, and Mr. Wisbottle, bowed like the mandarins in a grocer's shop; Tibbs rubbed hands, and went round in circles. He was observed to close one eye, and to assume a clock-work sort of expression with the other; this has been considered as a wink, and it has been reported that Agnes was its object. We repel the calumny, and challenge contradiction.

Mrs. Tibbs inquired after Mrs. Bloss's health in a low tone. Mrs. Bloss, with a supreme contempt for the memory of Lindley Murray, answered the various questions in a most satisfactory manner; and a pause ensued, during which the eatables disappeared with awful rapidity.

"You must have been very much pleased with the appearance of the ladies going to the Drawing-room the other day, Mr. O'Bleary?" said Mrs. Tibbs, hoping to start a topic.

"Yes," replied Orson, with a mouthful of toast.

"Never saw anything like it before, I suppose?" suggested Wisbottle.

"No—except the Lord Lieutenant's levees," replied O'Bleary.

"Are they at all equal to our drawing-rooms?"

"Oh, infinitely superior!"

"Gad! I don't know," said the aristocratic Wisbottle, "the Dowager Marchioness of Publiccash was most magnificently dressed, and so was the Baron Slappenbachenhausen."

"What was he presented on?" inquired Evenson.

"On his arrival in England."

"I thought so," growled the radical; "you never hear of these fellows being presented on their going away again. They know better than that."

"Unless somebody pervades them with an apintment," said Mrs. Bloss, joining in the conversation in a faint voice.

"Well," said Wisbottle, evading the point, "it's a splendid sight."

"And did it never occur to you," inquired the radical, who never would be quiet; "did it never occur to you, that you pay for these precious ornaments of society?"

"It certainly *has* occurred to me," said Wisbottle, who thought this answer was a poser; "it *has* occurred to me, and I am willing to pay for them."

"Well, and it has occurred to me too," replied John Evenson, "and I ain't willing to pay for 'em. Then why should I?—I say, why should I?" continued the politician, laying down the paper, and knocking his knuckles on the table. "There are two great principles—demand——"

"A cup of tea if you please, dear," interrupted Tibbs.

"And supply——"

"May I trouble you to hand this tea to Mr. Tibbs?" said Mrs. Tibbs, interrupting the argument, and unconsciously illustrating it.

The thread of the orator's discourse was broken. He drank his tea and resumed the paper.

"If it's very fine," said Mr. Alfred Tomkins, addressing the company in general, "I shall ride down to Richmond to-day, and come back by the steamer. There are some splendid effects of light and shade on the Thames; the contrast between the blueness of the sky and the yellow water is frequently exceedingly beautiful." Mr. Wisbottle hummed, "Flow on, thou shining river."

"We have some splendid steam-vessels in Ireland," said O'Bleary.

"Certainly," said Mrs. Bloss, delighted to find a subject broached in which she could take part.

"The accommodations are extraordinary," said O'Bleary.

"Extraordinary indeed," returned Mrs. Bloss. "When Mr. Bloss was alive, he was promiscuously obligated to go to

353

Ireland on business. I went with him, and raly the manner in which the ladies and gentlemen were accommodated with berths, is not creditable."

Tibbs, who had been listening to the dialogue, looked aghast, and evinced a strong inclination to ask a question, but was checked by a look from his wife. Mr. Wisbottle laughed, and said Tomkins had made a pun; and Tomkins laughed too, and said he had not.

The remainder of the meal passed off as breakfasts usually do. Conversation flagged, and people played with their tea-spoons. The gentlemen looked out at the window; walked about the room; and, when they got near the door, dropped off one by one. Tibbs retired to the back parlour by his wife's orders, to check the greengrocer's weekly account; and ultimately Mrs. Tibbs and Mrs. Bloss were left alone together.

" Oh dear ! " said the latter, " I feel alarmingly faint ; it's very singular." (It certainly was, for she had eaten four pounds of solids that morning.) " By-the-bye," said Mrs. Bloss, " I have not seen Mr. What's-his-name yet."

" Mr. Gobler ? " suggested Mrs. Tibbs.

" Yes."

" Oh ! " said Mrs. Tibbs, " he is a most mysterious person. He has his meals regularly sent up-stairs, and sometimes don't leave his room for weeks together."

" I haven't seen or heard nothing of him," repeated Mrs. Bloss.

" I dare say you'll hear him to-night," replied Mrs. Tibbs ; " he generally groans a good deal on Sunday evenings."

" I never felt such an interest in any one in my life," ejaculated Mrs. Bloss. A little double-knock interrupted the conversation ; Dr. Wosky was announced, and duly shown in. He was a little man with a red face,—dressed of course in black, with a stiff white neckerchief. He had a very good practice, and plenty of money, which he had amassed by in-variably humouring the worst fancies of all the females of all the families he had ever been introduced into. Mrs. Tibbs offered to retire, but was entreated to stay.

"Well, my dear ma'am, and how are we?" inquired Wosky, in a soothing tone.

"Very ill, doctor—very ill," said Mrs. Bloss, in a whisper.

"Ah! we must take care of ourselves;—we must, indeed," said the obsequious Wosky, as he felt the pulse of his interesting patient.

"How is our appetite?"

Mrs. Bloss shook her head.

"Our friend requires great care," said Wosky, appealing to Mrs. Tibbs, who of course assented. "I hope, however, with the blessing of Providence, that we shall be enabled to make her quite stout again." Mrs. Tibbs wondered in her own mind what the patient would be when she was made quite stout.

"We must take stimulants," said the cunning Wosky— "plenty of nourishment, and, above all, we must keep our nerves quiet; we positively must not give way to our sensibilities. We must take all we can get," concluded the doctor, as he pocketed his fee, "and we must keep quiet."

"Dear man!" exclaimed Mrs. Bloss, as the doctor stepped into his carriage.

"Charming creature indeed—quite a lady's man!" said Mrs. Tibbs, and Dr. Wosky rattled away to make fresh gulls of delicate females, and pocket fresh fees.

As we had occasion, in a former paper, to describe a dinner at Mrs. Tibbs's; and as one meal went off very like another on all ordinary occasions; we will not fatigue our readers by entering into any other detailed account of the domestic economy of the establishment. We will therefore proceed to events, merely premising that the mysterious tenant of the back drawing-room was a lazy, selfish hypochondriac; always complaining and never ill. As his character in many respects closely assimilated to that of Mrs. Bloss, a very warm friendship soon sprung up between them. He was tall, thin, and pale; he always fancied he had a severe pain somewhere or other, and his face invariably wore a pinched, screwed-up expression; he looked, indeed, like a man who had got his feet in a tub of exceedingly hot water, against his will.

For two or three months after Mrs. Bloss's first appearance in Coram-street, John Evenson was observed to become, every day, more sarcastic and more ill-natured; and there was a degree of additional importance in his manner, which clearly showed that he fancied he had discovered something, which he only wanted a proper opportunity of divulging. He found it at last.

One evening, the different inmates of the house were assembled in the drawing-room engaged in their ordinary occupations. Mr. Gobler and Mrs. Bloss were sitting at a small card-table near the centre window, playing cribbage; Mr. Wisbottle was describing semicircles on the music-stool, turning over the leaves of a book on the piano, and humming most melodiously; Alfred Tomkins was sitting at the round table, with his elbows duly squared, making a pencil sketch of a head considerably larger than his own; O'Bleary was reading Horace, and trying to look as if he understood it; and John Evenson had drawn his chair close to Mrs. Tibbs's work-table, and was talking to her very earnestly in a low tone.

" I can assure you, Mrs. Tibbs," said the radical, laying his forefinger on the muslin she was at work on; "I can assure you, Mrs. Tibbs, that nothing but the interest I take in your welfare would induce me to make this communication. I repeat, I fear Wisbottle is endeavouring to gain the affections of that young woman, Agnes, and that he is in the habit of meeting her in the store-room on the first floor, over the leads. From my bedroom I distinctly heard voices there, last night. I opened my door immediately, and crept very softly on to the landing; there I saw Mr. Tibbs, who, it seems, had been disturbed also.—Bless me, Mrs. Tibbs, you change colour ! "

"No, no—it's nothing," returned Mrs. T. in a hurried manner; "it's only the heat of the room."

"A flush!" ejaculated Mrs. Bloss from the card-table; "that's good for four."

"If I thought it was Mr. Wisbottle," said Mrs. Tibbs, after a pause, "he should leave this house instantly."

"Go!" said Mrs. Bloss again.

"And if I thought," continued the hostess with a most threatening air, "if I thought he was assisted by Mr. Tibbs—"

"One for his nob!" said Gobler.

"Oh," said Evenson, in a most soothing tone—he liked to make mischief—"I should hope Mr. Tibbs was not in any way implicated. He always appeared to me very harmless."

"I have generally found him so," sobbed poor little Mrs. Tibbs; crying like a watering-pot.

"Hush! hush! pray—Mrs. Tibbs—consider—we shall be observed—pray, don't!" said John Evenson, fearing his whole plan would be interrupted. "We will set the matter at rest with the utmost care, and I shall be most happy to assist you in doing so."

Mrs. Tibbs murmured her thanks.

"When you think every one has retired to rest to-night," said Evenson very pompously, "if you'll meet me without a light, just outside my bedroom door, by the staircase window, I think we can ascertain who the parties really are, and you will afterwards be enabled to proceed as you think proper."

Mrs. Tibbs was easily persuaded; her curiosity was excited, her jealousy was roused, and the arrangement was forthwith made. She resumed her work, and John Evenson walked up and down the room with his hands in his pockets, looking as if nothing had happened. The game of cribbage was over, and conversation began again.

"Well, Mr. O'Bleary," said the humming-top, turning round on his pivot, and facing the company, "what did you think of Vauxhall the other night?"

"Oh, it's very fair," replied Orson, who had been enthusi-astically delighted with the whole exhibition.

"Never saw anything like that Captain Ross's set-out —eh?"

"No," returned the patriot, with his usual reservation— "except in Dublin."

"I saw the Count de Canky and Captain Fitzthompson in the Gardens," said Wisbottle; "they appeared much delighted."

"Then it *must* be beautiful," snarled Evenson.

"I think the white bears is partickerlerly well done," suggested Mrs. Bloss. "In their shaggy white coats, they look just like Polar bears—don't you think they do, Mr. Evenson?"

"I think they look a great deal more like omnibus cads on all fours," replied the discontented one.

"Upon the whole, I should have liked our evening very well," gasped Gobler; "only I caught a desperate cold which increased my pain dreadfully! I was obliged to have several shower-baths, before I could leave my room."

"Capital things those shower-baths!" ejaculated Wisbottle.

"Excellent!" said Tomkins.

"Delightful!" chimed in O'Bleary. (He had once seen one, outside a tinman's.)

"Disgusting machines!" rejoined Evenson, who extended his dislike to almost every created object, masculine, femi-nine, or neuter.

"Disgusting, Mr. Evenson!" said Gobler, in a tone of strong indignation.—"Disgusting! Look at their utility— consider how many lives they have saved by promoting perspiration."

"Promoting perspiration, indeed," growled John Evenson, stopping short in his walk across the large squares in the pattern of the carpet—"I was ass enough to be persuaded some time ago to have one in my bedroom. 'Gad, I was in it once, and it effectually cured *me*, for the mere sight of it threw me into a profuse perspiration for six months afterwards."

A titter followed this announcement, and before it had subsided James brought up "the tray," containing the remains of a leg of lamb which had made its *début* at dinner; bread; cheese; an atom of butter in a forest of parsley; one pickled walnut and the third of another; and so forth. The boy disappeared, and returned again with another tray, containing glasses and jugs of hot and cold water. The gentlemen brought in their spirit-bottles; the housemaid placed divers plated bedroom candlesticks under the card-table; and the servants retired for the night.

Chairs were drawn round the table, and the conversation proceeded in the customary manner. John Evenson, who never ate supper, lolled on the sofa, and amused himself by contradicting everybody. O'Bleary ate as much as he could conveniently carry, and Mrs. Tibbs felt a due degree of indignation thereat; Mr. Gobler and Mrs. Bloss conversed most affectionately on the subject of pill-taking, and other innocent amusements; and Tomkins and Wisbottle "got into an argument;" that is to say, they both talked very loudly and vehemently, each flattering himself that he had got some advantage about something, and neither of them having more than a very indistinct idea of what they were talking about. An hour or two passed away; and the boarders and the plated candlesticks retired in pairs to their respective bedrooms. John Evenson pulled off his boots, locked his door, and determined to sit up until Mr. Gobler had retired. He always sat in the drawing-room an hour after everybody else had left it, taking medicine, and groaning.

Great Coram-street was hushed into a state of profound repose: it was nearly two o'clock. A hackney-coach now and then rumbled slowly by; and occasionally some stray lawyer's clerk, on his way home to Somers-town, struck his iron heel on the top of the coal-cellar with a noise resembling the click of a smoke-jack. A low, monotonous, gushing sound was heard, which added considerably to the romantic dreariness of the scene. It was the water "coming in" at number eleven.

"He must be asleep by this time," said John Evenson to himself, after waiting with exemplary patience for nearly an hour after Mr. Gobler had left the drawing-room. He listened for a few moments; the house was perfectly quiet; he extinguished his rushlight, and opened his bedroom door. The staircase was so dark that it was impossible to see anything.

"S—s—s!" whispered the mischief-maker, making a noise like the first indication a catherine-wheel gives of the probability of its going off.

"Hush!" whispered somebody else.

"Is that you, Mrs. Tibbs?"

"Yes, sir."

"Where?"

"Here;" and the misty outline of Mrs. Tibbs appeared at the staircase window, like the ghost of Queen Anne in the tent scene in Richard.

"This way, Mrs. Tibbs," whispered the delighted busy-body: "give me your hand—there! Whoever these people are, they are in the store-room now, for I have been looking down from my window, and I could see that they accidentally upset their candlestick, and are now in darkness. You have no shoes on, have you?"

"No," said little Mrs. Tibbs, who could hardly speak for trembling.

"Well; I have taken my boots off, so we can go down, close to the store-room door, and listen over the banisters;" and down-stairs they both crept accordingly, every board creaking like a patent mangle on a Saturday afternoon.

"It's Wisbottle and somebody, I'll swear," exclaimed the radical in an energetic whisper, when they had listened for a few moments.

"Hush—pray let's hear what they say!" exclaimed Mrs.

Tibbs, the gratification of whose curiosity was now paramount to every other consideration.

" Ah ! if I could but believe you," said a female voice coquettishly, " I'd be bound to settle my missis for life."

" What does she say ? " inquired Mr. Evenson, who was not quite so well situated as his companion.

"She says she'll settle her missis's life," replied Mrs. Tibbs. " The wretch ! they're plotting murder."

" I know you want money," continued the voice, which belonged to Agnes : "and if you'd secure me the five hundred pound, I warrant she should take fire soon enough."

" What's that ? " inquired Evenson again. He could just hear enough to want to hear more.

" I think she says she'll set the house on fire," replied the affrighted Mrs. Tibbs. " But thank God I'm insured in the Phœnix ! "

" The moment I have secured your mistress, my dear," said a man's voice in a strong Irish brogue, " you may depend on having the money."

" Bless my soul, it's Mr. O'Bleary ! " exclaimed Mrs. Tibbs, in a parenthesis.

" The villain ! " said the indignant Mr. Evenson.

" The first thing to be done," continued the Hibernian, " is to poison Mr. Gobler's mind."

" Oh, certainly," returned Agnes.

" What's that ? " inquired Evenson again, in an agony of curiosity and a whisper.

" He says she's to mind and poison Mr. Gobler," replied Mrs. Tibbs, aghast at this sacrifice of human life.

" And in regard of Mrs. Tibbs," continued O'Bleary.—Mrs. Tibbs shuddered.

" Hush ! " exclaimed Agnes, in a tone of the greatest alarm, just as Mrs. Tibbs was on the extreme verge of a fainting fit. " Hush ! "

" Hush ! " exclaimed Evenson, at the same moment to Mrs. Tibbs.

"There's somebody coming *up*-stairs," said Agnes to O'Bleary.

"There's somebody coming *down*-stairs," whispered Evenson to Mrs. Tibbs.

"Go into the parlour, sir," said Agnes to her companion. "You will get there, before whoever it is, gets to the top of the kitchen stairs."

"The drawing-room, Mrs. Tibbs!" whispered the astonished Evenson to his equally astonished companion; and for the drawing-room they both made, plainly hearing the rustling of two persons, one coming down-stairs, and one coming up.

"What can it be?" exclaimed Mrs. Tibbs. "It's like a dream. I wouldn't be found in this situation for the world!"

"Nor I," returned Evenson, who could never bear a joke at his own expense. "Hush! here they are at the door."

"What fun!" whispered one of the new-comers.—It was Wisbottle.

"Glorious!" replied his companion, in an equally low tone.—This was Alfred Tomkins. "Who would have thought it?"

"I told you so," said Wisbottle, in a most knowing whisper. "Lord bless you, he has paid her most extraordinary attention for the last two months. I saw 'em when I was sitting at the piano to-night."

"Well, do you know I didn't notice it?" interrupted Tomkins.

"Not notice it!" continued Wisbottle. "Bless you; I saw him whispering to her, and she crying; and then I'll swear I heard him say something about to-night when we were all in bed."

"They're talking of *us!*" exclaimed the agonised Mrs. Tibbs, as the painful suspicion, and a sense of their situation, flashed upon her mind.

362

THE VALOROUS TIBBS.

"I know it—I know it," replied Evenson, with a melancholy consciousness that there was no mode of escape.

"What's to be done? we cannot both stop here!" ejaculated Mrs. Tibbs, in a state of partial derangement.

"I'll get up the chimney," replied Evenson, who really meant what he said.

"You can't," said Mrs. Tibbs, in despair. "You can't—it's a register stove."

"Hush!" repeated John Evenson.

"Hush—hush!" cried somebody down-stairs.

"What a d—d hushing!" said Alfred Tomkins, who began to get rather bewildered.

"There they are!" exclaimed the sapient Wisbottle, as a rustling noise was heard in the store-room.

"Hark!" whispered both the young men.

"Hark!" repeated Mrs. Tibbs and Evenson.

"Let me alone, sir," said a female voice in the store-room.

"Oh, Hagnes!" cried another voice, which clearly belonged to Tibbs, for nobody else ever owned one like it. "Oh, Hagnes—lovely creature!"

"Be quiet, sir!" (A bounce.)

"Hag——"

"Be quiet, sir—I am ashamed of you. Think of your wife, Mr. Tibbs. Be quiet, sir!"

"My wife!" exclaimed the valorous Tibbs, who was clearly under the influence of gin-and-water, and a misplaced attachment; "I ate her! Oh, Hagnes! when I was in the volunteer corps, in eighteen hundred and——"

"I declare I'll scream. Be quiet, sir, will you?" (Another bounce and a scuffle.)

"What's that?" exclaimed Tibbs, with a start.

"What's what?" said Agnes, stopping short.

"Why that!"

"Ah! you have done it nicely now, sir," sobbed the frightened Agnes, as a tapping was heard at Mrs. Tibbs's

363

bedroom door, which would have beaten any dozen wood-peckers hollow.

"Mrs. Tibbs! Mrs. Tibbs!" called out Mrs. Bloss. "Mrs. Tibbs, pray get up." (Here the imitation of a woodpecker was resumed with tenfold violence.)

"Oh, dear—dear!" exclaimed the wretched partner of the depraved Tibbs. "She's knocking at my door. We must be discovered! What will they think?"

"Mrs. Tibbs! Mrs. Tibbs!" screamed the woodpecker again.

"What's the matter!" shouted Gobler, bursting out of the back drawing-room, like the dragon at Astley's.

"Oh, Mr. Gobler!" cried Mrs. Bloss, with a proper approximation to hysterics; "I think the house is on fire, or else there's thieves in it. I have heard the most dreadful noises!"

"The devil you have!" shouted Gobler again, bouncing back into his den, in happy imitation of the aforesaid dragon, and returning immediately with a lighted candle. "Why, what's this? Wisbottle! Tomkins! O'Bleary! Agnes! What the deuce! all up and dressed?"

"Astonishing!" said Mrs. Bloss, who had run down-stairs, and taken Mr. Gobler's arm.

"Call Mrs. Tibbs directly, somebody," said Gobler, turning into the front drawing-room.—"What! Mrs. Tibbs and Mr. Evenson!!"

"Mrs. Tibbs and Mr. Evenson!" repeated everybody, as that unhappy pair were discovered: Mrs. Tibbs seated in an arm-chair by the fireplace, and Mr. Evenson standing by her side.

We must leave the scene that ensued to the reader's imagina-tion. We could tell, how Mrs. Tibbs forthwith fainted away, and how it required the united strength of Mr. Wisbottle and Mr. Alfred Tomkins to hold her in her chair; how Mr. Evenson explained, and how his explanation was evidently disbelieved; how Agnes repelled the accusations of Mrs.

Tibbs by proving that she was negotiating with Mr. O'Bleary to influence her mistress's affections in his behalf; and how Mr. Gobler threw a damp counterpane on the hopes of Mr. O'Bleary by avowing that he (Gobler) had already proposed to, and been accepted by, Mrs. Bloss; how Agnes was discharged from that lady's service; how Mr. O'Bleary discharged himself from Mrs. Tibbs's house, without going through the form of previously discharging his bill; and how that disappointed young gentleman rails against England and the English, and vows there is no virtue or fine feeling extant, "except in Ireland." We repeat that we *could* tell all this, but we love to exercise our self-denial, and we therefore prefer leaving it to be imagined.

The lady whom we have hitherto described as Mrs. Bloss, is no more. Mrs. Gobler exists: Mrs. Bloss has left us for ever. In a secluded retreat in Newington Butts, far, far removed from the noisy strife of that great boarding-house, the world, the enviable Gobler and his pleasing wife revel in retirement: happy in their complaints, their table, and their medicine; wafted through life by the grateful prayers of all the purveyors of animal food within three miles round.

We would willingly stop here, but we have a painful duty imposed upon us, which we must discharge. Mr. and Mrs. Tibbs have separated by mutual consent, Mrs. Tibbs receiving one moiety of 43*l.* 15*s.* 10*d.*, which we before stated to be the amount of her husband's annual income, and Mr. Tibbs the other. He is spending the evening of his days in retirement; and he is spending also, annually, that small but honourable independence. He resides among the original settlers at Walworth; and it has been stated, on unquestionable authority, that the conclusion of the volunteer story has been heard in a small tavern in that respectable neighbourhood.

The unfortunate Mrs. Tibbs has determined to dispose of the whole of her furniture by public auction, and to retire from a residence in which she has suffered so much. Mr.

SKETCHES BY BOZ

Robins has been applied to, to conduct the sale, and the transcendent abilities of the literary gentlemen connected with his establishment are now devoted to the task of drawing up the preliminary advertisement. It is to contain, among a variety of brilliant matter, seventy-eight words in large capitals, and six original quotations in inverted commas.

CHAPTER II.

Mr. Augustus Minns was a bachelor, of about forty as he said—of about eight-and-forty as his friends said. He was always exceedingly clean, precise, and tidy; perhaps somewhat priggish, and the most retiring man in the world. He usually wore a brown frock-coat without a wrinkle, light inexplicables without a spot, a neat neckerchief with a remarkably neat tie, and boots without a fault; moreover, he always carried a brown silk umbrella with an ivory handle. He was a clerk in Somerset-house, or, as he said himself, he held "a responsible situation under Government." He had a good and increasing salary, in addition to some 10,000*l.* of his own (invested in the funds), and he occupied a first floor in Tavistock-street, Covent-garden, where he had resided for twenty years, having been in the habit of quarrelling with his landlord the whole time: regularly giving notice of his intention to quit on the first day of every quarter, and as regularly countermanding it on the second. There were two classes of created objects which he held in the deepest and most unmingled horror; these were dogs, and children. He was not unamiable, but he could, at any time, have viewed the execution of a dog, or the assassination of an infant, with the liveliest satisfaction. Their habits were at variance with his love of order; and his love of order was as powerful as his love of life. Mr. Augustus Minns had no relations, in or near London, with the exception of his cousin, Mr. Octavius

367

Budden, to whose son, whom he had never seen (for he disliked the father), he had consented to become godfather by proxy. Mr. Budden having realised a moderate fortune by exercising the trade or calling of a corn-chandler, and having a great predilection for the country, had purchased a cottage in the vicinity of Stamford-hill, whither he retired with the wife of his bosom, and his only son, Master Alexander Augustus Budden. One evening, as Mr. and Mrs. B. were admiring their son, discussing his various merits, talking over his education, and disputing whether the classics should be made an essential part thereof, the lady pressed so strongly upon her husband the propriety of cultivating the friendship of Mr. Minns in behalf of their son, that Mr. Budden at last made up his mind, that it should not be his fault if he and his cousin were not in future more intimate.

"I'll break the ice, my love," said Mr. Budden, stirring up the sugar at the bottom of his glass of brandy-and-water, and casting a sidelong look at his spouse to see the effect of the announcement of his determination, "by asking Minns down to dine with us, on Sunday."

"Then pray, Budden, write to your cousin at once," replied Mrs. Budden. "Who knows, if we could only get him down here, but he might take a fancy to our Alexander, and leave him his property?—Alick, my dear, take your legs off the rail of the chair!"

"Very true," said Mr. Budden, musing, "very true indeed, my love!"

On the following morning, as Mr. Minns was sitting at his breakfast-table, alternately biting his dry toast and casting a look upon the columns of his morning paper, which he always read from the title to the printer's name, he heard a loud knock at the street-door; which was shortly afterwards followed by the entrance of his servant, who put into his hands a particularly small card, on which was engraven in immense letters, "Mr. Octavius Budden, Amelia Cottage (Mrs. B.'s name was Amelia), Poplar-walk, Stamford-hill."

George Cruikshank.

Mr. Minns and his Cousin

" Budden ! " ejaculated Minns, " what can bring that vulgar man here !—say I'm asleep—say I'm out, and shall never be home again—anything to keep him down-stairs."

" But please, sir, the gentleman's coming up," replied the servant, and the fact was made evident, by an appalling creaking of boots on the staircase accompanied by a pattering noise ; the cause of which, Minns could not, for the life of him, divine.

" Hem—show the gentleman in," said the unfortunate bachelor. Exit servant, and enter Octavius preceded by a large white dog, dressed in a suit of fleecy hosiery, with pink eyes, large ears, and no perceptible tail.

The cause of the pattering on the stairs was but too plain. Mr. Augustus Minns staggered beneath the shock of the dog's appearance.

" My dear fellow, how are you ? " said Budden, as he entered.

He always spoke at the top of his voice, and always said the same thing half-a-dozen times.

" How are you, my hearty ? "

" How do you do, Mr. Budden ?—pray take a chair ! " politely stammered the discomfited Minns.

" Thank you—thank you—well—how are you, eh ? "

" Uncommonly well, thank you," said Minns, casting a diabolical look at the dog, who, with his hind legs on the floor, and his fore paws resting on the table, was dragging a bit of bread and butter out of a plate, preparatory to devouring it, with the buttered side next the carpet.

" Ah, you rogue ! " said Budden to his dog ; " you see, Minns, he's like me, always at home, eh, my boy !—Egad, I'm precious hot and hungry ! I've walked all the way from Stamford-hill this morning."

" Have you breakfasted ? " inquired Minns.

" Oh, no !—came to breakfast with you ; so ring the bell, my dear fellow, will you ? and let's have another cup and saucer, and the cold ham.—Make myself at home, you see ! "

continued Budden, dusting his boots with a table-napkin. "Ha!—ha!—ha!—'pon my life, I'm hungry."

Minns rang the bell, and tried to smile.

"I decidedly never was so hot in my life," continued Octavius, wiping his forehead; "well, but how are you, Minns? 'Pon my soul, you wear capitally!"

"D'ye think so?" said Minns; and he tried another smile. "'Pon my life, I do!"

"Mrs. B. and—what's his name—quite well?"

"Alick—my son, you mean; never better—never better. But at such a place as we've got at Poplar-walk, you know, he couldn't be ill if he tried. When I first saw it, by Jove! it looked so knowing, with the front garden, and the green railings, and the brass knocker, and all that—I really thought it was a cut above me."

"Don't you think you'd like the ham better," interrupted Minns, "if you cut it the other way?" He saw, with feelings which it is impossible to describe, that his visitor was cutting or rather maiming the ham, in utter violation of all established rules.

"No, thank ye," returned Budden, with the most barbarous indifference to crime, "I prefer it this way, it eats short. But I say, Minns, when will you come down and see us? You will be delighted with the place; I know you will. Amelia and I were talking about you the other night, and Amelia said—another lump of sugar, please; thank ye—she said, don't you think you could contrive, my dear, to say to Mr. Minns, in a friendly way—come down, sir—damn the dog! he's spoiling your curtains, Minns—ha!—ha!—ha!" Minns leaped from his seat as though he had received the discharge from a galvanic battery.

"Come out, sir!—go out, hoo!" cried poor Augustus, keeping, nevertheless, at a very respectful distance from the dog; having read of a case of hydrophobia in the paper of that morning. By dint of great exertion, much shouting, and a marvellous deal of poking under the tables with a stick and umbrella, the dog was at last dislodged, and placed on the landing outside the door, where he immediately commenced a most appalling howling; at the same time vehemently scratching the paint off the two nicely-varnished bottom panels, until they resembled the interior of a backgammon-board.

"A good dog for the country that!" coolly observed Budden to the distracted Minns, "but he's not much used to confinement. But now, Minns, when will you come down? I'll take no denial, positively. Let's see, to-day's Thursday. —Will you come on Sunday? We dine at five, don't say no—do."

After a great deal of pressing, Mr. Augustus Minns, driven to despair, accepted the invitation, and promised to be at Poplar-walk on the ensuing Sunday, at a quarter before five to the minute.

"Now mind the direction," said Budden: "the coach goes from the Flower-pot, in Bishopsgate-street, every half hour. When the coach stops at the Swan, you'll see, immediately opposite you, a white house."

"Which is your house—I understand," said Minns, wishing to cut short the visit, and the story, at the same time.

"No, no, that's not mine; that's Grogus's, the great iron-monger's. I was going to say—you turn down by the side of the white house till you can't go another step further—mind that!—and then you turn to your right, by some stables— well; close to you, you'll see a wall with 'Beware of the Dog' written on it in large letters—(Minns shuddered)—go along by the side of that wall for about a quarter of a mile —and anybody will show you which is my place."

"Very well—thank ye—good-bye."

"Be punctual."

"Certainly: good morning."

"I say, Minns, you've got a card."

"Yes, I have; thank ye." And Mr. Octavius Budden departed, leaving his cousin looking forward to his visit on

the following Sunday, with the feelings of a penniless poet
to the weekly visit of his Scotch landlady.

Sunday arrived; the sky was bright and clear; crowds of
people were hurrying along the streets, intent on their
different schemes of pleasure for the day; everything and
everybody looked cheerful and happy except Mr. Augustus
Minns.

The day was fine, but the heat was considerable; when Mr.
Minns had fagged up the shady side of Fleet-street, Cheapside, and Threadneedle-street, he had become pretty warm,
tolerably dusty, and it was getting late into the bargain. By
the most extraordinary good fortune, however, a coach was
waiting at the Flower-pot, into which Mr. Augustus Minns
got, on the solemn assurance of the cad that the vehicle
would start in three minutes—that being the very utmost ex-
tremity of time it was allowed to wait by Act of Parliament.
A quarter of an hour elapsed, and there were no signs of
moving. Minns looked at his watch for the sixth time.

"Coachman, are you going or not?" bawled Mr. Minns,
with his head and half his body out of the coach window.

"Di—rectly, sir," said the coachman, with his hands in his
pockets, looking as much unlike a man in a hurry as possible.

"Bill, take them cloths off." Five minutes more elasped:
at the end of which time the coachman mounted the box,
from whence he looked down the street, and up the street,
and hailed all the pedestrians for another five minutes.

"Coachman! if you don't go this moment, I shall get out,"
said Mr. Minns, rendered desperate by the lateness of the
hour, and the impossibility of being in Poplar-walk at the
appointed time.

"Going this minute, sir," was the reply;—and, accordingly, the machine trundled on for a couple of hundred
yards, and then stopped again. Minns doubled himself up
in a corner of the coach, and abandoned himself to his fate,
as a child, a mother, a bandbox and a parasol, became his
fellow-passengers.

The child was an affectionate and an amiable infant; the little dear mistook Minns for his other parent, and screamed to embrace him.

" Be quiet, dear," said the mamma, restraining the impetuosity of the darling, whose little fat legs were kicking, and stamping, and twining themselves into the most complicated forms, in an ecstasy of impatience. "Be quiet, dear, that's not your papa."

"Thank Heaven I am not!" thought Minns, as the first gleam of pleasure he had experienced that morning shone like a meteor through his wretchedness.

Playfulness was agreeably mingled with affection in the disposition of the boy. When satisfied that Mr. Minns was not his parent, he endeavoured to attract his notice by scraping his drab trousers with his dirty shoes, poking his chest with his mamma's parasol, and other nameless endearments peculiar to infancy, with which he beguiled the tediousness of the ride, apparently very much to his own satisfaction.

When the unfortunate gentleman arrived at the Swan, he found to his great dismay, that it was a quarter past five. The white house, the stables, the "Beware of the Dog,"— every landmark was passed, with a rapidity not unusual to a gentleman of a certain age when too late for dinner. After the lapse of a few minutes, Mr. Minns found himself opposite a yellow brick house with a green door, brass knocker, and door-plate, green window-frames and ditto railings, with "a garden" in front, that is to say, a small loose bit of gravelled ground, with one round and two scalene triangular beds, containing a fir-tree, twenty or thirty bulbs, and an unlimited number of marigolds. The taste of Mr. and Mrs. Budden was further displayed by the appearance of a Cupid on each side of the door, perched upon a heap of large chalk flints, variegated with pink conch-shells. His knock at the door was answered by a stumpy boy, in drab livery, cotton stockings and high-lows, who, after hanging his hat on one of the dozen brass pegs which ornamented the passage, denominated by courtesy "The Hall," ushered him into a front drawing-room commanding a very extensive view of the backs of the neighbouring houses. The usual ceremony of introduction, and so forth, over, Mr. Minns took his seat: not a little agitated at finding that he was the last comer, and, somehow or other, the Lion of about a dozen people, sitting together in a small drawing-room, getting rid of that most tedious of all time, the time preceding dinner.

"Well, Brogson," said Budden, addressing an elderly gentleman in a black coat, drab knee-breeches, and long gaiters, who, under pretence of inspecting the prints in an Annual, had been engaged in satisfying himself on the subject of Mr. Minns's general appearance, by looking at him over the tops of the leaves—"Well, Brogson, what do Ministers mean to do? Will they go out, or what?"

"Oh—why—really, you know, I'm the last person in the world to ask for news. Your cousin, from his situation, is the most likely person to answer the question."

Mr. Minns assured the last speaker, that although he was in Somerset-house, he possessed no official communication relative to the projects of his Majesty's Ministers. But his remark was evidently received incredulously; and no further conjectures being hazarded on the subject, a long pause ensued, during which the company occupied themselves in coughing and blowing their noses, until the entrance of Mrs. Budden caused a general rise.

The ceremony of introduction being over, dinner was announced, and down-stairs the party proceeded accordingly —Mr. Minns escorting Mrs. Budden as far as the drawing-room door, but being prevented, by the narrowness of the staircase, from extending his gallantry any farther. The dinner passed off as such dinners usually do. Ever and anon, amidst the clatter of knives and forks, and the hum of conversation, Mr. B.'s voice might be heard, asking a friend to take wine, and assuring him he was glad to see him; and a great deal of by-play took place between Mrs. B. and the servants, respecting the removal of the dishes, during which her countenance assumed all the variations of a weather-glass, from "stormy" to "set fair."

Upon the dessert and wine being placed on the table, the servant, in compliance with a significant look from Mrs. B., brought down "Master Alexander," habited in a sky-blue suit with silver buttons; and possessing hair of nearly the same colour as the metal. After sundry praises from his mother, and various admonitions as to his behaviour from his father, he was introduced to his godfather.

"Well, my little fellow—you are a fine boy, ain't you?" said Mr. Minns, as happy as a tomtit on birdlime.

"Yes."

"How old are you?"

"Eight, next We'nsday. How old are *you*?"

"Alexander," interrupted his mother, "how dare you ask Mr. Minns how old he is!"

"He asked me how old *I* was," said the precocious child, to whom Minns had from that moment internally resolved that he never would bequeath one shilling. As soon as the titter occasioned by the observation had subsided, a little smirking man with red whiskers, sitting at the bottom of the table, who during the whole of dinner had been endeavouring to obtain a listener to some stories about Sheridan, called out, with a very patronising air, "Alick, what part of speech is *be*."

"A verb."

"That's a good boy," said Mrs. Budden, with all a mother's pride. "Now, you know what a verb is?"

"A verb is a word which signifies to be, to do, or to suffer; as, I am—I rule—I am ruled. Give me an apple, Ma."

"I'll give you an apple," replied the man with the red whiskers, who was an established friend of the family, or in other words was always invited by Mrs. Budden, whether

Mr. Budden liked it or not, "if you'll tell me what is the meaning of *be*."

"Be?" said the prodigy, after a little hesitation—"an insect that gathers honey."

"No, dear," frowned Mrs. Budden; "B double E is the substantive."

"I don't think he knows much yet about *common* substantives," said the smirking gentleman, who thought this an admirable opportunity for letting off a joke. "It's clear he's not very well acquainted with *proper names*. He! he! he!"

"Gentlemen," called out Mr. Budden, from the end of the table, in a stentorian voice, and with a very important air, "will you have the goodness to charge your glasses? I have a toast to propose."

"Hear! hear!" cried the gentlemen, passing the decanters. After they had made the round of the table, Mr. Budden proceeded—"Gentlemen; there is an individual present——"

"Hear! hear!" said the little man with red whiskers.

"*Pray* be quiet, Jones," remonstrated Budden.

"I say, gentlemen, there is an individual present," resumed the host, "in whose society, I am sure we must take great delight—and—and—the conversation of that individual must have afforded to every one present, the utmost pleasure." ["Thank Heaven, he does not mean me!" thought Minns, conscious that his diffidence and exclusiveness had prevented his saying above a dozen words since he entered the house.] "Gentlemen, I am but a humble individual myself, and I perhaps ought to apologise for allowing any individual feelings of friendship and affection for the person I allude to, to induce me to venture to rise, to propose the health of that person—a person that, I am sure—that is to say, a person whose virtues must endear him to those who know him—and those who have not the pleasure of knowing him, cannot dislike him."

"Hear! hear!" said the company, in a tone of encouragement and approval.

376

"Gentlemen," continued Budden, "my cousin is a man who—who is a relation of my own." (Hear! hear!) Minns groaned audibly. "Who I am most happy to see here, and who, if he were not here, would certainly have deprived us of the great pleasure we all feel in seeing him. (Loud cries of hear!) Gentlemen, I feel that I have already trespassed on your attention for too long a time. With every feeling —of—with every sentiment of—of——"

"Gratification"—suggested the friend of the family.

"—Of gratification, I beg to propose the health of Mr. Minns."

"Standing, gentlemen!" shouted the indefatigable little man with the whiskers—" and with the honours. Take your time from me, if you please. Hip! hip! hip!—Za!—Hip! hip! hip!—Za!—Hip! hip!—Za—a—a!"

All eyes were now fixed on the subject of the toast, who by gulping down port wine at the imminent hazard of suffocation, endeavoured to conceal his confusion. After as long a pause as decency would admit, he rose, but, as the newspapers sometimes say in their reports, "we regret that we are quite unable to give even the substance of the honourable gentleman's observations." The words "present company —honour—present occasion," and "great happiness"—heard occasionally, and repeated at intervals, with a countenance expressive of the utmost confusion and misery, convinced the company that he was making an excellent speech; and, accordingly, on his resuming his seat, they cried "Bravo!" and manifested tumultuous applause. Jones, who had been long watching his opportunity, then darted up.

"Budden," said he, "will you allow *me* to propose a toast?"

"Certainly," replied Budden, adding in an under-tone to Minns right across the table, "Devilish sharp fellow that: you'll be very much pleased with his speech. He talks equally well on any subject." Minns bowed, and Mr. Jones proceeded:

"It has on several occasions, in various instances, under many circumstances, and in different companies, fallen to my lot to propose a toast to those by whom, at the time, I have had the honour to be surrounded. I have sometimes, I will cheerfully own—for why should I deny it?—felt the over-whelming nature of the task I have undertaken, and my own utter incapability to do justice to the subject. If such have been my feelings, however, on former occasions, what must they be now—now—under the extraordinary circumstances in which I am placed. (Hear! hear!) To describe my feelings accurately, would be impossible; but I cannot give you a better idea of them, gentlemen, than by referring to a circumstance which happens, oddly enough, to occur to my mind at the moment. On one occasion, when that truly great and illustrious man, Sheridan, was—— "

Now, there is no knowing what new villainy in the form of a joke would have been heaped on the grave of that very ill-used man, Mr. Sheridan, if the boy in drab had not at that moment entered the room in a breathless state, to report that, as it was a very wet night, the nine o'clock stage had come round, to know whether there was anybody going to town, as, in that case, he (the nine o'clock) had room for one inside.

Mr. Minns started up; and, despite countless exclamations of surprise, and entreaties to stay, persisted in his determination to accept the vacant place. But, the brown silk umbrella was nowhere to be found; and as the coachman couldn't wait, he drove back to the Swan, leaving word for Mr. Minns to "run round" and catch him. However, as it did not occur to Mr. Minns for some ten minutes or so, that he had left the brown silk umbrella with the ivory handle in the other coach, coming down; and, moreover, as he was by no means remarkable for speed, it is no matter of surprise that when he accomplished the feat of "running round" to the Swan, the coach—the last coach—had gone without him.

It was somewhere about three o'clock in the morning, when

MR. MINNS'S WILL

Mr. Augustus Minns knocked feebly at the street-door of his lodgings in Tavistock-street, cold, wet, cross, and miserable. He made his will next morning, and his professional man informs us, in that strict confidence in which we inform the public, that neither the name of Mr. Octavius Budden, nor of Mrs. Amelia Budden, nor of Master Alexander Augustus Budden, appears therein.

CHAPTER III.

THE Miss Crumptons, or to quote the authority of the inscription on the garden-gate of Minerva House, Hammersmith, "The Misses Crumpton," were two unusually tall, particularly thin, and exceedingly skinny personages: very upright, and very yellow. Miss Amelia Crumpton owned to thirty-eight, and Miss Maria Crumpton admitted she was forty; an admission which was rendered perfectly unnecessary by the self-evident fact of her being at least fifty. They dressed in the most interesting manner—like twins! and looked as happy and comfortable as a couple of marigolds run to seed. They were very precise, had the strictest possible ideas of propriety, wore false hair, and always smelt very strongly of lavender.

Minerva House, conducted under the auspices of the two sisters, was a "finishing establishment for young ladies," where some twenty girls of the ages of from thirteen to nineteen inclusive, acquired a smattering of everything, and a knowledge of nothing; instruction in French and Italian, dancing lessons twice a-week; and other necessaries of life. The house was a white one, a little removed from the roadside, with close palings in front. The bedroom windows were always left partly open, to afford a bird's-eye view of numerous little bedsteads with very white dimity furniture, and thereby impress the passer-by with a due sense of the luxuries of the

380

Sentiment

establishment; and there was a front parlour hung round with highly varnished maps which nobody ever looked at, and filled with books which no one ever read, appropriated exclusively to the reception of parents, who, whenever they called, could not fail to be struck with the very deep appearance of the place.

"Amelia, my dear," said Miss Maria Crumpton, entering the school-room one morning, with her false hair in papers: as she occasionally did, in order to impress the young ladies with a conviction of its reality. "Amelia, my dear, here is a most gratifying note I have just received. You needn't mind reading it aloud."

Miss Amelia, thus advised, proceeded to read the following note with an air of great triumph:

"Cornelius Brook Dingwall, Esq., M.P., presents his compliments to Miss Crumpton, and will feel much obliged by Miss Crumpton's calling on him, if she conveniently can, to-morrow morning at one o'clock, as Cornelius Brook Dingwall, Esq., M.P., is anxious to see Miss Crumpton on the subject of placing Miss Brook Dingwall under her charge.

"Adelphi.

"Monday morning."

"A Member of Parliament's daughter!" ejaculated Amelia, in an ecstatic tone.

"A Member of Parliament's daughter!" repeated Miss Maria, with a smile of delight, which, of course, elicited a concurrent titter of pleasure from all the young ladies.

"It's exceedingly delightful!" said Miss Amelia; whereupon all the young ladies murmured their admiration again. Courtiers are but school-boys, and court-ladies school-girls.

So important an announcement at once superseded the business of the day. A holiday was declared, in commemoration of the great event; the Miss Crumptons retired to their private apartment to talk it over; the smaller girls discussed the probable manners and customs of the daughter of a Member of Parliament; and the young ladies verging on eighteen wondered whether she was engaged, whether she was pretty, whether she wore much bustle, and many other *whethers* of equal importance.

The two Miss Crumptons proceeded to the Adelphi at the appointed time next day, dressed, of course, in their best style, and looking as amiable as they possibly could—which, by-the-bye, is not saying much for them. Having sent in their cards, through the medium of a red-hot looking footman in bright livery, they were ushered into the august presence of the profound Dingwall.

Cornelius Brook Dingwall, Esq., M.P., was very haughty, solemn, and portentous. He had, naturally, a somewhat spasmodic expression of countenance, which was not rendered the less remarkable by his wearing an extremely stiff cravat. He was wonderfully proud of the M.P. attached to his name, and never lost an opportunity of reminding people of his dignity. He had a great idea of his own abilities, which must have been a great comfort to him, as no one else had; and in diplomacy, on a small scale, in his own family arrangements, he considered himself unrivalled. He was a county magistrate, and discharged the duties of his station with all due justice and impartiality; frequently committing poachers, and occasionally committing himself. Miss Brook Dingwall was one of that numerous class of young ladies, who, like adverbs, may be known by their answering to a commonplace question, and doing nothing else.

On the present occasion, this talented individual was seated in a small library at a table covered with papers, doing nothing, but trying to look busy, playing at shop. Acts of Parliament, and letters directed to " Cornelius Brook Dingwall, Esq., M.P.," were ostentatiously scattered over the table; at a little distance from which, Mrs. Brook Dingwall was seated at work. One of those public nuisances, a spoiled child, was playing about the room, dressed after the most approved fashion—in a blue tunic with a black belt a quarter of a yard wide, fastened with an immense buckle—looking like a robber in a melodrama, seen through a diminishing glass.

After a little pleasantry from the sweet child, who amused himself by running away with Miss Maria Crumpton's chair as fast as it was placed for her, the visitors were seated, and Cornelius Brook Dingwall, Esq., opened the conversation.

He had sent for Miss Crumpton, he said, in consequence of the high character he had received of her establishment from his friend, Sir Alfred Muggs.

Miss Crumpton murmured her acknowledgments to him (Muggs), and Cornelius proceeded.

" One of my principal reasons, Miss Crumpton, for parting with my daughter, is, that she has lately acquired some senti-mental ideas, which it is most desirable to eradicate from her young mind." (Here the little innocent before noticed, fell out of an arm-chair with an awful crash.)

" Naughty boy ! " said his mamma, who appeared more surprised at his taking the liberty of falling down, than at anything else; " I'll ring the bell for James to take him away."

" Pray don't check him, my love," said the diplomatist, as soon as he could make himself heard amidst the unearthly howling consequent upon the threat and the tumble. " It all arises from his great flow of spirits." This last explanation was addressed to Miss Crumpton.

" Certainly, sir," replied the antique Maria : not exactly seeing, however, the connexion between a flow of animal spirits, and a fall from an arm-chair.

Silence was restored, and the M.P. resumed : " Now, I know nothing so likely to effect this object, Miss Crumpton, as her mixing constantly in the society of girls of her own age ; and, as I know that in your establishment she will meet such as are not likely to contaminate her young mind, I propose to send her to you."

The youngest Miss Crumpton expressed the acknowledgments of the establishment generally. Maria was rendered speechless by bodily pain. The dear little fellow, having recovered his animal spirits, was standing upon her most tender foot, by way of getting his face (which looked like a capital O in a red-lettered play-bill) on a level with the writing-table.

"Of course, Lavinia will be a parlour boarder," continued the enviable father; "and on one point I wish my directions to be strictly observed. The fact is, that some ridiculous love affair, with a person much her inferior in life, has been the cause of her present state of mind. Knowing that of course, under your care, she can have no opportunity of meeting this person, I do not object to—indeed, I should rather prefer—her mixing with such society as you see yourself."

This important statement was again interrupted by the high-spirited little creature, in the excess of his joyousness breaking a pane of glass, and nearly precipitating himself into an adjacent area. James was rung for; considerable confusion and screaming succeeded; two little blue legs were seen to kick violently in the air as the man left the room, and the child was gone.

"Mr. Brook Dingwall would like Miss Brook Dingwall to learn everything," said Mrs. Brook Dingwall, who hardly ever said anything at all.

"Certainly," said both the Miss Crumptons together.

"And as I trust the plan I have devised will be effectual in weaning my daughter from this absurd idea, Miss Crumpton," continued the legislator, "I hope you will have the goodness to comply, in all respects, with any request I may forward to you."

The promise was of course made; and after a lengthened discussion, conducted on behalf of the Dingwalls with the most becoming diplomatic gravity, and on that of the Crumptons with profound respect, it was finally arranged that

THE EVENING OF THE BALL

Miss Lavinia should be forwarded to Hammersmith on the next day but one, on which occasion the half-yearly ball given at the establishment was to take place. It might divert the dear girl's mind. This, by the way, was another bit of diplomacy.

Miss Lavinia was introduced to her future governess, and both the Miss Crumptons pronounced her "a most charming girl;" an opinion which, by a singular coincidence, they always entertained of any new pupil.

Courtesies were exchanged, acknowledgments expressed, condescension exhibited, and the interview terminated.

Preparations, to make use of theatrical phraseology, "on a scale of magnitude never before attempted," were incessantly made at Minerva House to give every effect to the forth-coming ball. The largest room in the house was pleasingly ornamented with blue calico roses, plaid tulips, and other equally natural-looking artificial flowers, the work of the young ladies themselves. The carpet was taken up, the folding-doors were taken down, the furniture was taken out, and rout-seats were taken in. The linen-drapers of Hammersmith were astounded at the sudden demand for blue sarsenet ribbon, and long white gloves. Dozens of geraniums were purchased for bouquets, and a harp and two violins were bespoke from town, in addition to the grand piano already on the premises. The young ladies who were selected to show off on the occasion, and do credit to the establishment, practised incessantly, much to their own satisfaction, and greatly to the annoyance of the lame old gentleman over the way; and a constant correspondence was kept up, between the Misses Crumpton and the Hamersmith pastrycook.

The evening came; and then there was such a lacing of stays, and tying of sandals, and dressing of hair, as never can take place with a proper degree of bustle out of a boarding-school. The smaller girls managed to be in every-body's way, and were pushed about accordingly; and the elder ones dressed, and tied, and flattered, and envied, one another, as earnestly and sincerely as if they had actually *come out.*

"How do I look, dear?" inquired Miss Emily Smithers, the belle of the house, of Miss Caroline Wilson, who was her bosom friend, because she was the ugliest girl in Hammersmith, or out of it.

"Oh! charming, dear. How do I?"

"Delightful! you never looked so handsome," returned the belle, adjusting her own dress, and not bestowing a glance on her poor companion.

"I hope young Hilton will come early," said another young lady to Miss somebody else, in a fever of expectation.

"I'm sure he'd be highly flattered if he knew it," returned the other, who was practising *l'été.*

"Oh! he's so handsome," said the first.

"Such a charming person!" added a second.

"Such a *distingué* air!" said a third.

"Oh, what *do* you think?" said another girl, running into the room; "Miss Crumpton says her cousin's coming."

"What! Theodosius Butler?" said everybody in raptures.

"Is *he* handsome?" inquired a novice.

"No, not particularly handsome," was the general reply; "but, oh, so clever!"

Mr. Theodosius Butler was one of those immortal geniuses who are to be met with in almost every circle. They have, usually, very deep, monotonous voices. They always persuade themselves that they are wonderful persons, and that they ought to be very miserable, though they don't precisely know why. They are very conceited, and usually possess half an idea; but, with enthusiastic young ladies, and silly young gentlemen, they are very wonderful persons. The individual in question, Mr. Theodosius, had written a pamphlet containing some very weighty considerations on the expediency of doing something or other; and as every sentence contained a good many words of four syllables, his admirers took it for granted that he meant a good deal.

" Perhaps that's he," exclaimed several young ladies, as the first pull of the evening threatened destruction to the bell of the gate.

An awful pause ensued. Some boxes arrived and a young lady—Miss Brook Dingwall, in full ball costume, with an immense gold chain round her neck, and her dress looped up with a single rose; an ivory fan in her hand, and a most interesting expression of despair in her face.

The Miss Crumptons inquired after the family, with the most excruciating anxiety, and Miss Brook Dingwall was formally introduced to her future companions. The Miss Crumptons conversed with the young ladies in the most mellifluous tones, in order that Miss Brook Dingwall might be properly impressed with their amiable treatment.

Another pull at the bell. Mr. Dadson the writing-master, and his wife. The wife in green silk, with shoes and cap-trimmings to correspond : the writing-master in a white waistcoat, black knee-shorts, and ditto silk stockings, displaying a leg large enough for two writing-masters. The young ladies whispered one another, and the writing-master and his wife flattered the Miss Crumptons, who were dressed in amber, with long sashes, like dolls.

Repeated pulls at the bell, and arrivals too numerous to particularise : papas and mammas, and aunts and uncles, the owners and guardians of the different pupils ; the singing-master, Signor Lobskini, in a black wig ; the piano-forte player and the violins ; the harp, in a state of intoxication ; and some twenty young men, who stood near the door, and talked to one another, occasionally bursting into a giggle. A general hum of conversation. Coffee handed round, and plentifully partaken of by fat mammas, who looked like the stout people who come on in pantomimes for the sole purpose of being knocked down.

The popular Mr. Hilton was the next arrival ; and he having, at the request of the Miss Crumptons, undertaken the office of Master of the Ceremonies, the quadrilles commenced with considerable spirit. The young men by the door gradually advanced into the middle of the room, and in time became sufficiently at ease to consent to be introduced to partners. The writing-master danced every set, springing about with the most fearful agility, and his wife played a rubber in the back-parlour—a little room with five book-shelves, dignified by the name of the study. Setting her down to whist was a half-yearly piece of generalship on the part of the Miss Crumptons; it was necessary to hide her somewhere, on account of her being a fright.

The interesting Lavinia Brook Dingwall was the only girl present, who appeared to take no interest in the proceedings of the evening. In vain was she solicited to dance; in vain was the universal homage paid to her as the daughter of a member of parliament. She was equally unmoved by the splendid tenor of the inimitable Lobskini, and the brilliant execution of Miss Lætitia Parsons, whose performance of "The Recollections of Ireland" was universally declared to be almost equal to that of Moscheles himself. Not even the announcement of the arrival of Mr. Theodosius Butler could induce her to leave the corner of the back drawing-room in which she was seated.

"Now, Theodosius," said Miss Maria Crumpton, after that enlightened pamphleteer had nearly run the gauntlet of the whole company, "I must introduce you to our new pupil."

Theodosius looked as if he cared for nothing earthly.

"She's the daughter of a member of parliament," said Maria.—Theodosius started.

"And her name is—— ?" he inquired.

"Miss Brook Dingwall."

"Great Heaven!" poetically exclaimed Theodosius, in a low tone.

Miss Crumpton commenced the introduction in due form. Miss Brook Dingwall languidly raised her head.

"Edward!" she exclaimed, with a half-shriek, on seeing the well-known nankeen legs.

Fortunately, as Miss Maria Crumpton possessed no remarkable share of penetration, and as it was one of the diplomatic arrangements that no attention was to be paid to Miss Lavinia's incoherent exclamations, she was perfectly unconscious of the mutual agitation of the parties; and therefore, seeing that the offer of his hand for the next quadrille was accepted, she left him by the side of Miss Brook Dingwall.

"Oh, Edward!" exclaimed that most romantic of all romantic young ladies, as the light of science seated himself beside her, "Oh, Edward, is it you?"

Mr. Theodosius assured the dear creature, in the most impassioned manner, that he was not conscious of being anybody but himself.

"Then why—why—this disguise? Oh! Edward M'Neville Walter, what have I not suffered on your account?"

"Lavinia, hear me," replied the hero, in his most poetic strain. "Do not condemn me unheard. If anything that emanates from the soul of such a wretch as I, can occupy a place in your recollection—if any being, so vile, deserve your notice—you may remember that I once published a pamphlet (and paid for its publication) entitled 'Considerations on the Policy of Removing the Duty on Bees'-wax.'"

"I do—I do!" sobbed Lavinia.

"That," continued the lover, "was a subject to which your father was devoted, heart and soul."

"He was—he was!" reiterated the sentimentalist.

"I knew it," continued Theodosius, tragically; "I knew it —I forwarded him a copy. He wished to know me. Could I disclose my real name? Never! No, I assumed that name which you have so often pronounced in tones of endearment. As M'Neville Walter, I devoted myself to the stirring cause; as M'Neville Walter I gained your heart; in the same character I was ejected from your house by your father's domestics; and in no character at all have I since been enabled to see you. We now meet again, and I proudly own that I am—Theodosius Butler."

The young lady appeared perfectly satisfied with this argumentative address, and bestowed a look of the most ardent affection on the immortal advocate of bees'-wax.

"May I hope," said he, "that the promise your father's violent behaviour interrupted, may be renewed?"

"Let us join this set," replied Lavinia, coquettishly—for girls of nineteen *can* coquette.

"No," ejaculated he of the nankeens; "I stir not from this spot, writhing under this torture of suspense. May I—may I—hope?"

"You may."

"The promise is renewed?"

"It is."

"I have your permission?"

"You have."

"To the fullest extent?"

"You know it," returned the blushing Lavinia. The contortions of the interesting Butler's visage expressed his raptures.

We could dilate upon the occurrences that ensued. How Mr. Theodosius and Miss Lavinia danced, and talked, and sighed for the remainder of the evening—how the Miss Crumptons were delighted thereat. How the writing-master continued to frisk about with one-horse power, and how his wife, from some unaccountable freak, left the whist-table in the little back-parlour, and persisted in displaying her green head-dress in the most conspicuous part of the drawing-room. How the supper consisted of small triangular sandwiches in trays, and a tart here and there by way of variety; and how the visitors consumed warm water disguised with lemon, and dotted with nutmeg, under the denomination of negus. These, and other matters of as much interest, however, we pass over, for the purpose of describing a scene of even more importance.

A fortnight after the date of the ball, Cornelius Brook Dingwall, Esq., M.P., was seated at the same library-table, and in the same room, as we have before described. He was alone, and his face bore an expression of deep thought and solemn gravity—he was drawing up "A Bill for the better observance of Easter Monday."

The footman tapped at the door—the legislator started from his reverie, and "Miss Crumpton" was announced. Permission was given for Miss Crumpton to enter the *sanctum*; Maria came sliding in, and having taken her seat with a due portion of affectation, the footman retired, and the governess was left alone with the M.P. Oh! how she longed for the presence of a third party! Even the facetious young gentleman would have been a relief.

Miss Crumpton began the duet. She hoped Mrs. Brook Dingwall and the handsome little boy were in good health.

They were. Mrs. Brook Dingwall and little Frederick were at Brighton.

"Much obliged to you, Miss Crumpton," said Cornelius, in his most dignified manner, "for your attention in calling this morning. I should have driven down to Hammersmith, to see Lavinia, but your account was so very satisfactory, and my duties in the House occupy me so much, that I determined to postpone it for a week. How has she gone on?"

"Very well indeed, sir," returned Maria, dreading to inform the father that she had gone off.

"Ah, I thought the plan on which I proceeded would be a match for her."

Here was a favourable opportunity to say that somebody else had been a match for her. But the unfortunate governess was unequal to the task.

"You have persevered strictly in the line of conduct I prescribed, Miss Crumpton?"

"Strictly, sir."

"You tell me in your note that her spirits gradually improved."

"Very much indeed, sir."

"To be sure. I was convinced they would."

"But I fear, sir," said Miss Crumpton, with visible emotion,

391

"I fear the plan has not succeeded, quite so well as we could have wished."

"No!" exclaimed the prophet. "Bless me! Miss Crumpton, you look alarmed. What has happened?"

"Miss Brook Dingwall, sir——"

"Yes, ma'am?"

"Has gone, sir"—said Maria, exhibiting a strong inclination to faint.

"Gone!"

"Eloped, sir."

"Eloped!— Who with — when — where — how?" almost shrieked the agitated diplomatist.

The natural yellow of the unfortunate Maria's face changed to all the hues of the rainbow, as she laid a small packet on the member's table.

He hurriedly opened it. A letter from his daughter, and another from Theodosius. He glanced over their contents— "Ere this reaches you, far distant—appeal to feelings—love to distraction—bees'-wax—slavery," &c., &c. He dashed his hand to his forehead, and paced the room with fearfully long strides, to the great alarm of the precise Maria.

"Now mind; from this time forward," said Mr. Brook Dingwall, suddenly stopping at the table, and beating time upon it with his hand; "from this time forward, I never will, under any circumstances whatever, permit a man who writes pamphlets to enter any other room of this house but the kitchen.—I'll allow my daughter and her husband one hundred and fifty pounds a-year, and never see their faces again : and, damme! ma'am, I'll bring in a bill for the abolition of finishing-schools."

Some time has elapsed since this passionate declaration. Mr. and Mrs. Butler are at present rusticating in a small cottage at Ball's-pond, pleasantly situated in the immediate vicinity of a brick-field. They have no family. Mr. Theodosius looks very important, and writes incessantly; but, in consequence of a gross combination on the part of publishers, none of his productions appear in print. His young wife begins to think that ideal misery is preferable to real unhappiness; and that a marriage, contracted in haste, and repented at leisure, is the cause of more substantial wretchedness than she ever anticipated.

On cool reflection, Cornelius Brook Dingwall, Esq., M.P., was reluctantly compelled to admit that the untoward result of his admirable arrangements was attributable, not to the Miss Crumptons, but his own diplomacy. He, however, consoles himself, like some other small diplomatists, by satisfactorily proving that if his plans did not succeed, they ought to have done so. Minerva House is *in statu quo*, and "The Misses Crumpton" remain in the peaceable and undisturbed enjoyment of all the advantages resulting from their Finishing-School.